THE GLOBAL DECLINE OF THE MANDATORY DEATH PENALTY

Historically, at English common law, the death penalty was mandatory for the crime of murder and other violent felonies. Over the last three decades, however, many former British colonies have reformed their capital punishment regimes to permit judicial sentencing discretion, including consideration of mitigating factors. Applying a comparative analysis to the law of capital punishment, Novak examines the constitutional jurisprudence and resulting legislative reform in the Caribbean, Sub-Saharan Africa, and South and Southeast Asia, focusing on the rapid retreat of the mandatory death penalty in the Commonwealth over the last thirty years.

The coordinated mandatory death penalty challenges—which have had the consequence of greatly reducing the world's death row population—represent a case study of how a small group of lawyers can sponsor human rights litigation that incorporates international human rights law into domestic constitutional jurisprudence, ultimately harmonizing criminal justice regimes across borders.

This book is essential reading for anyone interested in the study and development of human rights and capital punishment, as well as those exploring the contours of comparative criminal justice.

Novak provides a thorough comparative study of the movement away from the mandatory death penalty towards discretionary sentencing in Commonwealth countries, about which we know little. While much of the book deals with contemporary jurisprudence, legal analysis is discussed within an historical and sociological context that is informative and engaging.

Carolyn Hoyle, University of Oxford, UK

Professor Novak has made an enormous contribution to the eventual abolition of the death penalty, in an incisive study of one of the more insidious aspects of it: its mandatory nature in many states that still retain it. The rationale for the prohibition of mandatory sentences to death—so ably explained in these pages and famously embraced by the US Supreme Court in Woodson v. North Carolina—is quickly establishing itself as a rule of international human rights law.

Juan E. Mendez, Washington College of Law, USA

Even after formal abolition of the death penalty in the United Kingdom in the 1960s, the toxic legacy of mandatory execution was a threat to penal justice and human rights in many nations tied to the common law tradition. This book tells the story of the litigation and advocacy that has removed the ugly shadow of mandatory capital punishment from most common law nations.

Franklin E. Zimring, University of California, Berkeley, USA

To Dr. Alexandros Petersen

The Global Decline of the Mandatory Death Penalty
Constitutional Jurisprudence and Legislative Reform in Africa, Asia, and the Caribbean

ANDREW NOVAK
American University Washington College of Law, USA

LONDON AND NEW YORK

First published 2014 by Ashgate Publishing

Published 2016 by Routledge
2 Park Square, Milton Park, Abingdon, Oxon OX14 4RN
711 Third Avenue, New York, NY 10017, USA

Routledge is an imprint of the Taylor & Francis Group, an informa business

Copyright © Andrew Novak 2014

All rights reserved. No part of this book may be reprinted or reproduced or utilised in any form or by any electronic, mechanical, or other means, now known or hereafter invented, including photocopying and recording, or in any information storage or retrieval system, without permission in writing from the publishers.

Notice:
Product or corporate names may be trademarks or registered trademarks, and are used only for identification and explanation without intent to infringe.

Andrew Novak has asserted his right under the Copyright, Designs and Patents Act, 1988, to be identified as the author of this work.

British Library Cataloguing in Publication Data
A catalogue record for this book is available from the British Library

The Library of Congress has cataloged the printed edition as follows:
Novak, Andrew.
  The global decline of the mandatory death penalty : constitutional jurisprudence and legislative reform in Africa, Asia, and the Caribbean / by Andrew Novak.
      pages cm. – (Law, Justice and Power)
  Includes bibliographical references and index.
  ISBN 978–1–4724–2325–2 (hardback)
  1. Capital punishment.
  I. Title.
  K5104.N68 2014
  364.66–dc23   2013043986

ISBN 9781472423252 (hbk)

Contents

A Note on Sources		*vii*
About the Author		*ix*
Acknowledgments		*xi*
1	Introduction: The Mandatory Death Penalty in Historical and Comparative Perspective	1
2	An Excessive and Arbitrary Punishment: The Mandatory Death Penalty and Discretion in the United States of America	9
3	Restricting the Death Penalty to the "Rarest of the Rare": The Origins of a Discretionary Death Penalty in India and Bangladesh	31
4	A Successful Experiment: The Abolition of the Mandatory Death Penalty in the Commonwealth Caribbean	47
5	The Holdouts: The Survival of the Mandatory Death Penalty in Malaysia and Singapore	73
6	The New Frontier: Constitutional Challenges to the Mandatory Death Penalty in Sub-Saharan Africa	99
7	The Doctrine of Extenuating Circumstances: The Rise of Judicial Sentencing Discretion in Southern Africa	125
8	Conclusion: After the Mandatory Death Penalty	163
Index		*169*
Table of Authorities		*177*

A Note on Sources

This book cites to case law in a wide variety of jurisdictions, each with its own peculiarities as to citation format and case reporting. While the book generally uses the logic of *The Bluebook: A Uniform System of Citation*, which prefers print reporter citations to medium-neutral citations, inevitably some variation exists as not all jurisdictions regularly publish court decisions.[1] In order of preference, the book cites to print reporters, medium-neutral citations, docket numbers with identifying features of the case, and finally to internet citations. Print reporters are organized by volume and page number with the abbreviation for the reporter series. Medium-neutral citations instead are organized by year, a code for the court issuing the decision, and the sequential number of the decision as issued that year. Where a case or docket number must be used, citation is made to the full case name and any identifying information including the full date. In some jurisdictions, first names are used in case citations. This may be because of naming conventions in that jurisdiction (such as where the family name precedes the given name) or, alternatively, because some last names are extremely common. Because the Bluebook does not comprehensively include all of the world's jurisdictions, the following additional abbreviations for print reporter and medium-neutral citations are used in this book:

Print Reporter Abbreviations

A.C.	Appeals Cases (United Kingdom)
A.H.R.L.R.	African Human Rights Law Reports
A.I.R.	All India Reports
All N.L.R.	All Nigeria Law Reports
All S.A.	All South African Law Reports
B.L.C.	Bangladesh Law Chronicles
B.L.D.	Bangladesh Legal Decisions
Bots.L.R.	Botswana Law Reports
Bz.L.R.	Belize Law Reports
C.C.C.	Canadian Criminal Cases
D.L.R.	Dhaka Law Reports (Bangladesh)
E.A.L.R.	East African Law Reports
E.H.R.R.	European Human Rights Reports
E.L.R.	Eastern Districts Local Law Reports (South Africa)
G.L.R.	Ghana Law Reports
H.K.C.F.A.R.	Hong Kong Court of Final Appeal Reports
K.L.R.	Kenya Law Reports
L.A.C.	Lesotho Appeals Cases

---

1 *See* THE BLUEBOOK: A UNIFORM SYSTEM OF CITATION (Columbia Law Review Ass'n et al. eds., 19th ed. 2010).

L.L.R.-L.B.	Lesotho Law Reports and Legal Bulletin
L.R.C.	Law Reports of the Commonwealth
M.L.J.	Malaya Law Journal
O.P.D.	Orange Free State Provincial Division Law Reports (South Africa)
P.N.G.L.R.	Papua New Guinea Law Reports
R.L.R.	Rhodesian Law Reports
S.A.	South African Law Reports
S.A.C.R.	South African Criminal Law Reports
S.C.C.	Supreme Court Cases (India)
S.C.G.L.R.	Supreme Court of Ghana Law Reports
S.C.R. (India)	Supreme Court Reports (India)
S.C.R. (Can.)	Supreme Court Reports (Canada)
S.L.R.	Singapore Law Reports
Sri L.R.	Sri Lankan Reports
T.L.R.	Tanzania Law Reports
W.I.R.	West Indies Reports
W.L.R.	Weekly Law Reports (England)
Zam.L.R.	Zambia Law Reports
Zim.L.R.	Zimbabwe Law Reports

Court Abbreviations for Medium-Neutral Citations

BNHC	High Court of Brunei Darussalam
BWCA	Botswana Court of Appeal
BWHC	Botswana High Court
CCJ	Caribbean Court of Justice
HKCA	Hong Kong Court of Appeal
HKCFI	Hong Kong Court of First Instance
LSCA	Lesotho Court of Appeal
LSHC	Lesotho High Court
MWHC	Malawi High Court
MYFC	Malaysia Federal Court
MYSSHC	Malaysia High Court of Sabah and Sarawak
NASC	Namibia Supreme Court
PGSC	Papua New Guinea Supreme Court
SGCA	Singapore Court of Appeal
SZCA	Swaziland Court of Appeal
SZHC	Swaziland High Court
UGCC	Uganda Constitutional Court
UGHC	Uganda High Court
UGSC	Uganda Supreme Court
UKPC	Judicial Committee of the Privy Council
ZMSC	Zambia Supreme Court
ZWHHC	Zimbabwe High Court in Harare
ZWSC	Zimbabwe Supreme Court

About the Author

Andrew Novak is an adjunct professor of African law at American University Washington College of Law and an adjunct professor of criminology, law, and society at George Mason University, where he teaches international and comparative criminal justice. He received a Master of Science in African Politics from the London School of Oriental and African Studies and a Juris Doctor from Boston University School of Law. His articles on the death penalty in Sub-Saharan Africa have appeared in the *Suffolk University Law Review*, *Loyola Journal of Public Interest Law*, *Richmond Journal of Global Law and Business*, *Indiana International and Comparative Law Review*, *Boston University International Law Journal*, and the *Cardozo Journal of Law, Ethics, and Public Policy* among others.

Acknowledgments

Research on this book has taken place across three continents over six years. I would like to thank the Death Penalty Project, including Parvais Jabbar, Saul Leurfreund, Nicola Goldfinch-Palmer, and Annette So for their helpful assistance over the years. In addition to Parvais and Saul, other legal practitioners who worked on the cases in this book were invaluable sources of information: Joseph Middleton at Doughty Street Chambers and Ben Silverstone now at Matrix Chambers in London and Gerry Githonga and Timothy Bryant at Azania Legal Consultants in Nairobi. This book would not have been possible without the advice and support of innumerable professors, editorial boards, librarians, and reviewers over the years, none deserving of more praise than Dr. Jay Michaelson and Dr. Jesse Fecker. The Ditshwanelo Botswana Center for Human Rights in Gaborone, where I volunteered during the summer of 2007, was a useful repository of newspaper clippings and reports about the death penalty that benefited the Southern Africa chapter. Edmund Wong and his family were gracious hosts on my trip to Malaysia and Singapore. Finally, my family and friends were sources of constant moral support during the writing of this book; I would like to thank them, and perhaps most of all.

Chapter 1
Introduction: The Mandatory Death Penalty in Historical and Comparative Perspective

A process that accords no significance to relevant facets of the character and record of the individual offender or the circumstances of the particular offense excludes from consideration in fixing the ultimate punishment of death the possibility of compassionate or mitigating factors stemming from the diverse frailties of humankind. It treats all persons convicted of a designated offense not as uniquely individual human beings, but as members of a faceless, undifferentiated mass to be subjected to the blind infliction of the penalty of death.

Justice Potter Stewart, *Woodson v. North Carolina* (1976)[1]

To deny the offender the opportunity, before sentence is passed, to seek to persuade the court that in all the circumstances to condemn him to death would be disproportionate and inappropriate is to treat him as no human being should be treated and thus to deny his basic humanity …

Lord Bingham of Cornhill, *Reyes v. Queen* (2002)[2]

The death penalty is in rapid and irreversible retreat everywhere in the English-speaking world, even in the most intransigent holdouts like Texas and Singapore.[3] The common law mandatory death sentence, automatic upon conviction for homicide or a small number of other serious felonies, has declined even faster than this, to the point of extinction in the Commonwealth. The penalty simplifies the sentencing process for the resource-constrained legal systems of the developing world, but it works a harsh justice. By sweeping in mercy killing with sadistic killing and cold-blooded murder with heat-of-passion murder, the mandatory death penalty shifts sentencing discretion from a trial judge to an executive or a mercy committee that grants clemency or pardon in troublesome cases but fails to reduce all risk of arbitrariness or mistake.[4] In short a mandatory death regime overpunishes in a world in which the death penalty, as the ultimate expression of state power, must be treated with great care.

Because postcolonial independence constitutions generally contain fundamental rights provisions that include due process rights and a prohibition on cruel and degrading punishment, they possess uniform constitutional vulnerabilities that make collateral attacks

---

1   428 U.S. 280, 304 (1976).
2   [2002] 2 A.C. 235 (P.C.) (appeal taken from Belize).
3   In 2011, executions in Texas fell to their lowest level in 15 years. Sonia Smith, *Texas Executions Drop to Fifteen Year Low*, Tex. Monthly, Dec. 17, 2011, http://www.texasmonthly.com/story/texas-executions-drop-fifteen-year-low. Similarly, the number of executions in Singapore fell from an average of 66 per year in the mid-1990s to an average of four per year by 2004 and lower subsequently. David T. Johnson, *The Jolly Hangman, the Jailed Journalist, and the Decline of Singapore's Death Penalty*, 8 Asian J. Criminology 41 (2013).
4   Rob Turrell, *'It's a Mystery': The Royal Prerogative of Mercy in England, Canada, and South Africa*, 4 Crime, Hist. & Societies 83, 84–8 (2000).

on the death penalty possible.[5] Human rights litigation against the mandatory nature of the death penalty has succeeded in the establishment of discretionary capital punishment regimes throughout the English-speaking Caribbean; in the African countries of Kenya, Malawi, and Uganda; and in India and Bangladesh.[6] Because of similarities in the criminal justice systems that Commonwealth countries inherited from Great Britain, courts across the English-speaking world, including the United States, "share" death penalty jurisprudence by citing to one another and building a corpus of comparative case law that has successfully restricted the application of the death penalty.[7]

In practice, there are three ways to mitigate the harshness of the mandatory death penalty for murder. The first is to separate the crime of murder into two offenses, capital murder and non-capital murder, and retain the mandatory death sentence for only a small range of particularly heinous crimes. This is the system devised by Great Britain's Homicide Act of 1957 after the Royal Commission on Capital Punishment concluded that the "outstanding defect of the law of murder is that it provides a single punishment for a crime widely varying in culpability."[8] The Homicide Act limited the mandatory death penalty to special cases of aggravated murder, such as murder of a law enforcement officer or murder performed in the course of theft, by shooting or explosion, or while resisting arrest or escaping custody. All other murders fell outside the scope of mandatory death, which proved unsatisfactory as murders otherwise widely regarded as heinous, such as the sexual or sadistic murders of children, were considered "less serious," fueling pressure for eventual abolition of the death penalty for homicide in 1965.[9] More recently, other Commonwealth jurisdictions, notably Singapore in its sweeping legislative reform of 2012, have experimented with this alternative.

The other two ways in which the mandatory death penalty may be replaced by a more parsimonious regime require allocating sentencing discretion to the trial judge to determine whether the individual circumstances of the offense warrants the punishment of death. One option is to require the judge to articulate a specific *aggravating* factor in the case that places the murder in a special category of seriousness. This is the prevailing system in the United States after *Woodson v. North Carolina* and India after *Mithu v. State of Punjab*, which found mandatory death sentences unconstitutional and replaced them with pure discretionary death regimes.[10] The other alternative is the opposite, to require a judge to articulate a specific *mitigating* factor that removes the case from the category of seriousness warranting death. This is the regime ushered in by the Criminal Procedure and Evidence (Amendment) Act of 1935 in apartheid South Africa, which had the consequence of turning

---

5 WILLIAM A SCHABAS, THE DEATH PENALTY AS CRUEL TREATMENT AND TORTURE: CAPITAL PUNISHMENT CHALLENGED IN THE WORLD'S COURTS 4 (1996).

6 *See e.g.*, Reyes v. Queen, [2002] 2 A.C. 259 (P.C.) (appeal taken from Belize); Queen v. Hughes, [2002] 2 A.C. 259 (P.C.) (appeal taken from St. Lucia); Fox v. Queen, [2002] A.C. 284 (P.C.) (appeal taken from St. Kitts & Nevis); Kafantayeni v. A.G. [2007] MWHC 1 (Malawi); Kigula v. A.G., [2009] 2 E.A.L.R. 1, 17 (Uganda S.C.); Mutiso v. Republic, [2011] 1 E.A.L.R. 342 (Kenya C.A.); Mithu v. State of Punjab, (1983) 2 S.C.R. 690 (India); State v. Sukur Ali, (2004) 9 B.L.C. (H.C.D.) 238.

7 Paolo Carozza, *'My Friend is a Stranger': The Death Penalty and the Global Ius Commune of Human Rights*, 81 TEX. L. REV. 1031, 1036 (2003).

8 *Cited in* BARRY MITCHELL & JULIAN V. ROBERTS, EXPLORING THE MANDATORY LIFE SENTENCE FOR MURDER 31 (2012).

9 *Id.* at 33.

10 Woodson v. North Carolina, 428 U.S. 280 (1976); Mithu v. State of Punjab, (1983) 2 S.C.R. 690 (India).

a mandatory death sentence into a rebuttable presumption in favor of death.[11] Known as the "doctrine of extenuating circumstances," this alternative passed into the law of other Southern African countries and to the South Pacific nation of Papua New Guinea.

Of these three options, the second one has become by far the dominant model in the common law world because it both resolves the underlying dilemma created by a mandatory death sentence *and* because it accords with the international trend toward limiting use of the death penalty to only the "most serious crimes."[12] The first option creating a narrow class of mandatory capital offenses greatly reduces the scope of problematic cases because it inherently requires an aggravating factor for the death penalty's imposition. However, by failing to consider individual circumstances of the offense or the offender, this narrows the fundamental flaw of a mandatory death regime without completely resolving it, as some offenders guilty of even the most aggravated offenses may still have mitigating factors in their specific cases. Similarly, the third option, a presumption in favor of death as established by the doctrine of extenuating circumstances in Southern Africa, does not accord with the emerging global consensus that the death penalty should be limited to the rarest of the rare and the worst of the worst. Requiring a defendant to show why he or she should *not* be executed lacks the analytical clarity of a pure discretionary death penalty and places an extra burden on defense counsel.

The Origins of the Common Law Mandatory Death Penalty

Historically, at English common law the death penalty was mandatory upon conviction, a punishment that passed to the Empire and was retained in many colonies after independence.[13] Capital punishment reached its zenith in England during the 1700s with the decline of transportation to a penal colony as a criminal sanction, which in turn led to increased mercy and pardon requests from the gallows and squalid and overcrowded conditions in the gaol.[14] Beginning after the English Revolution, the cabinet was required to confirm every capital case by considering each condemned prisoner for reprieve or pardon, and on what conditions. After a final decision, only a petition made to the king for mercy through the secretary of state was available to the prisoner.[15] During the 1780s, as many as 56% of capital condemned prisoners were hanged, a "judicial carnage" of numbers that were unprecedented before then and unsustainable after. The proportion of pardons simply had to increase to prevent public unrest at the bloodshed, and more complex mercy procedures developed in which the Recorder of London, the head judicial administrative officer for the city, consulted with the home secretary in every case.[16] This process was the precursor to the

---

11 Criminal Procedure and Evidence (Amendment) Act 46 of 1935 § 61.

12 *See* International Covenant on Civil and Political Rights (ICCPR), *opened for signature* December 19, 1966, 999 U.N.T.S. 85 (entered into force March 23, 1976), art. 6(2).

13 Evan Mandrey, Capital Punishment: A Balanced Examination 239–40 (2005); Simon Coldham, *Criminal Justice Policies in Commonwealth Africa: Trends and Prospects*, 44 J. Afr. L. 218, 223, 225 (2000) (noting the "remarkable continuity" of modern African criminal justice with the colonial period).

14 J.M. Beattie, Policing and Punishment in London, 1660–1750, 362–3 (2001).

15 *See id.* at 448–9 for the period 1714–50.

16 V.A.C. Gatrell, The Hanging Tree: Execution and the English People, 1770–1868, at 544–5 (2006).

advisory committee on the prerogative of mercy that was installed in British colonies where it remains in many Commonwealth constitutions today.

Pardons were common; about half of those condemned to death during the eighteenth century were not sent to the gallows. It may be that mercy was ultimately a political decision. "Petitions were most effective from great men, and the common course was for a plea to be passed up through increasingly higher levels of the social scale, between men bound together by the links of patronage and obligation."[17] Many mercy petitions were written by gentlemen on behalf of their laborers. Indeed, the pardon "put the principle instrument of legal terror—the gallows—directly in the hands of those who held power," simultaneously appearing impartial "acts of grace," while reinforcing class division and patronage to special interests.[18] In general, however, the grounds for pardon—for the young, the old, the mentally and physically infirm, the potentially reformable and re-employable, the poor, those with strong character references, those who were potentially innocent, and those who committed no violence or deception—conformed to "a set of broadly held social ideals about how justice should work."[19]

Most of those hanged at the gallows in Tyburn in London during the seventeenth and eighteenth centuries were guilty of property crimes, as they violated the sacred social contract of respect for private property.[20] In this sense, executions represented—to a far greater degree than in the modern era—the infliction of the ultimate punishment of death on lower, economically disadvantaged classes by upper landed classes. By the turn of the nineteenth century, executions for juveniles declined to zero as a result of prosecutions based on downgraded (non-capital) charges, increasingly restive juries, and robust executive clemency.[21] By contrast, persons in their late teenage years and twenties were the most likely to receive the death sentence and the least likely to receive a reprieve. Men were more than twice as likely to be sentenced to death as women, and twice as likely to be transported to the penal colonies; by the second half of the eighteenth century, courts were very reluctant to sentence women to the gallows.[22] By the time colonial penal codes were drafted in the late nineteenth century, they uniformly included exceptions for juveniles and pregnant women from the scope of capital punishment.

The most obvious change to sentencing policy between 1740 and 1820 was the decline of physical and often publicly inflicted punishments such as whipping and branding, and the rise of imprisonment.[23] Like punishments generally, executions were elaborate symbols of state power, and the execution ritual changed as society changed. In 1868, the last public execution took place in England; from then until 1964, they always took place behind prison walls. But even before this, the process of execution was becoming more "civilized" with the curtailment of practices such as beheading traitors (1820); forcing condemned to

---

17 Douglas Hay et al., Albion's Fatal Tree: Crime and Society in Eighteenth-Century England 45 (1975).
18 Id. at 47–8.
19 Peter King, Crime, Justice, and Discretion in England, 1740–1820 at 332 (2000).
20 Peter Linebaugh, The London Hanged: Crime and Civil Society in the Eighteenth Century xx (1992). An exception may have been forgery, which required literacy and therefore fell more heavily on a slightly higher economic class than most capital crimes. For this crime, the wealth and respectable background of the accused were cited as reasons for *harsher* treatment. King, *supra* note 19 at 307.
21 Peter King, Crime and Law in England, 1750–1840: Remaking Justice from the Margins 120–23 (2006).
22 King, *supra* note 19 at 279–80, 289.
23 Id. at 263.

carry their own ropes to the scaffold (1824); and gibbeting, the public display of a hanged prisoner after death (1832). Black curtains began to be draped around the bases of the scaffold to prevent the public from seeing the gruesome death.[24] Uniformly in the colonies death was by hanging, but public executions persisted elsewhere in the Empire long after 1868. Criminal punishments in the British colonial world were tools of social control, just as they were in Britain, with the goal of changing behavior and showcasing state power.

Like transportation to penal colonies before it, capital punishment declined over time in favor of imprisonment. The falling crime rate in the early nineteenth century led to a sharp curtailment in the number of capital offenses by the start of Queen Victoria's reign in 1837, from 220 to 15, and within twenty years only four (murder, piracy with violence, treason, and arson in the royal dockyards).[25] In practice, however, the penalty was restricted to murder. By the second half of the nineteenth century, it became apparent that not all murders were equally serious, and reformers made several attempts to narrow the scope of mandatory capital punishment. The system of mercy became more prominent, in which juries made private recommendations to the Home Secretary, who was able to reduce sentences without providing reasons. "In this way, the penal system in England and Wales adopted what has sometimes been described as 'the least bad solution,' but one that no one—abolitionist, retentionist or those somewhere in between—supported."[26] Not until the Royal Commission on Capital Punishment was set up in 1948 were alternatives to the mandatory death penalty seriously considered among British political elites.

By the time India's penal code went through several rounds of drafting beginning in the 1830s, the Victorian-era reforms of England's Bloody Code and the brutal nature of public capital and corporal punishments were well under way, and India and later colonies benefited.[27] From this point, the diffusion process took place. Former British colonies in Africa, Southeast Asia, and the Caribbean received similar penal and criminal procedure codes, based on the Indian Penal Code or derivative ones from Australia or the Gold Coast, many of which remain in force. The drafting of a penal code was "an imperial and international endeavor in which lawmakers in distant geographical locations routinely cited each other's work," and the drafters of the Indian Penal Code for instance were influenced by those of Louisiana and New York before them.[28] The contemporaneous processes of codifying the criminal law of India and of Britain proper were deeply interrelated in a "globalized" (that is, Empire-wide) sharing process that in many ways foreshadowed the modern sharing of death penalty jurisprudence. Litigation to abolish the mandatory death penalty in the post-colonial English-speaking world is only possible because of the historical similarities in constitutional and statutory texts in many former British colonies.

---

24 V.A.C. Gatrell, The Hanging Tree: Execution and the English People, 1770–1868 at 589, 596 (1996).

25 Barry Mitchell & Julian V. Roberts, Exploring the Mandatory Life Sentence for Murder 25–6 (2012).

26 *Id.* at 26 (internal citation omitted).

27 David Skuy, *Macaulay and the Indian Penal Code of 1862: The Myth of the Inherent Superiority and Modernity of the English Legal System Compared to the Indian Legal System in the Nineteenth Century*, 32 Mod. Asian Stud. 513, 527–30 (1998).

28 Elizabeth Kolsky, *Codification and the Rule of Law Difference: Criminal Procedure in British India*, 23 L. & Hist. Rev. 631, 632 (2005).

A Uniform Constitutional Vulnerability

In the postcolonial world, the mandatory death penalty has faced a sustained retreat worldwide since the abolition of the death sentence in Great Britain in 1965. The penalty first fell in the United States and India, the major retentionist common law powers. Today the penalty has been found incompatible with human rights norms in most of the Commonwealth Caribbean, East Africa, and South Asia, where courts have found an automatic sentence of death unconstitutional and replaced mandatory schemes with discretionary ones that allow consideration of mitigating factors in the capital sentencing process.[29] The result are criminal justice regimes that operate closer to conformity with international human rights norms and that have explicitly adopted these standards in domestic legal systems.

This harmonization of death penalty regimes across borders is no accident: it was the deliberate intention of a small network of international human rights lawyers to create a body of transnational jurisprudence from which to draw in bringing incremental challenges in national courts.[30] By initially petitioning bodies such as the United Nations Human Rights Committee and the Inter-American Human Rights System, this core of advocates developed a corpus of persuasive reasoning to find the mandatory death penalty incompatible with human rights treaty obligations, on which they relied in challenges before domestic and supranational courts in the Caribbean and later in Africa. The strategy had worked before: the decision of the European Court of Human Rights in 1989 finding that undue delay in an execution and conditions of death row could render an otherwise constitutional sentence cruel and degrading was followed over the next decade by decisions arising out of such diverse jurisdictions as Canada, Jamaica, India, and Zimbabwe.[31]

The constitutions of former British colonies in the Caribbean and Africa are *in pari materia* with one another, created from a template used by departing colonial officials at Lancaster House in London where most constitutional negotiations hurriedly took place on the eve of independence.[32] The fundamental rights portions of the constitutions are heavily based on the European Convention of Human Rights, which applied to Britain's colonies after 1953.[33] Almost all of these constitutions contain a right to life provision that is clawed back by a subclause specifically saving the death penalty. In addition, every constitution contains a clause prohibiting torture and cruel, inhuman, or degrading treatment and

---

29 *See generally*, Andrew Novak, *Constitutional Reform and the Abolition of the Mandatory Death Penalty in Kenya*, 44 SUFFOLK UNIV. L. REV. 285 (2012); Andrew Novak, *The Decline of the Mandatory Death Penalty in Common Law Africa: Constitutional Challenges and Comparative Jurisprudence in Malawi and Uganda*, 11 LOY. J. PUB. INT. L. 19 (2009); Andrew Novak, *The Abolition of the Mandatory Death Penalty in Africa: A Comparative Constitutional Analysis*, 22 IND. INT'L & COMP. L. REV. 267 (2012).

30 This strategy is driven by the Death Penalty Project UK and its executive directors Saul Lehrfreund and Parvais Jabbar, as well as their partners on the ground. Interview, *Litigating Against the Death Penalty for Drug Offences: An Interview with Saul Lehrfreund and Parvais Jabbar*, 1 INT'L J. HUM. RTS. & DRUG POL'Y 53, 54–5 (2010).

31 Soering v. U.K., (1989) E.H.R.R. 439; Catholic Commission for Justice and Peace v. A.G. (1993) L.R.C. 277 (Zim. S.C.); Triveniben v. State of Gujarat (1989) 1 S.C.J. 383 (India); United States v. Burns, [2001] 1 S.C.R. 283 (Can.); Pratt and Morgan v. A.G. (1993) UKPC 1 (appeal taken from Jam.).

32 William Dale, *The Making and Remaking of Commonwealth Constitutions*, 42 INT'L & COMP. L.Q. 67 (1993).

33 Jennifer Widner, BUILDING THE RULE OF LAW: FRANCIS NYALALI AND THE ROAD TO JUDICIAL INDEPENDENCE IN AFRICA 161 (2001).

punishment. Because the constitution only prevented challenge to the death penalty per se and not textually to a mandatory death penalty, the argument went, courts could find that the mandatory death penalty qualified as cruel and inhuman punishment because it was disproportionately harsh, classifying all murders the same even though all were not equally heinous.

Human rights lawyers succeeded on another track as well. Because the mandatory death penalty provides for an automatic sentence of death upon conviction of murder, no sentencing hearing takes place. Courts have interpreted this as a violation of the right to a fair trial, another right that appears uniformly across common law constitutions in the Caribbean and Sub-Saharan Africa, which should include the right to present mitigating evidence on a defendant's behalf in a sentencing hearing. The United Nations Human Rights Committee, the Inter-American Commission on Human Rights, the Privy Council, and national courts of appeal accepted this argument in a series of challenges. Both lines of jurisprudence have the same two holdouts: Malaysia and Singapore, also former British colonies, which have constitutions that do not include protections against cruel, inhuman, or degrading punishment or the right to a fair trial. Although the mandatory death penalty has been extinguished in most of the Caribbean, it survives in Southeast Asia.

The mandatory death penalty is peculiarly vulnerable to these incremental challenges because of two fundamental assumptions about postcolonial common law countries. First, because the mandatory death penalty exists in similar form in almost all former British colonies, it possesses common characteristics across borders. Second, most former British colonies share constitutional frameworks and adhere to most international human rights treaties. Like a row of dominoes, legal challenges in one jurisdiction place pressure on neighboring countries with similar bills of rights. Where these two assumptions are true, as in the Commonwealth Caribbean, Sub-Saharan Africa, and South Asia, the mandatory death penalty has usually fallen. Where these two assumptions are modified, as in the different constitutional regimes of Malaysia and Singapore, the penalty has survived challenge.

These challenges are based on a transnational body of death penalty jurisprudence that domestic courts cite, follow, and distinguish in accordance with local constitutional and legal norms. Many of the decisions analyzed in this book relied heavily on foreign and international precedent, and each has made an important contribution of their own to the corpus of global death penalty jurisprudence. This sharing process is helping to install international human rights principles in domestic constitutional regimes, harmonizing criminal justice regimes across borders and eventually shaping international law. That many of these challenges were conceived and coordinated by a relatively small group of abolitionist lawyers underscores the promise of human rights litigation in turning aspirational principles into realities.

The Structure of the Book

The remainder of the book is divided into the specific regions of the common law world where challenges to the mandatory death penalty have taken place. Chapter 2 of this book looks at the abolition of the mandatory death penalty in the United States in *Woodson v. North Carolina* and the revolution in capital sentencing that followed.

The suspension of the death penalty in the United States in 1972, with its resulting backlash and eventual reinstatement, paralleled a contemporaneous process in India that resulted in the restriction of the death penalty without outright abolition, the subject of

Chapter 3. Courts in India and its near neighbor Bangladesh continue to refine this death penalty jurisprudence, balancing human rights principles and state security.

The decline of the mandatory death penalty in the Commonwealth Caribbean, the subject of Chapter 4, was the result of coordinated challenges by London-based defense lawyers who brought challenges before international human rights tribunals and used the resulting decisions before the Privy Council, the highest court of appeal for most Caribbean countries.

This successful process stands in contrast to Malaysia and Singapore, explored in Chapter 5, which have justified their robust mandatory death penalty regimes for drug trafficking and other crimes as based on "Asian values" and the need for communitarian-based social policy that places the state above the individual. The chapter also contrasts these countries with Hong Kong, a territory with close similarities to Singapore but one that has famously abolished the death penalty.

Chapter 6 looks at the new frontier of Sub-Saharan Africa, where constitutional challenges to the mandatory death penalty succeeded in Kenya, Malawi, and Uganda. The sentencing reform that followed in each jurisdiction provides a model for future resource-constrained developing countries in establishing discretionary death penalty regimes. Although a similar challenge failed in Ghana, cases remain pending elsewhere on the continent.

In Southern Africa, the subject of Chapter 7, the doctrine of extenuating circumstances turned a mandatory death penalty into a rebuttable presumption in favor of death. Unlike common law East and West Africa, the death penalty in Southern Africa (and, by extension, Papua New Guinea in the South Pacific) was not truly mandatory. Although the death penalty has been abolished in South Africa and Namibia, it survives elsewhere in the region, although even here the regional trend is toward a pure discretionary death regime.

Finally, the Conclusion answers the question of what happens after abolition of the mandatory death penalty, looking at the constitutional status of life imprisonment and mandatory minimum sentences, the creation of sentencing guidelines, and the judicial review of executive clemency decisions. Death may be different, to paraphrase Justice Stewart's words in *Furman v. Georgia*, but the constitutional implications of the mandatory death jurisprudence reach far beyond the hangman and the noose.

Chapter 2
An Excessive and Arbitrary Punishment: The Mandatory Death Penalty and Discretion in the United States of America

In 1976, the United States Supreme Court invalidated the mandatory death penalty for murder in *Woodson v. North Carolina*, the first country in the English-speaking world to do so, on the basis that the Eighth Amendment to the U.S. Constitution prohibited "cruel and unusual punishments."[1] This decision ran counter to the prevailing international consensus of the time. Earlier, in 1967, the Judicial Committee of the Privy Council in London upheld a mandatory death sentence in *Queen v. Runyowa*, distinguishing American jurisprudence on the basis of the different wording of the Rhodesian Bill of Rights, which prohibited "cruel, inhuman, and degrading punishment or other treatment."[2] Similarly, in 1977, the Supreme Court of Canada upheld the mandatory death penalty for murder of a police officer in *Miller v. Queen*, rejecting the *Woodson* rationale even though the Canadian Bill of Rights prohibited "cruel and unusual treatment or punishment" and the Canadian legislature had abolished the death penalty the prior year.[3] This Commonwealth consensus that the prohibition on cruel and degrading punishment applied only to the nature and type of punishment and not to the severity or appropriateness of punishment is no longer good law.[4] Today, *Woodson* is cited and followed worldwide for the proposition that a mandatory death sentence may be too harsh for a crime given the individual circumstances of the offense, making such a disproportionate sentence unconstitutionally cruel and degrading.

Despite the "evolving" standards of the Eighth Amendment, modern death penalty jurisprudence in the United States rarely follows, and even more rarely shapes, international trends. Indeed, American exceptionalist sentiment concerning the death penalty is well documented, and the country was among the last to abolish the death penalty for juveniles and persons with mental retardation.[5] The death penalty in the United States is emotionally divisive and its legal vulnerabilities have attracted significant scholarly attention. Today, the constitutional status of the death penalty exists as a negotiated compromise between the liberal and conservative wings of the Supreme Court and their competing interpretations of the Eighth Amendment. Nonetheless, constitutional challenges to the death penalty have succeeded in reducing the number of executions overall, perhaps not as much through

---

1 Woodson v. North Carolina, 428 U.S. 280 (1976); U.S. CONST. amend. VIII.
2 Queen v. Runyowa, [1967] R.L.R. 42 (P.C.) (appeal taken from Rhodesia & Nyasaland).
3 Miller v. Queen, [1977] 2 S.C.R. 680 (Can.).
4 *See e.g.*, Bowe v. Queen, (2006) 68 W.I.R. 10 (P.C.) (appeal taken from Bahamas) (noting that the Council in *Runyowa* "effectively abdicated its duty of constitutional adjudication"). *Miller* has been read as prohibiting "grossly disproportionate" punishments under the Canadian Bill of Rights (and subsequently the Canadian Charter of Rights and Freedoms). *See* Queen v. Latimer, [2001] 1 S.C.R. 3 (2001) (Can.).
5 *See, e.g.*, Carol S. Steiker, *Capital Punishment and American Exceptionalism*, 81 OR. L. REV. 97, 97–8 (2002).

shaping constitutional doctrine as through increasing the structural costs of the imposition of capital punishment. The abolition of the death penalty in the United States is a war of attrition rather than a drama; it is quietly fading as alternatives such as life imprisonment without parole become more cost effective and post-conviction litigation, including high profile exonerations based on DNA evidence, undermines public support.[6]

The Death Penalty and Society in the United States

Capital punishment is currently a permissible sentence in thirty-two U.S. states, as well as the federal government and the military, although not all of these have operative statutes or have performed executions since death penalty reinstatement in 1976.[7] Eighteen states, the District of Columbia, and Puerto Rico have abolished the practice, most of them clustered in New England and the upper Midwest. As of August 15, 2013, 1,343 condemned prisoners have been executed since 1976, more than half in just three states: Texas (503), Virginia (110), and Oklahoma (105).[8] These prisoners included only 13 women; about 56% were white and 34% were African-American. Nearly 87% were executed by lethal injection and another 11% by electric chair.[9] Currently, executions have only occurred for aggravated or premeditated homicide since 1976; while other capital crimes remain on the books, their use is likely unconstitutional.[10] Imposition of the death penalty has declined in frequency since the year 2000, and the decline will accelerate in the short term due to dwindling supplies of the lethal injection drugs sodium thiopental and pentobarbital as a result of a European Union embargo and the refusal by domestic manufacturers and their distributors to sell the drugs to corrections facilities.[11]

Scholars have widely documented persistent deficiencies in the capital punishment regime in the United States despite popular support.[12] Research has suggested that many capital prisoners have inadequate legal counsel and, in later stages of the appellate process,

---

6 Ethan Bronner, *Use of Death Sentences Continues to Fall in U.S.*, N.Y. TIMES, Dec. 21, 2012, at A24.

7 *States With and Without the Death Penalty*, Death Penalty Information Center, http://www.deathpenaltyinfo.org/states-and-without-death-penalty (last accessed Aug. 20, 2013). The current death penalty statutes of Arkansas and California are not constitutionally operable. Robbie Brown, *Arkansas Court Upends the Death Penalty*, N.Y. TIMES, June 22, 2012 at A11; Denny Walsh, *Appellate Court Upholds Halt to Death Penalty in California*, SACRAMENTO BEE, May 31, 2013, http://www.sacbee.com/2013/05/31/5460309/appellate-court-upholds-halt-to.html.

8 Statistics are drawn from *Searchable Execution Database*, Death Penalty Information Center, http://www.deathpenaltyinfo.org/views-executions (last accessed Aug. 20, 2013).

9 *Id. See also* Bureau of Justice Statistics, *Capital Punishment, 2011 – Statistical Tables*, U.S. Department of Justice, NCJ 242185, July 2013.

10 *Death Penalty For Offenses Other Than Murder*, Death Penalty Information Center, http://deathpenaltyinfo.org/death-penalty-offenses-other-murder (last accessed Aug. 20, 2013); Kennedy v. Louisiana, 554 U.S. 407 (2008).

11 Josh Sanburn, *The Hidden Hand Squeezing Texas' Supply of Execution Drugs*, TIME MAGAZINE, Aug. 7, 2013, http://nation.time.com/2013/08/07/the-hidden-hand-squeezing-texas-supply-of-execution-drugs/; Ed Pilkington, *Death Penalty Declines in U.S. as Disapproval Grows*, GUARDIAN (U.K.), Dec. 15, 2011, http://www.theguardian.com/world/2011/dec/15/death-penalty-declines-us-disapproval.

12 For an analysis of popular support of the death penalty, see generally Richard C. Dieter, *A Crisis of Confidence: Americans' Doubts About the Death Penalty*, *in* AGAINST THE DEATH PENALTY: INTERNATIONAL INITIATIVES AND IMPLICATIONS 187 (Jon Yorke ed., 2008). *See generally* Austin Sarat &

no counsel at all.[13] Death sentences are disproportionately imposed on persons of limited economic means and members of disadvantaged minority communities.[14] Chance plays a significant role in determining who dies, where, and when. Since the late 1990s, high profile exonerations, the successes of law school clinics devoted to innocence issues, and scientific advances in gathering evidence revealed that dozens of death sentences were erroneously imposed.[15] The high wrongful conviction rate is variously attributed to faulty forensic science, police and prosecutorial misconduct, and inadequate defense counsel.[16]

The disproportionate racial impact of the death penalty in the United States has produced some of the best empirical research on capital punishment anywhere in the world. Widely cited statistics reveal a high correlation between the race of a victim and the likelihood of death penalty imposition; the race of the defendant is also correlated.[17] A prosecutor's discretion in seeking the death penalty plays a role in producing the discriminatory consequences.[18] Female offenders are unlikely to be arrested for murder, only rarely sentenced to death, and almost never executed.[19] In addition, defendants are more likely to be sentenced to death when a victim is female.[20] The continued execution of prisoners with

---

Neil Vidmar, *Public Opinion, the Death Penalty, and the Eighth Amendment: Testing the Marshall Hypothesis*, 1976 WISC. L. REV. 171.

13 Stephen B. Bright, Essay, *Counsel for the Poor: The Death Sentence Not for the Worst Crime but for the Worst Lawyer*, 103 YALE L.J. 1835, 1836 (1994); Michael Mello, *Facing Death Alone: The Post-Conviction Attorney Crisis on Death Row*, 37 AM. U. L. REV. 513, 516, 531 (1988); Andrew Hammel, *Effective Performance Guarantees for Capital State Post-Conviction Counsel: Cutting the Gordian Knot*, 5 J. APP. PRAC. & PROCESS 347, 348 (2003).

14 The literature on the correlations among race, economic standing, and the imposition of the death penalty is voluminous. *See, e.g.*, DAVID COLE, NO EQUAL JUSTICE: RACE AND CLASS IN THE CRIMINAL JUSTICE SYSTEM 132–3 (1999); John Blume, Theodore Eisenberg & Martin T. Wells, *Explaining Death Row's Population and Racial Composition*, 1 J. EMPIRICAL LEGAL STUD. 165, 204 (2004).

15 STANLEY COHEN, THE WRONG MEN: AMERICA'S EPIDEMIC OF WRONGFUL DEATH ROW CONVICTIONS x–xi (2003). Scholars have posited the error rate to be between 0.5% and 3 to 5%. C. Ronald Huff, *Wrongful Convictions: The American Experience*, 46 CAN. J. CRIMINOLOGY & CRIM. JUST. 107, 109 (2004); D. Michael Risinger, *Innocents Convicted: An Empirically Justified Factual Wrongful Conviction Rate*, 97 J. CRIM. L. & CRIMINOLOGY 761, 762, 768–80 (2007).

16 Jean Coleman Blackerby, Note, *Life After Death Row: Preventing Wrongful Convictions and Restoring Innocence After Exoneration*, 56 VAND. L. REV. 1179, 1185–93 (2003). Other factors include eyewitness error, plea bargaining, community pressure for a conviction, and admission of character evidence at trial. C. Ronald Huff, Arye Rattner & Edward Sagarin, *Guilty Until Proved Innocent: Wrongful Conviction and Public Policy*, 32 CRIME & DELINQUENCY 518, 524, *et seq.* (1986). False confessions, particularly among persons with intellectual or developmental disabilities, may also be a cause. *See* Paul G. Cassell, *The Guilty and the "Innocent": An Examination of Alleged Cases of Wrongful Conviction from False Confessions*, 22 HARV. J. L. & PUB. POL'Y 523, 525 (1999).

17 Michael J. Songer & Isaac Unah, *The Effect of Race, Gender, and Location on Prosecutorial Decisions to Seek the Death Penalty in South Carolina*, 58 S.C. L. REV. 161, 206 (2006); Stephanie Hindson, Hillary Potter & Michael J. Radelet, *Race, Gender, Region and Death Sentencing in Colorado, 1980–1999*, 77 U. COLO. L. REV. 549, 581 (2006).

18 Michael Mears, *The Georgia Death Penalty: A Need for Racial Justice*, 1 JOHN MARSHALL L.J. 71, 86 (2008); Isaac Unah, *Choosing Those Who Will Die: The Effect of Race, Gender, and Law in Prosecutorial Decision to Seek the Death Penalty in Durham County, North Carolina*, 15 MICH. J. RACE & L. 135, 174 (2009).

19 Victor L. Streib, *Gendering the Death Penalty: Countering Sex Bias in a Masculine Sanctuary*, 63 OHIO ST. L.J. 433, 434 (2002).

20 *See, e.g.*, Jefferson E. Holcomb, Marian R. Williams & Stephen Demuth, *White Female Victims and Death Penalty Disparity Research*, 21 JUST. Q. 877, 877 (2004). Women statistically commit fewer offenses than men, but it may also be true that women are selected out of the death penalty pool of

emotional, developmental, or intellectual disabilities has attracted a great deal of academic criticism. Scientific and psychological research on mental health has outpaced criminal justice reform.[21] The Supreme Court has ruled that the execution of a prisoner who is insane or mentally retarded is unconstitutional, but it is unclear how this case law affects prisoners with other mental illnesses.[22]

Poor legal representation is characteristic of the death penalty almost everywhere in the common law world. In the United States, a death sentence resulting from ineffective assistance of counsel as guaranteed by the Sixth Amendment may also constitute cruel and unusual punishment.[23] "Because of constitutional requirements and the diligence of attorneys in capital cases, death penalty litigation is a long, expensive process," often with more pretrial motions, higher expert fees, longer voir dire of jurors, a bifurcated trial, and automatic appeals.[24] To make out a constitutional claim of ineffective assistance of counsel, a defendant must show first that the attorney's performance was unreasonable under professional norms; and second that the deficient performance resulted in prejudice.[25] As caseloads of capital defense attorneys become heavier and funding dries up, the potential for harm of constitutional magnitude grows, despite major advances toward legal aid reform in a number of states.[26] An excessive caseload and strained budgets can cause attorneys to employ substandard representation.[27] In addition to poor legal representation, misconduct by prosecutors or law enforcement has contributed to eroding public confidence in capital punishment.[28] Withholding exculpatory evidence or presenting false evidence violates both due process and the Eighth Amendment.[29]

Even more than sentencing disparities, lack of counsel, or prosecutorial misconduct, the risk of wrongful executions has greatly contributed to declining support for the death penalty in modern America, especially after the advent of DNA testing in the early 1990s. Despite high profile exonerations since that time, not all states allow the introduction of

---

defendants because of structural bias at earlier stages in the process, such as in prosecutorial discretion and plea-bargaining. According to one study, women account for 10% of murder arrests, 2% of death sentences, and only 1.1% of executions. Harry Greenlee & Shelia P. Greenlee, *Women and the Death Penalty: Racial Disparities and Differences*, 14 WM. & MARY J. WOMEN & L. 319, 321 (2007).

21 Liliana Lyra Jubilut, *Death Penalty and Mental Illness: The Challenge of Reconciling Human Rights, Criminal Law, and Psychiatric Standards*, 6 SEATTLE J. SOC. JUST. 353, 354, 356-7.

22 Ford v. Wainright, 477 U.S. 399 (1986); Atkins v. Virginia, 536 U.S. 304 (2002).

23 The Sixth Amendment states, "In all criminal proceedings, the accused shall enjoy the right…to have the Assistance of Counsel for his defence." U.S. CONST. amend. VI. *See also*, Note, *The Eighth Amendment and Ineffective Assistance of Counsel in Capital Trials*, 107 HARV. L. REV. 8, 8, *et seq.* (1994).

24 Margot Garey, Comment, *The Cost of Taking a Life: Dollars and Sense of the Death Penalty*, 18 U.C. DAVIS L. REV. 1221, 1245, *et seq.* (1985).

25 Carissa Byrne Hessick, *Ineffective Assistance at Sentencing*, 50 B.C. L. REV. 1069, 1072 (2009).

26 Roscoe C. Howard, Jr., *The Defunding of the Post-Conviction Defense Organizations As a Denial of the Right to Counsel*, 98 W.VA. L. REV. 863, 901-3, 920 (1996).

27 Bennett H. Brummer, *The Banality of Excessive Defender Workload: Managing the Systemic Obstruction of Justice*, 22 ST. THOMAS L. REV. 104, 106-7 (2009).

28 Welsh White, *Curbing Prosecutorial Misconduct in Capital Cases: Imposing Prohibitions on Improper Penalty Trial Arguments*, 39 AM. CRIM. L.REV. 1147, 1172, 1179, 1181 (2002); Natasha Minsker, *Prosecutorial Misconduct in Death Penalty Cases*, 45 CAL. W. L. REV.373, 401 (2009).

29 Gilbert Stroud Merritt, *Prosecutorial Error in Death Penalty Cases*, 76 TENN. L. REV. 677, 677 (2009).

DNA evidence in post-conviction proceedings to prove innocence.[30] Scholars have noted the increasing centrality of innocence in the death penalty debate due to the advent of more sophisticated forensic technology.[31] Indeed, no single issue has the power to transform public opinion on capital punishment as the risk of executing the innocent.[32]

Clemency holds an important place in the history of capital punishment in the United States, as it was the principal avenue of relief for individuals convicted of capital offenses before the right to appeal was constitutionalized, but it too contains an element of chance. Though every death penalty state has a provision for the governor or a board of advisors to grant clemency, the nature of pardon and parole is erratic.[33] Executive clemency "is idiosyncratic at best, and arbitrary at worst," overall seeming to "add, rather than subtract, an element of luck in the ultimate decision of who ends up being executed."[34]

Proportionality in Criminal Sentencing and the Eighth Amendment

Adopted in 1791, the Eighth Amendment of the United States Constitution states, "Excessive bail shall not be required, nor excessive fines imposed, nor cruel and unusual punishments inflicted," almost identical to a provision in the English Bill of Rights of 1689 although some American colonies possessed similar limitations as early as 1641.[35] The Amendment was the brainchild of the drafters of the 1776 Virginia Declaration of Rights, including George Mason and Patrick Henry, who sought a limitation on the types of punishments that a federal Congress could impose.[36] At a minimum, the Amendment probably was intended to prohibit "modes of punishments such as pillorying, disemboweling, decapitation, drawing and quartering, burning at the stake, crucifixion, breaking on the wheel, the rack and thumbscrew, and extreme instances of solitary confinement."[37] Scholars have posited that, by extension, the Eighth Amendment may prohibit such putatively cruel punishments as slavery-era chain gangs, torture for the purpose of eliciting confessions, banishment, and judicial whipping or caning, among others.[38]

---

30   Rachel Steinback, Comment, *The Fight for Post-Conviction DNA Testing is Not Yet Over: An Analysis of the Eight Remaining 'Holdout States' and Suggestions for Strategies to Bring Vital Relief to the Wrongfully Convicted*, 98 J. Crim. L. & Criminology 329, 333–4 (2007).

31   David S. Medwed, *Innocentrism*, 2008 U. Ill. L. Rev. 1549, 1551–2 (2008).

32   Lawrence Marshall, *The Innocence Revolution and the Death Penalty*, 1 Ohio St. J. Crim. L. 573, 579 (2004); Michael L. Radelet, *The Role of the Innocence Argument in Contemporary Death Penalty Debates*, 41 Tex. Tech L. Rev. 199, 219 (2008).

33   Cathleen Burnett, Justice Denied: Clemency Appeals in Death Penalty Cases 15, 155 (2002).

34   Michael L. Radelet & Barbara A. Zsembik, *Executive Clemency in Post-Furman Capital Cases*, 27 U. Rich. L. Rev. 289, 305 (1993).

35   U.S. Const. amend. VIII. *See* Stanley Mosk, *The Eighth Amendment Rediscovered*, 1 Loy. L.A. L. Rev. 4, 6–7 (1968) (noting early provisions in charters of Massachusetts and Connecticut).

36   Stephen T. Parr, *Symmetric Proportionality: A New Perspective on the Cruel and Unusual Punishment Clause*, 68 Tenn. L. Rev. 41, 47 (2000).

37   Margaret R. Gibbs, *Eighth Amendment: Narrow Proportionality Requirement Preserves Deference to Legislative Judgment*, 82 J. Crim. L. & Criminology 955, 956 (1992) (note).

38   Tessa M. Gorman, Comment, *Back on the Chain Gang: Why the Eighth Amendment and the History of Slavery Proscribe the Resurgence of Chain Gangs*, 85 Cal. L. Rev. 441 (1997); Wm. Garth Snider, *Banishment: The History of Its Use and a Proposal for Its Abolition under the First Amendment*, 24 New Eng. J. on Crim. & Civ. Confinement 455 (1998) (but using First Amendment approach); Christine Rebman, Comment, *Eighth Amendment and Solitary Confinement: The Gap in Protection from Psychological Consequences*, 49 DePaul L. Rev. 567 (2000); Daniel E. Hall, *When*

The Eighth Amendment's murky origins have led to considerable debate as to the intentions of the Amendment's drafters in 1791 and even the intentions of the drafters of Article 10 of the English Bill of Rights of 1689. The prohibition on "cruel and unusual punishments" may have been a reaction to either the Bloody Assizes under King James II, a special commission that tried, convicted, and executed hundreds of insurgents, or alternatively the trial of Titus Oates, who was convicted of capital perjury after his testimony sent more than a dozen men to the gallows for a fabricated Catholic plot against the King.[39] If the prohibition was a reaction to the Bloody Assizes, in which convicted prisoners were hanged, cut down while still alive, disemboweled, beheaded, and quartered, then the prohibition was likely intended to be a ban on certain barbarous and cruel punishments or punishments not in accordance with law.[40] On the other hand, the only contemporaneous use of the phrase "cruel and unusual punishment" before the drafting of the English Bill of Rights was in a minority report in the House of Lords condemning the overly harsh punishment on Titus Oates, including an excessive fine, life imprisonment, whipping, pillorying four times per year, and defrocking, none of which would have been considered barbarous or cruel per se at the time.[41] On this theory, the prohibition on cruel and unusual punishments was intended to prevent disproportionately harsh punishments. The drafters of the Eighth Amendment in 1791 may have been influenced by either or both of these events, and the tension between the two theories is evident in modern American case law.

Disproportionately harsh punishments existed long after the English Bill of Rights came into force: the number of capital crimes in England actually increased exponentially from eight in 1500 to fifty in 1689 and then to more than 200 by the year 1800.[42] This implies that Article 10 of the English Bill of Rights was not intended to prohibit disproportionately harsh punishments and certainly not to restrict application of the death penalty. Indeed, in the United States after ratification of the Eighth Amendment, one of the first acts of Congress was to enact a law creating offenses punishable by death and by corporal punishment.[43] Yet, the proportionality principle in American criminal sentencing has a long history in the United States and beyond since its articulation in Cesare Beccaria's book *On Crimes and Punishments* in 1764, which was widely read in the early American colonies by such important figures as John Adams, Thomas Jefferson, and George Mason.[44]

Caning Meets the Eighth Amendment: Whipping Offenders in the United States, 4 Widener J. Pub. L. 403 (1995); Celia Rumann, *Tortured History: Finding Our Way Back to the Lost Origins of the Eighth Amendment*, 31 Pepp. L. Rev. 3 (2004) (on torturous interrogations).

39 Rumann, *supra* note 38 at 670–71.

40 Charles Walter Schwartz, *Eighth Amendment Proportionality Analysis and the Compelling Case of William Rummel*, 71 J. Crim. L. & Criminology 378, 378 (1980); *see also* Anthony F. Granucci, *"Nor Cruel and Unusual Punishments Inflicted": The Original Meaning*, 57 Calif. L. Rev. 839 (1969). Granucci argued that the trial of Titus Oates formed the original basis for Article 10 of the English Bill of Rights. *Id.* at 859–60.

41 Schwartz, *supra* note 40 at 379.

42 *Id.* at 380.

43 Julian Killingley, *Constraining America's Death Penalty: The Eighth Amendment and Excessive Punishment*, in Against the Death Penalty: International Initiatives and Implications 127, 128–9 (Jon Yorke, ed. 2008), *citing* 1 Stat. 117 (1st Cong., 2d Sess. 1790), Act of April 30, 1790.

44 *Id.* at 381, *citing* Deborah A. Schwartz & Jay Wishingrad, Comment, *The Eighth Amendment, Beccaria, and the Enlightenment: An Historical Justification for the* Weems v. United States *Excessive Punishment Doctrine*, 24 Buffalo L. Rev. 783 (1975).

Still the debate rages. The Eighth Amendment prohibits excessive bail and excessive fines; it pointedly does not prohibit excessive punishments. On the other hand, it is not clear why excessive punishment would be permissible but excessive bail or fines not be. According to Claus, the purpose of the Eighth Amendment was to prohibit arbitrary or discriminatory application of criminal punishment rather than the excessiveness or type of punishment per se.[45] Stinneford has argued for an Eighth Amendment interpretation that includes the Founders' definition of "unusual" in addition to "cruel," and thus it was intended to prohibit foreign practices that were unknown at common law, or traditional punishments that fell out of usage and were later revived.[46] Granucci argues that the American drafters of the Eighth Amendment were as influenced by the early reformers Robert Beale and Nathanial Ward as they were by the English Bill of Rights.[47] Both Beale, a late sixteenth-century British lawyer, and Ward, a Puritan reformer in the Massachusetts Bay Colony, worked to prohibit "cruel" and barbaric punishments, principles first codified in the colony's Body of Liberties in 1641.

Regardless of the original purpose of the Eighth Amendment, it is clear today that it embodies some proportionality principle. The Supreme Court turned away a proportionality challenge to a criminal sentence under the Eighth Amendment as early as 1867 and limited the prohibition on cruel and unusual punishments only to barbarous forms of punishment themselves.[48] However, in an 1892 case, three justices dissented when the Court upheld a sentence of an enormous fine or lengthy term of imprisonment with hard labor for alcohol sales violations, believing that the Eighth Amendment prohibited "all punishments which by their excessive length or severity are greatly disproportioned to the offences charged."[49] This was the first explicit statement from the Court that the Eighth Amendment forbade not only inherently cruel punishments, but also otherwise permissible punishments that were excessive in relation to a crime.[50]

The first successful challenge to a form of punishment and its appropriateness for an offense under the Eighth Amendment was in *Weems v. United States* in 1910, a constitutional attack on the punishment of cadena temporal (chaining with hard labor) for the crime of forgery of an official document in American-occupied Philippines.[51] The Court's decision in *Weems* was the first to turn away from an "originalist" view of the Eighth Amendment and find that even forms of punishment in existence at the time the constitution entered into force could be unconstitutional. In *Trop v. Dulles*, the Court found that revocation of citizenship for wartime desertion was a cruel and unusual criminal punishment, famously noting that the Eighth Amendment "must draw its meaning from the evolving standards of decency that mark the progress of a maturing society."[52] These cases reactivated the Eighth

---

45 Laurence Claus, *The Antidiscrimination Eighth Amendment*, 28 HARV. J. L. & PUB. POL'Y 119, 120–21 (2004); Laurence Claus, *Methodology, Proportionality, Equality: Which Moral Question Does the Eighth Amendment Pose?* 31 HARV. J. L. & PUB. POL'Y 35, 37–8 (2008).

46 John F. Stinneford, *The Original Meaning of Unusual: The Eighth Amendment as a Bar to Cruel Innovation*, 102 Nw. U. L. REV.1745–6 (2008).

47 Granucci, *supra* note 40 at 848–51.

48 Pervear v. Massachusetts, 72 U.S. (5 Wall.) 608, 609–10 (1867); Wilkerson v. Utah, 99 U.S. 130 (1878); In re: Kemmler, 136 U.S. 436 (1890).

49 O'Neil v. Vermont, 144 U.S. 323, 339–40 (1892) (Field, J., dissenting).

50 James S. Campbell, *Revival of the Eighth Amendment: Development of Cruel-Punishment Doctrine by the Supreme Court*, 16 STAN. L. REV. 996, 1004 (1964).

51 Weems v. United States, 217 U.S. 349 (1910).

52 Trop v. Dulles, 356 U.S. 86 (1958). The Court had previously ruled that reliance on the customs or norms of the civilized world could establish standards for constitutional interpretation.

Amendment as a "living" clause, not tied to originalist notions of criminal punishment at the time of the founding of the American Republic.

Weems and *Trop* did not involve challenges to state law. Not until 1962 in *Robinson v. California* was the Eighth Amendment incorporated to the states via the due process clause of the Fourteenth Amendment.[53] *Robinson* was a challenge to a California law criminalizing the status of drug addiction; the sentence of 90 days imprisonment was not in itself a cruel and unusual punishment, but was unconstitutional for a "status" offense that did not involve criminal conduct. The decision in *Robinson* opened up state punishments to federal constitutional scrutiny for the first time, and was an indispensable tool for advocates seeking abolition of the death penalty. State courts were also active in striking down punishments that were deemed to be excessive for the crime involved based both on the Eighth Amendment and analogous provisions in state constitutions. Relying on *Weems*, the California Supreme Court invalidated an indeterminate sentence for a second conviction for public exposure, as the penalty could have amounted to life imprisonment, and threw out a mandatory 10 year minimum of imprisonment for a second drug-related felony.[54] The Michigan Supreme Court found unconstitutional a mandatory minimum sentence of twenty years for selling marijuana.[55] Similarly, the U.S. Court of Appeals for the Fourth Circuit found that a mandatory life sentence under West Virginia's habitual offender law violated the constitution as applied to conviction for perjury and check fraud.[56] While cases such as these were rare, the Eighth Amendment provided a constitutional minimum that prevented the worst abuses of legislatively enacted mandatory or determinate sentencing laws.

Other than death penalty challenges, the Supreme Court has only found a sentence to be unconstitutionally disproportionate in extreme cases. "The feeling that modern Eighth Amendment jurisprudence has gone off the rails has arisen, at least in part, from the wildly inconsistent rulings that have emanated from the Supreme Court over the past few decades, particularly regarding proportionality in sentencing and the death penalty."[57] For instance, in *Rummel v. Estelle*, the Court upheld a mandatory life sentence for a small-time recidivist who was convicted of obtaining about $120 by false pretenses, determining that the Eighth Amendment did not require any proportionality between the crime and the punishment.[58] Yet three years later in *Solem v. Helm*, the Court struck down a life sentence for another small-time recidivist who was convicted of uttering a fraudulent check in the amount of $100, finding such a punishment to be grossly extreme.[59] In 2003, the Court recognized proportionality as a constitutional principle, but upheld a sentence of twenty-five years to life for the theft of three golf clubs.[60]

The Paquete Habana, 175 U.S. 677, 712 (1900). *Trop* was a plurality decision, but the proposition for which it stood commanded majority support in Witherspoon v. Illinois, 391 U.S. 510 (1968), which invalidated the practice of "death qualifying" juries by removing from the panels any person who had moral objections to capital punishment.

53 Robinson v. California, 370 U.S. 660 (1962).
54 In re: Lynch, 8 Cal.3d 410 (1972); In re: Foss, 10 Cal.3d 910, (1974).
55 People v. Lorentzen, 387 Mich. 167, 194 N.W.2d 827 (1972).
56 Hart v. Coiner, 483 F.2d 136 (4th Cir. 1973), *cert. denied*, 415 U.S. 983 (1974).
57 Stinneford, *supra* note 46 at 1739, 1740.
58 Rummel v. Estelle, 445 U.S. 263 (1980).
59 Solem v. Helm, 463 U.S. 277 (1983).
60 Ewing v. California, 538 U.S. 11, 30–31 (2003).

While the Court focused on the appropriateness of a given punishment for an offense in non-capital cases, in death penalty cases the Court tended to determine whether a capital offense was grossly disproportionate as a matter of law.[61] In *Coker v. Georgia*, the Court invalidated the death penalty for rape solely because no life was taken; according to the Court, it was not germane to the proportionality analysis that Coker was a prison escapee who committed armed robbery and kidnapping along with the rape, or that he had previous convictions for other violent crimes including rape and murder.[62] The Court also summarily overturned a death sentence for non-fatal kidnapping.[63] *Coker*, a four justice plurality decision, was confirmed by a majority in *Kennedy v. Louisiana* in 2008, which invalidated the death penalty for the rape of a child under the age of 12 on the basis that the death penalty for a crime against an individual that did not result in death violated the Eighth Amendment.[64]

The Court has also limited application of the death penalty to accomplices who lacked intent to kill or played only a minor role in a crime. The Court has struggled with the category of felony murder, which "allows a conviction without a real examination of blameworthiness."[65] In *Enmund v. Florida*, the Court reversed a death sentence for an accomplice who remained in the car during an armed robbery and was not present at the scene of the killing.[66] Four years later, in *Cabana v. Bullock*, the Court held that a felony murder accomplice had to kill, attempt to kill, or intend to kill or use lethal force to be death penalty-eligible.[67] Less than a year later, a different five justice majority adopted a broader test in *Tison v. Arizona*, finding that a felony murder accomplice could be death penalty-eligible if the accomplice was a "major participant" in the underlying felony and displayed "reckless indifference" or "reckless disregard" for human life.[68]

Although it took some time, the Court has also removed certain categories of offenders from the scope of the death penalty. Only a year after the Court struck down the death penalty for juveniles under age 15, the justices upheld the death penalty for offenders aged 16 and 17 in *Stanford v. Kentucky*.[69] Sixteen years later, the Court invalidated such punishment in *Roper v. Simmons*.[70] Relying on *Roper*, the Court later invalidated life imprisonment without parole for juveniles in *Graham v. Florida* (non-homicide offenses) and *Miller v. Alabama* (homicide), finding that children are constitutionally different from adults for sentencing purposes, an unusual application of death penalty case law to non-capital sentencing.[71] Similarly, in *Penry v. Lynaugh* in 1989, the Court determined that execution of a person with mental retardation was not necessarily cruel and unusual punishment,

---

61   Richard A. Rosen, *Felony Murder and the Eighth Amendment Jurisprudence of Death*, 31 B.C. L. Rev. 1103, 1141 (1990).
62   Coker v. Georgia, 433 U.S. 584, 598 (1977).
63   Eberhart v. Georgia, 433 U.S. 584 (1977).
64   Kennedy v. Louisiana, 554 U.S. 407 (2008).
65   Rosen, *supra* note 61 at 1137.
66   Enmund v. Florida, 458 U.S. 782, 784 (1982).
67   Cabana v. Bullock, 474 U.S. 476 (1980).
68   Tison v. Arizona, 481 U.S. 137 (1987).
69   Thompson v. Oklahoma, 487 U.S. 815 (1988); Stanford v. Kentucky, 492 U.S. 361 (1989).
70   Roper v. Simmons, 543 U.S. 551 (2005).
71   Graham v. Florida, 560 U.S. __; 130 S.Ct. 2011 (2010); Miller v. Alabama, 567 U.S. __; 132 S.Ct. 2455 (2012). For a background on these cases, including the increasing juvenile crime rates that led to harsher penalties, as well as a comparative analysis with other retentionist countries, see Hillary J. Massey, Note, *Disposing of Children: The Eighth Amendment and Juvenile Life Without Parole After Roper*, 47 B.C.L. Rev. 1083, 1088, 1114-16 (2006).

while in 2002 the Court reversed course and found such execution unconstitutional in *Atkins v. Virginia*.[72] Was it the Constitution that changed, or the Court? The Court did not overrule its previous decisions when it decided *Roper* and *Atkins*; rather, these decisions were based on the notion that the Eighth Amendment evolved as society evolved.[73] In his *Roper* dissent, Justice Antonin Scalia wrote that the Court's decision was based on the proposition "that the meaning of our Constitution has changed over the past 15 years—not, mind you, that this Court's decision 15 years ago was *wrong*, but that the Constitution *has changed.*"[74] Scalia formulated an originalist interpretation of the Eighth Amendment, positing only that the Amendment prohibited punishments that were deemed to be inherently cruel as of 1791 and not punishments disproportionate for a specified offense.

The shifting contours of the Eighth Amendment, reactivated after *Trop v. Dulles* and applied to the states in *Robinson v. California*, created a constitutional platform from which to launch challenges to the death penalty. The Legal Defense Fund of the National Association for the Advancement of Colored People (NAACP), founded in 1940 by future Supreme Court Justice Thurgood Marshall, spearheaded a moratorium strategy to begin a constitutional attack on the discriminatory application of the death penalty by coordinating hundreds of challenges nationwide.[75] The strategy began working as a flurry of death penalty appeals reduced the number of executions in the United States from 42 in 1961 to just two in 1967, and none between 1968 and 1972, even as the number of death row prisoners increased in that period. The logjam pressured the United States Supreme Court to grant certiorari to one of the NAACP's challenges. As early as 1963, three justices dissented to the denial of certiorari in a case upholding a sentence of death for "a convicted rapist who has neither taken nor endangered human life."[76] On the other hand, as late as 1971, Justice John Marshall Harlan wrote that any attempt to rationalize capital punishment was futile, and consequently states had the freedom to choose how they used the penalty.[77] "By shifting majorities, the Court has steered a path between the extremes. Keeping the goal of minimizing arbitrariness, caprice, and discrimination in front of them, the Justices have scrutinized various state procedures, approving some and disallowing others."[78]

On June 29, 1972, in a pithy *per curiam* decision, five justices of the Supreme Court found that Georgia's statutory death penalty for murder and Georgia's and Texas's death penalties for rape constituted cruel and unusual punishment.[79] A pending appeal from California was dismissed as moot because of the intervening decision of the California Supreme Court in *People v. Anderson* invalidating the state's death penalty statute.[80] However, beyond the simple holding in the lead decision in *Furman v. Georgia*, the five justices in the majority agreed on very little. The decision included nine opinions for a total of 230 pages, the longest decision ever handed down by the Court. Two of these opinions, by Thurgood

---

72 Penry v. Lynaugh, 492 U.S. 302 (1989); Atkins v. Virginia, 536 U.S. 304 (2002).
73 Stinneford, *supra* note 46 at 1741.
74 *Roper*, 543 U.S. at 608 (Scalia, J., dissenting), *cited in* Stinneford, *supra* note 46 at 1741.
75 Killingley, *supra* note 43 at 137.
76 Rudolph v. Alabama, 375 U.S. 889 (1963) (Goldberg, J., dissenting from the denial of certiorari), *cited in* William J. Brennan, *Constitutional Adjudication and the Death Penalty: A View from the Court*, 100 HARV. L. REV. 313, 315 (1986).
77 McGautha v. California, 402 U.S. 183, 204 (1971).
78 Rosen, *supra* note 61 at 1113.
79 Furman v. Georgia, 408 U.S. 238 at 239–40 (1972) (consolidated with Jackson v. Georgia, No. 69–5030, and Branch v. Texas, No. 69–5031).
80 People v. Anderson, 6 Cal.3d 628 (1972).

Marshall and William Brennan, believed that the death penalty always violated the Eighth Amendment no matter how it was administered; for the rest of their time on the bench, both would dissent in every death sentence upheld by the Court over the next twenty years.[81] The opinions by William Douglas, Byron White, and Potter Stewart were narrower in scope and, for that reason, considered the controlling majority; they believed that Georgia's death penalty as applied was cruel and unusual because of racial discrimination in the penalty's application and because the infrequency of death sentences provided no meaningful basis for distinguishing the few cases in which death was imposed from the many in which it was not.[82] "These death sentences are cruel and unusual in the same way that being struck by lightning is cruel and unusual," Justice Stewart famously wrote.[83] He continued:

> For, of all the people convicted of rapes and murders in 1967 and 1968, many just as reprehensible as these, the petitioners are among a capriciously selected random handful upon whom the sentence of death has in fact been imposed. My concurring Brothers have demonstrated that, if any basis can be discerned for the selection of these few to be sentenced to death, it is the constitutionally impermissible basis of race. But racial discrimination has not been proved, and I put it to one side. I simply conclude that the Eighth and Fourteenth Amendments cannot tolerate the infliction of a sentence of death under legal systems that permit this unique penalty to be so wantonly and so freakishly imposed.[84]

A dissent by Chief Justice Warren Burger and Justices Harry Blackmun, Lewis Powell, and William Rehnquist, all appointees of President Richard Nixon, upheld the death penalty as permissible under common law tradition and the Eighth Amendment.[85]

For the next four years after 1972, the death penalty in the United States existed in constitutional limbo. No executions could occur until a state statute survived scrutiny by the Supreme Court—an unpredictable prospect given that none of the justices agreed on a single line of reasoning in *Furman*. State legislatures became laboratories, experimenting with both common law mandatory death regimes and Model Penal Code-influenced guided discretionary regimes. Thirty-seven states re-enacted death penalty statutes between 1972 and 1976. However, one thing that a majority of the Court did agree on in *Furman* was that *Weems v. United States* stood for the proposition that a punishment that was excessive for a crime constituted cruel and unusual punishment under the Eighth Amendment.[86] Even if the Court eventually upheld the constitutionality of the death penalty per se, the confluence of the two lines of Eighth Amendment jurisprudence—the arbitrariness in *Furman* and the

---

81 Furman v. Georgia, 408 U.S. 238, 257 (1972) (Brennan, J., concurring); 314 (Marshall, J., concurring).

82 *See id.* at 257 (Douglas, J., concurring); 309–10 (Stewart, J., concurring); 311–12 (White, J., concurring).

83 *Id.* at 309–10 (Stewart, J., concurring).

84 *Id.* (internal citations omitted).

85 *Id.* at 375 *et seq.* (Burger, J., dissenting). The Chief Justice distinguished capital punishment from other forms of criminal punishment that were "repugnant to all civilized standards," including burning at the stake. *Id.* at 385. Justice Brennan later noted that burning at the stake *was* capital punishment, and perhaps *Furman* would have been better reframed as a challenge to "frying in a chair." Brennan, *supra* note 76 at 330.

86 This is recognized at least in the concurring opinions by Justices Marshall and Brennan and by the four justice dissent. *See id.* at 280–81 (Brennan, J., concurring); 324–5 (Marshall, J., concurring); 393 (Burger, J., dissenting).

excessiveness in *Weems*—ensured that the mandatory death statutes at least were in grave constitutional danger.

The Abolition of the Mandatory Death Penalty for Murder in the United States

On July 2, 1976, the U.S. Supreme Court determined the fate of five state death penalty statutes for the first time since *Furman* four years earlier. In the lead decision *Gregg v. Georgia*, the Court, by a 7 to 2 majority, upheld the newly enacted death penalty statutes of Florida, Georgia, and Texas.[87] These three states had followed the Model Penal Code in guiding judicial discretion by requiring judges to articulate aggravating factors that warranted the special punishment of death and to weigh them against any mitigating factors that existed in the defendant's individual case. According to the Court in *Gregg*, these three statutes included objective criteria that directed and limited sentencing discretion with appellate review, and allowed the sentencing authority to consider the character and record of an individual defendant.[88] Justice Potter Stewart, who was in the majority in *Furman* but wrote the plurality decision in *Gregg*, reframed the Eighth Amendment standard not as prohibiting arbitrariness in the application of the death penalty, but rather as prohibiting a sentencing procedure that created a *substantial risk* of arbitrariness.[89] *Gregg* was a concession to practical reality.

Two of the challenged statutes did not survive the morning of July 2. In *Woodson v. North Carolina* and *Stanislaus Roberts v. Louisiana*, the Court found unconstitutional mandatory death statutes that removed *all* discretion from the judge to substitute a lesser sentence.[90] Mandatory capital punishment statutes had never been popular in the United States and had generally died out by the early twentieth century, but they faced a brief revival after *Furman* when twenty-two states reverted to the common law non-discretionary capital sentencing regime.[91]

James Tyrone Woodson was one of four men convicted of felony-murder in a robbery of a convenience store, even though he had waited in the automobile as the robbery took place. Unlike two of his accomplices, he maintained his innocence—he had been forced to participate against his will—and was convicted and sentenced to death along with the actual killer. Because North Carolina's death penalty for common law murder was mandatory, the jury could not hear mitigating evidence as to the defendant's lack of actual intent to kill or his minor role in the crime at the sentencing stage of the trial. The Court accepted an appeal in *Stanislaus Roberts v. Louisiana* with that of *Woodson*. The Louisiana statute was intended to be more narrowly tailored than the North Carolina law, confined only to murderers who possessed actual intent to kill, thus avoiding North Carolina's problematic cases. More surprisingly, the Louisiana law also fell, 5 to 4, with the same voting lineup as *Woodson*. As the Court noted, "[a]s in North Carolina, there are no standards provided to guide the jury

---

87 Gregg v. Georgia, 428 U.S. 153 (1976); Proffitt v. Florida, 428 U.S. 242 (1976); Jurek v. Texas, 428 U.S. 262 (1976).

88 *Gregg*, 428 U.S. at 156.

89 Janet C. Hoeffel, *Risking the Eighth Amendment: Arbitrariness, Juries, and Discretion in Capital Cases*, 46 B.C. L. Rev. 771, 773, 778–80 (2005).

90 Woodson v. North Carolina, 428 U.S. 280 (1976); Stanislaus Roberts v. Louisiana, 428 U.S. 325 (1976).

91 John W. Poulos, *The Supreme Court, Capital Punishment and the Substantive Criminal Law: The Rise and Fall of Mandatory Capital Punishment*, 28 Ariz. L. Rev. 143, 187–8, 226–7 (1986).

in the exercise of its power to select those first-degree murderers who will receive death sentences, and there is no meaningful appellate review of the jury's decision."[92]

The Court identified several fundamental flaws with a mandatory capital punishment regime that have since been widely cited around the world. First, a mandatory sentence "simply papered over the problem of unguided and unchecked jury discretion," because it exacerbated the problem of jury nullification: juries acquitted at higher rates in mandatory death penalty regimes, actually exacerbating the *Furman* problem of unfettered discretion.[93] In essence, because a jury was deciding guilt and sentence simultaneously, they risked merging the two decisions, choosing between acquittal on the murder charge and a death sentence upon conviction. The sentencing discretion ordinarily granted to a factfinder was transferred to other, less transparent, actors. If death was undeserved, prosecutors would prosecute for manslaughter or non-capital murder; appellate courts would use more robust review in sentencing inquiries; and executive clemency bodies would grant clemency at high rates. A trial judge, after weighing evidence and interpreting witness candor and demeanor, was especially well-placed to determine a defendant's sentence. By constraining a judge's sentencing discretion at trial, a mandatory death penalty made sentencing more arbitrary and opaque.

In addition, a mandatory sentence failed to individualize an appropriate sentence to the relevant aspects of the character and record of each defendant and consider appropriate mitigating factors.[94] While individualization was not necessarily required for all criminal sentencing, death was different, the Court noted: the "fundamental respect for humanity" underlying the Eighth Amendment required consideration of the person of the offender and the circumstances of the crime.[95] Justice Stewart's words in *Woodson* were as memorable as they were in *Furman* as he condemned a penalty that "treat[ed] all persons convicted of a designated offense not as uniquely individual human beings, but as members of a faceless, undifferentiated mass to be subjected to the blind infliction of the penalty of death":

> Instead of rationalizing the sentencing process, a mandatory scheme may well exacerbate the problem identified in *Furman* by resting the penalty determination on the particular jury's willingness to act lawlessly. While a mandatory death penalty statute may reasonably be expected to increase the number of persons sentenced to death, it does not fulfill *Furman*'s basic requirement by replacing arbitrary and wanton jury discretion with objective standards to guide, regularize, and make rationally reviewable the process for imposing a sentence of death.[96]

Woodson and *Stanislaus Roberts* concerned only the broadest categories of homicide; the Court subsequently considered the constitutionality of the mandatory death penalty as applied to narrower categories of prisoners. In *Harry Roberts v. Louisiana*, a 5 to 4 majority of the Supreme Court declared unconstitutional a law that restricted the mandatory death penalty for the intentional murder of a police officer.[97] Relying on *Stanislaus Roberts*, the Court conceded that the murder of an on-duty police officer was an aggravating circumstance

---

92 *Stanislaus Roberts*, 428 U.S. at 335–6.
93 *Woodson*, 428 U.S. at 303.
94 *Id.* at 303–4.
95 *Id.*
96 *Id.*
97 Harry Roberts v. Louisiana, 431 U.S. 633 (1977).

in a case, but it did not automatically outweigh all possible mitigating factors. According to the Court, "it is essential that the capital-sentencing decision allow for consideration of whatever mitigating circumstances may be relevant to either the particular offender or the particular offense."[98] Other state statutes modeled on the one at issue in *Harry Roberts* also fell.[99]

As a corollary to requiring consideration of individual circumstances in capital sentencing, the Court ruled in *Lockett v. Ohio* that a state could not constitutionally limit the mitigating factors that a defendant may put before a sentencing authority.[100] In that case, the petitioner argued that her death sentence was unconstitutional because the statute did not permit the judge to consider her character, prior record, age, lack of specific intent to cause death, and relatively minor role in the crime. The Court agreed: "we conclude that the Eighth and Fourteenth Amendments require that the sentencer, in all but the rarest kind of capital case, not be precluded from considering, as a mitigating factor, any aspect of a defendant's character or record and any of the circumstances of the offense that the defendant proffers as a basis for a sentence less than death."[101] The Ohio statute challenged in *Lockett* required imposition of the death penalty if at least one of seven aggravating factors were present, unless the defendant could show (a) that the victim induced or facilitated the crime; (b) the crime would not have been committed in the absence of duress or strong provocation; or (c) the offense was a product of the offender's psychosis or mental deficiency. The Ohio Supreme Court upheld the statute as indistinguishable from the one at issue in *Proffitt v. Florida*, noting that the mitigating factors were construed liberally in favor of the defendant. The U.S. Supreme Court disagreed, noting that a statute cannot unconstitutionally narrow the universe of mitigating options open to a defendant.[102] If *Woodson* held that a capital sentencing scheme required that defendants be permitted to present all relevant mitigating evidence to a sentencing authority, *Lockett* required that the sentencing authority listen to and consider that evidence.

In 1982, the *Lockett* plurality's holding won the backing of a majority of the Court in the 5 to 4 decision of *Eddings v. Oklahoma*.[103] Unlike the Ohio statute in *Lockett*, Oklahoma's statute in *Eddings* allowed a judge to consider "any mitigating circumstances" in the sentencing process. However, the trial judge, though finding the defendant's youth at age 16 to be a great mitigating factor, refused to consider the defendant's violent family life in sentencing the defendant to death. Although the Oklahoma appellate courts agreed that the trial judge was right to exclude these factors from consideration because they did not tend to show a legal excuse, the Supreme Court disagreed: "The sentencer, and the Court of Criminal Appeals on review, may determine the weight to be given relevant mitigating evidence. But they may not give it no weight by excluding such evidence from

---

98 *Id.* at 637.

99 *See, e.g.*, State v. Davis, 43 N.Y.2d 17 (1977) (striking down New York's statute).

100 Lockett v. Ohio, 438 U.S. 586 (1978).

101 *Id.* at 604. The Court's reference to "all but the rarest kind of capital case" was another deferral of the question left open in *Woodson*, namely, whether a mandatory death sentence for a life-term prisoner who committed murder could be constitutional.

102 Justice Blackmun's concurrence was narrower, believing that the Ohio statute permitted the death penalty even in the instances of vicarious liability or constructive intent to kill, and thus, based on *Coker v. Georgia*, was unconstitutionally disproportionate. *Id.* at 613–16 (Blackmun, J., concurring).

103 Eddings v. Oklahoma, 455 U.S. 104 (1982).

their consideration."[104] As the defendant was so young, a violent upbringing or background of child abuse was particularly relevant in his case.[105]

Although *Woodson* required individualized sentencing in capital cases, the Court later ruled that no such right existed in non-capital cases. In *Harmelin v. Michigan*, the Supreme Court limited the proportionality principle by upholding a mandatory sentence of life imprisonment without possibility of parole for a conviction of drug possession, finding that such a sentence did not violate the constitution.[106] Harmelin argued that the Court's death penalty jurisprudence required an individualized determination as to the appropriateness of mandatory life imprisonment without parole. According to the majority, however, the sentence of death was unique due to its irrevocability and the total rejection of the rehabilitative sentencing theory; by contrast, a mandatory life-term prisoner could benefit from retroactive legislation and executive clemency. *Harmelin* sharply curtailed the Court's jurisprudence on proportionality in sentencing, and the majority divided between Justice Antonin Scalia's opinion finding that the Eighth Amendment contained no proportionality principle at all, and Justice Anthony Kennedy's opinion that "*stare decisis* counsels our adherence to the narrow proportionality principle that has existed in our Eighth Amendment jurisprudence for 80 years."[107] The opinions, including the dissent by Justice White, read the murky origins of the Eighth Amendment very differently, even disagreeing on the scope and purpose of the cruel and unusual punishments clause of the English Bill of Rights. Nonetheless, backed by a majority, a narrow proportionality principle survives as a constitutional minimum in criminal sentencing in the United States.

Abolition of Mandatory Capital Punishment for Murder Committed by Life-Term Prisoners

One loophole remained open. The *Woodson* plurality expressly reserved the question of whether a mandatory death sentence could be constitutional as applied to an extremely narrow category of offenses in which the statute linked the definition of the crime to the character of the defendant.[108] In dicta, the Court noted in *Woodson* that the case did "not involve a mandatory death penalty statute limited to an extremely narrow category of homicide, such as murder by a prisoner serving a life sentence, defined in large part in terms of the character or record of the offender. We thus express no opinion regarding the constitutionality of such a statute."[109] Assuming the constitutionality of such a provision, a handful of states enacted narrowly defined mandatory death statutes limited to this scenario. However, by the late 1980s, all of these statutes had either been repealed or found unconstitutional by state courts, though two of them, in Nevada and Alabama, were not retroactive to prisoners already under a mandatory sentence of death.[110]

---

104   *Id.* at 114–15.
105   *See also* Hitchcock v. Dugger, 481 U.S. 393 (1987).
106   Harmelin v. Michigan, 501 U.S. 957 (1991).
107   *Id.* at 990 (Scalia, J., concurring); 996 (Kennedy, J., concurring in part and concurring in the judgment).
108   D. Michael Frink, *Mandatory Death Penalty Declared Unconstitutional for Failure to Permit Consideration of Any Mitigating Circumstances:* State v. Cline, 14 SUFFOLK U. L. REV. 578, 594 (1980).
109   *Woodson*, 428 U.S. at 287, n. 7.
110   *See* Sumner v. Shuman, 483 U.S. 66, 72 n. 2 (1987).

In 1977, a divided 5 to 4 decision by the Supreme Court of Alabama upheld the mandatory death sentence for homicide committed by a life-term prisoner in *Harris v. State*.¹¹¹ The Court ruled that a sentencing authority was not required to review mitigating circumstances where a life-term prisoner killed a prison guard during a riot as an aggravating factor was implicit in definition of the crime. According to the Alabama court, the U.S. Supreme Court recognized the "unique nature of statutes providing for the mandatory death penalty for life-term prisoners found guilty of murder and has been explicit in noting that it did not intend to pass on the validity of such statutes when addressing those statutes of a different nature" in *Woodson*.¹¹² The justices noted the deterrence effects of the statute, which "fulfill an otherwise unfulfillable public need: assurance that an otherwise unpunishable life-termer who commits a heinous crime of first degree murder shall not go unpunished." Four justices of the Alabama Supreme Court dissented, believing that mitigating circumstances could exist in a murder of a prison guard by a life-term prisoner; in the specific case at bar, the prisoner claimed he had been coerced to join the riot, and the trial judge was unable to consider this fact in sentencing.¹¹³ *Harris* came in for significant scholarly criticism for its cursory dismissal of the mitigating factors that could exist in such a case, though it was confirmed in a subsequent Alabama Supreme Court decision two years later.¹¹⁴

In early 1979, the Supreme Court of Rhode Island was the first to close the *Woodson* loophole by finding that a mandatory death sentence was unconstitutional for incarcerated prisoners who committed first-degree murder while imprisoned. In *State v. Cline*, the state supreme court relied on *Woodson* to invalidate the mandatory death sentence as incongruous with the Eighth Amendment, holding that a capital punishment statute must allow a sentencing authority to consider the circumstances of the particular offense and could not restrict the mitigating factors that a judge or jury may consider.¹¹⁵ Rhode Island's statute was broader than the *Woodson* loophole because it imposed an automatic capital sentence upon any inmate who committed first-degree murder, not just life-term prisoners. Nonetheless, it was not the prisoner's classification that proved fatal, but rather, the lack of a "provision for the trial justice, in imposing [a] sentence, to consider any mitigating factors whatsoever."¹¹⁶

Like the Rhode Island court, the California Court of Appeal in *Graham v. Superior Court of San Francisco* invalidated California's then-repealed (but not retroactive) statute that authorized the mandatory sentence of death for a life-term prisoner who committed malicious assault resulting in the death of a corrections officer.¹¹⁷ The Court of Appeal noted that California's statute only required a malicious killing, and defined as such could include both first- and second-degree murder, and therefore "encompass[ed] a wide range of personal culpability," particularly since the California statute encompassed all prisoners serving indeterminate terms.¹¹⁸ Following *Cline*, the Court noted that the classification,

---

111   Harris v. State, 352 So.2d 460 (Ala. 1977).
112   *Id*. at 484.
113   *Id*. at 487 (Torbert, J., dissenting); 489 (Jones, J., dissenting); 497 (Shores, J., dissenting); 498 (Beatty, J., concurring in part and dissenting in part).
114   David S. Frankel, *The Constitutionality of the Mandatory Death Penalty for Life-Term Prisoners Who Murder*, 55 N.Y.U. L. REV. 636, 661–4 (1980); Thigpen v. State, 355 So.2d 392 (Ala. Crim.App. 1977), *aff'd*, 355 So.2d 400 (Ala. 1977).
115   State v. Cline, 397 A.2d 1309 (R.I. 1979).
116   *Id*. at 1311.
117   Graham v. Superior Court of City and County of San Francisco, 98 Cal.App.3d 880 (1979).
118   *Id*. at 887.

though defective, was not the fundamentally unconstitutional flaw; rather, it was the lack of sentencing discretion. The Court also rejected the State's argument that a mandatory death sentence was required for its deterrence value because a life-term prisoner had nothing more to lose; the Court responded that life-term prisoners could be eligible for parole, and thus had a great deal to lose. In 1978, the California legislature provided for an alternative life sentence for a prisoner who committed murder, again undermining the deterrence rationale for the pre-existing law.

In New York, the Court of Appeals, the highest state court, squarely closed the loophole left open in *Woodson* by invalidating a mandatory death sentence for a first-degree murder committed by a prisoner already under a life sentence for a first-degree murder conviction in *People v. Smith*.[119] Because execution was not inevitable for every crime of murder, the Court reasoned, "a discretionary death penalty, which allows for the consideration of the character as well as the record of the individual offender and the circumstances of the particular offense, differs little in terms of deterrence from a mandatory death penalty and does not in fact detract from the value of capital punishment as a deterrent."[120] Certainly a prior conviction of first-degree murder is a powerful aggravating factor in determining the appropriate sentence for a subsequent murder. The Court, over a dissent, rejected the argument that the narrowness of the statute incorporated aggravating and mitigating factors directly into the definition, finding that "built-in defenses" related only to guilt and innocence while mitigating factors in sentencing did not necessarily need to relate to the crime itself.

The U.S. Supreme Court passed on reviewing *People v. Smith* in 1985. However, the Court accepted a challenge the following year in *Sumner v. Shuman*, a constitutional challenge to Nevada's mandatory death penalty statute for murder committed by a prisoner under a sentence of life imprisonment without possibility of parole.[121] The Nevada Supreme Court had upheld Shuman's death sentence, but the federal district court for Nevada reversed on constitutional grounds, a determination upheld by the U.S. Court of Appeals for the Ninth Circuit.[122] In a 6 to 3 decision, the U.S. Supreme Court finally closed the door to mandatory capital punishment in all cases under the Eighth Amendment. In a decision written by Justice Harry Blackmun, one of the dissenters in *Woodson*, the Court held that a sentencing authority was *always* required to consider as mitigating factors any aspect of the defendant's character or record and any of the circumstances of the particular offense. A statute that mandated a death sentence for a life-term prisoner who is convicted of murder while under a life term without possibility of parole violated the Eighth and Fourteenth Amendments.

Although the Court in *Woodson* and *Lockett* had previously declined to determine whether a mandatory statute applied to life-term inmates could withstand constitutional scrutiny based on extremely narrow circumstances or a particular deterrence concern, the majority in *Shuman* ruled that "a departure from the individualized capital-sentencing doctrine is not justified and cannot be reconciled with the demands of the Eighth and Fourteenth Amendments."[123] Without consideration of the nature of the underlying life-term

---

119 People v. Smith, 63 N.Y.2d 41 (1984), *cert. denied* 469 U.S. 1227 (1985).
120 *Id.* at 77.
121 Sumner v. Shuman, 483 U.S. 66 (1987).
122 *See* Shuman v. State, 94 Nev. 265 (1978); Shuman v. Wolff, 571 F.Supp.213 (D.Nev. 1983); Shuman v. Wolff, 791 F.2d 788 (9th Cir. 1986).
123 *Sumner v. Shuman*, 483 U.S. at 78.

offense, "the label 'life-term inmate' reveals little about the inmate's record or character."[124] In Shuman's case, a sentencing authority may find relevant his behavior during fifteen years of incarceration when he was sentenced for the murder he committed in prison. The Court also rejected the argument that a mandatory capital-sentencing procedure was necessary as a deterrent because a life-term prisoner had nothing to lose. The Court noted that by 1987 every state in the country had repealed mandatory death statutes for life-term prisoners. "The fact that the Nevada Legislature saw fit to repeal the specific statute at issue here a decade ago seriously undermines petitioners' contention that such a statute is required as a deterrent."[125] In addition, a life-term inmate did not evade the possibility of a death sentence in a discretionary regime; after individualized consideration, he still may be subjected to capital punishment. Finally, a narrowly enacted mandatory death statute still did not completely resolve the problem of jury nullification: if a jury did not believe that a defendant, even a life-term prisoner who kills, was deserving of death, the jury might merge the guilt and sentencing inquiries and acquit or convict of a lesser charge.[126] The life-term prisoner exception simply narrowed the unconstitutionality of mandatory death penalty statutes to smaller populations; it did not resolve the underlying defects.

Guided Judicial Discretion after *Woodson*

By the early 1980s, the Court's proportionality jurisprudence provided little check on the increasing rejection of rehabilitation as a penological goal in favor of a retributivist trend toward harsher criminal punishments. This shift is reflected in the decline of indeterminate sentencing, in which a sentence was determined by a judge or a sentencing authority after conviction based on the individual circumstances of the crime.[127] Around that period state legislatures began experimenting with determinate sentencing laws, which prescribed mandatory minimums or narrowly variable terms of imprisonment in lieu of judicially determined sentences with limited opportunities for parole and probation.[128] The contemporaneous abolition of the mandatory death penalty and the rise of guided judicial discretion in death penalty cases stand in stark contrast to the trend toward determinate sentencing in non-capital cases.

The beginnings of federal sentencing reform in the United States can be traced to the development of the Model Penal Code by the American Law Institute in 1962, which provided a modest blueprint for classifying crimes in an ordinary and consistent manner according to the gravity of the offense. Encouraged by the promise of reform of the criminal code, including sentencing, Congress established the National Commission on the Reform of Federal Criminal Laws, informally known as the Brown Commission, in 1966.[129] Congress had a relatively minor role in federal criminal sentencing until the 1980s, having enacted only piecemeal statutes to address disparities and balance the roles of trial judges and United States Parole Commission in determining the length of

---

124 *Id.* at 81.
125 *Id.* at 83.
126 *Id.* at 84, n. 13.
127 Martin R. Gardner, *The Determinate Sentencing Movement: Excessive Punishment Before and After* Rummel v. Estelle, 1980 DUKE L.J. 1103, 1107–8.
128 *Id.* at 1109–10.
129 Kenneth R. Feinberg, *Federal Criminal Sentencing Reform: Congress and the United States Sentencing Commission*, 28 WAKE FOREST L. REV. 291, 294 (1993).

imprisonment and the date of release.[130] By 1984, this system was outdated and in need of reform, lacking the certainty required to ensure public confidence and operate as a deterrent to crime. Unjustifiable sentencing disparities existed among judges in similar cases, and the Parole Commission compounded the problem by releasing prisoners according to its own judgment and not that of the sentencing judge. The bipartisan Sentencing Reform Act of 1984 was enacted to resolve some of these tensions, a rejection of the rehabilitative objective in criminal sentencing.[131]

The task of writing federal sentencing guidelines by the Act's three-year deadline of 1987 was wholly unprecedented in U.S. history. The federal criminal code had many more criminal offenses than most state codes, a total of 688, including several highly complex ones. In addition, unlike some states where resource allocation and prison population could impact sentencing policy, no national consensus existed as to the dominant objective of criminal punishment and their preferred length. With the new law, Congress abolished parole, absolving judges of the perilous task of trying to anticipate the date of parole in determining the length of sentences, and instituted a system by which judges would impose shorter sentences without the possibility of early release except for fifty-four days of "good time" per year after the first year.[132] To remedy the problem of sentencing disparities, Congress established the United States Sentencing Commission, comprised of seven members appointed by the President, instructed to write sentencing guidelines by April 1987 that were to automatically take effect six months later. The guidelines included a range for each sentence, with the maximum exceeding the minimum by no more than 25 %; a judge would be permitted to depart from the guidelines, but must state the reasons for doing so, subject to appellate review. Each crime included a "base level" period of imprisonment with "specific offense characteristics," such as dollar value of a robbery or use of a weapon, and allowed for "adjustments" such as the vulnerability of the victim, role in the offense, efforts to obstruct justice, and others.[133]

Guided by the review of more than 10,000 actual cases in the initial development of the sentencing guidelines, the U.S. Sentencing Commission is today a permanent body tasked with reviewing and altering the guidelines based on continuing data analysis of actual practice. The Sentencing Commission was intended to replace the U.S. Parole Commission, established in 1910 and made a full-time permanent body in 1930, after the drop in popular support for federal parole in the 1980s. However, the Parole Commission continues to retain jurisdiction over crimes committed prior to 1987 and certain offenses committed in the District of Columbia.[134] "Elimination of, or reduction in, parole eligibility for such cases would raise a serious *ex post facto* issue."[135] Nonetheless, this decline of flexibility in criminal sentencing reflects the inherent tension between preserving consistency in criminal sentencing and tailoring a sentence based on the individual circumstances of a crime that the Supreme Court first confronted in death penalty cases.

---

130 Orrin G. Hatch, *The Role of Congress in Sentencing: The United States Sentencing Commission, Mandatory Minimum Sentences, and the Search for a Certain and Effective Sentencing System*, 28 WAKE FOREST L. REV. 185, 186–7 (1993).

131 *Id.* at 187–9.

132 Stephen Breyer, *The Federal Sentencing Guidelines and the Key Compromises Upon Which They Rest*, 17 HOFSTRA L. REV. 1, 3–5 (2008).

133 *Id.* at 5–6.

134 U.S. PAROLE COMMISSION, HISTORY OF THE FEDERAL PAROLE SYSTEM 1 (2004).

135 *Id.* at 2.

A Note on the Canadian Supreme Court Decision in *Miller v. Queen*

Only a few months after the U.S. Supreme Court decided *Woodson v. North Carolina*, the Supreme Court of Canada unanimously rejected the *Woodson* Court's rationale and upheld the mandatory death penalty for murder of a police officer in *Miller v. Queen* even though the Canadian Parliament had abolished the death penalty earlier that year.[136] Similar to the U.S. Constitution, the Canadian Bill of Rights of 1960 (and later the Canadian Charter on Rights and Freedoms of 1982) included a ban on "cruel and unusual treatment or punishment."[137] The Court of Appeal for British Columbia had determined that the death penalty for murder was not unconstitutional in *Queen v. Miller* in 1975, though a dissent believed that "cruel and unusual" should be read disjunctively to proscribe cruel punishments, however usual.[138] The majority distinguished the American *Furman* jurisprudence, noting the different methods of constitutional interpretation used in Canada's southern neighbor. While death might have been cruel, it was not "unusual" in the sense required by Section 2 of the Canadian Bill of Rights. Separately, in 1976 the Court of Appeal for Ontario reversed a county court decision finding that a mandatory minimum sentence of seven years for narcotics possession was cruel and unusual; the county court had relied heavily on American Eighth Amendment jurisprudence for the proposition that "cruel and unusual punishment" included disproportionate punishment.[139]

According to the Canadian Supreme Court on appeal in *Miller*, the mandatory nature of the death penalty indicated that the punishment could not be discriminatorily or arbitrarily imposed.[140] In addition, the Court noted, public opinion was irrelevant to the question as to whether the death penalty constituted "cruel and unusual" punishment. The ultimate question was whether the mandatory nature of a capital sentence was excessive for a given crime. That Parliament had retained the death penalty in the drafting of the Canadian Bill of Rights in 1960 was evidence that it never intended the cruel punishment provision to encompass a death sentence. However, the Court confirmed that Section 2 of the Bill of Rights contained a proportionality principle and noted that "cruel and unusual punishment" encompassed more than just methods of punishment. The Court distinguished *Woodson* and *Stanislaus Roberts*, noting that the Canadian statute narrowed the mandatory death penalty to murder of a police officer rather than all forms of murder, and the U.S. Supreme Court had not yet decided *Harry Roberts v. Louisiana* finding otherwise. The Canadian justices followed Justice White's dissent in *Woodson* in determining that prosecutorial and jury discretion was an ordinary part of the criminal process, refusing to assume that this discretion would be incompetently exercised. Today, even after death penalty abolition in

---

136 Miller v. Queen, [1977] 2 S.C.R. 680 (Can. 1976); Criminal Law Amendment Act (No. 2), ch. 105 (1976) (Can.).

137 Canadian Bill of Rights, S.C. 1960, c. 44, art. 2(b); Canadian Charter of Rights and Freedoms, Part I of the Constitution Act of 1982, *being* Schedule B to the Canada Act, 1982, c. 11, art. 12 (U.K.).

138 Queen v. Miller, (1975) 24 C.C.C.2d 401 (B.C.C.A.). Because the Canadian Bill of Rights was not a true constitution—it was an interpretive statute passed by Parliament—the extent of the scope of judicial review permitted by the Canadian Supreme Court was still unclear at the time of *Miller*. See Jeffrey S. Leon, *Cruel and Unusual Punishment: Sociological Jurisprudence and the Canadian Bill of Rights*, 36 U. TORONTO FAC. L. REV. 222, 230–31 (1978).

139 Queen v. Shand, (1976) 30 C.C.C.2d 23 (Ont. C.A.), *reversing* Queen v. Shand, (1976) 29 C.C.C.2d 199 (Ont. Co. Ct.).

140 Miller v. Queen, [1977] 2 S.C.R. 680 (Can. 1976).

Canada, *Miller* continues to be cited for the proposition that the ban on cruel and unusual punishment includes a proportionality principle. In 1987, the Supreme Court finally struck down the seven-year mandatory minimum for drug possession under the Narcotics Control Act on the basis of *Miller*'s gross disproportionality test for excessive punishments.[141] Even though the Canadian Supreme Court failed to follow the *Woodson* holding in 1976, it is now settled law in both the United States and Canada that a disproportionately harsh or excessive punishment is unconstitutional.

Conclusion

After the establishment of a discretionary death penalty regime and subsequent challenges based on the death penalty for non-homicide offenses, the characteristics of the offender, and the factors that a judge may consider in sentencing, the Supreme Court has made only incremental changes to the machinery of capital punishment. In a 5 to 4 decision in 1987, the Supreme Court rejected the defining theory of the NAACP and racial justice advocates by refusing to find that racial disparities in criminal sentencing violated the Eighth Amendment without discriminatory purpose or intent in *McClesky v. Kemp*, a challenge based on the most exhaustive analysis of race and capital sentencing yet performed.[142] Challenges to methods of execution have been similarly unsuccessful. In 2008, the Supreme Court upheld the constitutionality of lethal injection in *Baze v. Rees*, lifting a de facto moratorium on executions.[143] These developments suggest, on paper at least, that the death penalty will retain some constitutional durability in the years to come.

Nonetheless, Eighth Amendment jurisprudence continues to "evolve." In the current era of death penalty litigation, two areas seem especially promising for restricting the scope of capital punishment still further. The first is the Supreme Court's difficult and erratic jurisprudence concerning mental illness and the death penalty, a constitutional door that opened in *Ford v. Wainright* in 1986 when the Court overturned a death sentence where a prisoner had become insane during his incarceration, as extended to persons with mental retardation in *Atkins v. Virginia* in 2002.[144] As psychological research and testing improve, the contours of these precedents for persons with other forms of mental illness will require further development. A second line of constitutional challenge concerns the death row phenomenon, the theory that delay in execution could render an otherwise permissible execution unconstitutional by working a psychological torture on a prisoner. Unlike other common law jurisdictions, the U.S. Supreme Court has never directly decided such a challenge, though Justices John Paul Stevens and Stephen Breyer persistently dissented to the denial of certiorari in several cases that the Court turned away.[145] Such cases, known as *Lackey* claims after Justice Stevens's dissent to the denial of certiorari in *Lackey v. Texas*

---

141 Queen v. Smith, [1987] 1 S.C.R. 1045 (Can.).
142 McClesky v. Kemp, 481 U.S. 279 (1987).
143 Baze v. Rees, 553 U.S. 35 (2008).
144 Ford v. Wainright, 477 U.S. 399 (1986); Atkins v. Virginia, 536 U.S. 304 (2002).
145 *See* Lackey v. Texas, 514 U.S. 1045 (1995) (Stevens, J., dissenting to denial of certiorari); Gomez v. Fierro, 519 U.S. 918 (Stevens, J., dissenting to denial of certiorari); Ellridge v. Florida, 525 U.S. 944 (1998) (Breyer, J., dissenting to denial of certiorari); Knight v. Florida, 528 U.S. 990, 993 (1999) (Breyer, J., dissenting to denial of certiorari); Foster v. Florida, 537 U.S. 990, 991 (2002) (Breyer, J., dissenting to the denial of certiorari).

in 1997, exhibit the tensions between the imposition of federal constitutional law on the states and the consideration of foreign case law in domestic death penalty jurisprudence.

The abolition of the mandatory death penalty in the United States accords with the broader international trend that the death penalty should be reserved only to the most serious crimes based on an individual determination that considers the circumstances of the offense. Since 1976, *Woodson v. North Carolina* has gone global. *Woodson* is a seminal case in what Carozza refers to as the global common law of the death penalty, one cited by courts across the common law world in decisions invalidating the mandatory death penalty.[146] In 1983, for instance, the Supreme Court of India decided *Mithu v. State of Punjab*, which tracked *Woodson* closely.[147] However, since the early 1980s, the progressive expansion of the U.S. Eighth Amendment especially in death penalty cases has fallen out of sync with international norms. *Furman* was, in retrospect, the high water mark of constitutional death penalty abolition in the United States even as the death penalty has declined in recent years.[148]

---

146 Paolo Carozza, *'My Friend is a Stranger': The Death Penalty and the Global* Ius Commune *of Human Rights*, 81 TEX. L. REV. 1031, 1036 (2003).

147 Mithu v. State of Punjab, (1983) 2 S.C.R. 690 (India Sup. Ct.).

148 David Heffernan, Comment, *America the Cruel and Unusual? An Analysis of the Eighth Amendment Under International Law*, 45 CATH. U. L.REV. 481, 559 (1996).

Chapter 3
Restricting the Death Penalty to the "Rarest of the Rare": The Origins of a Discretionary Death Penalty in India and Bangladesh

India's constitutional regime bears many similarities to the United States, governed by principles of federalism under a written constitution that protects the rights of the accused and limits the state power of criminal punishment in highly abstract terms. During the 1970s, both countries experienced the first constitutional challenges to the death penalty as a result of progressive advances in constitutional jurisprudence that made such challenges possible for the first time. India followed *Furman v. Georgia* and its successors closely in developing its own "worst of the worst" framework for discerning when the death penalty was appropriate, modeled on the American regime. The creation of the "rarest of the rare" formula in *Bachan Singh v. State of Punjab* was partly a reaction by the Supreme Court of India to the state-level backlashes that occurred in the United States after the U.S. Supreme Court's attempt to strike down the death penalty in *Furman v. Georgia* in 1972. The Court "deemed it imprudent to attempt the judicial abolition of capital punishment, electing instead to curtail the circumstances in which death could be imposed."[1] In this the Court was successful: executions have become astonishingly rare in modern India.

As India's restrictionist jurisprudence settled, it in turn provided a model to its neighbors. The abolition of the mandatory death penalty in Bangladesh, an expression of the country's own "rarest of the rare" doctrine, widely cited Indian case law and rested on similar reasoning to the Indian Supreme Court's establishment of a discretionary death penalty regime twenty-five years earlier. This occurred despite important constitutional differences between India's independence constitution and the more modern constitution of Bangladesh. This chapter will also briefly look at Sri Lanka, which has wrestled with its own death penalty challenges. This subregional sharing process is a microcosm of the Commonwealth-wide development of a body of persuasive transnational death penalty jurisprudence.

The Death Penalty and Society on the Indian Subcontinent

India has a long history of capital punishment under the Mughal dynasty, then under two centuries of Muslim control and two of British control, during which the death penalty remained an accepted and widespread punishment closely connected to caste and economic

---

[1] DAVID T. JOHNSON & FRANKLIN E. ZIMRING, THE NEXT FRONTIER: NATIONAL DEVELOPMENT, POLITICAL CHANGE, AND THE DEATH PENALTY IN ASIA 438 (2009).

class.[2] India lacked a written, uniform set of criminal laws and principles for much of its history. The drafting of the Indian Penal Code coincided with early Victorian-era reforms of England's notorious Bloody Code, which authorized the death sentence for more than 200 crimes. Consequently, India benefited from early progressive experiments with judicial discretion in capital cases, and since the early colonial period judges were permitted to substitute life imprisonment or banishment to a penal colony in place of death.[3]

If the continent of Asia is exceptional for the survival of capital punishment in the modern world, the Indian Subcontinent is exceptional in Asia. Among retentionist nations, India is extraordinary: in the ten years between 1998 and 2007, India executed only a single person for a rate of less than one execution per ten billion people per year. By contrast, China's execution rate was at least 50,000 times higher during the same period, and Japan's was 300 times higher.[4] The rate of executions in India has dramatically declined over time, from at least 140 per year between 1953 and 1963 to only one per year between 1996 and 2000, and still lower thereafter. In addition, as in the United States, executions in India are geographically clustered, with most taking place in the less-developed north of the country. "No retentionist nation in the world executes at a lower rate than India, and the only way India's own rate could go any lower is if it falls out of the retentionist category altogether," Johnson and Zimring write.[5]

At the same time, however, legislators repeatedly reaffirmed their commitment to legal capital punishment. Death row has grown exponentially, as Parliament expanded the scope of capital punishment to cover new offenses related to terrorism, organized crime, drug trafficking, and kidnapping for ransom, from 110 death row prisoners in 2001 to 563 in 2004.[6] In addition, India's homicide rate during the first decade of the twenty-first century was six times higher than Japan's, three times higher than Singapore's, and twice as high as China's, three countries where the death penalty has been historically more active.[7] Besides murder, the death penalty is available under the Indian Penal Code for abetting any capital offense; waging war against the government; abetting mutiny; fabricating false evidence in a capital trial; abetting the suicide of a child or insane person; kidnapping for ransom; gang robbery involving murder; and criminal conspiracy to commit a capital crime.[8] In addition, the Terrorist and Disruptive Activities (Prevention) Act of 1987, now repealed prospectively but not retroactively, provided the death penalty for a terrorist attack, broadly defined, that resulted in the death of any person.[9] Similarly, the similarly repealed Prevention of Terrorism Act of 2002 and the Unlawful Activities Prevention (Amendment) Act of 2004 also introduced the death penalty for terrorist-related crimes.[10] The criminal

---

2   *Id.* at 428.
3   David Skuy, *Macaulay and the Indian Penal Code of 1862: The Myth of the Inherent Superiority and Modernity of the English Legal System Compared to India's Legal System in the Nineteenth Century*, 32 MOD. ASIAN STUD. 513, 513, 518–20, 526–7 (1998).
4   JOHNSON & ZIMRING, *supra* note 1 at 423.
5   *Id.* at 429–32.
6   *Id.* at 433.
7   David T. Johnson, *The Death Penalty in India*, in CRIME AND JUSTICE IN INDIA 365, 372 (2013).
8   Indian Penal Code Act, 1860, No. 45, §§109, 120B(1), 121, 132, 194, 302, 303, 305, 307, and 396 (as amended). Kidnapping for ransom was introduced in 1993 by the Criminal Law (Amendment) Act, 1993, No. 42, and is contained at Section 364A of the Penal Code.
9   Terrorist and Disruptive Activities (Prevention) Act, 1987, No. 28, § 3(2)(i).
10 Prevention of Terrorism Act, 2002, No. 15, § 3(2)(a); Unlawful Activities Prevention (Amendment) Act, 2004, No. 29, § 6(b)(i).

codes of all three branches of the armed forces provide for the death penalty, as well as a host of additional laws related to organized crime and terrorism.[11]

The death penalty in India, though regularly imposed, is publicly marginal. Capital punishment appears as part of a criminal justice system that is constantly bemoaned as inefficient and cumbersome.[12] Public perceptions of the court system praise its neutrality and independence but condemn its delay—ten years for a single case is not abnormal. Because of the long duration of these cases, conviction rates are very low, about 6% for "heinous crimes," including capital crimes.[13] The consequence is a perception of impunity for criminals, making crime a high reward, low risk venture. The public perception of judicial inefficiency has created a culture of extrajudicial killing by state agents; police always return fire, especially against suspected extremists. The casual nature of extrajudicial executions has aroused public suspicion that police execute a suspected criminal either because they cannot find the right offender or fear that the offender will be acquitted in court.[14] "With the (public) conflation of individual security with national security, state killing—whether police encounters or capital punishment—gains a new legitimacy, and a new urgency."[15] Extrajudicial police killings are seen as the last bulwark against a deep state crisis.

At least on paper, the "rarest of the rare" formula succeeds in distinguishing the most heinous crimes from the rest. Among the worst of the worst was the 2002 sentence for the Islamic militants who committed an attack on the Indian Parliament. In 2003, death sentences were given to eight members of the Yadav caste for a massacre of nineteen Dalit villagers. Yet another was against Dara Singh, a Hindu nationalist, who killed an Australian missionary and her two sons in 1999 by setting their car on fire while they were asleep inside. "With these sentences the judiciary appeared supremely neutral, above the political divisions of Indian society: capital punishment was imposed for Muslim terrorism as much for caste violence and murder inspired by Hindu-nationalism."[16] But India pays a high price for such a low execution rate: a system with so many capital offenses resulting in only a tiny trickle of executions in response to more than 30,000 murders per year "is lawless in the sense that nothing about the nation's capital jurisprudence can explain who gets sentenced to death or hanged when hundreds of equally or more culpable offenders escape the death penalty altogether."[17] This "lethal lottery" undermines the doctrinal predictability of the "rarest of the rare" formula.[18] Despite the media attention to the most recent execution, of Dhananjoy Chatterjee in 2004, the overwhelming majority of executions are unknown and secretive. Even the names of the prisoners are unconfirmed and the sentencing and appeals decisions are unreported.[19] Public opinion in support of the death penalty is lukewarm. In

---

11 Army Act, 1950, No. 46, §§ 34, 37, 38, 66; Air Force Act, 1950, No. 45 §§ 34, 37, 38, 68; Navy Act, 1957, No. 62, §§ 34, 35, 36, 37, 38, 39, 43, 44, 49, 56, 59, 76. For a complete list of statutes authorizing the death penalty, including those related to terrorism and organized crime, see BIKRAM JEET BATRA, LETHAL LOTTERY: THE DEATH PENALTY IN INDIA: A STUDY OF SUPREME COURT JUDGMENTS IN DEATH PENALTY CASES, 1950–2006, 44 (2008).

12 Julia Eckert, *Death and the Nation: State Killing in India, in* THE CULTURAL LIVES OF CAPITAL PUNISHMENT: COMPARATIVE PERSPECTIVES 195, 196–7 (Austin Sarat & Christian Boulanger eds., 2005).

13 *Id.* at 197.

14 *Id.* at 198–9.

15 *Id.* at 212.

16 *Id.* at 196.

17 JOHNSON & ZIMRING, *supra* note 1 at 438.

18 *See generally* BATRA, *supra* note 11.

19 *Id.* at 38.

a recent survey of college age students, 44% supported retention in various forms, 43% supported abolition, and 13% were unsure.[20]

The Constitutional Framework of the Death Penalty in India

Like the United States—and unlike most other Commonwealth nations—India's constitution is notable for its vagueness as to the permissibility of capital punishment. In the absence of a cruel and unusual punishment clause and an explicit protection of due process rights for accused prisoners, the Indian Supreme Court operated with a nearly blank slate. Article 21 of the Constitution of India provides the constitutional minimum: "No person shall be deprived of his life or personal liberty except according to procedure established by law."[21] And not just any procedure: according to the Court in *Maneka Gandhi v. Union of India*, the procedure prescribed by law had to be fair, just, and reasonable and not oppressive, fanciful, or arbitrary.[22] In that case, a challenge to the Government's unlawful withholding of a passport to prevent an Indian citizen from traveling abroad, the Court ruled that any procedure which impaired the right to personal liberty without a reasonable opportunity to be heard was unfair and unjust based on principles of natural law.[23] Through *Maneka Gandhi* and a successor case *Sunil Batra v. Delhi Administration*, which imported principles of just and proportionate punishment into Article 21, the content of due process and cruel and unusual punishment clauses are now part of Indian constitutional doctrine.[24]

The Indian Penal Code, first drafted in 1860, punished murder with death or life imprisonment, and with possibility of a fine, at Section 302. The following section of the Code, Section 303, punished murder committed by life-term prisoners with a mandatory death sentence.[25] Section 303 had one particular circumstance in mind: the murder by a prisoner of a jail official, in the colonial era usually an Englishman. The Constitution of 1950 retained capital punishment, and subsequent attempts to abolish it failed in subsequent years. Until the revision of the Code of Criminal Procedure in 1973, the death penalty was the usual punishment for murder, and sentencing judges had to record the special reasons why they chose to impose non-capital sentences when the statute gave them discretion. The revised Code reversed this presumption, turning death into an exceptional punishment and requiring judges to articulate aggravating factors for issuing a capital sentence after a separate sentencing phase of a trial.[26] Where two views are possible about the quantum of a sentence, a view which favors the grant of life imprisonment is generally accepted.[27]

Under Section 354(5) of the Code of Criminal Procedure of 1973, all death sentences must be carried out by hanging. In *Deena v. Union of India*, the Supreme Court ruled that the execution of a punishment of death must be as quick and simple as possible; produce

---

20 Eric G. Lambert, et al., *Views on the Death Penalty Among College Students in India*, 10 PUNISHMENT & SOC. 207, 215 (2008).
21 INDIA CONST. art. 21.
22 Maneka Gandhi v. Union of India, A.I.R. 1978 S.C. 597.
23 J.N. PANDEY, CONSTITUTIONAL LAW OF INDIA 209 (39th ed. 2003).
24 Sunil Batra v. Delhi Administration, (1980) 2 S.C.R. 557.
25 Indian Penal Code Act, 1860, No. 45, §§ 302, 303.
26 Code of Criminal Procedure Act, 1898, No. 5, § 367(5), *as amended by* Code of Criminal Procedure Act of 1973, 1974, No. 2.
27 Subhash Chander v. Krishan Lal, A.I.R. 2001 S.C. 1903, 1909.

immediate unconsciousness; and not involve mutilation.[28] In *Deena*, the Court upheld the constitutional validity of Section 354(5) of the Code of Criminal procedure of 1973, which selected death by hanging over electric chair, shooting, or lethal injection, finding that *Maneka Gandhi* only required that a procedure for taking human life be fair and reasonable and did not favor any method of execution. However, three years later the Court found public hangings to be unconstitutional, as these did not comport with Article 21.[29] India has also wrestled with the persistent problem of undue delay in carrying out the executions of condemned prisoners. As early as 1981, the Supreme Court held that delay in execution of a death sentence exceeding two years was sufficient grounds to commute a sentence to life imprisonment.[30] In *Triveniben v. State of Gujurat* in 1989, the Court held that undue long delay in execution of the death sentence entitled a condemned prisoner to a reduction of sentence; the court was to examine the nature of the delay and circumstances of the case, but without a bright-line rule fixing a period of delay that would commute a death sentence.[31]

In addition, executive clemency is provided for at Article 72(1), which specifically references the pardon power for capital sentences.[32] All convicted criminals have the right to submit petitions for clemency to the president of India. The executive must act on the advice of the cabinet, and clemency decisions may be subject to judicial review. The scope of clemency is broad and processing a mercy request may take years; as a result, repetitive petitions can indefinitely postpone an execution.[33] In *Maru Ram v. Union of India*, the Supreme Court ruled that a grant of mercy or pardon that was "wholly irrelevant, irrational, discriminatory or *mala fide*" was unconstitutional.[34] In a subsequent case, *Kehar Singh v. Union of India*, the petitioner, the convicted assassin of former Prime Minister Indira Gandhi, brought a constitutional challenge against the denial of his mercy petition under Article 72.[35] In *Kehar Singh*, the Court wrote that the President "acts in a wholly different plane from that in which the Court acted. He acts under a constitutional power, the nature of which is entirely different from the judicial power and cannot be regarded as an extension of it."[36] Article 161 of the constitution provides an accused a mirror right to apply for clemency or pardon from a state governor, which may also be reviewable in certain circumstances.[37] Under this precedent, the Court may only review the decision-making process and not the ultimate grant or denial of clemency or pardon.

---

28 Deena v. Union of India, (1983) 4 S.C.C. 645.
29 Attorney General of India v. Devi, A.I.R. 1986 S.C. 467, 468 ("a barbaric crime does not have to be visited with a barbaric penalty such as public hanging").
30 Vatheeswaran v. State of Tamil Nadu, A.I.R. 1983 S.C. 361, 363, 367.
31 Triveniben v. State of Gujarat, A.I.R. 1989 S.C. 142, 143.
32 INDIA CONST. art. 72(1).
33 JOHNSON & ZIMRING, *supra* note 1 at 439.
34 Maru Ram v. Union of India, (1981) 1 S.C.R. 1196, 1248.
35 Kehar Singh v. Union of India, (1989) 3 S.C.R. Supp. 1102.
36 *Id*. at 1103.
37 INDIA CONST. art. 161. *See also* Swaran Singh v. State of Uttar Pradesh, (1998) 4 S.C.C. 75 (reversing a grant of clemency where the governor was unaware of the prisoner's bad behavior and his prior convictions).

Restricting the Death Penalty to the Rarest of the Rare

Although a judge was historically permitted to substitute a sentence of life imprisonment for a death sentence under the Penal and Criminal Procedure Codes, the lack of standards for doing so formed the basis for a constitutional challenge. In 1973, the Supreme Court of India rejected a challenge to the death penalty in *Jagmohan Singh v. State of Uttar Pradesh*.[38] The condemned prisoners argued that the discretion vested in judges to choose between death and life imprisonment was not based on any legislative policy and, left unguided, violated the right to equality because two persons found guilty of murder could be treated differently. The absence of a procedure established by law violated Article 21. The judges, however, refused to be persuaded by the decision of the United States Supreme Court in *Furman v. Georgia*, which declared the death penalty then in existence as cruel and unusual punishment. The Court held that deprivation of life was constitutionally permissible as it was imposed after a trial in accordance with procedure established by law. Over time, the Court began elaborating on how to weigh mitigating and aggravating factors. The following year, the justices reduced a death sentence to life imprisonment after considering factors such as age, gender, socio-economic background, and mental disability, and not just the circumstances of the crime itself.[39]

Maneka Gandhi required that every law of punitive detention pass a test of reasonableness both as to procedure and substance, which allowed the Court to accept collateral challenges to the death penalty notwithstanding the implicit constitutionality of the death penalty in *Jagmohan Singh*.[40] Based on that interpretation, the following year the Court determined that the special reasons necessary for imposing the death penalty must relate to the criminal, awarded only if the security of society, public order, and the interests of the general public required such a course. This decision, *Rajenda Prasad v. State of Uttar Pradesh*, came breathtakingly close to abolishing the death penalty in India and noted the legislative trend toward limiting rather than broadening the penalty.[41] Restrictively interpreting the procedural imperatives required by Article 21, the Court reasoned that the death penalty can only be imposed in the narrowest circumstances of "a habitual murder or given to chronic violence," where it was clear that the accused literally "poses a grave peril to societal survival" and his "being alive will involve more lives being lost at his hands." [42]

Although the Court came close to abolition in *Rajendra Prasad*, the next case of consequence—the defining decision on the death penalty in India—walked the Court's jurisprudence back to equilibrium. In 1980, the Supreme Court upheld the constitutionality of a renewed challenge in *Bachan Singh v. State of Punjab*, on the basis of a new criminal procedure code provision at Section 354(3), requiring that a judgment sentencing a person to death state the reasons for such a sentence.[43] The majority of four judges upheld *Jagmohan* and reversed *Rajendra Prasad* insofar as it sought to restrict application of the death penalty only to cases involving endangerment to the security of the state or the public good. *Bachan Singh* allowed the Court to clarify when a case fell into the "rarest of the rare" category, suggesting as possible aggravating circumstances murder committed after

---

38   Jagmohan Singh v. State of Uttar Pradesh, (1973) 1 S.C.C. 20.
39   Anamma v. State of Andhra Pradesh, A.I.R. 1974 S.C. 799, 806.
40   Maneka Gandhi v. Union of India, (1978) 2 S.C.R. 621.
41   Rajendra Prasad v. State of Uttar Pradesh, A.I.R. 1979 S.C. 916.
42   *Id.* at 932, 933, 944.
43   Bachan Singh v. State of Punjab, A.I.R. 1980 S.C. 898, 929.

previous planning, murder involving exceptional depravity, or murder of any member of the armed forces, police officer, or public servant that was committed while the member was on duty. The Court did not intend these as an exhaustive list, noting only that they were "relevant circumstances."[44] Among the mitigating factors identified by the Court were where the offense was committed under extreme mental or emotional disturbance, the age of the accused, the possibility for rehabilitation, murder under duress, or mental illness. Although the Court upheld the constitutionality of the death penalty per se in *Jagmohan Singh* and *Bachan Singh*, its reasoning indicated that the manner in which the death penalty was carried out was not immune from constitutional challenge.

Although it had resisted laying down firm criteria for considering aggravating and mitigating circumstances, the Court filled this gap in *Machhi Singh v. State of Punjab*: "A balance-sheet of aggravating and mitigating circumstances has to be drawn up and in doing so the mitigating circumstances have to be accorded full weightage and a just balance has to be struck between the aggravating and the mitigating circumstances before the option is exercised."[45] The Court reaffirmed the "rarest of the rare" doctrine, finding that a sentencing court was required to ask whether the circumstances of the crime included something unusually heinous such that a sentence of life imprisonment was inadequate, and whether the circumstances of the crime were such that no alternative existed but to impose the death sentence even after according maximum weight to the mitigating factors.

With this line of cases, the Supreme Court favored discretion over predictability, which came at a cost: "in practice the broad discretion afforded by the rarest of the rare doctrine simply allows the courts to arbitrarily impose the death penalty as they see fit."[46] Instead of a searching interpretation of the Supreme Court's precedential decisions, every case followed a cookie-cutter analysis, blindly reiterating legal principles without applying them to the facts. A number of times courts "simply cut and pasted, word for word, the entirety of a lengthy legal analysis about weighing and balancing, the rarest of the rare doctrine, extreme circumstances, severe punishment, [and] aggravating and mitigating factors," and came to a rote conclusion.[47] On the one hand, the Court succeeded in reducing the number of death sentences; indeed they had become the "rarest of the rare." But it did not succeed in developing satisfactory criteria for when the ultimate penalty should be imposed and no discernible pattern emerged as to when a death sentence would be chosen.[48]

A paradigm shift was needed, and in 2009, it came, in *Santosh Bariyar v. State of Maharashtra*.[49] In *Bariyar*, the Court ruled that in order to issue a death sentence, the prosecution must prove by leading evidence that there was no possibility of rehabilitation of the accused and that life imprisonment would serve no purpose. The sentencing court must find that imposition of life imprisonment was not sufficient as the death penalty was a sentence of last resort; a trial court is required to provide clear evidence as to why the convict was not fit for any kind of reformatory or rehabilitative scheme. In *Bariyar*, the judiciary continued to "prune the application of the death penalty in India, with the intention of restricting its use and making it more difficult to apply."[50] Whether the commands of

---

44   *Id.* at 944.
45   Macchi Singh v. State of Punjab, A.I.R. 1983 S.C. 957, 966.
46   A.G. NOORANI, CHALLENGES TO CIVIL RIGHTS GUARANTEES IN INDIA 123 (2012).
47   *Id.* at 124.
48   Jill Cottrell, *Wrestling with the Death Penalty in India*, 7 S. AFR. J. ON HUM. RTS. 185, 186 (1991).
49   Santosh Bariyar v. State of Maharashtra, (2009) 6 S.C.C. 498.
50   Autri Saha & Pritika Rai Advani, *The Death Penalty: A New Perspective in Light of Santosh Bariyar Case*, 2 N.U.J.S. L. REV. 669, 693 (2009).

Bariyar will be implemented in practice remains to be seen. Just as the Court walked back from *Rajendra Prasad*, "it is not inconceivable that subsequent decisions of the Court may perpetuate the very inconsistency that *Bariyar* sought to obviate."[51] However, *Bariyar* has the potential to provide a more workable test for courts dispensing death sentences, and, as long as it remains good law, it is a welcome development.

The Abolition of the Mandatory Death Penalty in India: *Mithu v. State of Punjab*

Section 303 of the Indian Penal Code of 1860 provided for a mandatory death sentence in cases where a murder was committed by a person already serving a life sentence of imprisonment. The Supreme Court upheld several mandatory death sentences under this provision as late as the 1970s, and a bill to repeal the mandatory sentence was defeated in Parliament in 1972.[52] In 1973, the Supreme Court extended Section 303 to the case of a life prisoner who committed murder while on parole, but three years later refused to extend the section to a prisoner who committed murder while his life sentence was still on appeal.[53] In the latter case, the Court observed that "the Court has no discretion but to award the sentence of death, notwithstanding mitigating circumstances which by normal judicial standards and modern notions of penology do not justify the imposition of the capital penalty. Viewed from this aspect, the section is draconian in severity, relentless and inexorable in operation."[54] This decision highlighted the constitutional vulnerability of Section 303.

In 1983, the Indian Supreme Court found the mandatory death sentence under Section 303 unconstitutional in *Mithu v. State of Punjab*.[55] The Court determined that no rational justification existed for treating murder by life-term prisoners differently from all other murders, and therefore the classification was arbitrary and bore no nexus with the object of the statute. The circumstance that a person was undergoing a sentence of life imprisonment did not minimize the importance of other mitigating factors that were relevant at sentencing; life prisoners were subject to extreme pressures and strains, and in some cases more deserving of sympathy for the murder charge than for the underlying life-term offense. Judicial sentencing discretion was one of the most profound safeguards that a prisoner had in the sentencing process; certainly, mitigating factors such as age, provocation, emotional disturbance, or the motive of a crime were relevant to the question of sentence.

Citing to *Maneka Gandhi* and *Sunil Batra*, the Court confirmed that a "procedure" under Article 21 had to be in accordance with due process of law.[56] The right of the prisoner to be heard on the question of sentence under Section 235(2) of the Code of Criminal Procedure became meaningless when the sentence in question was mandatory. The Indian Supreme Court was concerned about the lack of regard given to the underlying offense warranting the sentence of life imprisonment. To prescribe a mandatory death sentence for

---

51 NOORANI, *supra* note 46 at 132.
52 BATRA, *supra* note 11 at 138, *citing* Mahabir Gope v. State of Bihar, A.I.R. 1963 S.C. 118; Oyami Ayatu v. State of Madhya Pradesh, (1974) 3 S.C.C. 299.
53 Pratap v. State of Uttar Pradesh, (1973) 3 S.C.C. 690; Dilip Kumar Sharma v. State of Madhya Pradesh, A.I.R. 1976 S.C. 133.
54 *Dilip*, A.I.R. 1976 S.C. at 138 (Sarkaria, J., concurring).
55 Mithu v. State of Punjab, (1983) 2 S.C.R. 690.
56 *Id.* at 697–8.

murder for a prisoner serving a life sentence for forgery, for instance, would be an arbitrary application of the provision because the fact of the forgery conviction had no nexus to the heightened penalty for murder. In addition, because some prisoners serving sentences of life imprisonment would eventually have their sentences reprieved or paroled, the law created the odd circumstance of treating condemned prisoners currently serving life sentences more harshly than prisoners who had completed their life sentences.

Chief Justice Yeshwant Vishnu Chandrachud's opinion in *Mithu* carried echoes of the decision by Justice Potter Stewart in *Woodson*, not only in substance but in elegance:

> A provision of law which deprives the court of the use of its wise and beneficent discretion in a matter of life and death, without regard to the circumstances in which the offence was committed and, therefore without regard to the gravity of the offence, cannot but be regarded as harsh, unjust and unfair. The legislature cannot make relevant circumstances irrelevant, deprive the courts of their legitimate jurisdiction to exercise their discretion not to impose the death sentence in appropriate cases, compel them to shut their eyes to mitigating circumstances and inflict upon them the dubious and unconscionable duty of imposing a pre-ordained sentence of death.[57]

In addition, because India's revised Criminal Procedure Code required judges to articulate the "special circumstances" meriting a heightened penalty of death, a mandatory death sentence made compliance with this provision impossible. This augmented the arbitrariness of the statute by depriving the life-term offender of a procedural safeguard provided to all other capital defendants. The Court ultimately found that the provision violated the constitution's right to life provision, as the procedure was not "fair, just, and reasonable," and the equality provision, because separating life convicts from all other persons was an arbitrary distinction. A concurrence reflected on Section 303's denial of judicial sentencing discretion: "So final, so irrevocable and so irrestitutable is the sentence of death that no law which provides for it without involvement of the judicial mind can be said to be fair, just and reasonable."[58] *Mithu* was confirmed by several additional Supreme Court decisions arising under the constitutionally inoperable Section 303, though the provision was not repealed.[59]

The passage of a mandatory death sentence in the Terrorism and Detention Act of 1985 tested *Mithu*. Because the mandatory death sentence provision under the Act eventually lapsed, the result was overlapping sentences of death and life imprisonment for different prisoners. The Court resolved this contradiction in *State through CBI, Delhi v. Gian Singh*, finding that the mandatory death sentence was superseded by the subsequently enacted alternatives to the death sentence.[60] Trial courts have also awarded mandatory death sentences under the Narcotic and Psychotropic Drugs Act, though these appear to have been reversed on appeal.[61] The Supreme Court avoided directly addressing the constitutionality of the mandatory death sentence under Section 27(3) of the Arms Act of 1959 by reversing several convictions, and nearly thirty years passed before the Court confirmed *Mithu*'s holding.[62]

---

57 *Id.* at 704.
58 *Id.* at 713 (Chinnappa Reddy, J., concurring).
59 Bhagwan Bax Singh v. State of Uttar Pradesh, (1984) 1 S.C.C. 278, and Surjit Singh v. State of Punjab, A.I.R. 1983 S.C. 838.
60 State through CBI, Delhi v. Gian Singh, (1999) 9 S.C.C. 312.
61 BATRA, *supra* note 11 at 142–3.
62 Subhash Ramkumar Bind v. State of Maharashtra, A.I.R. 2003 S.C. 269 (convicting of murder under the Penal Code but not under the Arms Act; substituting sentence of life imprisonment);

In June 2011, the Bombay High Court found the mandatory death penalty under Section 31A of the Narcotic and Psychotropic Drugs Act of 1985 unconstitutional in *Indian Harm Reduction Network (on behalf of Gulam Mohammed Malik) v. Union of India*, the first time that a Commonwealth court directly found a mandatory death sentence for drug trafficking unconstitutional.[63] The Attorney General attempted to distinguish murder by life-term prisoners from narcotics trafficking offenses, noting that India's provision for an automatic sentence of death only for repeat offenses was narrower than similar laws in countries such as Malaysia and Singapore, as those prescribed the mandatory death sentence for *first-time* offenders. "There is no reason to doubt that the offences relating to narcotics drug[s] or psychotropic substances are more heinous than culpable homicide," the Court wrote, noting the societal and economic devastation of the drug trade. Nonetheless, the judges were unconvinced by the attempt to distinguish *Mithu*: Section 31A of the Act "completely takes away the judicial discretion, nay, abridges the entire procedure for administration of criminal justice of weighing the aggravating and mitigating circumstances in which the offence was committed as well as that of the offender."[64] *Mithu* controlled and required invalidation of Section 31A.

Unlike the Supreme Court's determination in *Mithu* that a person's status as a life-term prisoner was irrelevant to the heinousness of a murder charge, the Bombay High Court found that the repeat status of an offender was not an arbitrary distinction—rather, it was based on an intelligible distinction that bore a nexus to criminal culpability. As a consequence, the death penalty for drug trafficking did not necessarily violate the equal protection of law provision of Article 14 of the constitution. In addition, the Court rejected the argument that the death sentence was disproportionate to drug trafficking offenses because the crime did not result in death and was thus not among the "rarest of the rare," instead noting that drug trafficking jeopardized the social fabric of the nation. Rather than strike Section 31A completely, however, the Court opted to construe the mandatory sentencing provision as discretionary and replace "shall" with "may" so that a trial court retained discretion to substitute death or a lesser punishment depending on the circumstances of the case.[65]

In February 2012, the Supreme Court of India finally invalidated the mandatory death penalty under the Arms Act of 1959, an anti-terrorist law criminalizing use of heavy arms or ammunition resulting in death.[66] In this decision, *State of Punjab v. Dalbir Singh*, the Court cited global precedent for the proposition that the mandatory death penalty violated the right to a fair trial because it precluded a sentencing hearing for a defendant convicted of murder. Although the Court ultimately acquitted the defendant of homicide, the justices struck down Section 27(3) of the Arms Act.[67] The Court found that the mandatory death penalty in the Arms Act violated constitutionally protected judicial review of criminal sentences and undermined the statutory sentencing structure of the Indian Penal Code and

---

Gyasuddin Khan v. State of Bihar, A.I.R. 2004 S.C. 210 (finding that the gun used may not fall within protected category and therefore it was "not appropriate to convict the appellant under S. 27(3) in which the extreme punishment of death is provided for").

63 Indian Harm Reduction Network (on behalf of Gulam Mohammed Malik) v. Union of India, Crim. Writ Petition No. 1784 of 2010 (June 11, 2010) (Bombay H.C.).
64 *Id.*
65 *Id.*
66 State of Punjab v. Dalbir Singh, A.I.R. 2012 S.C. 1040.
67 *Id.* at 1043, 1062; Arms Act, 1959, No. 54, *as amended by* Arms (Amendment) Act, 1988, No. 42, § 6(3) (introducing mandatory death sentence).

Criminal Procedure Code.⁶⁸ In addition to reviewing domestic precedent, the Court engaged in a searching analysis of American, Caribbean, and African authority, deeply influenced by the truly global nature of mandatory death penalty case law despite the unique features of India's constitutional regime.

With the invalidation of the mandatory death penalty under Section 303 of the Penal Code, Section 27(3) of the Arms Act of 1959, and Section 31A of the Narcotic Drugs and Psychotropic Substances Act of 1985, the clear weight of constitutional authority is that the mandatory death sentence is never constitutionally permissible. The Scheduled Castes and Scheduled Tribes (Prevention of Atrocities) Act of 1989 still has the mandatory death penalty, but only for an extremely narrow class of crime that is virtually never prosecuted: false witness or fabrication of evidence that results in the execution of an innocent person.⁶⁹ In addition, some prisoners may still be under mandatory sentence of death for a law that has lapsed, the Terrorist and Disruptive Activities (Prevention) Act of 1985, and absent a broad ruling may need to bring original writs challenging their individual sentences.⁷⁰ While these laws are likely unconstitutional, they may remain on the books until challenged.

Bangladesh and the Reach of Indian Death Penalty Jurisprudence

Indian death penalty jurisprudence had outsized consequences for Bangladesh, though the country has a more robust modern history of capital punishment than India. Bangladesh carried out about five known executions per year between 2005 and 2010, though statistics are not publicly released and executions are secret. About 90 prisoners were on death row at one facility outside of the capital Dhaka, out of a total penal population of about 2,300 prisoners. Roughly 100 to 200 death sentences are handed down per year.⁷¹ Unlike India, the 1972 Constitution of Bangladesh contains both an explicit death penalty savings clause and a prohibition on cruel, inhuman and degrading punishment on the Commonwealth model.⁷² Bangladesh's right to life provision differs materially from India's in that it does not contain the phrase "according to a procedure established by law": "No person shall be deprived of life or personal liberty save in accordance with law." Despite these differences, Bangladesh has generally followed the rough contours of Indian jurisprudence.

Under the Penal Code of Bangladesh, the death penalty exists for murder, mutiny, waging war against the state, assisting the suicide of a child or an insane person, attempted murder by life-convicts, aggravated kidnapping, and armed robbery resulting in murder, a similar list to the Indian Penal Code, and one that dates to 1860 when a common British-style penal code applied to a united India and Bangladesh.⁷³ In addition, the Special Powers (Amendment) Act of 1974 also added sabotage, illicit trafficking, counterfeiting, smuggling,

---

68 *Dalbir Singh*, A.I.R. 2012 S.C. at 1061. A proposal to amend the Arms Act to conform to the Indian Constitution was already pending in Parliament. Arms (Amendment) Act, 2011, No. 120 (Parliament of India, introduced Nov. 17, 2011).

69 Scheduled Castes and Scheduled Tribes (Prevention of Atrocities) Act, 1989, No. 33, § 2(i).

70 BATRA, *supra* note 11 at 137.

71 INTERNATIONAL FEDERATION FOR HUMAN RIGHTS (FIDH), BANGLADESH: CRIMINAL JUSTICE THROUGH THE PRISM OF CAPITAL PUNISHMENT AND THE FIGHT AGAINST TERRORISM 13–14 (2010).

72 BANGLADESH CONST. art. 32, 35(5).

73 Bangladesh Penal Code, 1860, No. 45, §§ 121 (waging war), 132 (mutiny), 302 (murder), 305 (assisting suicide), 307 (attempted murder by life-prisoner), 364A (kidnapping), 396 (armed robbery resulting in murder). Aggravated kidnapping added by Criminal Law (Amendment) Act, 1958, No. 34, § 2.

and poisoning as capital offenses.[74] A host of firearms and explosives-related offenses as well as terrorist-related crimes are punishable by death under separate laws.[75] Finally, laws protecting women and children from violence also attract the death penalty: murder or attempted murder with fire or acid; grievous bodily harm by fire or acid if the damage is to eyesight, face, hearing, or reproductive organs; trafficking of women or children; kidnapping; sexual assault resulting in death; dowry murder; and maiming of children for begging purposes.[76] In 1978, the Code of Criminal Procedure (inherited from British India) was amended to require a court to explain reasons for passing a sentence, whether death or life imprisonment, modeled on the Indian revision of 1973.[77]

Bangladeshi judges are increasingly influenced by comparative constitutional developments, especially from the Subcontinent. The achievements of Indian human rights litigation helped Bangladesh transcend perceptions of the traditional judicial role of technically applying law as written.[78] Nonetheless, the development of global human rights jurisprudence in Bangladesh is a work in progress, and the judiciary has at times failed adequately to stand up for the cause of justice due to a concern for strict legal positivism, political considerations, and institutional conservatism. The most radical step forward was the Appellate Division's invalidation of the Eighth Amendment to the Constitution of Bangladesh, holding that Parliament's amendment power is subject to the unalterability of "basic structures" of the constitution, a decision that followed the famous Indian decision *Kesavananda Bharati v. State of Kerala* in 1973, which authoritatively established the doctrine of inviolability of the "basic structure" of the Indian Constitution.[79] In 2005, the High Court Division declared unconstitutional the Constitution (Fifth Amendment) Act that sought to give constitutional protection to martial law, which likely acted as a deterrent to a military takeover during the 2007 Emergency.[80] At other times, Bangladesh has resisted the pull of Indian case law. Because the Indian constitutional regime was "radically different" on matters of preventive detention, the Appellate Division found that it was "dangerous" to take persuasive guidance from Indian decisions.[81]

Bangladesh has long wrestled with its own version of the "rarest of the rare" doctrine. In *Sarder v. State*, the Appellate Division reduced a death sentence based on the "bitter matrimonial relationship" between the appellants' family and the deceased, noting that Section 302 of the Penal Code "does not specify in which case the death sentence should

---

74 Special Powers (Amendment) Act, 1974, No. 49, §§ 25A (counterfeiting), 25B (smuggling), 25C (adulteration of food or drink).

75 Arms Act, 1878, No. 9, § 20A (use of unlicensed firearms for murder); Explosives Act, 1884, No. 4, § 12 (abetting or attempting capital offense); Explosive Substances Act, 1908, No. 6, § 3 (causing explosion likely to endanger life or property). *See* FIDH, *supra* note 71 at 11.

76 Bangladesh Code of Criminal Procedure Act, 1898, No. 5, § 367(5), *as amended by* Schedule of the Law Reforms Ordinance, 1978, No. 49.

77 MAHMUDUL ISLAM, CONSTITUTIONAL LAW OF BANGLADESH 195 (2d ed. 2002).

78 Ridwanul Hoque, *Constitutionalism and the Judiciary in Bangladesh*, *in* COMPARATIVE CONSTITUTIONALISM IN SOUTH ASIA 303, 309 (Sunil Khilnani, Vikram Raghavan & Arun K. Thiruvengadam eds., 2013).

79 *Id.* at 314, 315, *citing* Anwar Hossain Chowdhury v. Bangladesh, (1989) B.L.D. (A.D.) 1; Kesavananda Bharati v. State of Kerala, (1973) 4 S.C.R. 225.

80 *Id.* at 317–18, *citing* Bangladesh Italian Marble Works Ltd. v. Bangladesh, (2006) B.L.T. (H.C.D.) 1 (Aug. 29, 2005).

81 RIDWANUL HOQUE, JUDICIAL ACTIVISM IN BANGLADESH: A GOLDEN MEAN APPROACH 242 (2011), *citing* Sajenda Parvin v. Bangladesh, (1988) 40 D.L.R. (A.D.) 178, 183.

be given," but rather "leaves the matter to the discretion of the court."[82] According to the Court, "[e]very case should be considered in the facts and circumstances of that case only." However, the Court refused to find that the long period between the sentence and the disposition of the appeal to be a ground for commutation of sentence, despite the appellants' "great mental agony." In 1998, the High Court Division reduced a death sentence to life imprisonment where a condemned prisoner was awaiting execution of his sentence for four years and eleven months, finding that he had been "suffering mental agony of death" and a "sentence of life imprisonment instead of death will meet the ends of justice."[83] The Court also noted that the condemned man was so poor that he was unable to file an application for bail and could not engage a lawyer to defend his case; he was represented by state-appointed counsel both at trial and on appeal. However, the High Court Division found that it had no discretion to reduce a sentence of life imprisonment where the penal code authorized either death or life imprisonment for rape, considering itself bound by the minimum non-capital sentence in the Penal Code.[84]

The Appellate Division reduced a death sentence to life imprisonment where the accused witnessed a cruel and gruesome murder by his friends, but did not participate in the actual killing.[85] According to the Court, "we think that some extenuating circumstances has visibly appeared as would permit us to take a lenient view in the matter of sentence."[86] In a case involving three brothers who murdered two victims in a confrontation, the High Court opted to reduce the sentence of the two brothers who did not actually administer fatal blows to the victims, finding that they were only vicariously liable for the offense of murder.[87] In 2009, the Appellate Division reduced a sentence to life imprisonment where the defendant committed ordinary murder without premeditation.[88] "Since this is not the rarest of the rare cases," the Court indicated, "ends of justice will be met if the sentence of death of accused…is converted into one of imprisonment for life."[89] At a minimum, Bangladeshi courts weigh aggravating and mitigating circumstances similarly to Indian courts, and with the same resulting problem of arbitrariness in the death penalty's application.

Besides a mandatory death sentence for murder and attempted murder by a life-term prisoner, Bangladesh also possessed a mandatory death sentence from 1995 to 2000 under the Oppression of Women and Children (Special Enactment) Act for three crimes: first, the murder of a woman or child using explosives, corrosive substances, or poison; second, dowry murder, in which a woman is killed by her husband or his family after suffering harassment or torture to extort a higher dowry; and third, murder following rape.[90] The mandatory death sentence was replaced by a discretionary one under the Women and Children Repression Prevention Act of 2000, but without retroactive application. In 1995, a 14-year-old boy was given a mandatory death sentence for the rape and murder of a 7-year-old girl. In the resulting case, *State v. Sukur Ali*, the High Court Division of Bangladesh ruled that "[n]o alternative punishment has been provided for the offence that the condemned prisoner has

---

82 Sarder v. State, (1987) 7 B.L.D. (A.D.) 324, 328.
83 State v. Mohammed Monir Ahmed, (1998) 18 B.L.D. (H.C.D.) 605, 610.
84 Biswas v. State, (2002) 22 B.L.D. (H.C.D.) 575, 580.
85 Abdul Awal v. State, (1994) 14 B.L.D. (A.D.) 224.
86 *Id.* at 229.
87 State v. Akkel Ali, (2000) 20 B.L.D. (H.C.D.) 484, 492.
88 State v. Pinto, (2009) 29 B.L.D. (A.D.) 73.
89 *Id.* at 78.
90 Oppression of Women and Children (Special Enactment) Act, 1995, No. 18, §§ 4, 6(2), and 10(1).

been charged and we are left with no other discretion but to maintain the sentence if we believe that the prosecution has been able to prove the charge beyond reasonable doubt."[91] In that decision, the High Court Division reasoned that it could not defy the language of the concerned special statute that provided for the mandatory death penalty for "any person" guilty of the offense. According to one commentator, this was "a questionable interpretation of the law which the Appellate Division later endorsed," though it "lent an impetus to the ongoing legal activism by civil-society members."[92] The statute itself did not define any limits on the person of the offender.

In 2010, in an original writ brought on behalf of Sukur Ali, the High Court Division of the Supreme Court of Bangladesh invalidated the mandatory death penalty in *Bangladesh Legal Aid and Services Trust (Sukur Ali) v. Bangladesh*, following the persuasive decisions of the Supreme Court of India.[93] The Court refused to disturb the death sentence on Sukur Ali, as it had been upheld by the Appellate Division, but reached the ultimate issue of whether the mandatory sentence of death was constitutional, specifically addressing the two crimes for which it remained authorized under the Penal Code: murder and attempted murder by a person under a sentence of life imprisonment. Citing to *Reyes v. Queen*, the Court acknowledged the decline of the mandatory death penalty in the Commonwealth but upheld the constitutionality of a discretionary death penalty for the most heinous crimes, including murder, murder during rape, and death by acid.

The High Court Division's holding as to the separation of powers was similar to the Indian Supreme Court's decision in *Mithu*. When the legislature prescribes a mandatory punishment "the hands of the court are tied" and the "court becomes a simple rubberstamp of the legislature."[94] It was "the duty of the court to take into account [an accused's] character and antecedents in order to come to a just and proper decision," but where a sentence was mandatory the court was precluded from considering mitigating or extenuating facts and circumstances. In Bangladesh, no provision existed for a sentencing hearing for an accused prisoner. "It is our view that it is imperative that such provision should exist, particularly in view of the fact that in our country the adversarial system denies the accused any opportunity to put forward any mitigating circumstances before the court."[95]

The Court ensured that its decision was far reaching: "any mandatory provision of law takes away the discretion of the court and precludes the court from coming to a decision which is based on the assessment of all the facts and circumstances surrounding any given offence or the offender, and that is not permissible under the Constitution."[96] A court must always have "the discretion to determine what punishment a transgressor deserves and to fix the appropriate sentence for the crime he is alleged to have committed." Considering the particularly grave consequences of a death sentence, the Court acknowledged the role of mistake and wrongful convictions in the abolition of the death penalty elsewhere in the world, but noted that abolition in Bangladesh "must be left to the public, parliament and researchers to debate extensively and decide after thorough and threadbare discussion

---

91 State v. Sukur Ali, (2004) 9 B.L.C. (H.C.D.) 238.
92 Hoque, *supra* note 78 at 325.
93 Bangladesh Legal Aid and Services Trust (BLAST) v. Bangladesh, (2010) 30 B.L.D. (H.C.D.) 194.
94 *Id.* at 208.
95 *Id.* at 209.
96 *Id.* at 210.

whether the death penalty is to be retained."[97] Section 6(2) of the Oppression of Women and Children (Special Enactment) Act was declared *ultra vires* to the Constitution.

The High Court Division's decision in *BLAST* may be criticized because it did not fully resolve the situation of petitioner Sukur Ali, a juvenile sentenced to death more than a decade ago. Instead of reversing Sukur Ali's death sentence, the Court hid behind a false guise of judicial restraint, leaving it to the Appellate Division to pronounce on his particular death sentence. The failure of the High Court Division to alter the death sentence under the guise of judicial restraint "actually disguises studious avoidance of the issue of unjustness of the death penalty already awarded to the minor convict."[98] Because of the case, however, both organizations and individuals are allowed to bring abstract judicial review challenges to legislation or constitutional amendments on the basis that they are *ultra vires* to the constitution, a "liberalization of public interest judicial review standing," allowing unprecedented constitutional challenges.[99] The decision makes Sukur Ali's resentencing likely, and the Court's sweeping holding aligns Bangladesh with the clear emerging consensus in the Commonwealth that not all murders are equally heinous and deserving of death and that a trial judge is best placed to consider the circumstances of the offense and of the offender in determining an appropriate sentence.

A Note on the Mandatory Death Penalty in Sri Lanka

Sri Lanka's constitutional regime possesses the same constitutional vulnerabilities of other common law countries. The 1978 constitution includes a prohibition on cruel, inhuman, and degrading punishment, though the right to life provision parallels the Indian language: "No person shall be punished with death or imprisonment except by order of a competent court, made in accordance with procedure established by law."[100] Sri Lanka retains the mandatory death sentence for murder, although the country has not carried out an execution since 1978.[101] In *Van Der Jhultes v. Attorney General* in 1988, the Sri Lanka Court of Appeal ruled that the death penalty for drug trafficking under the Poisons, Opium, and Dangerous Drugs Ordinance was not mandatory, as the statute stated that a convicted offender "shall be liable" to suffer death instead of "shall" suffer death.[102] In a subsequent case, *Weerawardane v. State*, the Court of Appeal reversed a lower court decision in which a High Court judge "decided to impose a term of life imprisonment on the accused-appellant without sentencing him to death as required by law."[103] The Court acquitted, finding that the attempt to impose a lesser sentence indicated equivocation about the conviction. However, the decision confirmed that the death penalty was mandatory and that a judge did not possess the discretion to substitute a lesser sentence.

---

97 *Id.* at 210.
98 Hoque, *supra* note 78 at 325.
99 HOQUE, *supra* note 81 at 159.
100 SRI LANKA CONST. art. 11, 13(4).
101 Sri Lanka Penal Code, Ord. 2 of 1883, § 295.
102 Van Der Jhultes v. Attorney General, (1989) 1 Sri L.R. 204 (28 June 1988).
103 Weerawardane v. State, [2000] 2 Sri L.R. 391 (21 Oct. 1999).

Conclusion

India is exceptional among retentionist nations for its low execution rate and high thresholds for death sentences, though courts have struggled with producing a workable test that clearly separates the most heinous crimes from the rest. The constitutional regime created by *Bachan Singh v. State of Punjab* in 1980 granted wide discretion to judges to determine an appropriate sentence in death penalty-eligible cases, but did so at the expense of predictability in sentencing. Like the United States Supreme Court, the Supreme Court of India narrowed the sentencing options open to legislators by invalidating mandatory death sentences and moving to a regime of guided discretion. In 2009, the Court's decision in *Santosh Bariyar* provided a much-needed paradigm shift, again narrowing the scope of capital punishment while providing a more workable test that requires trial judges to determine that no rehabilitative or custodial sentence would serve a useful purpose.

India's death penalty jurisprudence had an outsized impact on neighboring Bangladesh, which has a more modern constitution that closely follows the Commonwealth template. In 2010, relying on Indian case law, the High Court Division succeeded in striking down the mandatory death penalty. Sri Lanka, an abolitionist country in practice, has also shown a willingness to modify or limit its operative mandatory death provisions. Just as Commonwealth countries engage in a sharing process of building and sharing a corpus of death penalty jurisprudence that has helped harmonize best practices across borders, the Indian Subcontinent is engaged in a regional sharing process of its own, one in which India plays a prominent role.

Chapter 4
A Successful Experiment: The Abolition of the Mandatory Death Penalty in the Commonwealth Caribbean

Following fifteen years of litigation, the mandatory death penalty for murder has been invalidated in nearly every Commonwealth Caribbean country, a process that highlighted the tensions between global and local perspectives on international human rights law. With drastically rising crime rates during the 1990s, Caribbean nations began calling for more robust use of the death penalty, conflicting with the international trend toward abolition. This retentionist sentiment came into conflict with the increasingly broad jurisdiction of international human rights tribunals and pressure from Great Britain. The result was "an unprecedented political and juridical struggle over the conditions under which capital punishment would continue to be utilized in the Caribbean region," forcing the small, resource-poor Caribbean states to choose between their English common law heritage on the one hand, and their hard-won independence on the other.[1]

Until the twentieth century, capital punishment was widely used in the colonial period by British colonizers, particularly against slaves in the Caribbean plantation economy. Slave revolts were often suppressed by the public execution of rebel leaders. The Jamaican Slave Rebellion of 1865, for instance, resulted in 354 executions and excessive floggings.[2] For ordinary crimes, the tiny free population was tried in assize courts, modeled on magistrates' courts in England; the much larger slave population had a separate system of slave courts. Slaves, as valuable property, would typically only be executed for very severe crimes such as rebellion or the murder of a European. The majority of slave punishments were private, meted out by the slaveholder or overseer in the form of flogging or bodily mutilation; imprisonment was a punishment reserved for free populations.[3] A communal system of compensation in Antigua and other plantation economies provided recompense to slaveholders whose slaves were executed by the state, and slaveholders often compensated one another for the crimes of their slaves.[4] The death penalty was mandatory upon conviction of a capital crime, though the slaveholder could petition the governor for pardon or reprieve on behalf of a slave.[5]

---

1 Brian Tittemore, *The Mandatory Death Penalty in the Commonwealth Caribbean and the Inter-American Human Rights System*, 13 WM. & MARY BILL RTS. J. 445, 464 (2004).

2 Quincy Whitaker, *Challenging the Death Penalty in the Caribbean: Litigation at the Privy Council*, in AGAINST THE DEATH PENALTY: INTERNATIONAL INITIATIVES AND IMPLICATIONS 101, 103 (Jon Yorke ed., 2008).

3 Diana Paton, *Punishment, Crime, and the Bodies of Slaves in Eighteenth Century Jamaica*, 34 J. SOC. HIST. 923, 926, 927, 928 (2001).

4 David Barry Gaspar, *"To Bring Their Offending Slaves to Justice": Compensation and Slave Resistance in Antigua, 1669–1763*, 30 CARIB. Q. 45, 45 (1984).

5 Anthony De V. Phillips, *Doubly Condemned: Adjustments to the Crime and Punishment Regime in the Late Slavery Period in the British Caribbean Colonies*, 18 CARDOZO L. REV. 699, 711 (1996).

The modern history of the Caribbean began in May 1962, when Great Britain dissolved the Federation of the West Indies, allowing Jamaica and Trinidad and Tobago to move rapidly toward independence. The eight remaining members of the former Federation attempted to form a rump political union, but negotiations faltered and Barbados achieved independence in 1966; the others entered into a voluntary association with Britain. Guyana's path to independence in 1966 resulted in a state of emergency, widespread strikes, and the presence of British troops. The constitutions of all four independent territories were modeled on that of the United Kingdom, but with modifications in the structure of government and including bills of rights.[6] Jamaica, Guyana, and Trinidad and Tobago were early ratifiers of the International Covenant on Civil and Political Rights, though acceptance of the Inter-American Human Rights System, originally created without Caribbean participation, was a slower process.[7]

For the remaining microstates of the Caribbean, independence came later: Bahamas in 1973, Grenada in 1974, Dominica in 1978, Saint Lucia and Saint Vincent and the Grenadines in 1979, Belize and Antigua and Barbuda in 1981, and Saint Kitts and Nevis in 1983. These countries also adopted legal systems with elaborate constitutional bills of rights. Except for two decades of authoritarianism in Guyana and a four-year period after the 1979 coup in Grenada, Westminster-style constitutions installed a post-independence tradition of liberal democratic rule in most of the Commonwealth Caribbean. However, tiny populations and sharp resource constraints ensured that the island nations remained dependent on Great Britain. Challenges facing each nation included rising rates of transnational criminal activity, adversarial and highly personal politics with endemic corruption, relatively low levels of technocratic expertise, and high distribution costs of government services.[8] Attempts by the small island states to move out of the shadows of Great Britain largely failed, as when a homegrown Republican constitution for Saint Vincent and the Grenadines lost in a referendum in 2009.[9] Despite the foibles, the Caribbean ranks well above the global average in the enjoyment of civil and political rights, with detailed constitutional protections and a moderately good record of protecting human rights in domestic legal systems, backed by a network of non-governmental organizations and ombudsmen.[10]

The Death Penalty and Society in the Caribbean

After independence, death sentences were imposed extremely rarely in postcolonial Commonwealth Caribbean states.[11] Except for Saint Kitts and Nevis, which last carried out an execution in 2008, at least ten years have passed—and in some cases, much more—since

---

6 J.H. PARRY & PHILIP SHERLOCK, A SHORT HISTORY OF THE WEST INDIES 299–302 (1983).

7 Laurence R. Helfer, *Overlegalizing Human Rights: International Relations Theory and the Commonwealth Caribbean Backlash Against Human Rights Regimes*, 102 COLUMBIA L. REV. 1832, 1864 (2002).

8 Matthew Louis Bishop, *Slaying the "Westmonster" in the Caribbean? Constitutional Reform in St. Vincent and the Grenadines*, 13 BRIT. J. POL. & INT'L REL. 420, 421, 425–6 (2011).

9 *Id.* at 421, 431–2.

10 Helfer, *supra* note 7 at 1863 (2002).

11 Farley Brathwaite, *Some Aspects of Sentencing in the Criminal Justice System of Barbados*, 42 CARIB. Q. 101, 103 (1996).

a Commonwealth Caribbean territory carried out an execution.[12] Indeed, several legislatures considered bills to divide murder into capital murder, non-capital murder, and intentional homicide in order to restrict application of the death penalty.[13] In recent years, Trinidad and Tobago has been the most enthusiastic proponent of capital punishment and shocked international opinion with the execution of Glen Ashby in July 1994 while his appeal was still pending before the Privy Council.[14]

The Caribbean region has historically had among the highest violent crime rates in the developing world.[15] This is true even though the region's tiny societies are less anonymous and strongly family- and community-based.[16] The drug trade has profoundly affected crime. Belize was a major producer of marijuana due to the combination of jungle cover and isolated air strips without radar coverage. Similarly, the scattered islands of the Bahamas, with low-cost commercial flights to the United States, served as important drug trade routes. Money laundering is a byproduct of drug cultivation, transport, and use. The web of drug criminality had "no economic, social, or political boundaries" and could be "deep and wide enough to shake the political foundation of a nation," as it did when the ruling party of Saint Kitts and Nevis lost the 1995 elections after a series of prominent drug scandals encompassed high-level officials.[17] With high levels of economic inequality, unemployment, and inflation, Jamaica entered a structural adjustment program in the late 1970s that improved its nationwide economic output and increased foreign investment, especially in the tourism sector, but also limited opportunities for low-skilled labor.[18] Poverty launched the country into a cycle of drugs and crime.

Criminologists have extensively studied the high rates of gun violence in the Caribbean. In Jamaica, 55 people per 100,000 were killed by gunfire in 2008, up from 20 per 100,000 in the 1980s; Bahamas, Guyana, and Saint Kitts and Nevis have also experienced large increases in homicide rates. The number of gun-related homicides in Trinidad and Tobago rose threefold to over 500 in 2008 from 137 in 1994. The percentage of murders involving a firearm has also increased, related to the proliferation of small arms in the Eastern Caribbean.[19] Gun homicides in Trinidad and Tobago are less likely to be solved than other forms of homicide; about 90% of the victims of gun violence are male, and

---

12 According to Capital Punishment UK, the last execution in Antigua and Barbuda was in 1991; Bahamas in 2000; Barbados 1984; Dominica 1986; Grenada 1978; Guyana 1997; Jamaica 1988; St. Kitts and Nevis 2008; St. Lucia 1995; St. Vincent and the Grenadines 1995; and Trinidad and Tobago 1999. Capital Punishment UK, *Capital Punishment in the Commonwealth*, http://www.capitalpunishmentuk.org/common.html (last accessed June 18, 2013).

13 *See e.g.*, Offences Against the Person (Amendment) Act, 1992, No. 14 (Jam.); Criminal Justice Act, 1994, No. 22 (Belize).

14 Julian B. Knowles, *Capital Punishment in the Commonwealth Caribbean: Colonial Inheritance, Colonial Remedy?*, *in* CAPITAL PUNISHMENT: STRATEGIES FOR ABOLITION 282, 288 (Peter Hodgkinson & William Schabas eds., 2004).

15 Klaus de Albuquerque, *A Comparative Analysis of Violent Crime in the Caribbean*, 33 SOC. & ECON. STUD. 93, 97 (1984).

16 Maureen Cain, *Crime and Criminology in the Caribbean: An Introduction*, 42 CARIB. Q. v, vii (1996).

17 Ivelaw L. Griffith, *Drugs and Criminal Justice in the Caribbean*, 42 CARIB. Q. 72, 73–6, 78 (1996).

18 Anthony Harriott, *The Changing Social Organization of Crime and Criminals in Jamaica*, 42 CARIB. Q. 54, 56 (1996).

19 Biko Agozino, *et al.*, *Guns, Crime, and Social Order in the West Indies*, 9 CRIMINOLOGY & CRIM. JUST. 287, 290–91, 294 (2009).

about 80% are of African descent. Jamaica is at the center of the gun problem: in 2006, five people per day were killed, mostly in gunfire.[20] The proliferation of small weaponry and the high rates of gun violence are inextricably linked to the drug trade, robust in the global economic downturn.[21]

At independence, Caribbean states did not sever their legal ties to Britain, retaining the Judicial Committee of the Privy Council in London as the court of final appeal. Composed of a panel of British judges chosen from among members of the House of Lords, the Privy Council exercised narrow, conservative interpretation of constitutional fundamental rights clauses. By the 1980s, however, the Council's jurisprudence zigzagged between a narrow interpretation and a broad, progressive interpretation of fundamental rights depending on the panel of judges.[22] With a relatively small docket and British-funded operations, this constitutional structure went unchallenged until the 1990s when increasingly robust appellate review disrupted this equilibrium and made the Privy Council deeply unpopular in the Caribbean basin. Death penalty cases were the center of the firestorm.[23] The Privy Council likely became more vigilant due to stricter oversight of British jurisprudence from the European Court of Human Rights and growing awareness of the poor quality of legal representation in the Caribbean.[24]

Unlike the independent states, those territories that remained British colonies benefited from the abolition of the death penalty in British law. The death penalty was abolished in British dependent territories in the Caribbean (Anguilla, British Virgin Islands, Cayman Islands, Montserrat, and Turks and Caicos) in 1991, except in Bermuda due to its autonomous status.[25] Although Bermuda voters favored retention by an overwhelming margin in an August 1990 referendum, the House of Assembly narrowly voted to abolish the death penalty and corporal punishment in December 1999 under pressure from London. Bermuda last carried out an execution in 1977, the final execution to occur on British soil anywhere in the world.[26] Resistance engendered by Britain's heavy hand in death penalty abolition in the dependent territories foreshadowed the angry protests directed at the Privy Council a decade later when capital punishment regimes came under heavy scrutiny. Consternation was especially acute as citizens of dependent territories have restricted rights to apply for British citizenship.[27]

---

20 *Id.* at 291, 301.

21 Ronald Sanders, *Crime in the Caribbean: An Overwhelming Phenomenon*, 92 ROUND TABLE: COMMONW. J. OF INT'L AFF. 377, 383, 384–5 (2010).

22 Helfer, *supra* note 7 at 1865–6.

23 *Id.* at 1866–7. The European Court of Human Rights has not completely resolved the question of whether the Privy Council is an organ of the British Government, such that it would be bound by the anti-death penalty mandate of the European Convention on Human Rights. If so, it would be a violation of the Convention (and of Britain's implementing legislation, the Human Rights Act of 1998) for the Privy Council to rule in favor of the death penalty. *See* Rachel Murray, *The Human Rights Act: The End for the Privy Council and Death Penalty Cases?*, 6 J. CIVIL LIBERTIES 35, 38–40 (2001).

24 Knowles, *supra* note 14 at 290.

25 Caribbean Territories (Abolition of the Death Penalty for Murder) Order 1991 (S.I. No. 988 of 1991).

26 *"Bring the Death Penalty Back" – We Can't*, BERNEWS, April 11, 2010, http://bernews.com/2010/04/bring-the-death-penalty-back-we-cant; *Bermuda Retains Death Penalty*, ASSOCIATED PRESS, August 29, 1990 (retrieved from APNewsArchive.com).

27 Colleen Ballerino Cohen & Frances E. Mascia-Lees, *The British Virgin Islands as Nation and Desti-Nation: Representing and Siting Identity in a Post-colonial Caribbean*, 33 SOC. ANALYSIS: INT'L

A series of reports on the mandatory death penalty in Trinidad and Tobago by the London-based Death Penalty Project and the Rights Advocacy Project of the University of the West Indies Faculty of Law constitute the most extensive public opinion research ever performed in the Caribbean on the mandatory nature of the death penalty. The first report, published in 2006, was an exhaustive study of every reported homicide over a five-year period (a total of 633 cases) and all defendants prosecuted during the same period (297 completed prosecutions).[28] The results showed that only a tiny fraction of murderers were ever brought to justice: only about 5% of actual perpetrators were convicted of murder, with another 13% convicted of manslaughter at the end of the five-year span. The mandatory death penalty overpunished the small proportion of cases successfully won by the prosecution, masking serious deficiencies in law enforcement, investigations, and forensics. For instance, drug-related murders made up 33% of recorded killings, but only 2% of the convictions. On the other hand, domestic murders in which the victim and perpetrator were known to one another constituted 17% of recorded murders but 52% of capital murder convictions.[29] A second report in 2009 surveyed the judiciary and legal profession in Trinidad and Tobago, at a time when the country's murder rate had skyrocketed.[30] More than half the judges, prosecutors, and defense counsel interviewed could recall instances where they believed a death sentence was excessively harsh given the circumstances of a crime and where a jury convicted of a lesser crime in order to avoid a death sentence. The overwhelming majority (63%) favored a discretionary death penalty, and another 18% favored dividing murder into capital and non-capital offenses.

In 2011, the Death Penalty Project and the Rights Advocacy Project published the third report with survey results from the general public.[31] A representative sample of 1,000 residents were given crime hypotheticals, some of which contained a possible aggravating or mitigating factor, and respondents were asked to determine whether the death penalty was appropriate for the crime. The results were predictable, showing overwhelming support for the death penalty (89%), but much lower levels of support (26%) for a mandatory death sentence for murder.[32] As expected, responses expressing support for the death penalty fell dramatically when presented with an actual fact pattern compared to an abstract question. The polling confirmed that the mandatory death penalty overpunished: most respondents favored retention for precisely those types of murders that were the least-often prosecuted, namely, drug or gang murders, while disfavoring the penalty for domestic murders, a category that resulted in more frequent convictions. The reports showed that there was virtually no correlation between the severity of a crime and the punishment of death.

The Death Penalty Project and the Independent Jamaican Council for Human Rights collaborated on an exhaustive report on the prison conditions in Jamaica in 2011, including

---

J. OF SOC. & CULTURAL PRAC. 130, 143–4 (1993) (noting no hangings have ever occurred in the British Virgin Islands in modern times and all death sentences were commuted in sync with British law).

28   ROGER HOOD & FLORENCE SEEMUNGAL, A RARE AND ARBITRARY FATE: CONVICTION FOR MURDER, THE MANDATORY DEATH PENALTY, AND THE REALITY OF HOMICIDE IN TRINIDAD AND TOBAGO (2006).

29   *See* ROGER HOOD & FLORENCE SEEMUNGAL, PUBLIC OPINION ON THE MANDATORY DEATH PENALTY IN TRINIDAD 2 (2011) ("HOOD & SEEMUNGAL, PUBLIC OPINION").

30   Roger Hood & Florence Seemungal, *Experiences and Perceptions of the Mandatory Death Sentence for Murder in Trinidad and Tobago: Judges, Prosecutors, and Counsel, in* A PENALTY WITHOUT LEGITIMACY: THE MANDATORY DEATH PENALTY IN TRINIDAD AND TOBAGO (2009).

31   HOOD & SEEMUNGAL, PUBLIC OPINION, *supra* note 29.

32   *Id.* at vii–viii.

the "abominable" conditions on death row.[33] Housed in rooms without windows, three of the eight inmates then on death row used cardboard or thin sheets in lieu of mattresses and were covered in insects. No cells contained lights. Bulbs and electrical wires had to be provided from outside the facility or purchased on the black market; inmates could be denied access to electrical sockets as punishment. The cells did not contain toilets, but rather slop buckets to be emptied into pit toilets during the period in which the prisoners were allowed out of their cells. The cell block lacked temperature control in the hot Jamaican climate, and the prison did not provide water vessels for inmates.[34]

The Savings Clause Minefield in Caribbean Constitutions

Under the constitutions of the former British Caribbean colonies, the death penalty by hanging was uniformly a permissible sentence because of a constitutional clause specifically insulating the death penalty from constitutional challenge, the death penalty "savings clause." Article 16(1) of the Constitution of the Bahamas is representative of this type of clause: "No person shall be deprived intentionally of his life save in execution of the sentence of a court in respect of a criminal offence of which he has been convicted."[35] Modeled on a similar provision at Article 2(1) of the European Convention on Human Rights, this clause immunizes the death penalty from direct constitutional challenge as a violation of the right to life.

In addition to the death penalty savings clause, Commonwealth Caribbean constitutions possess an unusual quirk. With the exception of Belize, all the constitutions prevent challenge to capital punishment on the basis of the cruel, inhuman, and degrading treatment provisions through so-called "partial" savings clauses, which immunize any form of punishment legal at the time the constitution went into force.[36] Article 7 of the Constitution of Antigua and Barbuda is representative of this type of clause:

(1) No person shall be subjected to torture or to inhuman or degrading punishment or other such treatment;

(2) Nothing contained in or done under the authority of any law shall be held to be inconsistent with or in contravention of this section to the extent that the law in question authorizes the infliction of any description of punishment that was lawful in Antigua on 31st October 1981.

---

33 DEATH PENALTY PROJECT, PRISON CONDITIONS IN JAMAICA: A REPORT BASED ON JAMES ROBOTTOM'S VISIT IN AUGUST 2009 (2011).

34 *Id.* at 20–24.

35 ANTIGUA & BARBUDA CONST. art. 4(1); BAHAMAS CONST. art. 16(1); BARBADOS CONST. art. 12(1); BELIZE CONST. art. 4(1); DOMINICA CONST. art. 2(1); GRENADA CONST. art. 2(1); GUYANA CONST. art. 138(1); JAMAICA CONST. art. 14(1); ST. KITTS & NEVIS CONST. art. 7; ST. LUCIA CONST. art. 5; ST. VINCENT CONST. art. 5; TRINIDAD & TOBAGO CONST. art. 5(2)(b).

36 ANTIGUA & BARBUDA CONST. art. 7(2); BAHAMAS CONST. art. 17(2); BARB. CONST. art. 15(2); DOMINICA CONST. sched. 2, art. 11; GRENADA CONST. art. 5(2); GUYANA CONST. art. 141(2); JAM. CONST. art. 17(2); ST. KITTS & NEVIS CONST. sched. 2, art. 9; ST. LUCIA CONST. sched. 2, art. 10; ST. VINCENT CONST. sched. 2, art. 10; TRIN. & TOBAGO CONST. art. 6. Savings clauses vary, Burnham notes, leading to inconsistent case law that limits application across jurisdictions. Margaret A. Burnham, *Saving Constitutional Rights from Judicial Scrutiny: The Savings Clause in the Law of the Commonwealth Caribbean*, 36 U. MIAMI INTER-AM. L. REV. 249, 251 (2005).

The consequence of this provision is that any form of punishment legal at the time the Constitution entered into force (usually the date of independence or autonomous status) cannot be challenged on the basis that the form of punishment is cruel, inhuman or degrading. For instance, adult corporal punishment continues to be used in Jamaica and Trinidad, perpetually insulated from challenge.[37]

In addition, five countries—Bahamas, Barbados, Guyana, Jamaica, and Trinidad and Tobago—possess a broader savings clause, known as a "general" savings clause, which protects from challenge any law in existence at independence on the basis of the fundamental rights provisions of the constitution.[38] These five countries were, not coincidentally, the first in the English-speaking Caribbean to become independent. Article 26(8) of the Constitution of Jamaica is representative of general savings clauses:

> Nothing contained in any law in force immediately before the appointed day shall be held to be inconsistent with any of the provisions of this Chapter; and nothing done under the authority of any such law shall be held to be done in contravention of any of these provisions.

Guyana's 1980 constitution also saves laws that were repealed and re-enacted after independence or laws that were altered after independence in a manner constitutionally consistent with the prior enactment.[39] Jamaica's constitution similarly protects laws that were consolidated or revised after independence in a non-substantive manner.[40] Otherwise constitutionally vulnerable laws are immune from challenge on the basis of the fundamental rights provisions of the constitution, unless those laws were modified after independence. The anti-sodomy laws in force at independence are one example of this, a major constraint on expanding legal protections for sexual minorities in the Caribbean.[41]

Human rights lawyers led by the Death Penalty Project developed a legal strategy in the Caribbean to maneuver around this two-part minefield by challenging the consequences that flowed from the death penalty's imposition, rather than frontally assaulting the punishment itself, as the time, conditions, and manner in which the death penalty is carried out are not necessarily saved.[42] These anachronistic savings clauses preserve British colonial justice methods in perpetuity. The irony is that, in the modern death penalty debate, Commonwealth Caribbean nations seize on them as an expression of national independence from the London-based Privy Council (itself a colonial anachronism), which has gone to great lengths to narrowly interpret these clauses in light of evolving international human rights norms.[43]

---

37 Whitaker, *supra* note 2 at 104.

38 Saul Lehrfreund, *International Legal Trends and the 'Mandatory' Death Penalty in the Commonwealth Caribbean*, 1 OXFORD U. COMMW. L.J. 171, 180–81 (2001). *See also*, TRIN. & TOBAGO CONST. art. 6(1); GUYANA CONST. art. 152; BARB. CONST. art. 26(1); BAHAMAS CONST. art. 30(1).

39 GUYANA CONST. art. 151 (1980). Guyana's independence constitution had a narrower clause. *See* GUYANA CONST. art. 141 (1970).

40 JAM. CONST. art. 26(9).

41 Celine Abramschmitt, *Is Barbados Ready for Same-Sex Marriage? Analysis of Legal and Social Constructs*, 57 SOC. & ECON. STUD. 61 (2008) (on constitutionality of the Barbados Sexual Offenses Act, which criminalizes sodomy and buggery, and the Marriage Act, which defines marriage as one man and one woman).

42 Joanna Harrington, Comment, *The Challenge to the Mandatory Death Penalty in the Commonwealth Caribbean*, 98 AM. J. INT'L. L. 126, 128 (2004).

43 Whitaker, *supra* note 2 at 105.

Finally, one country has a savings clause that does not precisely fit the template: Belize. By the time Belize gained independence in 1981, savings clauses were already seen as anachronistic, constraining postcolonial constitutional jurisprudence. As a consequence, Belize has a general savings clause with an unusual feature: an expiration date. According to Article 21 of the Constitution of Belize, "Nothing contained in any law in force immediately before Independence Day nor anything done under the authority of any such law shall, *for a period of five years after Independence Day*, be held to be inconsistent with or done in contravention of any provisions of" the fundamental rights chapter of the Constitution.[44] According to Smith, "the framers of the Belize Constitution... were alert to some of the challenges that had emerged from the region's experience with constitutional interpretation."[45] As Lehrfreund writes, "In contrast to the constitutions of other Caribbean jurisdictions Belize has a living instrument which is no longer tied to the colonial status quo."[46] For this reason, the death penalty in Belize was peculiarly vulnerable to constitutional challenge.

The Death Row Phenomenon Challenges: A Prologue

The death row "phenomenon," or "syndrome," refers to the mental torture or distress that takes place in the mind of a prisoner as he or she awaits execution, validated by the research of psychiatrist Dr. Stuart Grassian into the mental deterioration of fourteen death row inmates placed in solitary confinement in the mid-1980s.[47] As the death row phenomenon began appearing in the jurisprudence of international human rights tribunals and Commonwealth courts, judges wrestled with the length of the delay required and whether the delay could be the fault of the convicted prisoner.[48] Ironically, Schabas writes, prolonged detention on death row was the consequence of efforts to limit and eventually abolish the death penalty by seeking judicial and constitutional review, petitions for clemency or pardon, review by international or regional tribunals, or political moratoria on executions.[49]

The Commonwealth Caribbean, where delays were particularly extensive, became a battleground in death row phenomenon appeals.[50] In *de Freitas v. Benny* in 1975, the Privy Council upheld the constitutionality of the death penalty in Trinidad and Tobago and turned away a constitutional challenge to undue delay between sentence and execution.[51] The Lords also refused to inquire into the process of executive clemency, finding that it "has

---

44 Emphasis added. *See* BELIZE CONST. art. 21.
45 Godfrey Smith, *Constitutionalism in Belize: Lessons for the Commonwealth Caribbean?*, University of the West Indies Faculty Working Paper 12 (Sept. 18, 2008), http://www.flashpointbelize. com/Portals/0/Constitutionalism%20in%20Belize%20%20Lessons%20for%20the%20Commonwealth%20 Caribbean.pdf.
46 Lehrfreund, *supra* note 38 at 181.
47 Stuart Grassian & N. Friedman, *Effects of Sensory Deprivation in Psychiatric Seclusion and Solitary Confinement*, 8 INT'L J. L. & PSYCHIATRY 49 (1986).
48 *See, e.g.*, Soering v. U.K., 11 E.H.R.R. 439 (1989) (Eur. Ct. H.R.); Trinveniben v. State of Gujarat, A.I.R. 1989 S.C. 142 (India S.C.); U.S. v. Burns, [2001] S.C.R. 283 (Can.); Catholic Comm'n for Justice and Peace v. Attorney General, (1993) L.R.C. 277 (Zimbabwe S.C.).
49 WILLIAM A. SCHABAS, THE DEATH PENALTY AS CRUEL TREATMENT AND TORTURE: CAPITAL PUNISHMENT CHALLENGED IN THE WORLD'S COURTS 97–8 (1996).
50 Hamid A. Ghany, The Death Penalty, Human Rights, and British Law Lords: Judicial Opinion on Delay of Execution in the Commonwealth Caribbean, 4 INT'L J. OF HUM. RTS. 30, 33 et seq. (2000).
51 De Freitas v. Benny, [1975] 27 W.I.R. 318 (P.C.) (appeal taken from Trin. & Tobago).

always been a matter which lies solely in the discretion of the sovereign."[52] Similarly, in *Abbott v. Attorney General of Trinidad and Tobago* in 1979, the Privy Council dismissed the appeal of a condemned prisoner who claimed a breach of fundamental rights because nearly a year passed on his petition for reprieve, and five years since his conviction.[53] Nonetheless, the Lords accepted the theoretical argument: "That so long a period should have been allowed to pass between the passing of a sentence of death and its being carried out is, in their Lordships' view, greatly to be deplored." It was possible to imagine a delay between sentencing and execution that was "so prolonged" as to arouse "a reasonable belief that [a] death sentence must have been commuted to life imprisonment," but this scenario would "involve delay measured in years, rather than in months."[54] The Lords deferred to local judges who had better knowledge of local procedures and were better placed to judge whether delay was unwarranted.

Three years later, the Privy Council addressed the question squarely. In 1982, the Privy Council rejected a death row phenomenon challenge by a vote of 3 to 2 in *Riley v. Attorney General of Jamaica*, finding that delay in executing a lawful death sentence could not render the execution unlawful, regardless of the reasons for or the length of the delay.[55] The dissent reasoned that delay beyond the time necessary for appeal and petition for clemency could amount to cruel, inhuman, and degrading punishment, perceiving the effects of delay from the perspective of the condemned prisoner.[56] According to the famous dissent by Lords Scarman and Brightman, "the jurisprudence of the civilized world, much of which is derived from common law principles and the prohibition against cruel and unusual punishments in the English Bill of Rights, has recognized and acknowledged that prolonged delay in executing a sentence of death can make the punishment when it comes inhuman and degrading."[57]

In 1993, the dissents of Lords Scarman and Brightman finally won majority support, and the Privy Council invalidated the death sentence of a prisoner in Jamaica who had been sentenced to death nearly fifteen years prior in *Pratt and Morgan v. Attorney General of Jamaica*.[58] The Privy Council held that execution must follow within a reasonable time after sentencing lest it become unconstitutional. In words reminiscent of U.S. Supreme Court Justice Potter Stewart, Lord Griffiths appealed to the humanity of prisoners in accepting the death row phenomenon: "There is an instinctive revulsion against the prospect of hanging a man after he has been held under sentence of death for many years. What gives rise to this instinctive revulsion? The answer can only be our humanity; we regard it as an inhuman act to keep a man facing the agony of execution over a long extended period of time."[59] To argue, as Jamaica did, that because the death sentence is constitutionally saved the manner

---

52 Id. at 322.
53 Abbott v. A.G. Trin. & Tobago, (1979) 32 W.I.R. 347 (P.C.).
54 Id. at 344, 352.
55 Riley v. A.G. Jam., (1983) 35 W.I.R. 279 (P.C.).
56 *Id.* at 294 (Scarman & Brightman, Lords, dissenting). *See* Lord Scarman & Philip Sapsford, *The Death Penalty: Can Delay Render Execution Unlawful?*, 25 ANGLO-AM. L. REV. 265, 267–8 (1996).
57 *Riley*, 35 W.I.R. at 293.
58 Pratt & Morgan v. A.G. Jam., (1993) 43 W.I.R. 340, 360 (P.C.) ("To execute these men now after holding them in custody in an agony of suspense for so many years would be inhuman punishment... In the last resort the courts have to accept the responsibility of saying whether the threshold has been passed in any given case and there may be difficult borderline decisions to be made. This, however, is not a borderline case. The delay in this case is wholly unacceptable and this appeal must be allowed"). *See* FRED PHILLIPS, THE DEATH PENALTY AND HUMAN RIGHTS 27 (2009).
59 *Id.* at 356.

in which it is carried out must also be saved interpreted the savings clause too broadly; the clause saved merely the sentence itself and not the manner of execution. The Council also refused to place the blame for delay on a defendant: if the appellate system allowed a defendant to unreasonably delay, it was the system and not the defendant to blame.

Because of the similar wording of most Commonwealth Caribbean constitutions and the similarities in their death row practices, the decision was followed by mass commutations of 105 prisoners in Jamaica, 53 in Trinidad and Tobago, and 9 in Barbados. The decision radically altered public and elite perceptions of the Privy Council in the Caribbean, who condemned the usurpation of legislative power and the radical break from prior precedent.[60] Petitions to the U.N. Human Rights Committee and to the Inter-American Human Rights System increased as defendants and their counsel came to recognize the significance of *Pratt*, particularly in Jamaica and Trinidad and Tobago, which had the region's largest death rows.[61] The process of exhausting domestic appeals and appealing international tribunals often took so long that Caribbean states exceeded the five-year window and were forced to commute death sentences.

The decision in *Pratt* bolstered the campaign to whittle away at the death penalty in the courts.[62] With challenges appearing before regional and international tribunals as well as national courts, the decisions began to form a cohesive body of death penalty jurisprudence from which later courts drew, in the Caribbean and beyond. The result is "an extensive body of Caribbean death penalty jurisprudence," which has placed on record the shortcomings of Caribbean penal systems.[63] In 1995, the Privy Council rejected an appeal by Barbados, which argued that the five-year time frame was unreasonably short because petitions to international tribunals took two years on average.[64] However, in a case arising from the Bahamas, the Privy Council shortened the length of the delay applicable to condemned prisoners in that country to three and a half years as the Bahamas was outside jurisdiction of the U.N. Human Rights Committee.[65] Jamaica, Trinidad and Tobago, and Guyana each moved to withdraw from the jurisdiction of the U.N. Human Rights Committee and the Inter-American Human Rights Commission.[66]

In 1995, the Privy Council extended *Pratt*'s reasoning in *Guerra v. Baptiste*, a death row phenomenon challenge arising from Trinidad and Tobago.[67] The Privy Council determined that the clock started ticking even before the disposition of the final appeal, for the "simple fact...that, following conviction and sentence to death, the condemned man is placed on death row and has there to contemplate the prospect even though, in some cases but not in others, he may have a real hope of a successful appeal."[68] In addition, the Privy Council found that a condemned prisoner should be given reasonable notice of the time of his execution, to enable him to arrange his affairs, be visited by family members, receive spiritual advice and comfort, or seek a stay of execution. The Council found that the notice given to Guerra, 17 hours, constituted cruel and degrading treatment even though the defendant was able to receive a stay of execution in that short time frame.

---

60 Helfer, *supra* note 7 at 1871.
61 *Id*. at 1875.
62 Harrington, *supra* note 42 at 129.
63 *Id*.
64 Bradshaw v. A.G. Barb., (1995) 46 W.I.R. 62, 68 (P.C.).
65 Henfield v. A.G. Bahamas, [1997] A.C. 413 (P.C.).
66 Helfer, *supra* note 7 at 1881.
67 Guerra v. Baptiste, (1995) 47 W.I.R. 439 (P.C.) (appeal taken from Trin. & Tobago).
68 *Id*. at 453.

In 1999, the Privy Council issued a divided ruling in *Thomas v. Baptiste*, holding that Trinidad and Tobago could not constitutionally execute prisoners whose challenges to unconstitutionally cruel and degrading prison conditions were still pending before international tribunals.[69] The Council issued a stay of execution until the Inter-American Commission on Human Rights could complete the appeal, finding that "due process of law" required consideration of the decisions of international tribunals.[70] In ever-parsimonious fashion, the Privy Council held that the Bahamas did not have to wait until international appeals were concluded, as the Constitution of the Bahamas did not possess a "due process of law" clause.[71] A year later, however, in *Lewis v. Attorney General of Jamaica*, the Council found that carrying out a death sentence without regard for the decisions of international tribunals was always unconstitutional.[72] The Lords noted that due process of law was a fundamental common law principle.

In a subsequent case, the Lords excluded *pre-trial* delay from the calculus as to whether the undue delay before execution constituted cruel or inhuman treatment.[73] However, the Council quashed death sentences when defendants were subjected to multiple trials such that delays of several years would accrue, on the basis that such repeated prosecutions were abuses of the criminal process.[74] In another case, *Reckley v. Minister of Public Safety*, the Council found that a violation of the right to seek commutation or pardon was justiciable, but the actual exercise of executive discretion was not reviewable in court, because by "its very nature the...discretion, if exercised in favor of the condemned man, will involve a departure from the law."[75] *Lewis* reversed *Reckley* by finding that a prisoner had the right to make representations to a mercy committee, to see all the material that the committee considered, and even to have an oral hearing.[76] The mercy committee must give reasons for departing from the recommendation of an international human rights body if it did so. The Council has been more cautious in addressing prison conditions, perhaps concerned about

---

69   Thomas v. Baptiste, [2000] 2 A.C. 1, 21–4 (P.C. 1999) (appeal taken from Trin. & Tobago).

70   The Privy Council limited the reasoning of *Pratt* in *Thomas* on the theory that the violation of cruel and unusual treatment was in the execution of a death sentence following prolonged delay and not inherently in the delay itself.

71   Fisher v. Minister of Public Safety, [2000] A.C. 434 (P.C.) (appeal taken from Bahamas); Higgs v. Minister of Public Safety, [2000] 2 W.L.R. 1368 (P.C.) (appeal taken from Bahamas).

72   Lewis v. A.G. Jam., [2001] 2 A.C. 50, 85 (P.C. 2000). *Lewis* reversed *de Freitas v. Benny* in stating that the prerogative of mercy was entirely at the discretion of the executive and prisoners had no right of access to the material on which the clemency committee relied. Dennis Morrison, *The Judicial Committee of the Privy Council and the Death Penalty in the Commonwealth Caribbean: Studies in Judicial Activism*, 30 NOVA L. REV. 403, 418 (2005).

73   Fisher v. Minister of Public Safety, [1998] A.C. 673 (P.C.) (appeal taken from Bahamas). *Fisher* closed the question left open in *Henfield* as to whether time spent on death row prior to trial "counted" for the purposes of reaching the requisite time limit. *See* Henfield v. A.G. Bahamas, [1997] A.C. 413, 426–7 (P.C.). *Fisher* was a 3 to 2 majority decision and triggered a strong dissent.

74   Charles v. State, [2000] 1 W.L.R. 384 (P.C.) (appeal taken from Trin. & Tobago); Flowers v. Queen, [2000] 1 W.L.R. 2396 (P.C.) (appeal taken from Jam.).

75   Reckley v. Minister for Public Safety, (1996) 47 W.I.R. 9, 19 (P.C.) (appeal taken from Bahamas). One consequence of *Reckley* may have been that the executive will laxly exercise the discretion because he or she knows that their decisions are not reviewable. Christopher Gelber, *Reckley (No 2) and the Prerogative of Mercy: Act of Grace or Constitutional Safeguard?*, 60 MOD. L. REV. 572, 576, 581 (1997).

76   Lewis v. A.G. Jam., [2000] 3 W.L.R. 1785, 1805–6 (P.C.).

the significant costs for Caribbean governments.⁷⁷ The interventionism of the Privy Council, sometimes erratic, narrowed the scope and increased the costs of capital punishment. In February 2001, immediately before a wave of challenges to the mandatory death penalty, the restless governments of eleven Caribbean nations finalized an agreement to replace Privy Council jurisdiction with a new Caribbean Court of Justice.⁷⁸

The Invalidation of the Mandatory Death Penalty in the Caribbean by International Tribunals

The strategy of using international human rights tribunals to build persuasive jurisprudence later relied on by national courts was successful in instilling the death row phenomenon in the domestic constitutional jurisprudence of the Commonwealth Caribbean. In *Pratt and Morgan*, the Privy Council extensively relied on the prior decisions of the U.N. Human Rights Committee in determining that extensive delay on death row constituted cruel, inhuman, and degrading punishment.⁷⁹ Advocates built up a substantial body of persuasive jurisprudence, a kind of transnational "common law," that domestic courts cited and relied on. To this end, challenges to the U.N. Human Rights Committee and to the Inter-American Commission and Court on Human Rights helped define the treaty obligations of Commonwealth Caribbean nations who had ratified the First Optional Protocol to the International Covenant on Civil and Political Rights (ICCPR) or the American Convention on Human Rights. In turn, domestic courts, including the Privy Council, attempted to interpret constitutional obligations in accordance with international treaty commitments. This is the strategy by which the mandatory death penalty receded so rapidly in the region, as no international human rights tribunal has ever found a mandatory death penalty regime compatible with human rights norms.⁸⁰

The United Nations Human Rights Committee

Composed of independent experts who hear individual complaints, the U.N. Human Rights Committee has jurisdiction over and monitors the records of countries that have ratified the First Optional Protocol to the ICCPR.⁸¹ According to the ICCPR:

---

77 James Gray, *Evolving Constitutional Protection in the Caribbean Commonwealth and the Judicial Committee of the Privy Council*, 4 OXFORD U. COMMW. L.J. 77, 100–101 (2004).

78 The Caribbean Court of Justice has two types of jurisdiction, original jurisdiction for disputes arising under the Treaty of Chaguaramas, which established the Caribbean Community, and appellate jurisdiction as the court of last resort for those countries that abolished appeals to the Privy Council. Nearly all members of the Commonwealth Caribbean recognize the first type of jurisdiction; only Barbados, Belize, and Guyana recognize the second.

79 Pratt & Morgan v. A.G. Jam, (1993) 43 W.I.R. 340, 349–51, 353 (P.C.).

80 Alex Bailin & Julian Knowles, *Hanged by a Comma?*, 9 JUD. REV. 250, 252 (2004).

81 Office of the United Nations High Commissioner for Human Rights, Introduction to the Human Rights Committee, http://www.unhchr.ch/html/menu2/6/a/introhrc.htm (last visited: Feb. 19, 2009). Jurisdiction over the English-speaking Caribbean is light. Barbados and Saint Vincent and the Grenadines have ratified the Optional Protocol recognizing the jurisdiction of the UNHRC. Guyana, Jamaica, and Trinidad and Tobago have either denounced their ratification or issued a reservation preventing the Committee from hearing death penalty challenges. *See*, Amnesty International, *Unacceptably Limiting Human Rights Protection* (March 1999), http://www.amnesty.org/es/library/

6(2): In countries which have not abolished the death penalty, sentence of death may be imposed only for the most serious crimes in accordance with the law in force at the time of the commission of the crime and not contrary to the provisions of the present Covenant and to the Convention on the Prevention and Punishment of the Crime of Genocide. This penalty can only be carried out pursuant to a final judgement rendered by a competent court.

7: No one shall be subjected to torture or to cruel, inhuman or degrading treatment or punishment.

The Committee has heard challenges to the mandatory death penalty several times.[82] In *Thompson v. Saint Vincent and the Grenadines*, the Committee found the mandatory death sentence to violate the right to life since the penalty is not individually tailored to fit the crime.[83] Although the state argued that the death sentence was only mandatory for murder, a crime that necessarily involved the taking of human life, the Committee disagreed that the sentence was proportionate. The sharply split Committee also found that the right to seek commutation or pardon under the Covenant did not cure the basic defect of a mandatory death penalty: the failure to permit consideration of individual circumstances. Five Committee members dissented, believing that the Covenant permitted the death penalty to be carried out so long as it was not cruel, inhuman, or degrading (Article 7), and reserved solely for the most serious crimes (Article 6.2). The Covenant, they wrote, did not require that courts have sentencing discretion.[84]

The Committee reached a unanimous result, however, in *Kennedy v. Trinidad and Tobago*, which involved the imposition of the mandatory death penalty for felony murder in which the victim died from a head trauma during a robbery and not from the fired gun.[85] Executing a death sentence in this case was an arbitrary deprivation of life in violation of Article 6.1, because the defendant was not able to present mitigating evidence to the domestic court that he lacked actual intent to kill.[86] The dissenters in *Thompson* distinguished that case on the grounds that *Kennedy* did not involve an intentional murder, and thus was not a "most serious crime" as required by Article 6.2.[87] The Committee found Trinidad and Tobago's denunciation of the First Optional Protocol to the Covenant, ousting the Committee's jurisdiction, inapplicable in *Kennedy* as the case was submitted for consideration before the denunciation. The Committee also rejected Trinidad's reservation on the Optional Protocol that attempted to remove only death row prisoners from the Committee's jurisdiction.[88]

In two later cases, the U.N. Human Rights Committee returned to the topic of the mandatory death penalty. In the case of *Carpo v. Philippines*, the Committee found that

---

asset/AMR05/001/1999/es/dom-AMR050011999en.pdf (condemning the decision to withdraw from the Protocol).

82 The Committee found the mandatory death sentence for aggravated robbery violated Art. 6.2 of the Covenant in *Lubuto v. Zambia*, although this was not a direct challenge to the mandatory nature of the death sentence. Lubuto v. Zambia, U.N. Doc. CCPR/C/55/D/390/1990/Rev. 1 (1995), ¶ 7.2.

83 Thompson v. St. Vincent, Comm. No. 806/1998, U.N. Doc. CCPR/C/70/D/806/1998 (2000) at ¶ 8.2. *See also*, International Covenant on Civil and Political Rights (ICCPR), *opened for signature* December 19, 1966, 999 U.N.T.S. 85 (entered into force March 23, 1976), art. 6(1).

84 *Thompson, supra* note 83 at ¶ 9 (dissenting).

85 Kennedy v. Trinidad & Tobago, Comm. No. 845/1998, U.N. Doc. CCPR/C/67/D/845/1999 ¶ 7.3 (2002) (U.N.H.R.C.).

86 *Id.* ¶ 7.3.

87 *See id.* (Kretzmer, Mr., concurring).

88 Knowles, *supra* note 14 at 298–9.

the reinstatement of the mandatory death penalty in the Philippines was a violation of the Covenant.[89] Dissenters in *Carpo* noted that the death sentence was only mandatory for willful murder "with treachery," which required an aggravating circumstance and was thus a "most serious crime." Ultimately the Committee required judicial sentencing discretion in capital cases and not merely limiting the scope of mandatory capital crimes. In *Chan v. Guyana*, the Committee found the imposition of a mandatory death sentence for felony murder and accomplice liability to be a violation of Article 6.1 of the Covenant, a unanimous decision on that point.[90] However, in 2010, Guyana's legislature unanimously abolished the mandatory death penalty for ordinary murder, retaining it only for persons convicted of murdering law enforcement officials, prison officers, or members of the judiciary.[91]

Inter-American Commission on Human Rights

Mandatory death penalty challenges also appeared before the Inter-American Commission on Human Rights, established in 1959 to apply the 1948 American Declaration on the Rights and Duties of Man and the 1969 American Convention on Human Rights. The Convention established the Inter-American Court of Human Rights, but only Trinidad and Tobago (from 1991 to 1998) and Barbados (since 2000) have ever accepted the Court's jurisdiction. The Court's jurisprudence is heavily tilted toward the Spanish-speaking Western Hemisphere and Brazil, where the death penalty is almost universally abolished. As a result, while challenges have arisen before the Court and the Commission, the Commission's jurisprudence is considerably more extensive.

According to the American Convention on Human Rights at Article 4,

> (1) Every person has the right to have his life respected. This right shall be protected by law and, in general, from the moment of conception. No one shall be arbitrarily deprived of his life.

> (2) In countries that have not abolished the death penalty, it may be imposed only for the most serious crimes and pursuant to a final judgment rendered by a competent court and in accordance with a law establishing such punishment, enacted prior to the commission of the crime. The application of such punishment shall not be extended to crimes to which it does not presently apply.[92]

---

89   Carpo v. Philippines, Comm. No. 1077/2002, UN Doc. CCPR/C/77/D/1077/2002 (2002).

90   Chan v. Guyana, Comm. No. 913/2000, UN Doc. CCPR/C/85/D/913/2000 ¶ 6.5 (2006). *See* Arif Bulkan, *Democracy in Disguise: Assessing the Reforms to the Fundamental Rights Provisions in Guyana*, 32 GA. J. INT'L & COMP. L. 613, 620–21 (2004) (noting new capital offenses related to terrorism and drug use). Guyana ousted Privy Council jurisdiction in 1970 and is not a member of the Inter-American Human Rights System. Margaret A. Burnham, *Indigenous Constitutionalism and the Death Penalty: The Case of the Commonwealth Caribbean*, 3 INT'L J. CON. L. 582, 585 (2005) ("Burnham, *Indigenous*").

91   Criminal Law Offences (Amendment) Act, 2010, No. 21 (Guyana). *See also*, *Guyana Keeps Death Penalty for Killers of Police, Soldiers, and Judges*, JAM. OBSERVER, Oct. 16, 2010, http://www.jamaicaobserver.com/Guyana-keeps-death-penalty-for-killers-of-police-soldiers-and-judges_8061054; *Unanimous Support for Criminal Law Offences (Amendment) Bill in the National Assembly*, GUYANA CHRONICLE ONLINE, Oct. 15, 2010 (available at www.guyanachronicle.com).

92   American Convention on Human Rights, November 22, 1969, 1144 U.N.T.S. 143, O.A.S.T.S. No. 36, art. 4 (entered into force July 18, 1978).

In addition, the Convention prohibits the reinstatement of the death penalty after abolition and the imposition of capital punishment for political crimes or where the offender is under age 18, over age 70, or a pregnant woman. Finally, the Convention requires that a condemned prisoner have the right to apply for amnesty or pardon, and forbids execution while appeals are still pending.[93] For its part, the American Declaration on the Rights and Duties of Man states at Article 1: "Every human being has the right to life, liberty, and the security of his person."[94]

The Inter-American Commission on Human Rights found the mandatory death penalty to violate the Declaration in *Edwards v. Bahamas*, as the Bahamas had not ratified the Convention.[95] In interpreting the drafting history of Article 1 of the Declaration, the Commission determined that the right to life provision intended to restrict capital punishment to only the gravest crimes, and the mandatory death sentence constituted an arbitrary deprivation of life since it did not consider individualized circumstances.[96] According to the Commission, "the crime of murder can be perpetrated in the context of a wide variety of mitigating and aggravating circumstances, with varying degrees of gravity and culpability," and mandatory sentencing by its very nature precluded consideration as to whether a death sentence was appropriate. The due process requirements of the Declaration encompassed judicial review of a criminal sentence, and while a process for seeking executive clemency was necessary, it did not sufficiently individualize sentences.[97]

The Commission extended this holding to Grenada and Jamaica under the Convention. In *Baptiste v. Grenada*, the Court found the mandatory death sentence violated the right to life (Article 4), the right to humane treatment (Article 5), and the right to a fair trial (Article 8).[98] In addition, the absence of effective appellate review of sentence violated the right to due process. In a subsequent case *Knights v. Grenada*, the Commission wrote that "the defendant is entitled to present submissions and evidence in respect of all potentially mitigating circumstances relating to himself and his or her offense, and the court imposing sentence is afforded discretion to consider these factors in determining whether the death penalty is a permissible or appropriate punishment."[99] A year later in *Jacob v. Grenada*, the Commission again determined that the death sentence was imposed "without principled distinction or rationalization" as to whether it was appropriate, and precluded effective appellate review.[100] In *Lallion v. Grenada*, the Commission confirmed these holdings and also found that the conditions of the defendant's detention and the delay in informing him of the charges violated the Covenant.[101]

---

93   *Id.* at arts. 4.3–4.6.
94   American Declaration of the Rights and Duties of Man, adopted in 1948, O.A.S. Res. XXX, O.A.S. Off. Rec. OEA/Ser.L/V/I.4 Rev. (1965).
95   Edwards v. Bahamas, Case 12.067, Inter-Am. Comm'n H.R., Report No. 48/01, OEA/Ser.L/V/II.111, doc. 20 (2000).
96   *Id.* ¶¶ 128, 137–8.
97   *Id.* ¶¶ 149, 165–6.
98   Baptiste v. Grenada, Case 11.743, Inter-Am. Comm'n H.R., Report No. 38/00, OEA/Ser.L/V/II.106 doc. 3 (1999).
99   Knights v. Grenada, Case 12.028, Inter-Am Comm'n H.R., Report No. 47/01, OEA/Ser.L/V/II.111 doc. 20 (2000).
100 Jacob v. Grenada, Case 12.158, Inter-Am. Comm'n H.R., Report No. 56/02, OEA/Ser.L/V/II.117 doc. 1 (2002).
101 Lallion v. Grenada, Case 11.765, Inter-Am. Comm'n H.R., Report No. 55/02, OEA/Ser.L/V/II.117 doc. 5 (2002).

Just as it had ruled in the cases from the Bahamas and Grenada, the Commission found that Jamaica's mandatory death penalty violated the Convention in *McKenzie v. Jamaica*, in which it also addressed conditions and delay on death row as well as insufficient legal representation.[102] The Commission also found a violation of the rights to life and human dignity. In *Lamey v. Jamaica*, decided the following year, the Commission also faulted Jamaica for "failing to guarantee [petitioners] an effective right to apply for amnesty, pardon or commutation of sentence," or "to make representations, in person or by counsel, to the Jamaican Privy Council," and to receive a decision in a reasonable time.[103] In several subsequent cases, the Commission found the conditions of detention to constitute cruel and degrading treatment.[104]

The Commission's jurisprudence is stable and consistent as a result of this line of cases. The stress on human dignity was "particularly strong in holding together the overall approach of the Commission," finding that the mandatory death penalty violated human dignity by failing to consider individualized circumstances.[105] The Commission also struck down the mandatory death sentence in Guatemala, a civil law country. In *Raxcacó-Reyes v. Guatemala*, the Commission ruled that "[m]andatory capital punishment makes no rational distinctions between persons who may have committed the same crime—in this case, kidnapping—under very diverse personal circumstances and, consequently, takes the perpetrator's life without recognizing that, as a unique individual, he merits individual consideration."[106] Guatemala is de facto abolitionist, and its constitutional court has suspended executions in the absence of a proper procedure for seeking clemency; the president has twice vetoed legislation authorizing such a procedure and thereby reinstating the death sentence.[107]

In August 2012, the Inter-American Commission on Human Rights called for a moratorium on executions for all members of the Organization of American States, an announcement made in conjunction with publication of its new report on the death penalty in the Inter-American Human Rights System.[108] The Commission noted the "worrisome challenges [that] persist regarding the lack of compliance" with the Convention by member

---

102 McKenzie v. Jam., Case 12.023, Inter-Am. Comm'n H.R., Report No. 41/00, OEA/Ser.L/V/II.106 doc. 3 (2000).

103 Lamey v. Jam., Case 11.826, Inter-Am. Comm'n H.R., Report No. 49/01, OEA/Ser.L/V/II.111 doc. 20 (2000).

104 Thomas v. Jam., Case 12.183, Inter-Am. Comm'n H.R., Report No. 127/01, OEA/Ser./L/V/II.114, doc. 5 (2001); Aitken v. Jam., Case 12.275, Inter-Am. Comm'n H.R., Report No. 58/02, doc. 5 (2002); Sewell v. Jam., Case No. 12.347, Inter-Am. Comm'n H.R., Report No. 76/02, Doc. 5 rev. 1 at 763 ¶ 97–9, 118 (2002).

105 Paolo G. Carozza, *'My Friend Is a Stranger': The Death Penalty and the Global Ius Commune of Human Rights*, 81 TEX. L. REV. 1031, 1071 (2002), *citing Baptiste, supra* note 98 ¶ 88–90; *McKenzie, supra* note 102 ¶ 201–3; *Lamey, supra* note 103 ¶ 133–5; and *Edwards, supra* note 95 at ¶ 145–7.

106 Raxcacó-Reyes v. Guatemala, Case 12.402, Inter-Am. Comm'n H.R., Report No. 49/03 ¶¶ 45–58, 73 (2004).

107 Inter-American Comm'n on Hum. Rts., *The Death Penalty in the Inter-American Human Rights System: From Restrictions to Abolition*, OEA/Ser. L/V.II, Doc. 68, Dec. 31, 2011.

108 Press Release, *IACHR Calls on a Moratorium in the Application of the Death Penalty*, Organization of American States, August 3, 2012, http://www.oas.org/en/iachr/media_center/PReleases/2012/100.asp.

states, including several executions that were carried out in violation of the Commission's own provisional measures.[109]

Inter-American Court of Human Rights

In the Commonwealth Caribbean, the Inter-American Court of Human Rights has only had jurisdiction over Barbados and Trinidad and Tobago. In three mandatory death penalty challenges, the Court followed the lead of the Commission by striking down the mandatory death penalty as incompatible with the rights enshrined in inter-American human rights instruments. In 2002, the Court found Trinidad and Tobago's mandatory death penalty to conflict with its obligations under the American Convention in *Hilaire, Constantine, and Benjamin v. Trinidad and Tobago*.[110] *Hilaire* was an omnibus challenge brought by thirty-two prisoners on death row, challenging the mandatory nature of the death penalty; the process for granting amnesty, pardon, or commutation; delay in criminal proceedings; deficiencies in conditions of detention; due process violations; and lack of access to legal aid. Trinidad and Tobago denounced its ratification of the American Convention as a result of the pending challenge, but the case was referred to the Court by the Commission before this time limit expired and jurisdiction could not be ousted. Trinidad and Tobago refused to comply with the Court's preliminary orders and executed one petitioner in violation of the Court's stay.[111]

In *Hilaire*, the Court found that because the mandatory death sentence can be imposed on crimes without regard to circumstances, the penalty was not restricted to the "most serious crimes" in violation of Article 4.2.[112] That the death penalty was constitutional in Trinidad and Tobago was no defense to violating treaty obligations. The mandatory death penalty statute "automatically and generically mandates the application of the death penalty for murder and disregards the fact that murder may have varying degrees of seriousness." As a consequence, the statute compelled the "indiscriminate imposition of the same punishment for conduct that can be vastly different."[113] The result was arbitrary deprivation of life in violation of Article 4(1) of the Convention. The Court unanimously found that the State violated the rights to life and humane treatment and the right to apply for commutation or pardon, and that it was obligated to retry all of the petitioners.

In 2007, the Court decided *Boyce v. Barbados*, again finding that the mandatory application of the death penalty constituted an arbitrary deprivation of life.[114] That such a penalty was immunized from challenge based on the general savings clause of the Constitution of Barbados denied defendants "the right to seek judicial protection against violations of their right to life." As the Court noted, "Barbados is bound to comply with its obligations under the American Convention in good faith, and it may not invoke the provisions of its internal law as justification for its failure to comply with its treaty obligations."[115] The mandatory capital punishment statute in Barbados also failed to

---

109 Inter-American Commission on Human Rights, *The Death Penalty in the Inter-American Human Rights System: From Restrictions to Abolition*, OEA/Ser. L/V.II, Doc. 68, December 31, 2011.
110 Hilaire, Constantine & Benjamin v. Trin. & Tobago, Inter-Am. Ct. H.R. (ser. C) No. 94 (June 21, 2002).
111 *Id.* ¶¶ 21–33.
112 *Id.* ¶ 106.
113 *Id.* ¶ 103.
114 Boyce v. Barb., Inter-Am. Ct. H.R. (ser. C) No. 169 (Nov. 20, 2007).
115 *Id.* at 21, ¶ 77.

consider the level of participation of the accused in the commission of a crime; because an accomplice was punished the same as a principal, a person could be sentenced to death for having only a small role in the commission of a crime.[116]

In early 2009, the Court issued a ruling in *Cadogan v. Barbados*, confirming that a sentence that does not consider the individual circumstances of a crime, including degree of culpability and participation by an offender, violated the right to life under the American Convention and was not saved by a right to seek executive mercy.[117] While the Court avoided making a factual finding as to the petitioner's mental illness, the judges found that the State violated his right to a fair trial because he had never had a psychiatric evaluation and was unable to raise a defense of diminished responsibility. Finally, as in *Boyce*, the Court found that the general savings clause of the Constitution of Barbados immunizing pre-existing laws from constitutional challenge violated Article 2 of the Convention, which required state parties to provide for judicial redress of human rights violations. The State respondent conceded that its constitution would need to be amended to comply with the Convention.[118]

The Privy Council and Partial Savings Clauses: Antigua and Barbuda, Belize, Dominica, Grenada, Saint Kitts and Nevis, Saint Lucia, and Saint Vincent and the Grenadines

The jurisprudence of the non-binding human rights tribunals assisted anti-death penalty advocates in challenging the mandatory death sentence before binding courts of appeal by creating a reservoir of precedents and reasoning. In April 2001, the Eastern Caribbean Court of Appeal invalidated the mandatory death sentences of Saint Lucia and Saint Vincent and the Grenadines in the consolidated cases of *Spence and Hughes v. Queen*.[119] The Court interpreted the identical savings clauses of Saint Lucia and Saint Vincent restrictively, ruling that while the death penalty itself was insulated from challenge, the mandatory nature of the death penalty was not a "punishment," but only a mode of application.[120] In addition, the Court attempted to read the statutes in accordance with Saint Vincent's and Saint Lucia's international treaty obligations. The Court found the mandatory death penalty to qualify as inhumane treatment in violation of Article 5 of the Constitution, holding that a court "must have the discretion to take into account the individual circumstances" of an offender "if the sentencing is to be considered rational, humane and rendered in accordance with the requirements of due process," within the parameters of legislatively enacted sentencing guidelines. This was "the first time that a Caribbean court has significantly reduced the

---

116 Sergio Garcia Ramirez, *The Inter-American Court of Human Rights and the Death Penalty*, 3 MEXICAN L. REV. 99, 113 (2010).

117 Cadogan v. Barb., Inter-Am. Ct. H.R. (ser. C) No. 204 (Sept. 24, 2009).

118 *Id.* at ¶ 67.

119 *Spence and Hughes v. Queen*, Crim. App. Nos. 20 of 1998 and 14 of 1997 (Apr. 2, 2001) (E. Carib.).

120 As the Court wrote, the automatic nature of the death penalty "merely refers to the lack of judicial discretion in imposing the punishment. The sentence of death could be imposed with or without the exercise of judicial discretion. In my view therefore what is saved is the sentence of death by hanging." *Id.* ¶ 19. *See, e.g.*, ST. LUCIA CONST. sched. 2, art. 10: "Nothing contained in or done under the authority of any law shall be held to be inconsistent with or in contravention of Section 5 of the Constitution to the extent that the law in question authorises the infliction of any description of punishment that was lawful in St. Lucia immediately before 1 March 1967." *See also*, ST. VINCENT CONST. sched. 2, art. 10 (virtually identical provision).

application of the death penalty," going "further than the Privy Council has ever gone," Lehrfreund wrote at the time. "It is of great importance that it is a domestic court in the Caribbean that has taken this step."[121]

The Privy Council accepted the appeal of Saint Lucia and consolidated the case with *Reyes v. Queen* from the Court of Appeal of Belize and *Fox v. Queen* from Saint Kitts and Nevis. The Privy Council invalidated the mandatory death sentence in Belize as the unique general savings clause expired five years after independence.[122] The Council further found that executive clemency proceedings could not save a mandatory death sentence. In this, the Court reversed *Lauriano v. Belize*, a decision of the Belize Court of Appeal holding that the ability to seek commutation or pardon provided the necessary flexibility for a mandatory capital punishment regime.[123] According to the Privy Council, a non-judicial body does not have the ability to determine an appropriate sentence after criminal proceedings. The Privy Council discerned a Commonwealth, indeed global, consensus that the respect for the individual humanity of the offender required consideration of the specific circumstances of the crime.[124]

Saint Lucia, unlike Belize, had an extant partial savings clause preserving any form of criminal punishment legal at the time the constitution went into effect.[125] Like the Eastern Caribbean Court of Appeal, the Privy Council in *Queen v. Hughes* interpreted the provision narrowly, as it would with any other fundamental rights limitation, finding that a mandatory death sentence was not itself a punishment but a method of sentencing.[126] The statute of Saint Lucia provided that an offender was "liable to suffer death" rather than "shall suffer death," and therefore did not unequivocally establish a mandatory death sentence. The Privy Council rejected this argument as the death sentence was mandatory in Britain at the time and would have been in the colonies as well. Nonetheless, the Privy Council followed *Pratt* in holding that the clause immunized forms of punishment alone, and not the manner in which they were administered. In the third case, *Fox v. Queen*, the Privy Council confirmed the *Hughes* judgment under the partial savings clause of Saint Kitts and Nevis.[127] The constitutional and statutory provisions in force in Saint Kitts and Nevis were virtually identical to those in Saint Lucia.

The Privy Council extended the holdings of *Reyes* and *Hughes* to Dominica in 2005 and Grenada in 2007, invalidating the mandatory death penalty in both countries. In *Balson v. State*, the Council noted that Dominica's constitution required that the "culpability of the accused must be assessed by the particular sentencing judge in the light of his own particular circumstances."[128] In 2007, the Privy Council ruled that the mandatory death penalty in Grenada was unconstitutional in *Coard v. Attorney-General*, finding that even though the appellants' death sentences had been commuted to life imprisonment, they never

---

121 Lehrfreund, *Caribbean*, *supra* note 38 at 183.
122 Reyes v. Queen, (2002) 60 W.I.R. 42 (P.C.) (appeal taken from Belize).
123 Lauriano v. Attorney General of Belize, (1995) 3 Bz.L.R. 77.
124 *Reyes*, 60 W.I.R. at 57–8, 69.
125 St. Lucia Const. sched. 2 ¶10.
126 Queen v. Hughes, [2002] 2 A.C. 259 (P.C.). Subsequently to *Hughes*, the Court of Appeal of Saint Lucia upheld the discretionary death penalty as constitutional. Phillip v. Queen, Crim. App. No. 4 of 2003 (May 24, 2004) (St. Lucia C.A.).
127 Fox v. Queen, [2002] 2 A.C. 284. *See* St. Kitts & Nev. Const. sched. 2 ¶ 2. This provision, the Council noted, was virtually identical to that of Saint Lucia.
128 Balson v. State, [2005] 4 L.R.C. 147 (P.C.) (appeal taken from Dominica).

had an opportunity to present mitigating evidence at a sentencing hearing.[129] Consequently, the Privy Council remanded for the resentencing of the thirteen appellants, including former deputy prime minister Bernard Coard, who were implicated in the coup murder of Prime Minister Maurice Bishop in 1983. The Privy Council refused to find that principles of finality and of mootness applied, even though the appeals were exhausted long before; the sentences were unconstitutional when they were passed and had never been rectified.[130] In 2008, the High Court of Justice of Antigua and Barbuda applied a discretionary death penalty in a murder case, citing *Spence and Hughes* as authority, completing the abolition of the mandatory death penalty in the "partial savings clause" jurisdictions.[131]

Subsequent case law from Belize and Saint Lucia indicates that trial judges now engage in sentencing inquiries by weighing mitigating and aggravating factors. In *Queen v. Reyes*, the Supreme Court of Belize found that "in order to exercise the discretion whether to sentence the prisoner to death or to life imprisonment, the Court must have regard to all the circumstances attendant on the commission of the crime and to the personal circumstances and factors that might have influenced the prisoner's conduct."[132] The Court found that there was a presumption against the death penalty and in favor of life; "it is the imposition of the death penalty rather than its non-imposition for murder, that requires special justification." In the case of *Moise v. Queen*, the Court of Appeal of Saint Lucia agreed that the constitution established a presumption in favor of an unqualified right to life and the death penalty should be imposed "only in the most exceptional and extreme cases of murder."[133] The convicted person must raise mitigating factors by presenting evidence to the court unless they were otherwise discernible, but the prosecution maintained the burden of proving the absence of mitigating factors beyond a reasonable doubt.

The Privy Council and General Savings Clauses: Bahamas, Barbados, Jamaica, and Trinidad and Tobago

The question of general savings clauses proved to be more difficult, because these clauses saved all existing laws in force at the time the constitution went into effect, and not simply the manner of punishment. A Privy Council panel in *Roodal v. Trinidad and Tobago* found in a 3 to 2 decision that the death penalty statute in that country should be interpreted as discretionary in order to conform to Trinidad and Tobago's international obligations.[134] A dissent noted that the constitution had a general savings clause, thus protecting any pre-existing law from challenge on the basis of the fundamental rights provisions of the constitution.[135] Later, in 2004, the full Privy Council accepted appeals from Jamaica, Barbados, and Trinidad and Tobago in order to review this interpretation of general savings clauses. As Lehrfreund predicted, general savings clauses were a "far greater obstacle" to a constitutional attack on the mandatory nature of the death penalty.[136] Lehrfreund believed

---

129   Coard v. A.G., [2007] UKPC 7 (appeal taken from Barb.).
130   *See* FRED PHILLIPS, THE DEATH PENALTY AND HUMAN RIGHTS 87–8 (2009).
131   Queen v. Monelle, Crim. Case No. 15/2007 (Sept. 18, 2008) (Antigua & Barbuda H.C.J.).
132   Queen v. Reyes, available at http://www.internationaljusticeproject.org/pdfs/Reyes-2.pdf (Oct. 25, 2002) (Belize S.C.) (unrep.).
133   Moise v. Queen, Crim. App. No. 8 of 2003 (July 15, 2005) (St. Lucia C.A.).
134   Roodal v. State, (2003) 64 W.I.R. 270, 285–6 (P.C.) (appeal taken from Trin. & Tobago).
135   *Id.* at 297 (Millet and Rodger, Lords, dissenting).
136   Lehrfreund, *supra* note 38 at 184.

that the mandatory death penalty in these countries could still be vulnerable on a separation of powers basis—a mandatory sentence transferred sentencing discretion from a judicial officer to an executive one—because the separation of powers framework is outside the fundamental rights provisions of the constitutional text.[137]

The full Privy Council narrowly reversed *Roodal*. In the Barbados case *Boyce and Joseph v. Queen*, a 5 to 4 majority found that the mandatory death penalty law was saved under a "general" savings clause.[138] The government defended the mandatory death penalty by arguing that it provided maximum deterrence value while allowing for executive clemency and pardon, which provided the necessary flexibility and humanity in its practical application. The Lords rejected this argument, finding that the mandatory death penalty was cruel and inhuman punishment, as found in *Reyes*. In Barbados, however, the mandatory death penalty for murder was saved as it predated independence and was never substantially altered. The Council believed that the general savings clause provision "defies rational explanation," as it saved not only existing laws, but also all conceptually similar laws, or altered laws that were not changed in substance, forcing a court to perform the difficult task of parsing whether a change was simply linguistic or whether it made a fundamental change.[139] The majority conceded that the Constitution of Barbados was a living instrument, and one that should be interpreted to conform to the country's international obligations. In this case, however, there was no ambiguity. By contrast, the dissent believed that the majority interpretation "puts a narrow and over-literal construction on the words used..., gives little or no weight to the human rights guarantees which the people of Barbados intended to embed in their Constitution and puts Barbados in flagrant breach of its international obligations."[140] The dissenters believed that the Privy Council could have construed the death penalty statute as being discretionary without immunizing from challenge a manner of punishment that was already found to be cruel and degrading.

The Council reached the same conclusion in *Matthew v. State* on appeal from Trinidad and Tobago, even though the country had had more than one constitution since independence, each saving the laws that existed under the previous one.[141] The Council found that "the principle of the separation of powers is not an overriding supra-constitutional principle" that could invalidate the mandatory death penalty.[142] The four-judge dissent, quoting the line of jurisprudence from the United Nations Human Rights Committee and Inter-American Human Rights System, found that the savings clause only applied to the "invalidation" of laws and the Council could interpret laws consistently with the international human rights obligations undertaken by Trinidad and Tobago without running afoul of the clause.[143]

The Council limited the holdings of *Boyce* and *Matthew* by ruling unanimously the opposite way in *Watson v. The Queen*, an appeal from Jamaica.[144] Even though Jamaica's mandatory death penalty was more restrictive than those of Barbados and Trinidad and Tobago, the law had been changed in 1992 to make it less harsh.[145] As this was well after Jamaica's independence, the law was not enacted at the time the constitution was

---

137   *Id.* at 185.
138   Boyce & Joseph v. Queen, (2004) 64 W.I.R. 37, 49–50 (P.C.) (appeal taken from Barb.).
139   *Id.* at 51.
140   *Id.* at 63 (Bingham, Lord, *et al.*, dissenting).
141   Matthew v. State, (2004) 64 W.I.R. 412 (P.C.) (appeal taken from Trin. & Tobago).
142   *Id.* at 423.
143   *Id.* at 436, 441 (Bingham, Lord, *et al.*, dissenting).
144   Watson v. Queen, (2004) 64 W.I.R. 241, 262 (P.C.) (appeal taken from Jam.).
145   *Id.* at 268–9 (Bingham, Lord, *et al.*, concurring).

implemented, and thus not saved. The dissenters in *Matthew* and *Boyce* wrote separately in *Watson* to lament that the Privy Council was striking down the least arbitrary of the three mandatory death penalty laws at issue in the appeals, finding a "gross anomaly" in the holdings of *Boyce*, *Matthew*, and *Watson*: "Jamaica would have succeeded in maintaining an objectionable nineteenth century law if it had not attempted to mitigate its harshness."[146] The concurrence eloquently restated the fundamental objection that "prevailing levels of crime and violence, however great the anxiety and alarm they understandably cause, cannot affect the underlying legal principle at stake, which is that no one, whatever his crime, should be condemned to death without an opportunity to try and persuade the sentencing judge that he does not deserve to die."

Felony murder, in which a defendant did not possess actual intent to kill, presented a different problem. The 3 to 2 decision of the Privy Council in *Khan v. State* invalidated Trinidad and Tobago's mandatory death sentence for felony murder. Although felony murder existed prior to independence, the 1979 abolition of the distinction between misdemeanors and felonies was determined to have stricken the offense of felony murder in the 1996 Privy Council decision *Moses v. State*.[147] In response to that decision, Trinidad and Tobago reinstated the offense of felony murder; however, the Privy Council determined that this was a substantive change to the existing criminal law and not saved by the general savings clause. Likewise in *Miguel v. State*, the Council ruled that the felony murder statute (properly called "violent arrestable offence murder" because it included felonies beyond those under the common law) was not "an existing law" under Trinidad and Tobago's general savings clause, and was not immune from direct constitutional challenge.[148] The 1997 statute did not repeal and re-enact an earlier statute; it "simply enacted a new provision which was no doubt intended to reproduce something very similar to the common law rule," but which swept more broadly and was therefore substantively different.[149]

The Privy Council limited the holding in *Khan* by upholding the common law felony murder statute of Barbados in *Griffith v. Queen*.[150] The felony murder statute dated to 1868 and was undoubtedly a pre-existing law at the time the Constitution of Barbados entered into force. Although Barbados abolished felony murder in 1994, this was not retroactive to the defendant's crime and conviction. Because the mandatory death penalty for murder was constitutional as a pre-existing law as of the date of conviction in 1992, the definition of "murder" could change subsequently without invalidating the death sentences previously imposed. As the Lords noted, "*Khan* concerned a new statutory rule which had the effect of bringing within the scope of the death penalty a class of persons who had previously not been exposed to it. Here, by contrast, the Board is dealing with the felony murder rule which always formed part of the common law of Barbados until it was abolished in 1994."[151]

---

146 *Id.* at 268–9. The majority's response was literal: "In their Lordships' opinion the language which these provisions have used is plain and unambiguous. In *Matthew* and *Boyce and Joseph* the laws in question are existing laws. In the present case the law in question is not." *Id.* at 262–3.

147 Moses v. State, (1996) 49 W.I.R. 455, 468 (P.C.) (appeal taken from Trin. & Tobago). Khan v. State, [2003] UKPC 79 (appeal taken from Trin. & Tobago).

148 Miguel v. State, [2011] UKPC 14 (P.C.) (appeal taken from Trin. & Tobago).

149 *Id.* at ¶ 62.

150 Griffith v. Queen, (2004) 65 W.I.R. 50 (P.C.) (appeal taken from Barb.). *See* Graeme Broadbent, *Trinidad and Tobago: Murder and the Constitutionality of Constructive Malice and Mandatory Death Sentence*, 68 J. Crim. L. 301, 303–5 (2004) (comment); Graeme Broadbent, *Barbados: Felony Murder Rule; Mandatory Sentences*, 69 J. Crim. L. 322, 322 (2005) (comment).

151 *Griffith*, 65 W.I.R. at 58.

These are fine distinctions, but perhaps theoretically consistent. *Watson* and *Khan* involved statutes that were repealed and replaced in different forms subsequent to independence; *Griffith* involved a statute that had pre-existed the constitution unmodified until its abolition.

As it did with Jamaica, the Privy Council closely parsed Bahamian law. In *Pinder v. Queen*, the Lords saved the Bahamas' use of flogging as a method of corporal punishment, relying on the *partial* savings clause to uphold the punishment.[152] This was true even though the Bahamas abolished corporal punishment in 1984 and reinstated it under public pressure in 1991 as a result of increased crime rates. The Lords noted, "flogging is an inhuman and degrading punishment and, unless protected from constitutional challenge under some other provision of the Constitution, is rendered unconstitutional by article 17(1)," the prohibition on cruel and inhuman punishment.[153] They reasoned that the punishment could not be saved under the *general* savings clause because it was not an existing law as of 1973 when the Constitution entered into force. Unlike the mandatory death penalty, at issue in the corporal punishment challenge was the *form* of punishment itself, and not the manner in which it was administered. As a result, the partial savings clause "saved" flogging. As Burnham writes, this decision was a precursor for what was to follow because it was an early indication that the Privy Council considered itself trapped by the savings clause. "Taken to its logical extreme, *Pinder* stands for the proposition that as long as the special punishment savings clause exists, future legislatures can always return to the barbarism of a penalty sanctioned at the time of the adoption of the constitution."[154]

Pinder was not enough to save the mandatory death penalty in the Bahamas, even though the constitution had a general savings clause. Widely citing Commonwealth and American case law on the mandatory death penalty, the Privy Council found that the mandatory death penalty in the Bahamas was unconstitutional in *Bowe v. Attorney General*.[155] According to the Council, the Bahamas' 1973 constitution contained a general savings clause immunizing laws from challenge, but the Bahamas' 1963 Order-in-Council and its 1969 Constitution did not contain such clauses. Because the mandatory nature of the death penalty for murder predated all of these documents, it became unconstitutional in 1963 when the Bahamas first passed a constitutional prohibition on cruel, inhuman, and degrading punishment, and consequently was no longer "existing law" in 1973 when the new constitution entered into force. "The Crown cogently argues that it is unreal to hold that the effect of the law was otherwise than was understood at the time," the Lords acknowledged. "It is, however, clear that it took some time for the legal effect of entrenched human rights guarantees to be appreciated, not because the meaning of the rights changed but because the jurisprudence on human rights and constitutional adjudication was unfamiliar and, by some courts, resisted."[156] By reading 40-year-old constitutional provisions in accordance with the modern understanding, post-*Reyes*, of cruel, inhuman, and degrading punishment, the Privy Council held the Bahamas' constitutional document to be a living instrument, one not to be construed in narrow, originalist fashion.

---

152 Pinder v. Queen, (2002) 61 W.I.R. 13 (P.C.) (appeal taken from Bahamas).
153 *Id.* at 17.
154 Margaret A. Burnham, *Saving Constitutional Rights from Judicial Scrutiny: The Savings Clause in the Law of the Commonwealth Caribbean*, 36 U. MIAMI INTER-AM. L. REV. 249, 261–2 (2005).
155 Bowe v. Queen, (2006) 68 W.I.R. 10 (P.C.) (appeal taken from Bahamas).
156 *Id.* at 35.

The Caribbean Court of Justice and Challenges from Barbados

The Privy Council's early round of decisions created enormous resistance. Barbados attempted to amend its constitution, though it had not executed a prisoner in twenty years.[157] The decisions indirectly led to the abolition of Privy Council appeals in Barbados and Belize, which opted for the jurisdiction of the Caribbean Court of Justice (the Jamaican Parliament attempted to do the same, though the Privy Council invalidated its attempt as unconstitutional).[158] Critics claimed that the Caribbean Court would become a "hanging court," a disguised attempt to maneuver around the Privy Council's decisions.[159] Advocates of the tribunal's jurisdiction, however, argued that the Privy Council's jurisprudence was still strongly persuasive before the new tribunal.[160] The Court also came in for criticism for its poor legal aid system for indigent defendants, paying appointed attorneys low levels of remuneration, and for its failure to permit English-barred attorneys from representing Caribbean clients.[161]

The persistent case of *Attorney General v. Joseph and Boyce* reached the Caribbean Court in 2006 after the Privy Council narrowly upheld the mandatory death sentences, the Inter-American Court of Human Rights invalidated them, and the Barbados Court of Appeal commuted them to life imprisonment.[162] The Court did not take the bait, dismissing the Government's appeal of the commutation of sentences, and holding that the Privy Council's decision in *Pratt* would prevent the prisoners' execution since five years had elapsed since their convictions.[163] The Caribbean Court of Justice ruled that the decision by authorities in Barbados to deny clemency to the petitioners and move forward with their pending executions even after they petitioned the Court violated their right to the protection of law. In addition, the Court found that mercy petitions were reviewable and that the condemned men had legitimate expectations that they would not be executed while their cases were on appeal to the Inter-American Court of Human Rights, in light of the ratification of the American Convention by Barbados.[164] At the same time, the Court showed independence

---

157 Harrington, *supra* note 42 at 138 (noting similar attempts in Belize, Trinidad and Tobago, and Jamaica). The Parliament of Barbados considered a constitutional amendment that would have amended Article 15 (the prohibition on cruel, inhuman, and degrading punishment) to include provisions specifically saving from constitutional challenge the mandatory nature of the death sentence, delay, and prison conditions then in force. Constitution (Amendment) Act, 2002, No. 14 (Barb.). The Amendment did not pass. Trinidad and Tobago entertained a similar proposal. Knowles, *supra* note 14 at 306–7.

158 *See* Burnham, *Indigenous*, *supra* note 90 at 584–5. The CCJ was launched in April 2005, though the Bahamas, with its mature banking and financial sector, is more reluctant to join. *Id.* at 584–5, 588 n. 24.

159 See Leonard Birdsong, *The Formation of the Caribbean Court of Justice: The Sunset of British Colonial Rule in the English Speaking Caribbean*, 36 U. MIAMI INTER-AM. L. REV. 197, 203–4 (2005).

160 Kenny Anthony, *The Caribbean Court of Justice: Will It Be a Hanging Court?*, Address at Norman Manly Law School (June 28, 2003), http://www.stlucia.gov.lc/primeminister/former_prime_ministers/kenny_d_anthony/statements/2003/the_caribbean_court_of_justice_will_it_be_a_hanging_court_june_28_2003.htm. (Anthony is the former prime minister of St. Lucia).

161 Knowles, *supra* note 14 at 306–7.

162 Birdsong, *supra* note 159 at 203–4. *See also*, Jane Cross, *A Life and Death Compromise: The Mandatory Death Penalty in the Caribbean Court of Justice*, Powerpoint presentation before the Northeast People of Color Legal Scholarship Conference (September 2008), http://www.bu.edu/law/nepoc/documents/abstracts/JaneCrossMandatory.ppt.

163 A.G. v. Joseph, [2006] CCJ 1 (A.J.) (appeal taken from Barb.).

164 PHILLIPS, *supra* note 130 at 45.

by distinguishing its reasoning from earlier Privy Council precedent. The Court highlighted the tension in the Privy Council's prior rulings that a five-year delay in carrying out a death sentence rendered an execution unlawful, while requiring state officials to wait for a convicted person to exhaust their appeals to human rights treaty bodies regardless of the length of time that it took. The Court also disagreed with the Privy Council's suggestion that human rights treaty obligations are binding on countries such as Barbados that have not incorporated those treaty provisions into domestic law.[165]

In 2009, the Caribbean Court of Justice upheld the conviction of Clyde Anderson Grazette in Barbados, but invited submissions as to the constitutionality of the mandatory nature of his death sentence.[166] The case remains pending as Barbados committed to abolishing the mandatory death penalty in accordance with the decisions of the Inter-American Court of Human Rights, though a draft bill has not yet been introduced. In the future, counsel for Grazette may re-engage the Caribbean Court of Justice to place additional pressure on Barbados to comply.

The mandatory death penalty jurisprudence of the Caribbean Court of Justice has, thus far, shown both the Court's independence from the Privy Council and its compliance with international human rights norms. As Lord Gifford wrote, the Caribbean Court of Justice "will be less costly, more accessible, and above all more credible as a final court of appeal" than the expensive and distant tribunal in London. "But no one should imagine that the CCJ will reverse the decisions of the Privy Council. Those decisions were based on a consensus of authority from courts around the world, and the CCJ has already shown that it respects that consensus."[167] Although the global "consensus" on the mandatory death penalty is still emerging, the sensitivity the Court has shown to international precedent suggests that Lord Gifford's prediction is correct.

Later Incremental Challenges to the Death Penalty in the Caribbean

As the line of mandatory death penalty cases became settled, death row appeals began appearing before the Privy Council concerning a defendant's right to a psychiatric evaluation in a capital trial. In 2009, the Privy Council invalidated a death sentence in *Trimmingham v. Queen*, finding that the murder involved, though grisly, was not among the "worst of the worst," which included multiple murders, premeditation, abduction, sexual or sadistic conduct, murder for political or ideological reasons, or where the perpetrator had previous convictions for murder.[168] In a subsequent case, the Privy Council quashed a death sentence where the state failed to obtain psychiatric reports or conduct a social welfare inquiry to determine the defendant's probability of reform and social re-adaptation.[169]

Following *Trimmingham*, the Privy Council ruled that psychiatric and psychological reports were necessary before a death sentence could be handed down, even if no issue as to the defendant's mental state arose at trial.[170] *Trimmingham*'s requirement that there be no reasonable prospect of reform is a condition that required professional medical advice.

---

165 A.G. v. Joseph, [2006] CCJ 1 (A.J.) (appeal taken from Barb.).
166 Grazette v. Queen, [2009] CCJ 2 (A.J.) (appeal taken from Barb.).
167 Anthony Gifford, *The Death Penalty: Developments in Caribbean Jurisprudence*, 37 INT'L J. LEGAL INFO. 196, 202 (2009).
168 Trimmingham v. Queen, [2009] UKPC 25 (P.C.) (appeal taken from St. Vincent).
169 White v. Queen, [2010] UKPC 22 (P.C.) (appeal taken from Belize).
170 Tido v. Queen, (2011) 79 W.I.R. 1, 14–15 (P.C.) (appeal taken from Bahamas).

In *Lockhart v. Queen*, the Council ruled, "in every case in which the death penalty is being considered, the report of a consultant psychiatrist is needed before the question whether the reasonable possibility of reform can be properly addressed."[171] The Privy Council has not directly ruled whether a sentence of death on a mentally impaired person constitutes cruel, inhuman, and degrading punishment. However, it has implied such a violation would occur if a mentally impaired person were sentenced to death; consequently, courts must consider medical evidence in order to make a determination as to a person's mental illness. The Court has remanded a number of cases to the Court of Appeal of Trinidad and Tobago to determine whether the defendant had a mental disability in fact.[172] These cases remain pending.

Conclusion

The abolition of the mandatory death penalty throughout the Commonwealth Caribbean was a striking success of the incrementalist litigation strategy pursued by human rights activists working toward the goal of total abolition. By bringing petitions before the U.N. Human Rights Committee and the Inter-American Human Rights System, these advocates succeeded in building up a persuasive body of death penalty jurisprudence under international treaty obligations. National courts of appeal and eventually the Privy Council, the court of highest appeal for most countries of the Commonwealth Caribbean, drew from this persuasive jurisprudence in a series of constitutional challenges that led to the dramatic restriction of the scope of the death penalty in the region. This success came at a cost. Because of wide public support for the death penalty as a result of increasing crime rates and the colonial underpinnings of the Privy Council appeals process, these strides toward death penalty abolition had the appearance of being externally imposed by Britain, the former colonial power. The result was the creation of a new Caribbean Court of Justice as a regional court of final appeal, though the Court has thus far adhered to the parameters of the Privy Council's earlier judgments.

The Privy Council's earliest decisions invalidating the mandatory death sentence, and *Reyes v. Queen* in particular, have contributed immeasurably to a transnational body of Commonwealth death penalty jurisprudence followed and distinguished throughout the English-speaking world. Like *Woodson v. North Carolina* and *Mithu v. State of Punjab*, *Reyes* has gone "viral" and courts in Africa, South Asia, and Southeast Asia have relied on its reasoning to determine that the death penalty should be reserved for the "worst of the worst" based on the individualized circumstances of an offender and an offense. Although *Reyes* was handed down by a "colonial" court, the decision followed the contours of earlier homegrown Caribbean case law, such as *Spence and Hughes v. Queen* at the Eastern Caribbean Court of Appeal. Despite the Privy Council's anachronistic standing in the Caribbean, the region is not simply the passive recipient of death penalty jurisprudence imposed from London or by human rights tribunals; rather, it is an active contributor to building this body of case law, and for this reason the new Caribbean Court of Justice provides an opportunity more than it does a challenge.

---

171 Lockhart v. Queen, (2011) 80 W.I.R. 1, 8 (P.C.) (appeal taken from Bahamas).
172 Most recently, these include Benjamin v. State, [2012] UKPC 8 (P.C.) (appeal taken from Trin. & Tobago) and Taitt v. State, [2012] UKPC 38 (P.C.) (appeal taken from Trin. & Tobago).

Chapter 5
The Holdouts: The Survival of the Mandatory Death Penalty in Malaysia and Singapore

Malaysia and Singapore share a common law heritage with other former British colonies in the Caribbean, South Asia, and Sub-Saharan Africa. English common law in Malaysia and Singapore is imprinted on heterogeneous societies in prosperous phases of economic development, which possess strong self-identities and a durable combination of democracy and authoritarianism. In Malaysia, the ethos of the strong state is infused with a light brand of implicitly political, "tolerant" Islam, while in secular Singapore the developmental state is centered in a broader theory of economic and social progress. As for capital punishment, both countries are robustly retentionist and profess a philosophical justification for capital punishment based on "Asian values," communitarian in nature and skeptical of outsiders.[1]

As a result of this purported cultural exceptionalism, Malaysia and Singapore have constitutions that differ from other former British colonies, advocating strong executive power and weak fundamental rights protections. Unlike virtually all other former British colonies, neither constitution explicitly prohibits cruel, inhuman, and degrading treatment or punishment.[2] Both countries retain mandatory judicial caning; in Singapore, strokes of a cane are automatic upon conviction for rape, robbery, drug trafficking, and vandalism.[3] Second, neither constitution recognizes a right to a fair trial, either in the constitutional document itself or through acceptance of international customary law or ratification of treaties, though they do include the right to be tried in a speedy manner, a prohibition on ex post facto laws and double jeopardy, and a ban on arbitrary arrest.[4] Finally, both constitutions allow broad derogations and the suspension of certain liberties if "necessary or expedient in the interest of the security" of the government.[5] Both countries stand in sharp contrast to the Hong Kong Special Administrative Region, a former British colony that has abolished the death penalty. Although Hong Kong has retroceded to the People's Republic of China, the world's leading retentionist state, the territory—which possesses similar demographics and economic development as Singapore—continues to justify its death penalty abolition on the basis of its commitment to liberal democracy. The strikingly different path of Hong Kong shows the limitations of the cultural exceptionalism used by Singapore and Malaysia to justify robust death penalty regimes.

---

1   On the death penalty and "Asian cultural exceptionalism," see Sangmin Bae, *Is the Death Penalty an Asian Value?*, 39 ASIAN AFF. 47, 49 (2008).
2   For the fundamental rights provisions of the constitutions, see SING. CONST. arts. 9–16 and MALAY. CONST. arts. 5–13.
3   DAVID T. JOHNSON & FRANKLIN E. ZIMRING, THE NEXT FRONTIER: NATIONAL DEVELOPMENT, POLITICAL CHANGE, AND THE DEATH PENALTY IN ASIA 415 n. 10 (2009). In 1993, 3,244 persons were caned in Singapore; in 2004, there were 11,790 arrests for immigration violations, which carries a sentence of three strokes. *Id.*
4   *See* SING. CONST. arts. 9(2)–(4), 11(1)–(2); MALAY. CONST. arts. 5(2)–(4), 7(1)–(2).
5   *See* SING. CONST. arts. 149–51; MALAY. CONST. arts. 149–50.

Both Malaysia and Singapore justify death penalty retention in terms of broader development goals. "The practice of capital punishment in Singapore was, and remains, an integral part of the wider effort to enforce a culture of developmentalism designed to underpin a postcolonial project of nation building."[6] A criminal act is viewed as a crime against the nation, indeed against the entire nation-building ethos, and is punished harshly. High penalties are imposed for even minor transgressions as a strong deterrent. In sentencing, the retributive nature of criminal justice is prominent. Criminals are subjected to a ritual of public shaming and humiliation in the form of intense media scrutiny, with personal details, photographs, and graphic coverage.[7] The combination of mass consumerism with heavy-handed justice has led to the characterization of Singapore as "Disneyland with the death penalty."[8]

In rapidly developing Malaysia, like Singapore, the criminal justice regime is part of a broader state-centered philosophy of unity among diversity, including skepticism of foreigners on whom the death penalty for drug trafficking falls heavily. Unlike Singapore's plurality-Chinese Buddhist population, Malaysia's state religion is Islam, to which about 60% of the population adheres, with the remainder including Buddhists (20%), Christians (10%), and Hindus (7%). Malaysia officially professes a "tolerant" version of Islam peacefully co-existing within a multi-religious society, although a more conservative strain is also increasingly visible in public life. An Islamic party enjoys strong support in the rural conservative north of peninsular Malaya, and controls two state governments.[9]

The death penalty in majority-Islamic countries is rooted in a philosophy of crime and punishment that differs from English common law: namely, certain punishments are authorized by sacred religious texts.[10] In 1993, the Malaysian state of Kelantan passed a *shari'a* criminal code that incorporated traditional *hudud* offenses, including amputation for theft, stoning for adultery, and crucifixion for robbery.[11] Several other state assemblies followed. While the *hudud* offenses in the *shari'a* criminal code are not constitutionally operable because they are pre-empted by federal criminal law, the existence of *shari'a* criminal law for minor offenses highlighted a tension in Malaysia between the demands of Islam and of a modern developmental state.[12] The Chief Justice of Malaysia stirred controversy in 2007 when he advocated replacing Malaysia's common law with Islamic law.[13] While Malaysia tolerates religious minorities, ethnic Malay Muslims are unable to

---

6 Alfred Oehlers & Nicole Tarulevicz, *Capital Punishment and the Culture of Developmentalism in Singapore, in* THE CULTURAL LIVES OF CAPITAL PUNISHMENT: COMPARATIVE PERSPECTIVES 291, 292 (Austin Sarat & Christian Boulanger eds., 2005).

7 *Id.*

8 William Gibson, *Disneyland with the Death Penalty*, WIRED MAGAZINE (Sept.–Oct. 1993). *See also* John Clammer, *Framing the Other: Criminality, Social Exclusion and Social Engineering in Developing Singapore*, 31 SOC. POL'Y & ADMIN. 136 (1997).

9 Andrew Harding, *The Keris, the Crescent, and the Blind Goddess: The State, Islam, and the Constitution in Malaysia*, 6 SING. J. INT'L & COMP. L. 154, 154 (2002).

10 William Schabas, *Islam and the Death Penalty*, 9 WM. & MARY BILL OF RTS. J. 223, 230–34 (2000).

11 Mohammad Hashim Kamali, *Punishment in Islamic Criminal Law: A Critique of the Hudud Bill of Kelantan, Malaysia*, 13 ARAB L.Q. 203, 204–5 (1998).

12 *See, e.g.*, Syariah Criminal Offences (Federal Territories) Act, 1997, No. 559 (applying to the Federal Territories of Kuala Lumpur and Labuan).

13 Thomas Bell, *Malaysia Considers Switch to Islamic Law*, TELEGRAPH (London), Sept. 1, 2007, http://www.telegraph.co.uk/news/worldnews/1561896/Malaysia-considers-switch-to-Islamic-law.html.

leave the faith without the consent of the *shari'a* courts, despite the constitutional guarantee of religious freedom.[14]

Despite the barriers imposed by statist constitutions, a culture of law and order, and a weakness of abolitionist civil society, use the mandatory death penalty in Malaysia and Singapore is on the sharp decline and legislative skepticism toward the mandatory death sentence for drug trafficking has risen. In November 2012, Singapore enacted a wide-ranging reform to its death penalty regime, limiting the mandatory death sentence to aggravated or premeditated murder, and sharply increasing the quantity thresholds necessary to trigger the death penalty for drug trafficking.[15] A similar thaw appears to be developing in Malaysia, where the Cabinet is reviewing the deterrent success of the mandatory death penalty for drug trafficking; legislative change is likely.[16] While both countries have upheld the constitutionality of such laws while articulating brave philosophical justifications based on "Asian values" and cultural exceptionalism, neither is immune from the global trends that render the mandatory sentence of death politically unacceptable.

The Law of the Death Penalty in Malaysia and Singapore

Malaysia received independence from Great Britain in 1957 in the midst of a twelve-year long state of emergency due to Communist guerrilla rebel activity, uniting peninsular Malaya with the Borneo territories of Sabah and the Sarawak protectorate. After independence, Malaysia established a delicate political–religious balance, tolerant of its minority citizens but with a culturally Malay identity. While the balance ushered in high rates of economic growth, it did so at some cost in the form of racial unrest and a state of emergency beginning in 1969. Singapore achieved self-government in 1959, threatened by a lack of natural resources, the decline of regional trade routes, and ethnic and religious tension. As a consequence, Singapore joined the Federation of Malaysia in 1963, but received independence in 1965. Singapore's developmental model, similar to Taiwan and South Korea, focused on the promotion of export-oriented industries with a powerful state role. This form of state-led development was extremely successful, turning Singapore into a major international financial center. In neither country has economic success resulted in democratic consolidation.

As Article 5(1) of the Constitution of Malaysia states, "No person shall be deprived of his life or personal liberty save in accordance with law," a clear if less-than-explicit death penalty savings provision. The Malaysian Penal Code authorizes the mandatory death penalty for murder, attempted murder for life-term prisoners, fatal terrorist acts, and offenses against the lives of the country's political leaders. In addition, the Penal Code authorizes the death penalty or life imprisonment with corporal punishment for waging war against the state, kidnapping or abduction with intent to murder, and gang-robbery

---

14 Shad Saleem Faruqi, *The Malaysian Constitution, the Islamic State, and Hudud Laws*, in ISLAM IN SOUTHEAST ASIA: POLITICAL, SOCIAL, AND STRATEGIC CHALLENGES FOR THE 21ST CENTURY 256, 261, 263 (K. S. Nathan, Mohammad Hashim Kamali eds. 2005).

15 Penal Code (Amendment) Act, 2012, No. 33; Criminal Procedure Code (Amendment) Act, 2012, No. 34; Misuse of Drugs (Amendment) Act, 2012, No. 27 (Sing.).

16 Edmund Ngo, *Death Penalty May Be Scrapped for Drug Offences*, THE STAR (Kuala Lumpur), Oct. 21, 2012, http://thestar.com.my/news/story.asp?file=/2012/10/21/nation/12204175 (noting that Prime Minister's Office was reviewing the death penalty under the Dangerous Drugs Act).

with murder.[17] The Dangerous Drugs Act of 1952 authorizes the mandatory death penalty for drug trafficking.[18] The mandatory death sentence for unauthorized possession of arms or ammunition in a security area under the Internal Security Act of 1960 was repealed in 2012.[19] According to Malaysia's Criminal Procedure Code, when a conviction for a capital crime becomes final, the judge passing the sentence forwards to the Chief Minister (*Menteri Besar*) of the state in which the crime was committed a copy of the trial evidence notes and a report written by the judge setting out his opinion as to whether the death sentence should or should not be carried out. The Chief Minister then issues an order stating the time and place of the execution or, alternatively, substituting a death sentence with a lesser punishment or a pardon. In both Singapore and Malaysia, the death sentence is carried out by hanging.[20]

Article 9(1) of the Constitution of Singapore is identical to Article 5(1) of the Constitution of Malaysia. In Singapore, the death penalty is mandatory for murder, drug trafficking, and a handful of rarely prosecuted offenses such as mutiny, genocide, piracy, and terrorist-related crimes. The death penalty is discretionary for a host of additional offenses, including hostage-taking, kidnapping, economic crimes, treason, and arms trafficking.[21] The Misuse of Drugs Act of 1973 was amended in 1975 to include a mandatory death sentence for drug trafficking in quantities that exceeded a statutory schedule.[22] Singapore's homicide provisions are closely modeled on Scots law under Penal Code sections 299 (culpable homicide) and 300 (murder), the latter of which encompasses four distinct *mens rea*: intention of causing death; intention of causing bodily injury that the offender knows is likely to cause death; commission of an act "so imminently dangerous that it must in all probability cause death"; and commission of an act "with the intention of causing bodily injury" severe enough that it would cause death "in the ordinary course of nature."[23] Until the law reform of November 2012, all four *mens rea*, even the controversial fourth one, triggered the mandatory death sentence.

Malaysia and Singapore stand out in the common law world because the two countries have upheld their mandatory death penalty schemes from constitutional challenge. Singapore has one of the highest execution rates in the world relative to its population size,

---

17 Penal Code Act, 1936, No. 574, §§ 121, 121A, 130C, 302, 307, 364, 396.

18 Dangerous Drugs Act, 1952, No. 234, § 39B.

19 Security Offenses (Special Measures) Act, 2012, No. 747, *repealing* Internal Security Act, 1960, No. 82.

20 Criminal Procedure Code, 1935, No. 593, §§ 277, 281.

21 Following the legislative changes of November 2012, the death penalty is mandatory for piracy with murder or attempted murder (§ 130B), genocide with death (§ 130E), abetment of mutiny (§ 131), and premeditated or aggravated murder (§ 302), or murder or attempted murder by a life-term convict (§ 307). Penal Code, Cap. 224, Laws of Singapore (rev. 2013). In addition, the death penalty is discretionary for waging war against the government (§ 121), committing offenses against the President (§ 121A), false testimony in a capital case (§ 194), ordinary murder (§ 302), abetment of suicide by a child or insane person (§ 305), kidnapping for purposes of murder (§ 364), and gang robbery with murder (§ 396). For aggravated arms possession, see Internal Security Act, Cap. 143, Laws of Singapore, § 58 (mandatory). For arms trafficking, see Arms Offences Act, Cap. 14, Laws of Singapore, § 6 (discretionary). For terrorist bombings resulting in death, see Terrorism (Suppression of Bombings) Act, Cap. 324A, Laws of Singapore, § 3 (mandatory).

22 Misuse of Drugs Act, 1973, No. 5; Misuse of Drugs (Amendment) Act, 1975, No. 49. The Misuse of Drugs Act is codified at Cap. 185, Laws of Singapore.

23 Tsun Hang Tey, *Death Penalty Singapore-Style: Clinical and Carefree*, 39 Comm. L. World Rev. 315, 347–8 (2010).

performing at least 369 executions since 1991.[24] Both countries historically have had high execution rates even for the region: in 2000, Singapore, with 5.2 executions per million, was second only to China in per capita executions; Malaysia, with 0.092 executions per million, was fifth.[25] The number of executions in both countries has declined since 2000. In 2007, Singapore only had 0.45 executions per million; Malaysia had zero that year.[26] Singapore's statistics seem even more out of place because Singapore has the third highest per capita income in Asia, and wealth is generally correlated to abolition.[27] The explanation for this phenomenon lies in the political culture in both countries: a strong executive with relatively weak judicial power, a law and order ethos, and a general intolerance of political dissent.[28]

Malaysia's three-tiered superior court system is composed of two high courts for East and West Malaysia, an intermediate Court of Appeal, and a court of final appeal known as the Federal Court.[29] Singapore has a two-tiered court system: a High Court with original jurisdiction in serious criminal cases and a Court of Appeal with appellate jurisdiction. The constitutional jurisprudence of the Singapore Court of Appeal has emphasized the "fundamental values of Singapore society," which are "communitarian" and serve "the common good."[30] The highest courts of both countries regularly engage in comparative constitutional interpretation, looking to foreign constitutional law as models or anti-models, despite their professed intention to develop national jurisprudence in line with an "Asian" value system that prizes social order rather than democracy as a precursor to national development.[31] Neither Malaysia nor Singapore are signatory to the International Covenant on Civil and Political Rights, which states that a "sentence of death may be imposed only for the most serious crimes" in retentionist countries.[32] Neither recognizes the jurisprudence of the Covenant's enforcing judicial body, the United Nations Human Rights Committee, which has found that a death sentence for drug trafficking violates Art. 6(2) of the Covenant.[33]

---

24   Oehlers & Tarulevicz, *supra* note 6 at 291.
25   JOHNSON & ZIMRING, *supra* note 3 at 23, 34–5 (2009).
26   *Id.* at 34–5.
27   *Id.* at 408, 420.
28   "Singapore's system of capital punishment may be the logical culmination of the government's penchant for 'crushing dissent' and micromanaging the social affairs and experiences of the residents of this nation's 63 islands." *Id.* at 413 (internal citations omitted).
29   WAN ARFAH HAMZAH, A FIRST LOOK AT THE MALAYSIAN LEGAL SYSTEM 94, 100–101, 104, 204 (2009). The Privy Council was the court of final appeal for Malaysia until December 31, 1984, when a constitutional amendment abolished appeals to the Privy Council and established a Supreme Court, though in constitutional and criminal appeals Privy Council jurisdiction was ousted earlier, on December 31, 1978. The modern court system, with the Supreme Court's jurisdiction divided between the Court of Appeal and the Federal Court, was installed in 1994. Singapore ousted Privy Council jurisdiction in 1994.
30   Thio Li-Ann, *"It Is a Little Known Legal Fact": Originalism, Customary Human Rights Law, and Constitutional Interpretation*, [2010] SING. J. LEGAL STUD. 558, 558.
31   Li-Ann Thio, *Beyond the "Four Walls" in an Age of Transnational Judicial Conversations: Civil Liberties, Rights Theories, and Constitutional Adjudication in Malaysia and Singapore*, 19 COLUM. J. ASIAN L. 428, 458 (2006).
32   *Id. See also*, Second Optional Protocol to the International Covenant on Civil and Political Rights, Aiming At Abolition of the Death Penalty, *opened for signature* December 15, 1989, 1642 U.N.T.S. 414 (entered into force July 11, 1991). Malaysia and Singapore are not signatories.
33   First Optional Protocol to the International Covenant on Civil and Political Rights, 999 U.N.T.S. 302 (entered into force March 23, 1976). Malaysia and Singapore are not signatories.

Given the harshness of the death penalty, courts are willing to substitute lesser, non-capital charges where the evidence permits: for instance, from a charge of discharging a weapon during a robbery (a capital offense) to a charge of causing grievous hurt with a firearm (a non-capital offense),[34] or from murder to culpable homicide.[35] For the crime of waging war against the Malaysian head of state (*Yang di-Pertuan Agong*, an elected monarch), the law permits discretion between death and life imprisonment, discretion that the Federal Court has occasionally invoked.[36] In addition, where a sentence is mandatory upon conviction, procedural due process issues have exaggerated importance; courts are searching, but firm, in their review.[37] Where a death sentence was imposed without procedural due process, the Federal Court of Malaysia found the sentence to violate the right to life as not "in accordance with law" and the right to a fair trial.[38] In that case, the Federal Court cited jurisprudence from Commonwealth jurisdictions as far as Barbados, Botswana, and India in interpreting the boundaries of procedural due process. However, a divided Singapore Court of Appeal upheld a death sentence even where it ruled that an accomplice's statement was prejudicial and self-serving, and should never have been admitted.[39]

Compared to the vast constitutional jurisprudence concerning the mandatory death penalty for drug trafficking in Singapore, similar jurisprudence for the crime of homicide is minimal. Singapore's Court of Appeal has never decided the constitutionality of the mandatory death sentence for murder, even though the definition of "murder" sweeps in felony murder and constructive intent murder.[40] In a 1981 appeal from Singapore, the Privy Council in *Ong Ah Chuan v. Public Prosecutor* distinguished murder from drug trafficking, noting that some crimes permitted "considerable variation in moral blameworthiness, despite the similarity in legal guilt of offenders upon whom the same mandatory death penalty must be passed." For murder, often committed in heat of passion, "the likelihood of this is very real; it is perhaps more theoretical than real in the case of large scale trafficking in drugs, a crime of which the motive is cold calculated greed."[41] As the Privy Council noted, however, Article 12(1) of Singapore's constitution (the right to equality) was "not concerned with equal punitive treatment for equal moral blameworthiness; it is concerned with equal punitive treatment for similar legal guilt," rendering the variation in moral blameworthiness irrelevant.[42]

The existence of the mandatory death penalty undermines a collateral attack on capital punishment on the basis of the death row phenomenon. In *Jabar v. Public Prosecutor*, the Singapore Court of Appeal distinguished Indian and Caribbean case law finding that

---

34 *E.g.*, Low Soo Song v. Public Prosecutor, [2009] MYFC 11 (Feb. 19, 2009). In Malaysia, discharge of a weapon during a robbery is a capital crime under the Firearms (Increased Penalties) Act, 1971, No. 37, § 3.

35 *E.g.*, Public Prosecutor v. Gunus Sagena, [2010] MYSSHC 375 (Nov. 2, 2010); Pathip Selvan s/o Sugumaran v Public Prosecutor, [2012] SGCA 44 (Aug. 15, 2012).

36 Mohd. Amin bin Mohd. Razali v. Pendakwa Raya, [2003] MYFC 6 (June 26, 2003).

37 Shamim Reza Bin Abdul Samad v. Public Prosecutor, [2009] MYFC 63 (Sept. 15, 2009) (failing to find ineffective assistance of counsel where it was not "flagrant"); Tan Ewe Huat v. Pendakwa Raya, [2004] MYFC 2 (Jan. 5, 2004) (finding confession involuntary and acquitting defendant, noting "we are not prepared to run the risk of sending the wrong person to the gallows").

38 Lee Kwan Woh v Public Prosecutor, [2009] MYFC 54 (July 31, 2009).

39 Lee Chez Kee v. Public Prosecutor, [2008] 3 S.L.R. 447 (Sing. C.A.).

40 Tsun Hang Tey, *supra* note 23 at 326–7.

41 Ong Ah Chuan v. Public Prosecutor, [1981] A.C. 648, 674 (P.C. 1980) (appeal taken from Sing.).

42 *Id.* at 673.

extensive delay could render a death sentence cruel and inhuman.[43] According to the Court, the intention of the Indian legislature "was clearly to make life imprisonment the general rule and the death sentence an exception," which allowed an appellate court to "readily take notice of any delay in the judicial process and make an order of commutation of the sentence to life imprisonment."[44] In Singapore, by contrast, the death penalty was mandatory. The Court accepted "that condemned prisoners on death-row should not be subjected to a prolonged period of imprisonment" and recognized "that they suffer a certain level of anguish and mental agony whilst awaiting execution." Courts in Singapore did not have jurisdiction to consider that events subsequent to the judicial process amounted to a constitutional violation. The wording of Singapore's death penalty savings clause ("save in accordance with law") differed from India's ("except according to a procedure established by law"), and as a result Singapore's courts could only inquire into legality and not into process. "Any law which provides for the deprivation of a person's life or personal liberty, is valid and binding so long as it is validly passed by Parliament," and a court may not inquire as to "whether it is also fair, just and reasonable as well."[45] The holding that a court could not inquire into the fairness or reasonableness of a penalty was a considerable detour from *Ong Ah Chuan*'s holding that "law" in Article 9(1) included principles of natural justice.

In Singapore, the scope of the mandatory death penalty for murder is still broader because it sweeps in group liability as well. Section 34 of the Penal Code provides, "When a criminal act is done by several persons, in furtherance of the common intention of all, each of such persons is liable for that act in the same manner as if the act were done by him alone." The Court of Appeal has loosened the standards; an accomplice merely needs to have intent "consistent" with the intention to kill and not possess the same intent as the actual offender.[46] More recently, the Court has held that a group criminal can be liable as long as he or she knew that the actual offender was likely to commit a crime.[47] Tsun writes: "The ramifications are disturbing. Merely participating in a plan to rob, assault or kidnap—which inevitably envisages some sort of injury—may render the accused liable for murder and the death penalty."[48] However, the Court severely admonished prosecutors for bringing homicide charges against a putative accomplice in a murder case, despite a lack of evidence that the accomplice was even present at the murder site.[49] This case may narrow prosecutors' willingness to bring such charges in close cases.

The weakness of civil society in Singapore undermines a public death penalty abolition movement. The Law Society of Singapore is prevented by law from commenting on legislation unless the government submits it to the Society for comment. State control of the media ensures coverage favorable to the government, and news reports rarely use the word "mandatory" in describing the death penalty. Only one political party in the country has called for abolition, and not until October 2005 was a campaign finally formed against the death penalty in Singapore. The contempt of court prosecution of British author Alan Shadrake for publishing a book on the death penalty in the country had chilling effects even

---

43   Jabar v. Public Prosecutor, [1995] 1 S.L.R. 617 (Sing. C.A.).
44   *Id.* at 630.
45   *Id.* at 631.
46   Mimi Wong v. Public Prosecutor, [1972] 2 M.L.J. 75 (Sing. C.A.).
47   Lee Chez Kee v. Public Prosecutor, [2008] 3 S.L.R. 447 (Sing. C.A.).
48   Tsun Hang Tey, *supra* note 23 at 356.
49   Muhammed bin Kadar v. Public Prosecutor, [2011] 3 S.L.R. 1205, 1298–9, 1300–1304 (Sing. C.A.).

as it made international headlines.[50] The 2005 execution in Singapore of a prominent athlete and civil servant for possession of a kilogram of marijuana prompted the first outpouring of dissent by civil society, despite media censorship.[51] Total abolition faces better odds in Malaysia, where the Bar Council has advocated the abolition of the death penalty, especially for drug trafficking. A multi-partisan caucus of legislators supports abolition of the death penalty, and in June 2011 the parliament moved a resolution ending the mandatory death penalty for drug trafficking.[52]

In July 2013, the Death Penalty Project and the Bar Council of Malaysia released a public opinion survey as to the mandatory sentence of death in Malaysia, reaching a representative sample of over 1,500 people.[53] While 80% favored the death penalty, when asked about a mandatory sentence of death the number fell to 56% for murder, between 25% and 44% for drug trafficking (depending on the drug), and 45% for firearms offenses. As in Trinidad and Tobago, however, the survey found that public opinion in favor of the mandatory death sentence in the abstract dropped dramatically when presented with an actual fact pattern: only 8% of respondents favored the mandatory death sentence for all of the drug trafficking scenarios, only 14% for the murder scenarios, and only 13% and 20%, respectively, for the two arms trafficking scenarios. "It was clear that, when faced with the reality of punishment, the majority of Malaysians favoured being able to exercise discretion whether or not to sentence persons convicted of murder to death," according to the report.[54]

Drug Trafficking and the Mandatory Death Penalty

Most troubling about the mandatory death penalty in Malaysia and Singapore is the extensive application of the penalty to drug-related crimes. Drug use is perceived as a crime committed by foreigners who seek to undermine Malaysia and Singapore, erode the social fabric, and limit the economic development of both countries.[55] Of 174 executions recorded in Singapore by Amnesty International between 1993 and 2003, 93 were of foreigners, usually migrant workers.[56] This feeds into the notion that Singaporeans are superior to their neighbors, in danger of subversion by outsiders. Only a handful of other countries besides Singapore and Malaysia treat drug trafficking as a capital crime, mostly in Asia.[57] Mental health and addiction professionals have criticized the death penalty for drug trafficking

---

50   M. Ravi, *Wanted for Mercy: Singapore and Its Mandatory Death Penalty*, 1 E. ASIAN L.J. 107, 109, 112 (2010).

51   JOHNSON & ZIMRING, *supra* note 3 at 417, n. 15 (describing trial and execution of Shanmugam Murugesu).

52   Churchill Edward, *Abolition of the Death Penalty in Malaysia?*, The Borneo Post (October 30, 2011), http://www.theborneopost.com/2011/10/30/abolition-of-death-penalty-in-malaysia/.

53   ROGER HOOD, THE DEATH PENALTY IN MALAYSIA: PUBLIC OPINION ON THE MANDATORY DEATH PENALTY FOR DRUG TRAFFICKING, MURDER, AND ARMS OFFENSES (2013).

54   *Id.* at 14.

55   Oehlers & Tarulevicz, *supra* note 6 at 291.

56   Johnson and Zimring note that 53% of executions in Singapore between 1993 and 2003 were of foreign nationals. JOHNSON & ZIMRING, *supra* note 3 at 416. They also note that Malaysia is one of the few countries in Asia, with Brunei, Macao, and Hong Kong, to have a higher percentage of foreign nationals in their prisons. *Id.* at 417 n. 14.

57   These countries include Egypt, Indonesia, Kuwait, Peoples' Republic of China, Saudi Arabia, Thailand, and Vietnam.

because the penalty falls most heavily on drug runners and "mules" rather than on big-time "lords," undermining the deterrence arguments in favor of the law.[58]

The execution rate in Singapore increased as the homicide rate declined because of an increasingly aggressive drug enforcement policy that punished possession with intent to distribute 15 grams of heroin, 30 gram of cocaine, 250 grams of methamphetamines, or 500 grams of cannabis.[59] As of 2012, more than 900 prisoners were on death row in Malaysia, of whom 640 were under conviction for drug trafficking.[60] The same is true of actual executions: drug trafficking offenses may account for as many as 69% of judicial executions in Malaysia and 76% of executions in Singapore.[61]

Malaysia made trafficking a capital crime in 1975, and made the penalty mandatory in 1983.[62] At the time, the government announced that abuse of drugs was the country's most serious national security challenge, noting that "life imprisonment and whipping were not an effective deterrent against drug trafficking activities, which were increasing" and affecting persons of all ages.[63] In the first fifteen years, about three hundred persons had been sentenced to death for trafficking, and about one hundred were executed. According to Harring, anti-trafficking legislation showed a consistent trend toward relaxing traditional due process standards of criminal law in drug cases, supplemented by mandatory whippings, forced rehabilitation, and preventive detention.[64]

Both Malaysia's Dangerous Drugs Act and Singapore's Misuse of Drugs Act create a presumption of trafficking if any person is found in possession of defined quantities of certain drugs.[65] This presumption is so strong that a Nigerian drug mule was unable to overcome the presumption even when he took a possibly lethal dose of the pills in front of law enforcement because he was convinced that the pills he was commissioned to deliver contained an African herbal supplement.[66] The presumption of trafficking in certain cases of possession is not the only one in the Act: any person found to have drugs in his custody or under his control is deemed to have possession and to know the nature of the drugs; a master of a ship or aircraft is presumed to have knowledge of any drugs imported on the vessel; and the occupier of a premises is presumed to have knowledge of drug concealment on the premises.[67] Malaysia's preventive detention laws for drug traffickers have even been

---

58 Griffith Edwards et al., *Drug Trafficking: Time to Abolish the Death Penalty*, 8 INT'L J. MENTAL HEALTH ADDICTION 616, 618 (2010).

59 JOHNSON & ZIMRING, *supra* note 3 at 414–15. As Professors Johnson and Zimring note, these are relatively small amounts.

60 Stephanie Sta Maria, *Bar Pushes for Abolition of Death Penalty*, THE EDGE (Dec. 10, 2012), http://www.theedgemalaysia.com/index.php?option=com_content&task=view&id=226829&Itemid=77.

61 The Malaysia statistics are for the period between July 2004 and July 2005. Rick Lines, *The Death Penalty for Drug Offences: A Violation of International Human Rights Law*, Powerpoint Presentation to the Commission on Narcotic Drugs (March 10, 2008), *available at*: http://www.ihra.net/files/2010/06/21/Lines-DeathPenaltyCND2008.pdf. The Singapore statistics are for the period between 1994 and 1999. *Id.*

62 Sidney L. Harring, *Death, Drugs and Development: Malaysia's Mandatory Death Penalty for Traffickers and the International War on Drugs*, 29 COLUM. J. TRANSNAT'L L. 365, 365 (1991).

63 Abdul Rani Kamarudin, *The Misuse of Drugs in Malaysia: Past and Present*, 1 JURNAL ANTIDADAH MALAYSIA 1, 16 (2007).

64 Harring, *supra* note 63 at 372.

65 *See* Dangerous Drugs Act, § 37(da) (note: section "da" is an amendment added between 37(d) and 37(e)) (Malay.); Misuse of Drugs Act, § 5(2) (Sing.).

66 Ravi, *supra* note 51 at 108.

67 Harring, *supra* note 63 at 374.

used to detain opposition party leaders and government critics; in 1990, an amendment removed drug trafficking detentions from judicial review.[68]

Law enforcement, prosecutors, and the judiciary engage in some selective enforcement of the drug trafficking statutes to prevent large-scale executions. The Malaysian law has a high level of acquittals, and prosecutors do not hesitate to seek lesser penalties for drug possession. The judiciary has developed a strict interpretation of the drug trafficking statutes. "As the process works out, the state gets its perceived deterrent benefit of the threat of mandatory death, but is spared both much of the difficulty of administering it and the international embarrassment of too many executions."[69] In fact, so broad are the exceptions that Harring calls the mandatory death sentence for drug trafficking, "in reality, not mandatory because so many trafficking arrests lead to dispositions other than the death penalty."[70] The mandatory death penalty for drug trafficking in Malaysia, in the eight years following its codification, resulted in well over 2,000 people facing trafficking charges and at least 200 mandatory death sentences. In the first decade after codification of the penalty, the proportion of convictions declined, likely because of the unwillingness of judges to convict under charges leading to mandatory death sentences. The high proportion of acquittals induced the public prosecutor to drop many cases before trial. The government has not criticized the high acquittal rate, suggesting some equilibrium has been reached.[71]

The case law's intricate distinctions bear out this equilibrium. In 1997, the Singapore Court of Appeal ruled that a traditional Chinese medical practitioner's use of opium in an external procedure to relieve joint pain was not "trafficking," even though he bought, sold, and distributed a narcotic.[72] According to the Court, "trafficking" required a purpose to use the substance as a narcotic drug. Courts in both Malaysia and Singapore forbid "double presumptions" when a person is found in control of (but not actual possession of) a quantity of narcotic that creates a presumption of trafficking. The defendant cannot have the burden of showing that he did not have possession *and* of showing that he was not trafficking.[73] This sharply narrows the scope of the presumptions.[74] The mental state of an accused is also searchingly scrutinized; awareness that one is trafficking in illegal drugs is not enough unless the defendant also "knows" the nature of the drug being trafficked.[75] Courts have acquitted defendants where the amount of drugs seized by police differs even slightly from the amount produced for inspection at trial, finding the chain of custody broken.[76]

---

68   *Id.* at 377.
69   *Id.* at 404.
70   *Id.*
71   Harring, *supra* note 63 at 400–401.
72   Ng Yang Sek v. Public Prosecutor, [1997] 3 S.L.R. 661 (Sing. C.A.).
73   For Malaysia, see Tan Tatt Eek v. Public Prosecutor, [2005] MYFC 5 (Feb. 3, 2005), *citing* Muhammed bin Hassan v. Public Prosecutor, [1998] 2 M.L.J. 273 (Malay. F.C.); Ibrahim Mohamad v. Pendakwa Raya, [2011] MYFC 15 (March 11, 2011).
74   For Singapore, see Mohd Halmi bin Hamid and Another v. Public Prosecutor, [2005] SGCA 56 (Dec. 9, 2005). However, where direct evidence rendered the presumptions unnecessary, the Court of Appeal has upheld the conviction. Tang Hai Liang v. Public Prosecutor, [2011] SGCA 38 (Aug. 2, 2011).
75   Tan Kiam Peng v. Public Prosecutor, [2007] SGCA 38 (Sept. 28, 2007).
76   *See, e.g.*, Yusri Bin Pialmi v. Pendakwa Raya, [2010] MYFC 29 (June 14, 2010).

Constitutional Challenges to the Mandatory Death Penalty for Drug Trafficking

The mandatory death sentence for drug trafficking has come under constitutional attack in both Malaysia and Singapore. In 1981, the Privy Council, then the highest court of appeal for cases arising from Singapore, ruled that the mandatory death penalty did not violate Arts. 9(1), 12(1), and 93 of the Constitution, which provide for, respectively, the right to life, equal protection of the law, and the separation of powers.[77] The case, *Ong An Chuan v. Public Prosecutor*, has formed the basis of Malaysian and Singaporean jurisprudence even though the case is limited in its persuasive value elsewhere in the Commonwealth after *Reyes v. Queen* and its progeny. *Ong An Chuan* provided the basis for the Malaysian challenge upholding the mandatory death sentence for aggravated arms possession in *Public Prosecutor v. Lau Kee Hoo* (1983) and the later drug trafficking challenges in Singapore in *Nguyen Tuong Van v. Public Prosecutor* (2004) and *Yong Vui Kong v. Public Prosecutor* (2010).[78]

In *Ong Ah Chuan*, the Privy Council faced the question as to whether the death penalty for drug trafficking was "in accordance with law," as required by the savings clause of Singapore's constitutional right to life provision at Article 9(1), and whether the Misuse of Drugs Act violated the right to equality under Article 12(1) because it distinguished among drug traffickers only on the basis of the amount of drugs that they possessed and not based on their moral or legal culpability for a crime.[79] The Council initially determined that the presumption of trafficking upon possession of a certain quantity of controlled drugs did not violate the presumption of innocence in criminal cases. While the constitution did not specifically recognize the presumption of innocence, the Council rejected the Public Prosecutor's argument that "law" in Article 9(1) and 12(1) meant any law passed by Parliament, which would render the phrase "a mockery." Instead, in a Westminster-style constitution, "law" referred "to a system of law which incorporates those fundamental rules of natural justice that had formed part and parcel of the common law of England that was in operation in Singapore at the commencement of the constitution."[80] Natural justice required that a court have material evidence before it that is logically probative of facts sufficient to constitute the offense of which an accused person is charged. The Privy Council upheld the constitutionality of the presumption of trafficking, finding that, in a specific intent crime, the accused alone knew his purpose; there was nothing unfair in requiring him to satisfy the court that he acted for a less heinous purpose if it indeed that was the case.

According to the Privy Council, the legislature of Singapore could reasonably find that society particularly abhorred drug trafficking committed for profit by an offender who took a calculated risk. "There is nothing unusual in a capital sentence being mandatory," the Council noted. "Indeed its efficacy as a deterrent may be to some extent diminished if it is not. At common law all capital sentences were mandatory."[81] The Council also rejected the argument that the drug trafficking law violated the constitutional right of equality, finding that all criminal laws involved the classification of individuals for purposes of punishment according to a defined set of circumstances, typically conduct and mental state. "Equality

---

77 Ong An Chuan v. Public Prosecutor, [1981] A.C. 648 (P.C. 1980).
78 Public Prosecutor v. Lau Kee Hoo, [1983] M.L.J. 157 (Malay. F.C.); Nguyen Tuong Van v. Public Prosecutor, [2005] 1 S.L.R. 103 (Sing. C.A.); Yong Vui Kong v. Public Prosecutor, [2010] 3 S.L.R. 489 (Sing. C.A.).
79 *Ong Ah Chuan*, [1981] A.C. at 660, 670.
80 *Id.* at 670.
81 *Id.* at 673.

before the law and equal protection of the law require that like should be compared with like," but it does not "forbid discrimination in punitive treatment between one class of individuals and another class in relation to which there is some difference in the circumstances of the offence that has been committed." The drug trafficking law discriminated "between class and class," namely those who trafficked in 15 grams of heroin or more, and those who trafficked in less than 15 grams.[82] The dissimilarity in circumstances between these two classes of crime was a question of social policy properly left to the legislature. The Court concluded *Ong Ah Chuan* with an argument that it would reject twenty years later: "the prerogative of mercy is available to mitigate the rigidity of the law and is the long-established constitutional way of doing so in Singapore as in England."[83]

In *Ong Ah Chuan*, the Privy Council indicated its unwillingness to undertake a proportionality inquiry as to whether the mandatory death penalty was too harsh for drug trafficking. Rawlings argues that this is a wise decision: "The Privy Council is in practice staffed by British Law Lords, accustomed to British norms of conduct and aware of the pressures on British society," he writes. "Singapore and Malaysian societies are very different, and subject to very different pressures—it would take a very bold, or possibly very foolish, Privy Council to assert that in response to those different pressures...the local legislature had adopted a quite disproportionate response."[84] Twenty years later, the Privy Council did not show this same hesitation in the Caribbean appeals.

In Malaysia, the mandatory death penalty for drug trafficking was initially a de facto creation of the judiciary and not a parliamentary enactment. In 1975, the legislature imposed a choice between a life sentence and the death penalty for drug trafficking cases, but until 1980 the judiciary treated this provision as essentially a mandatory life sentence. In eight cases between 1980 and 1985, however, the Federal Court (renamed the Supreme Court between 1985 and 1994) developed the doctrine that public policy mandated a presumptive death penalty for traffickers by reversing the life sentences of lower courts.[85] In the first of these cases, *Loh Hock Seng* in 1980, the Federal Court increased a life sentence to death, the first time in thirty-two years the court had made such an enhancement. According to the Court, "judges should not develop a phobia" of passing a death sentence "out of a sense of compassion to exercise mercy."[86] Following the case, High Court judges interpreted the holding narrowly, imposing the death penalty only in the absence of mitigating circumstances. In *Chang Liang Sang* in 1982, the Federal Court required the imposition of the death sentence "[o]ther than in the most exceptional circumstances."[87] According to Harring, the doctrine was likely the creation of a single powerful judge, Chief Justice Azlan Shah, who later became the elective monarch of Malaysia, and was a symptom of an increasingly activist judiciary seeking to assert its power.[88]

---

82   *Id.*
83   *Id.* at 674.
84   H.F. Rawlings, *Constitutionality of the Death Penalty*, 25 MALAYA L. REV. 148, 152 (1983).
85   *See* Harring, *supra* note 63 at 379, *citing* Public Prosecutor v. Oon Lai Hin, [1985] M.L.J. 66 (Malay. F.C.); Loh Hock Seng v. Public Prosecutor, [1980] 2 M.L.J. 13 (Malay. F.C. 1979); Public Prosecutor v. Mohamed Ismail, [1984] M.L.J. 134 (O.Cr.J. Penang 1983); Public Prosecutor v. Neoh Wan Kee, [1985] M.L.J. 368 (O.Cr.J. Penang 1984); Public Prosecutor v. Tan Gong Wai, [1985] M.L.J. 355 (O.Cr.J. Penang 1984); Public Prosecutor v. Tan Hock Hai, [1983] M.L.J. 163 (Malay. F.C. 1982); Chang Liang Sang v. Public Prosecutor, [1980] 2 M.L.J. 231 (Malay. F.C.).
86   *Loh Hock Seng*, [1980] 2 M.L.J.at 14.
87   *Chang Liang Sang*, [1980] 2 M.L.J.
88   Harring, *supra* note 63 at 380–81.

Parliamentary enactment of the mandatory death sentence grew out of the Federal Court's inability to specify the appropriate "exceptional circumstances" that would justify a life sentence. In *Public Prosecutor v. Saubin Beatrice*, a French woman accused of trafficking more than 500 grams of heroin was sentenced to life in prison, a sentence increased to death on appeal, and then reduced to life imprisonment by the Federal Court because of unstated "exceptional circumstances."[89] The Court never again found extenuating circumstances in a trafficking case; *Saubin Beatrice* gave the controversial impression that white European women faced disparate treatment from Malaysian men and women.

A year later, in *Tan Hock Hai*, a different panel of the Federal Court reversed a sentence of life imprisonment and imposed a death sentence, denying the lower court's finding of "exceptional circumstances" on the grounds that *Saubin Beatrice* never specified what those circumstances were, in essence limiting the holding of *Saubin Beatrice* to its facts.[90] Considering the rampant drug abuse in the country, the Court also determined that the crime had a deleterious effect on public health and required vigorous deterrence. The sentence of death "should be imposed for trafficking in dangerous drugs other than in the most exceptional circumstances."[91] *Tan Hock Hai*, coupled with the racial undertones of *Saubin Beatrice*, played a role in persuading the legislature to pass the 1983 amendment making the death penalty mandatory for drug trafficking, which crystallized the judicial consensus that the death penalty should virtually always be mandatory because of strong deterrent considerations.[92]

The Malaysian Court of Appeal upheld the constitutionality of the mandatory nature of the death penalty in *Public Prosecutor v. Lau Kee Hoo*, a challenge to Malaysia's aggravated arms possession law under the Internal Security Act of 1960.[93] Distinguishing earlier cases from India, Rhodesia, and Trinidad on the basis that the Malaysian constitution lacked a prohibition on cruel and degrading punishment, the Court instead adopted the holding of the Privy Council in *Ong Ah Chuan*, which it cited extensively. While not strictly concerning drug trafficking, the case in effect closed the door to a future constitutional challenge to the Dangerous Drugs Act.

Once upheld by *Ong Ah Chuan*, the window to challenge the mandatory death penalty under Singapore's Misuse of Drugs Act did not reopen until the Privy Council decided the Caribbean line of cases, rendering *Ong Ah Chuan* dubious authority. In the 2004 case *Nguyen Tuong Van v. Public Prosecutor*, the Singapore Court of Appeal upheld the mandatory death sentence from constitutional challenge by a 24-year-old Australian national of Vietnamese origin, who had been sentenced to death for importing nearly 400 grams of diamorphine.[94] The appellant challenged the mandatory death sentence on the grounds that the mandatory death sentence prescribed under the Misuse of Drugs Act was constitutionally impermissible and should be read as a discretionary death penalty.[95] Considering the line of Privy Council decisions arising from the Caribbean, the Court distinguished the Caribbean jurisprudence on the basis of their different constitutional structures.[96] The Court rejected

---

89   Public Prosecutor v. Saubin Beatrice, [1983] 1 M.L.J. 307 (O.Cr.J. Penang 1982).
90   Public Prosecutor v. Tan Hock Hai, [1983] 1 M.L.J. 163 (Malay. F.C.).
91   *Id.* at 164.
92   Stanley Yeo Meng Heong, *Judicial Policy on Sentencing Drug Traffickers*, 25 Malaya L. Rev. 415, 418 (1983).
93   Public Prosecutor v. Lau Kee Hoo, [1983] 1 M.L.J. 157 (Malay. F.C.).
94   Nguyen Tuong Van v. Public Prosecutor, [2005] 1 S.L.R. 103, 107 (Sing. C.A.).
95   *Id.* at 111.
96   *Id.* at 121.

appellant's argument that the mandatory death penalty was not "in accordance with law" and consequently not saved, because the constitutional foundation for upholding the law had since been reversed.

The Court also found that customary international law did not import the prohibition of cruel, inhuman, or degrading punishment into Singaporean constitutional law through the "in accordance with law" clause when such law had not been codified by Parliament. "We agree with the trial judge's reasoning on the effect of a conflict between a customary international law rule and a domestic statute," the Court indicated. "The trial judge held that even if there was a customary international law rule prohibiting execution by hanging, the domestic statute providing for such punishment would prevail in the event of inconsistency."[97] Although the European Convention on Human Rights applied to Britain's colonies after 1953, the Singapore Court of Appeal rejected the suggestion that the Convention was indicative of present international customary law.[98] In addition, the Court rejected the argument that the mandatory death penalty violated the constitutionally enshrined separation of powers because the legislature delegated judicial sentencing power to the executive branch.[99]

In assessing whether the mandatory death penalty for drug trafficking violated the equality provision at Article 12(1), the Court of Appeal elaborated on *Ong Ah Chuan* by noting that a classification will be upheld if it is based on intelligible differentia and the differentia bears a rational relation to the object sought to be achieved by the law in question.[100] The Court acknowledged the recent Privy Council decision of *Watson v. Queen*, in which the Privy Council indicated that it was "no longer acceptable, nor is it any longer possible to say, as Lord Diplock did on behalf of the Board in *Ong Ah Chuan*... that there is nothing unusual in a death sentence being mandatory." The Court of Appeal tersely dismissed the argument, noting that the sentence was "sufficiently discriminating to obviate any inhumanity in its operation." The judiciary had the responsibility to enforce laws that were "concomitant with the civil and civilised society which every citizen of Singapore must endeavor to preserve and protect," the Court noted in characteristic communitarian language.[101]

In 2010, an appeal in the case of *Yong Vui Kong* allowed the Court of Appeal an even more detailed analysis of the constitutionality of the mandatory death penalty under the Misuse of Drugs Act at a time when Singapore's mandatory death penalty law looked increasingly anachronistic.[102] The appellant argued that the mandatory death penalty violated the right to life and was not "in accordance with law" because the mandatory death penalty was an inhuman form of punishment and because it conflicted with international customary law.[103] In addition, the differentia laid out in the Misuse of Drugs Act among the amounts of drugs that triggered prescribed penalties, including death, were arbitrary, and consequently violated Article 12(1) of the constitution, providing for the equal protection of law.[104] The Court interpreted *Woodson*, *Mithu*, and the Caribbean jurisprudence in great detail and distinguished them on the basis of Singapore's different constitutional structure.

---

97 *Id.* at 128.
98 *Id.* at 126.
99 *Id.* at 128–9.
100 *Id.* at 123.
101 *Id.* at 126–7.
102 Yong Vui Kong v. Public Prosecutor, [2010] 3 S.L.R. 491 (Sing. C.A.).
103 *Id.* at 496–7.
104 *Id.* at 497–8.

The appellant's argument in *Yong Vui Kong* never overcame a circularity that would have allowed the conservative judges to invalidate the mandatory death penalty. The appellant argued that the mandatory death penalty was not saved because it constituted cruel, inhuman, and degrading punishment under customary international law, but failed to convince the judges of a mechanism by which the customary international law of the death penalty could be incorporated in Singapore's constitution in the absence of domestic law or international treaties.[105] The Court also rejected the appellant's 12(1) challenge against unequal protection of the law since Parliament had constitutionally justifiable reasons for setting up a schedule of drug trafficking penalties that could result in automatic death.[106] This argument was, essentially, that two drug traffickers carrying different amounts of drugs could be subjected to different penalties even though their mental state and legal culpability were the same. The Court found that two drug traffickers carrying different amounts of drugs were not equal at all; they were, in fact, distinguishable, and Parliament could distinguish them by assigning differing penalties.[107] Unlike the mandatory death penalty for murder, this was no colonial relic; it was a modern and deliberate legislative scheme.

International law was not completely irrelevant. The Singapore government conceded that it employed the death penalty only for the "most serious crimes," although it defined "most serious crimes" to include drug trafficking.[108] Singapore has also been a slippery target for a death row phenomenon challenge, as executions are carried out with speedy efficiency.[109] This makes Singapore a difficult target for international death penalty experts, and, at least until November 2012, the country was running "against what is widely perceived to be a strong move in the international community, if not to abolish the death penalty, then to use it more parsimoniously and with greater due process rights than is usual."[110]

What Yong Vui Kong's defense team attempted to do was to convince the Court of Appeal that the mandatory death penalty for drug trafficking was a breach of "those fundamental rules of natural justice that had formed part and parcel of the common law of England" after the line of Caribbean decisions from the Privy Council.[111] Scholars argued that Article 9 *must* incorporate some limits on disproportionate punishment if the Privy Council's assertion in *Ong Ah Chuan* was correct that "in accordance with law" included principles of natural justice.[112] The Singapore Court of Appeal, however, has preferred a purely positivist approach: in essence, all "law" must be written, and all that is written is "law". The Court also dismissed the argument that the European Convention on Human

---

105 *Id.* at 519–21. The Court placed special emphasis on the constitutional commission's findings in 1966 that specifically recommended that Singapore not adopt a prohibition on cruel, inhuman, or degrading treatment or punishment.

106 *Id.* at 536 *et seq.*

107 *Id.* at 538–9.

108 Michael Hor, *The Death Penalty in Singapore and International Law*, 8 SINGAPORE Y.B. INT'L L. 105, 106 (2004).

109 Jabar v. Public Prosecutor, [1995] S.L.R. 617, 629–30 (Sing. C.A.).

110 Hor, *supra* note 108 at 116. As Hor writes, since independence Singapore has increased the number of capital offenses to include kidnapping, drug trafficking, and arms offenses, and created presumptions in favor of death in both arms and drug trafficking cases to make convictions easier. Capital trial courts have abolished jury trials and replaced panels of judges with a single judge. While it was once a capital offense to traffic in a certain quantity of drugs, now it is enough to possess that amount; the intention to traffic will be assumed. *Id.*

111 Yap Po Jen, *Constitutionalising Capital Crimes: Judicial Virtue or "Originalism" Sin?*, [2011] SING. J. LEGAL STUD. 281, 282–3.

112 Tsun Hang Tey, *supra* note 23 at 320.

Rights applied to Singapore for ten years prior to independence, noting that the mandatory death penalty existed in the Singapore penal code since 1872, and also existed in some form in Great Britain through the end of the colonial period.[113] Even if the Convention bequeathed some "inhuman punishment" standard to Singapore, it would not include a prohibition on the mandatory death penalty.

In Singapore, customary international law is not accepted as applicable in domestic law until it is passed by statute.[114] Elsewhere in the constitution, the definition of "law" includes written law *and* common law, as well as customs or usages having the force of law in the country; it does not restrict the word "law" to written law.[115] The Court could have avoided this interpretive problem by simply saying that it had insufficient evidence of state practice to discern a norm of customary international law against the mandatory death penalty for drug trafficking.[116] This was an unspoken weakness in the case: the Attorney General had argued, with some justification, that the recent Commonwealth-wide authority striking down the mandatory nature of the death penalty was not necessarily reflective of an international legal consensus that the mandatory death penalty is prohibited as a rule of customary international law, noting that the widespread state practice and the *opinio juris* required to form such a rule were still lacking.[117]

For the principle that the mandatory death sentence was cruel and inhuman punishment, the Court of Appeal had recourse to American, Caribbean, and African cases, which it easily distinguished. Singapore's own constitutional history showed that the absence of a cruel and inhuman punishment clause was not unintentional; the drafters of the Malaysian constitution, on which Singapore's is based, specifically considered and rejected the need for such a provision.[118] As Thio writes, Singapore has opted for a "political constitutionalism" in which rights are determined by the political branches of government as a way of making them accountable, over the "rights-based legal constitutionalism" characterized by Western liberal democracies.[119] Parliament, not courts, have the power to determine the substantive content of law, and issues concerning the desirability of the death penalty are matters of social policy. The Court's decision in *Yong Vui Kong* accords with this constitutional theory.

The Court's attempt to use an "originalism" approach to constitutional interpretation is problematic. Singapore's constitutional bill of rights was wholly adopted from Malaysia's constitution via the Republic of Singapore Independence Act; consequently, it is possible to overrely on drafters' intent, oddly requiring Singaporean judges to attempt to discern the intent of another nation's constitutional drafters. The legislature specifically rejected a constitutional prohibition on cruel and degrading punishment in 1969, but as this was four years after independence, it is debatable that it represented the intent of the constitutional

---

113 *Yong Vui Kong*, [2010] 3 S.L.R. at 528.

114 Aravind Ganesh, *Insulating the Constitution:* Yong Vui Kong v. Public Prosecutor, *[2010] SGCA 20*, CRIDHO Working Paper No. 2010/01, Catholic University of Louvain.

115 *See, e.g.*, Singapore Const. art. 2(1).

116 Jack Tsen-Ta Lee, *The Mandatory Death Penalty and a Sparsely Worded Constitution*, 127 L. Q. Rev. 192, 195 (2011).

117 *Yong Vui Kong*, [2010] 3 S.L.R. at 513.

118 Thio Li-Ann, *supra* note 30 at 562, 565.

119 *Id.* at 570. Thio defends the Court of Appeal. "While critics of the Singapore judiciary may lament the failure to adopt a rights-oriented liberal constitutionalist orientation in treating rights as defeasible interests and not 'trumps,' contrary to the rights-prioritising, individualist dogma of legal liberalism, this modesty avoids the situation of 'rule by judges' which subverts the rule of law." *Id.* at 560.

drafters.[120] Even the Court of Appeal could not bear to bring their argument to its logical conclusion: the justices conceded that if the legislature legalized torture, it would not become lawful simply because a constitutional ban on torture was likewise rejected in 1969.[121] The end result is that "law" in article 9(1) includes some international customary prohibition on torture, but not on other forms of cruel, inhuman, or degrading punishment.

Turning the appellant's argument that the mandatory death sentence for drug trafficking violates the equality provision at Article 12(1) of the constitution, the Court purported to use a deferential "rational basis" test. However, the Court's reasoning lent itself to judicial manipulation: how a court defined the legislative purposes behind a law's classifications invariably determined whether the law's classifications were constitutional. "In other words, the courts can often either sustain or reject the rationality of the legislation by manipulating the level of abstraction of the legislative object."[122] The rational connection test thus becomes a tool for justifying the legality, and not for determining the constitutionality, of a statute.

Yong Vui Kong's defense lawyers brought a subsequent challenge arguing that the President's failure to consider his clemency petition was a constitutional violation. The High Court determined that the President of Singapore was required to act on the advice of his Cabinet in considering clemency petitions and did not possess his own discretionary power. In addition, clemency determinations were not reviewable by the judicial system.[123] According to Singapore's constitution, judges at the trial and appeal stages of the case must make a mercy report to the President, which is then forwarded to the Attorney General for an opinion.[124] The Court of Appeal upheld the High Court, finding that the President must constitutionally confer with the Cabinet and engage in good-faith review of the defendant's case, but the ultimate decision granting or denying clemency was unreviewable. However, the Court did not identity a constitutional mechanism by which a defendant could challenge whether the procedure was properly followed since the procedure is conducted in private.[125]

Yong Vui Kong's challenge to the arbitrariness of clemency proceedings was followed by a challenge to prosecutorial discretion in *Ramalingam Ravinthran v. Attorney-General*, arguing that bringing different charges to co-conspirators resulted in the arbitrary infliction of capital punishment and violated the prohibition on equality before the law.[126] In *Ravinthran* the prosecutor brought a charge of drug trafficking against two co-defendants who together engaged in the same criminal act; the only difference was the quantity of drugs each was charged with transporting such that one faced the mandatory death penalty and the other did not. The Court acknowledged outer limits on prosecutorial discretion: the Attorney General as represented by the Public Prosecutor must give every case unbiased

---

120 Yap Po Jen, *Constitutionalising Capital Crimes: Judicial Virtue or "Originalism" Sin?*, [2011] SING. J. LEGAL STUD. 281, 283–4. As Professor Yap notes, the right to vote is not contained in the Singaporean constitution and a similar amendment was also specifically rejected, and yet the country remains an electoral majoritarian democracy. *Id.* at 284–5.
121 *Id.* at 285.
122 Po Jen Yap, *The "Dead" Constitution: Crime and Punishment in Singapore*, 40 HONG KONG L.J. 577, 587–8 (2010).
123 Ravi, *supra* note 51 at 111, *citing* Yong Vui Kong v. Public Prosecutor, [2010] 3 S.L.R. 489 (Sing. C.A.).
124 Shubhankar Dan, *Presidential Pardon in Singapore: A Comment on* Yong Vui Kong v. Attorney General, 42 COMM. L. WORLD REV. 48, 55 (2013).
125 *Id.* at 54–5, 56–7.
126 Ramalingam Ravinthran v. Attorney-General, [2012] SGCA 2 (10 January 2012).

consideration and avoid taking into consideration irrelevant criteria. "He must compare and treat like with like, and must not unlawfully discriminate against one offender as compared to another," but he also had to take into consideration a wide array of other factors from the sufficiency of evidence to the willingness of a co-accused to testify. "Where relevant, these factors may justify offenders in the same criminal enterprise being prosecuted differently."[127] The Court refused to inquire into prosecutorial discretion given the myriad of factors that a prosecutor considers in weighing charges against an accused.

Singapore's courts declined to give content to constitutional due process rights despite the Privy Council's ruling in *Ong Ah Chuan* that the definition of "law" in Article 9(1) imported some principles of natural justice. According to the Court, the constitution does not require that an accused be told of his right to counsel, though he or she has the right to *have* counsel.[128] A right to be informed of the right against self-incrimination is also unrecognized, even though the death penalty could in theory be handed down by virtue of an accused's silence.[129] The Singaporean constitution does not specifically provide for a presumption of innocence or proof beyond a reasonable doubt in criminal cases.[130] *Ong Ah Chuan*'s cavalier treatment of the presumption of innocence in drug trafficking cases has been repudiated by courts around the world.[131] The inescapable conclusion is that Singaporeans as colonial subjects had some due process rights under the European Convention on Human Rights, but "now, as citizens of an independent republic, they have nothing."[132]

Singapore's capital punishment culture does not exist in a vacuum. Despite the weakness of Singapore's death penalty abolition movement, the case of *Yong Vui Kong* had a major media breakthrough when the Parliament of Malaysia took an active interest in his case. The opposition party promised to debate support for Yong Vui Kong, and the Malaysian Foreign Minister wrote to the Singaporean government to plead for his life. The resulting press conference was covered by all Malaysian media outlets and local activists in Singapore were re-energized.[133] In November 2012, Singapore abolished the mandatory death penalty for most categories of drug trafficking offenses and homicide, such that all persons under sentence of death had to be resentenced under the new law. The Penal Code (Amendment) Bill amended the Penal Code to provide for either death or life imprisonment with corporal punishment for persons who commit ordinary murder. The death sentence remained mandatory for premeditated or aggravated murder.[134] The Bill reframed the offense of culpable homicide, providing for a mandatory minimum sentence and corporal punishment if the killing was intentional, and a lower threshold if done with knowledge that the crime was likely to cause death.

The change in law also required that all death sentences be confirmed by the Singapore Court of Appeal, either pursuant to an appeal by the accused or by a petition

---

127 *Id.* at ¶ 52.
128 Rajeevan Edakalavan v. Public Prosecutor, [1998] 1 S.L.R. 815 (Sing. C.A.).
129 Public Prosecutor v. Mazan, [1993] 1 S.L.R. 512 (Sing. C.A.). *See* Tsun Hang Tey, *supra* note 23 at 354.
130 Tsun Hang Tey, *supra* note 23 at 339–40.
131 Queen v. Lambert [2002] 2 A.C. 545 (U.K.H.L.); Queen v. Oakes, (1987) 26 D.L.R. (4th) 200 (Can. S.C.).
132 Aravind Ganesh, *Insulating the Constitution:* Yong Vui Kong v. Public Prosecutor, *[2010] SGCA 20*, CRIDHO Working Paper No. 2010/01, Catholic University of Louvain.
133 Ravi, *supra* note 51 at 112.
134 Penal Code (Amendment) Act, 2012, No. 33.

for confirmation by the Public Prosecutor where the accused did not appeal.[135] The Bill created a new procedure for the review of death sentences where no appeal was filed by the accused such that the Court of Appeal had to examine the record of proceedings and the grounds of decision and satisfy itself as to the correctness of both conviction and sentence.[136] One consequence of the Bill was that it aligned the provision authorizing the mandatory death penalty for a murder carried out in the course of a robbery with a separately-enacted provision authorizing either death or life imprisonment for gang-robbery with murder, defined as robbery carried out by five or more people together. The Court of Appeal chafed at the inconsistency as gang-robbery was the worse crime since it involved the greater number of robbers.[137]

Finally, the Misuse of Drugs (Amendment) Bill empowered courts to impose a life sentence instead of a death sentence in most cases; enhanced punishments for repeat drug traffickers or those who target vulnerable persons; and created a drug rehabilitation system for abusers.[138] The Bill also allowed hair analysis as a supplementary tool to enhance detection of drug consumption and created two new offenses, arranging gatherings where controlled drugs are to be consumed or trafficked and causing a vulnerable person to commit a drug crime. The Bill empowered a court to impose a life sentence instead of a death sentence where the following requirements were met: (1) the offender must prove, on a balance of probabilities, that his role in the offense was limited to that of a courier who transported, sent, or delivered a controlled drug, or offered to do so; (2) the offender must have substantively assisted the Bureau in disrupting drug trafficking activities, or must prove, on a balance of probabilities, that he was suffering from such abnormality of mind as substantially impaired his mental responsibility. "Substantive assistance" could include provision of information leading to the arrest, detention, or prosecution of any person involved in drug trafficking activity.

In November 2013, the Singapore High Court resentenced Yong Vui Kong in accordance with this change in law, opting for a sentence of life imprisonment with fifteen strokes of a cane over a death sentence.[139] According to the Attorney General's office, Yong Vui Kong assisted the Central Narcotics Bureau in disrupting drug trafficking activities in Singapore and only played the role of a courier in the crime.[140] Only two years after the sweeping decision in *Yong Vui Kong*, Singapore's death penalty regime is unrecognizable, and one consequence is the rising pressure on Singapore's nearest neighbor Malaysia to follow suit. Yong Vui Kong's resentencing was widely reported in Malaysia, and opposition Members of Parliament in that country used the occasion to call for the discretionary resentencing of the nearly one thousand offenders on death row and the abolition of mandatory capital punishment.[141]

---

135   Criminal Procedure Code (Amendment) Act, 2012, No. 34, § 12.
136   *Id.* § 13.
137   Daniel Vijay v. Public Prosecutor, [2010] 4 S.L.R. 1119, 1210–11 (Sing. C.A.).
138   Misuse of Drugs (Amendment) Act, 2012, No. 27.
139   Rashvinjeet S. Bedi, *Singapore Spares Yong Vui Kong the Noose, Resentences Him to Life Imprisonment, 15 Strokes*, THE STAR ONLINE, Nov. 14, 2013, http://www.thestar.com.my/News/Nation/2013/11/14/Yong-Vui-Kong-spared-death-sentence-Singapore.aspx.
140   *Id.*
141   *Death Sentence for Drug Trafficking Should Be Abolished, Says DAP Leader*, MALAYSIAN INSIDER, Nov. 15, 2013, http://www.themalaysianinsider.com/malaysia/article/death-sentence-for-drug-trafficking-should-be-abolished-says-dap-leader.

The Limits of "Asian Values": The Abolition of the Mandatory Death Penalty in Hong Kong Special Administrative Region

Singapore led the world in executions with a rate of 20 per million between 1994 and 1996—twenty times higher than Texas and at least double that of the People's Republic of China (P.R.C.) during that period—justified by a brave philosophy of cultural exceptionalism and developmental goals.[142] By contrast, Hong Kong, which had not carried out an execution in twenty-five years, abolished the death penalty without fanfare in 1993. Although Singapore and Hong Kong have comparable legal systems and domestic contexts—similar demographics, population density, crime rates, and economic growth—their recent history shows strikingly different trajectories on capital punishment.[143] While Singapore justifies its death penalty based on cultural exceptionalism or "Asian values," Hong Kong justifies its abolition based on its commitment to Western-style liberal democracy. Hong Kong's colonial status until 1997 and the prevailing uncertainty pending its transfer to the P.R.C. in 1997 gave London more control over the nonuse and eventual abolition of the death penalty, similar to the British dependent territories in the Caribbean. The death penalty remains abolished in Hong Kong even after its incorporation into mainland Peoples' Republic of China, the world's leading retentionist state.[144]

During the colonial period, use of the death penalty in Hong Kong and Singapore was comparable; statistics indicate that the death penalty was used more robustly in Hong Kong than in Great Britain proper.[145] The death penalty was mandatory for the crime of murder and a handful of other offenses. However, Hong Kong's colonial status ensured that British law had a profound impact on the territory in a way that was not true for Singapore. Following abolition of the death penalty in Great Britain, Hong Kong's colonial governors were forced by edict to commute all death sentences to life imprisonment, even as the number of death sentences increased sixfold between 1966 and 1992. As in the Caribbean, the externally imposed moratorium was unpopular, but public support in favor of the death penalty softened as Hong Kong's transfer to the P.R.C. was formalized. In 1991, the Legislative Council passed the Bill of Rights Ordinance, which prohibited cruel, inhuman, and degrading punishment at Article 3. In addition, Article 2(2) stated that the death penalty shall only be imposed for the "most serious crimes," but Article 2(6) indicated that nothing in the article should be invoked to delay or prevent abolition of capital punishment.[146]

Anxiety about P.R.C.'s reacquisition of Hong Kong contributed to the abolition of capital punishment in 1993, undermining previously robust public support for retention.[147]

---

142 Franklin E. Zimring, Jeffrey Fagan & David T. Johnson, *Execution, Deterrence, and Homicide: A Tale of Two Cities*, 7 J. EMPIRICAL LEGAL STUD. 1, 2–3, 8–9 (2010).

143 For a comparison, see Michael Hor, *Criminal Due Process in Hong Kong and Singapore: A Mutual Challenge*, 37 HONG KONG L.J. 65, 66–7 (2007).

144 *See* HONG LU & TERANCE D. MIETHE, CHINA'S DEATH PENALTY: HISTORY, LAW AND CONTEMPORARY PRACTICES 7 (2007) (noting that China accounts for up to 70% of the world's executions).

145 JOHNSON & ZIMRING, *supra* note 3 at 366, 368–9 (2009) (noting that Hong Kong's per capita execution rate was 12 times higher than England and Wales from 1946 to 1955 and 18 times higher from 1956 to 1964).

146 Bill of Rights Ordinance, 1991, No. 59, §§ 2–3 (H.K.).

147 As Hor writes, in the mid-1970s, more than 90% of respondents favored retention of the death penalty for murder, and a majority supported expanding it to other crimes. As Johnson and Zimring note, however, after the massacres in Tiananmen Square in June 1989, enthusiasm for capital punishment fell to 50%, while less than 30% believed such death sentences should actually be carried out. Hor, *supra* note 140 at 165–6; JOHNSON & ZIMRING, *supra* note 3 at 369–70.

While P.R.C. pledged to allow Hong Kong's pre-existing laws to continue into force in the transfer agreement with Britain (the Basic Law), this pledge did not include subsequent legislation, and P.R.C. objected to a number of laws passed in Hong Kong on the eve of transfer.[148] Hong Kong experienced almost no backlash after abolition, and P.R.C. is unlikely to attempt to reintroduce the penalty before the current Special Administrative Region arrangement expires in 2047, particularly as Hong Kong has an extremely low homicide rate despite having one of the world's highest population densities. The provision in the transfer agreement allowing British or Commonwealth expatriate judges to serve on Hong Kong's Court of Final Appeal after 1997 was one factor contributing to the continuing influence of common law on the territory.[149] In 1997, the Long-Term Prison Sentences Review Board was empowered to consider a prisoner's rehabilitation and review sentences for parole five years into a life sentence and every two years thereafter. The 1997 Review Ordinance also exempted juveniles from the mandatory life sentence for murder, which was substituted for the death penalty upon abolition in 1993.[150]

A comparison of homicide rates in Singapore and Hong Kong shows a dramatic and nearly identical decrease in homicides in the two jurisdictions between 1980 and 2010, despite their divergence in capital punishment policy.[151] This is particularly true as Singapore's execution rate increased twenty-fold between 1994 and 1996, shortly after Hong Kong's abolition, before falling again by 95% over the next eleven years. "Homicide levels and trends are remarkably similar in these two cities over 35 years after 1973, with neither the surge in Singapore executions nor the more recent steep drop producing any differential impact."[152] Zimring, Fagan, and Johnson conclude that Singapore's exuberant claims of deterrence are overstated, as the control experiment of Hong Kong suggests that the death penalty has little impact on homicide rates.

The death sentence existed for three crimes in Hong Kong: murder, treason, and piracy with violence.[153] Any time a death sentence was imposed, the territory's Executive Council reviewed the sentence with the help of a report prepared by the trial judge. The Governor was required to consult with the Council but was not bound to their views. If the Governor upheld the sentence, the condemned prisoner could appeal to the Queen for a royal pardon through the Privy Council. Historically, with one exception in 1973, all death sentences were commuted by the Governor; the one time the Governor refused, the condemned man was pardoned by the Queen. Upon commutation, almost invariably the prisoner was sentenced to life imprisonment without parole.[154] In 1980, the Hong Kong Court of Appeal ruled that a judge had not misdirected a jury when he explained that although murder carried a mandatory death sentence, such a sentence would likely never be carried out as all sentences were commuted.[155]

---

148   Jon Vagg, *Robbery, Death, and Irony: How an Armed Robbery Wave in Hong Kong Led to the Abolition of the Death Penalty*, 36 HOWARD J. 393, 403 (1997).
149   Hor, *supra* note 143 at 166–7.
150   Long Term Prison Sentences Review Ordinance, (1997) Cap. 524, § 11 (H.K.).
151   Zimring, Fagan & Johnson, *supra* note 142 at 5–8.
152   *Id.* at 27.
153   Laws of Hong Kong, Cap. 212, § 2 (murder); Cap. 200, § 2 (treason); Cap. 119, § 19 (piracy) (rev. ed. 1972).
154   Andrew Scobell, *Strung Up or Shot Down? The Death Penalty in Hong Kong and China and Implications for Post-1997*, 20 CASE W. RES. J. INT'L L. 147, 154–6 (1988).
155   Cheung Wai Bun v. Queen, [1980] HKCA 109 (July 15, 1980). Note that prior to 1997, Hong Kong's court system was composed of a High Court and a Court of Appeal. After 1997, death penalty cases originated in the Court of First Instance and appealed to the Court of Final Appeal.

Because the sentence of death was mandatory, the jurors' verdict had to be unanimous. The defendant argued that this created a subtle incentive for jurors to convict for murder, as some of them may have opted for a manslaughter conviction if they believed death was not warranted.

The Legislative Council debated restoration the death penalty with a wave of armed robberies in the early 1990s, though given the colony's status, restoration would have been inoperable. During the debate on death penalty restoration, Legislative Council member Martin Lee offered an amendment abolishing the death penalty, raising concerns that the P.R.C. could use the sanction against citizens of Hong Kong after 1997.[156] The amendment passed in the Council by a vote of 24 to 12, with five abstentions. Formal abolition took place with the passage of the Crimes (Amendment) Ordinance, which received royal assent on April 22, 1993.[157] Following abolition, Hong Kong has wrestled with whether to extradite offenders who fled to Hong Kong from the P.R.C. through the process of "rendition," and how to react to Hong Kong citizens who are tried and executed in the P.R.C. "Despite the formal abolition that occurred in 1993, the death penalty remains a reality in Hong Kong because of its close proximity to the PRC and because of the PRC's willingness to use the death penalty against a wide variety of offenders."[158] Currently, under Hong Kong law, the Chief Executive cannot extradite a prisoner to a requesting country without assurances that capital punishment would not be imposed.[159]

In *Lau Cheong v. Hong Kong Special Administrative Region*, the Court of Final Appeal upheld the constitutionality of the mandatory sentence of life imprisonment for murder on the grounds that it was not arbitrary or disproportionate because of the inherent gravity of the offense and the deterrence function.[160] The defendants argued that because the crime of murder encompassed such a broad array of circumstances, from mercy killing to sadistic killing, the punishment was arbitrary and degrading as it did not permit judicial discretion to consider the accused's degree of culpability. The Court reviewed the legislative history of the provision, noting that the death penalty was mandatory for murder from 1842 when Britain acquired Hong Kong, until 1993, when it was replaced with mandatory life imprisonment for murder and discretionary life imprisonment for treason and piracy. Ultimately, death penalty abolition had been "achieved only on the basis that it would be replaced by the mandatory life sentence."[161] The Court confirmed that a disproportionate sentence could amount to cruel and degrading punishment, but indicated that the mandatory life sentence was a reasonable expression of legislative power.

The Court noted that considerable reliance had been placed on the mandatory death penalty cases from India and the Caribbean, but distinguished them on the basis that death and life were fundamentally different sentences: "In our view, because they are concerned with the death penalty, such assessments proceed on a qualitatively different footing and provide no authority for the assessment of proportionality regarding mandatory life sentences."[162] The Court instead relied on Canadian precedent finding that mandatory

---

156 Vagg, *supra* note 148 at 399–401.
157 Crimes (Amendment) Ordinance, 1993, No. 24.
158 JOHNSON & ZIMRING, *supra* note 3 at 372.
159 Order for Surrender, Amended Ordinance, 1999, No. 71, § 3, Cap. 503, § 13.
160 Lau Cheong v. Hong Kong Special Administrative Region, (2002) 5 H.K.C.F.A.R. 415.
161 *Id.* at 449.
162 *Id.* at 455–6.

sentencing was not unconstitutional in a case involving mercy killing.[163] Mandatory life imprisonment did not violate Article 11(4) of the Bill of Rights, which provided that everyone convicted of a crime shall have the right of appellate review of conviction and sentence. According to the Court, this right did not confer a separate right to appeal against sentence when the sentence was fixed by law. However, at the end of the decision the Court added a caveat, emphasizing that its holding was limited to the mandatory sentence for murder, based on the unique seriousness of the crime and its peculiar legislative framework; the reasoning was "not applicable to any other crime or any other sentence fixed by law."[164]

The Court of Final Appeal in *Lau Cheong* permitted legislative and executive decision makers a certain margin of discretion in determining the appropriate means to achieve policy goals. "The Court concluded in that case that the legislature's judgment that murder, though it may involve different degrees of culpability, merited life imprisonment was rational and tenable and should be respected."[165] Hor viewed the decision as upholding the legislative compromise that brought about abolition of the death penalty on the assurance that the substitute would be mandatory life imprisonment.[166] The decision simultaneously validated Hong Kong's death penalty abolition by distinguishing life from death *and* justified retention of mandatory life imprisonment for many of the same reasons that Singapore upheld the mandatory death penalty, including judicial deference to legislative policymaking and communitarian values. *Lau Cheong* illustrated the tension in Hong Kong jurisprudence between "Asian values" and liberal democratic ones.

In a subsequent challenge, the Court of First Instance rejected the argument that a court was required to specify a minimum term when passing a mandatory life sentence, as was required for discretionary life sentences for rape and kidnapping.[167] The defendant argued that this practice was inherently arbitrary because it treated like sentences of life imprisonment differently, and therefore constituted cruel and degrading treatment. According to the Court, even though the words pronounced by the judge were the same, a mandatory life sentence and a discretionary life sentence were different in philosophy, statutory framework, and executive policy. The Chief Executive still was required to take into account the recommendations of the parole board, a statutory body obliged to give consideration to individual circumstances. Relying on *Lau Cheong*, the Court found that the legislature could fairly determine that a class of crimes was of sufficient gravity to warrant a unique penalty. In addition, the Court rejected the notion that a mandatory life sentence left an accused person in a state of uncertainty. "A mandatory life prisoner knows that, in principle, he has forfeited his liberty for the rest of his days.... If he has any expectation it is only that, at appropriate times and in an informed manner, executive clemency will be considered."[168] The Court also rejected the argument that an accused had the right to make an oral hearing for the parole board, noting that the board only exercised an administrative and not a judicial function.

---

163   *Id.* at 456–69, *citing* Queen v. Luxton, [1990] 2 S.C.R. 711 (Can.); Queen v. Latimer, [2001] 1 S.C.R. 3 (Can.).

164   *Id.* at 465.

165   Anthony Mason, *The Place of Comparative Law in the Jurisprudence on the Rule of Law and Human Rights in Hong Kong*, 37 HONG KONG L.J. 299, 314 (2007).

166   Hor, *supra* note 143 at 74.

167   Tong Yu Lam v. Long Term Prison Sentences Review Board, [2006] HKCFI 321 (March 24, 2006).

168   *Id.*

A Note on the Mandatory Death Penalty in Brunei Darussalam

Brunei Darussalam—like Singapore, originally envisaged as a province of the Federation of Malaysia—also maintains the mandatory death penalty for murder and drug trafficking, as well as for lesser crimes including kidnapping, aggravated arson, terrorism, and gang robbery.[169] Like Malaysia and Singapore, Brunei's unexpected economic success after independence created a strong developmental state with a law and order ethos and the attendant problems of organized crime and drug trafficking. Because Brunei's constitution lacks even the most basic fundamental rights and judicial review provisions of the Malaysian and Singaporean constitutions, and because its population and crime rate are a tiny fraction of its two larger neighbors, the mandatory death penalty regime has gone unchallenged thus far. Still, as in its two neighbors, the legislative impulse has been to increase rather than decrease penalties, as in 2002 when it decreased the quantity thresholds for triggering the mandatory death sentence for drug trafficking.[170] No executions have occurred since Brunei's independence in 1957, though courts have apparently handed down death sentences in the past.[171] Like Malaysia and Singapore, Brunei has not signed the International Covenant on Civil and Political Rights and regularly votes against UN General Assembly resolutions advocating moratoria on executions. Brunei retains an avenue of appeal to the Judicial Committee of the Privy Council in some civil cases, but criminal appeals to the Privy Council in London were abolished in 1995.[172] As a consequence, the mandatory death penalty is immune from the vulnerabilities inherent in other Commonwealth constitutions.

Conclusion

For death penalty abolition, countries in East and Southeast Asia "are as culturally distinct and economically autonomous from Western European influence as any group of moderately industrialized nations can be."[173] Due to the unique structure of the Singaporean and Malaysian constitutional orders—strong executive branches, weak fundamental rights protections, and an isolation from international human rights treaties—the mandatory death

---

169 *See* Brunei Penal Code, Ch. 22, Laws of Brunei, arts. 302 (murder), 364 (kidnapping for purposes of murder), 396 (gang robbery with murder), and 435 (arson or explosives resulting in death, or arson to public utilities). The death penalty also exists as the most serious punishment available (non-mandatory) for waging war against the head of state (art. 121), abetment of mutiny (art. 132), abetment of suicide of a child or insane person (art. 305), false testimony in a capital case (art. 194), or culpable homicide by a convict (art. 307). For terrorism-related crimes, including aggravated arms possession, see Internal Security Act, Ch. 133, Laws of Brunei, arts. 40–41, Public Order Act, Ch. 148, Laws of Brunei, art. 28.

170 Hamzah Sulaiman, *Negara Brunei Darussalam: Socio-Economic Concerns Amid Stability and Plenty*, 2003 SOUTHEAST ASIAN AFF. 71, 72–3.

171 *See, e.g.*, Public Prosecutor v. Samer Klom Klom, [1996] BNHC 6 (January 31, 1996); Mohd Noh Bin Ramli v. Public Prosecutor, [1995] BNHC 32 (May 15, 1995). In a case where a defendant was under age 18, the Court determined that the death penalty was not mandatory. Public Prosecutor v. Abdul Bin Turkey, [1996] BNHC 44 (July 6, 1996).

172 E. Ann Black, *Brunei Darussalam: Ideology and Law in a Malay Sultanate*, *in* LAW AND LEGAL INSTITUTIONS OF ASIA: TRADITIONS, ADAPTATIONS AND INNOVATIONS 299, 310 (E. Ann Black & Gary F. Bell eds., 2011).

173 Franklin E. Zimring & David T. Johnson, *Law, Society, and Capital Punishment in Asia*, 10 PUNISHMENT & SOC. 103, 111 (2008).

penalty continues to survive in both countries and likely will in some form for the foreseeable future. Justified by cultural exceptionalism and "Asian values," courts in Malaysia and Singapore have resisted the pull of Commonwealth death penalty jurisprudence, emphasizing their own distinctiveness over possible similarities with other constitutional regimes. This chapter contrasts this exceptionalism with the very different path taken by Hong Kong Special Administrative Region, despite demographic and economic similarities to Singapore in particular, which justifies its abolition of the death penalty on the basis of its commitment to democratic ideals.

But even Malaysia and Singapore are not immune from the global consensus that the death penalty should be reserved for the most serious crimes based on judicial consideration of the circumstances of the crime and the background of the offender. Only two years after the Singapore Court of Appeal's decision in *Yong Vui Kong*, the Parliament of Singapore passed a major reform of criminal laws restricting the mandatory death penalty to crimes of aggravated murder and the most serious drug trafficking offenses. Even Malaysia has seen something of a thaw, as public support for the mandatory death penalty is weak and retention of the death penalty is now under legislative and executive review. In the coming years, the two countries may well align with the rest of the Commonwealth in restricting the death penalty to the rarest cases and in developing a framework for individualized sentencing discretion in capital cases. The abolition of the mandatory death penalty faces even longer odds in Brunei Darussalam as it is legally and politically immunized from constitutional challenge, though unlike Malaysia and Singapore, Brunei has not carried out an execution since independence.

Chapter 6
The New Frontier: Constitutional Challenges to the Mandatory Death Penalty in Sub-Saharan Africa

A dramatic revolution in Privy Council jurisprudence led to the near-extinction of the mandatory death penalty in the Commonwealth Caribbean in less than a decade. The weight of this authority had its greatest immediate impact in the East African countries of Kenya, Malawi, and Uganda, which have similar legacies of British colonial criminal justice and postcolonial constitutions that recognize due process rights and prohibitions on cruel and degrading punishment. To a greater extent than in the tiny Caribbean legal systems, the mandatory death penalty in East Africa created large death rows that grew as the number of actual executions dwindled, straining courts, correctional systems, and legal aid resources. Kenya faced the greatest crisis, with a mandatory death sentence for aggravated robbery and attempted robbery with violence that resulted in one of the largest death rows ever recorded in the developing world and one that surpassed even the United States at its peak in 2000.[1] A mandatory death regime may have been attractive to resource-constrained legal systems because it simplified the sentencing process, but it was a crude tool that papered over deficiencies elsewhere in the criminal justice system.

The abolition of the mandatory death penalty in constitutional challenges before the Kenya Court of Appeal, the Malawi Constitutional Court, and the Supreme Court of Uganda accords with the Commonwealth-wide trend toward the establishment of discretionary death penalty regimes.[2] All three countries have legacies of politicized criminal justice abuses, and only an irregular tradition of precolonial capital punishment displaced by a culturally foreign penal code and correctional system. The three countries have similar constitutional frameworks, including bills of rights originally drafted during independence negotiations and expanded in later constitutional reforms. For human rights lawyers such as the London-based Death Penalty Project, constitutional similarities translate into similar constitutional vulnerabilities and ensure that a decision in any one country is persuasive authority for its neighbors.

The trend, however, is not completely unidirectional. The Supreme Court of Ghana rejected a constitutional mandatory death penalty challenge in March 2011 by a four to one

---

1 At the time of President Mwai Kibaki's August 2009 commutation of all death sentences in Kenya—the largest commutation ever made—about 4,000 people were on death row, nearly a quarter of the world's entire death row population, in a country that had not carried out an execution since 1987. *Four Thousand Kenyans on Death Row Get Life*, AMNESTY INT'L, August 5, 2009, www.amnesty.org/en/news-and-updates/good-news/4000-kenyans-death-row-get-life-20090805. By contrast, the United States had 3,593 prisoners on death row in the year 2000, the highest recorded number since death penalty reinstatement in 1976. University of Alaska Anchorage Justice Center, *Capital Punishment 2000 and 2001*, 19(1) ALASKA JUSTICE F. 4–5 (2002).

2 Kafantayeni v. A.G., [2007] MWHC 1 at 6–7; Kigula v. A.G., [2009] 2 E.A.L.R. 1, 17 (Uganda S.C.); Mutiso v. Republic, [2011] 1 E.A.L.R. 342 (Kenya C.A.).

majority, carefully considering the persuasive authority from Kenya, Malawi, and Uganda, as well as from the Privy Council's Caribbean line of cases.[3] The majority upheld the constitutionality of Ghana's mandatory death penalty based on a narrow, textual reading of the constitution. A dissent insisted that authority from other Commonwealth jurisdictions on matters concerning international human rights was strongly persuasive in Ghana. Because of the "universalist dimension of human rights," the presiding judge wrote, "this court should be very slow to reject interpretations of human rights provisions *in pari materia* with provisions in our Constitution, when these interpretations have become widely-accepted orthodoxies in jurisdictions with a similar history to ours."[4] Like the majority of the Supreme Court of Ghana, in October 2013 a different bench of the Kenya Court of Appeal appeared to reject the court's earlier rationale by issuing an opinion that purported to uphold the mandatory death penalty as constitutional.[5] The decision is now on appeal to the Supreme Court of Kenya, which will be the final arbiter.[6] Despite these setbacks, however, the trend across the African continent is toward abolition of the mandatory death sentence. The result is that criminal justice regimes are harmonizing across borders and operating closer to conformity with prevailing international human rights and due process norms.

The Death Penalty and Society in Sub-Saharan Africa

The harsh nature of the mandatory death penalty was out of sync with African legal cultures. Outside of Islamic-majority Africa, much of the continent had only a spotty precolonial history of capital punishment, closely tied to local understandings of death, burial, and afterlife.[7] In countries with strong executive power, the transfer of sentencing discretion from an impartial trial judge to an appointed clemency committee risked politicization of the sentencing process, particularly for crimes such as treason, sabotage, or sedition, a dangerous scenario in the era of one-party regimes and military rule.[8] Finally, the risk of error was not negligible in heterogeneous countries where the language of the courtroom was foreign, where court delays complicated even routine motions, and where the right to effective assistance of counsel for indigent defendants was often more aspiration than reality.

---

3 Dexter Johnson v. Republic, (2011) 2 S.C.G.L.R. 601.

4 *Id.*, at 631 (Date-Bah, J., dissenting).

5 Mwaura v. Republic, Crim. App. 5/2008 (Oct. 18, 2013) (Kenya C.A.).

6 Sam Kiplagat, *Death Row Convict Goes to Supreme Court to Overturn Sentence*, THE STAR, Nov. 5, 2013 (retrieved from AllAfrica.com).

7 Where the death penalty did exist, it was often used only when other forms of economic compensation were inadequate, and the method used had cultural underpinnings. *See, e.g.*, Robin Law, *'My Head Belongs to the King': On the Political and Ritual Significance of Decapitation in Pre-Colonial Dahomey*, 30 J. AFR. HIST. 399, 415 (1989) (describing how the king of Dahomey "owned" heads of his subjects and executions would be by beheading). For the philosophy and practice of capital punishment under Islamic law, see SAYED SIKANDAR SHAH HANEEF, HOMICIDE IN ISLAM: LEGAL STRUCTURE AND THE EVIDENCE REQUIREMENTS 86 *et seq.* (2000).

8 This is particularly true in countries where the clemency or mercy committee is composed of political appointees or ex officio political officeholders such as an attorney general or minister of justice. *See* Lilian Chenwi, *Fair Trial Rights and Their Relation to the Death Penalty in Africa*, 55 INT'L & COMP. L. Q. 609, 631 (2006).

The death penalty is in rapid decline on the African continent.[9] With the abolition of capital punishment in law or in practice in most of French- and Portuguese-speaking Africa, the penalty persists almost exclusively in common law Africa and those countries governed by modified Islamic criminal law.[10] Even in retentionist common law Africa, the death penalty faces a crisis of legitimacy among political elites. Death penalty abolition may seem a distant prospect in tiny Gambia, a transit point for drug traffickers and organized crime, but a moratorium is currently in place after international outrage following nine controversial executions in August 2012.[11] Likewise, the death penalty appears to retain political durability in sprawling Nigeria as a result of the government's persistent battles against the Islamic terror group Boko Haram and separatist movements in the Niger Delta, though a recent case suggests the mandatory nature of the death penalty is constitutionally vulnerable.[12] Elsewhere, the penalty's decline is evident. The unexpectedly decisive re-election of President John Atta Mills in Ghana in December 2012 preserved the government's proposed White Paper calling for abolition, now a near-certain prospect, and constitutional reform efforts in Tanzania, Zambia, and Zimbabwe have provided political elites with a ready-made opportunity to drastically restrict the scope of capital punishment.[13]

---

9 LILLIAN MANKA CHENWI, TOWARD THE ABOLITION OF THE DEATH PENALTY IN AFRICA: A HUMAN RIGHTS PERSPECTIVE 53–6 (2007).

10 According to Amnesty International, the following countries are abolitionist for all crimes: Angola, Burundi, Cape Verde, Cote d'Ivoire, Djibouti, Gabon, Guinea-Bissau, Mauritius, Mozambique, Namibia, Rwanda, Sao Tome e Principe, Senegal, Seychelles, South Africa, and Togo. The following countries are abolitionist in practice, defined as countries that have not performed a judicial execution in ten years and are believed to have an internal policy against future executions: Burkina Faso, Cameroon, Central African Republic, Congo (Republic of), Eritrea, Ghana, Kenya, Liberia, Madagascar, Malawi, Mali, Mauritania, Niger, Swaziland, Tanzania, and Zambia. Amnesty defines the following countries as retentionist: Botswana, Chad, Democratic Republic of the Congo, Equatorial Guinea, Ethiopia, Nigeria, Somalia, South Sudan, Sudan, Uganda, and Zimbabwe. *Abolitionist and Retentionist Countries*, AMNESTY INT'L, http://www.amnesty.org/en/death-penalty/abolitionist-and-retentionist-countries (last accessed May 9, 2013). Hands Off Cain, an Italian anti-death penalty organization, also considers Benin, Comoros, Lesotho, and Sierra Leone as de facto abolitionist. *Country Status on the Death Penalty*, HANDS OFF CAIN, http://english.nessunotocchicaino.it/bancadati/index.php?tipotema=arg&idtema=17000605 (last accessed May 9, 2013).

11 Andrew Novak, *The Rule of Law, Constitutional Reform, and the Future of the Death Penalty in The Gambia*, 12 RICHMOND J. GLOBAL L. & BUS. 217 (2013).

12 Proposals to expand the death penalty for kidnapping, corruption, terrorism, and rape, for instance, have arisen in Nigeria recently. *See, e.g.*, Edegbe Odemwingie, *Senate Prescribes Death Penalty for Terrorists*, LEADERSHIP, February 21, 2013; *Justice Odunowo Advocates Death Penalty for Corruption*, VANGUARD, April 11, 2013; *Women Affairs Minister Advocates Death Penalty for Rapists*, THIS DAY, April 11, 2013; Austin Ogwuda, *Death Penalty for Kidnappers: Delta House Overrides Uduaguan*, VANGUARD, April 18, 2013 (noting state legislature overrode governor's veto of death penalty for kidnapping). All articles were retrieved from AllAfrica.com. However, news reports in September 2012 indicate that the High Court of Lagos State found the mandatory death penalty unconstitutional. *See* Precious Igbonwelundu, *Court Restraints Govt. from Executing Five by Hanging*, THE NATION, September 25, 2012, http://thenationonlineng.net/new/law/court-restrains-govt-from-executing-five-by-hanging. The decision was not available at the time of writing.

13 Republic of Ghana, *White Paper on the Report of the Constitution Review Commission of Inquiry*, W.P. No. 1/2012, June 2012, at 44; Rose Athumani, *No Death Penalty in New Constitution: Call*, TANZANIA DAILY NEWS, January 23, 2013 (noting the opposition of former Prime Minister Edward Lowassa to retaining the death penalty); Andrew Novak, *The Death Penalty and the Right to Life in the Draft Constitutions of Zambia and Zimbabwe*, AFRICLAW.ORG, April 18, 2013, http://africlaw.com/2013/04/18/the-death-penalty-and-the-right-to-life-in-the-draft-constitutions-of-zambia-and-zimbabwe

South Sudan, which has carried out eight executions since independence in July 2011, voted in favor of a December 2012 vote of the Third Committee of the United Nations General Assembly calling for a moratorium on the death penalty; eventual abolition is likely.[14] Eroding public and elite support for the death penalty is, in part, the result of abuses during the late colonial era and the post-independence period of authoritarian rule in which the criminal justice apparatus fell harshly on political dissidents. A swirl of changing religious attitudes on the continent, including the rise of conservative evangelical Christianity and conservative forms of Islam, has also moved the guideposts on death penalty opinion.

African regional human rights mechanisms have been relatively quiet on the issue of the death penalty, in contrast to their Inter-American and European counterparts. While African human rights instruments prohibit executions of juveniles and expectant mothers or mothers of infants and young children, the African Charter on Human and Peoples' Rights makes no mention of the death penalty.[15] In 1999 the African Commission passed a resolution advocating a moratorium on the death penalty and in 2005 created a Working Group on the Death Penalty, which is mandated to develop strategy for continent-wide abolition.[16] While the Commission has never ruled on a direct death penalty challenge, it has adopted procedural benchmarks in capital cases and has ruled that execution after an unfair trial is an arbitrary deprivation of life contrary to the Charter.[17] In an appeal from Zambia, the United Nations Human Rights Committee has also found a violation of the right to life following an unfair trial.[18] Regional tribunals also show promise: two challenges to the death penalty in The Gambia pending before the Community Court of Justice of the Economic Community of West African States (ECOWAS) may help further abolition efforts in that country.[19]

(noting that the death penalty is sharply curtailed in both Zimbabwe's new constitution and Zambia's draft constitution).

14 South Sudan operates under a transitional constitution and is in the process of drafting a permanent replacement. Courts still hand out death sentences despite the moratorium. The constitution contains an explicit cause restricting the death penalty solely to "extremely serious offences," excluding persons over age 70 and under 18, as well as pregnant or lactating women. This clause is independent of the right to life clause, which is at art. 11. S. SUDAN CONST. art. 11, 21; *South Sudan Says Death Penalty Remains Until Constitution Amended*, SUDAN TRIBUNE, May 4, 2013, http://www.sudantribune.com/spip.php?article46452.

15 These are the African Charter on the Rights and Welfare of the Child, OAU Doc. CAB/LEG/24.9/49 (1990), arts. 5(3) & 30(e) (entered into force November 19, 1999); and the Protocol to the African Charter on the Rights of Women in Africa, adopted July 11, 2003, art. 4(2) (j).

16 Lilian Chenwi, *Taking the Death Penalty Debate Further: The African Commission on Human and Peoples' Rights*, in AGAINST THE DEATH PENALTY: INTERNATIONAL INITIATIVES AND IMPLICATIONS 75, 78–80 (Jon Yorke ed., 2008).

17 Amnesty International (on behalf of Orton and Vera Chirwa) v. Malawi, Comm. 68/92 and 78/92, 8th Annual Activity Report: 1994–5 (A.C.H.P.R.); Constitutional Rights Project (in respect of Akamu and Others) v. Nigeria, Comm. 60/91, (2000) A.H.R.L.R. 180 (A.C.H.P.R. 1995); Forum of Conscience v. Sierra Leone, Comm. 223/98, (2000) A.H.R.L.R. 293 (A.C.H.P.R. 2000); Interights *et al.* (on behalf of Bosch) v. Botswana, Comm. 240/2001, (2003) A.H.R.L.R. 55 (A.C.H.P.R. 2003).

18 Lubuto v. Zambia, Comm.390/1990, (2001) A.H.R.L.R. 37 (U.N.H.R.C. 1995).

19 One suit was filed by a coalition of Gambian NGOs, and another was filed by a Nigerian NGO on behalf of the two Nigerians on death row. S.E.R.A.P. v. The Gambia, ECW/CCJ/AAP/11/12 (E.C.O.W.A.S. Sept. 2012) (Nigeria), *available at* http://serap-nigeria.org/the-filed-court-paper/; Press Release, Civil Soc'y Ass'ns Gam., CSAG Sues Gambia Government over Execution of Death Row Inmates (Oct. 12, 2012), *available at* http://civilsociety-gambia.org/csag-sues-gambia-government-over-execution-of-death-row-inmates/.

The British Colonial Legacy of Crime and Punishment

Prior to the advent of colonialism, the use and frequency of capital punishment varied enormously among precolonial African societies.[20] Because of the high value of labor in the lesser population-dense areas of precolonial Africa, punishment for crimes against person or property often relied on a system of economic compensation to the victim's family in lieu of or in addition to a personal penalty such as banishment or ostracism.[21] The criminal justice systems of many precolonial African societies directed their major focus to the victim rather than the offender, differentiating classes of homicide based on the victim's status rather than the perpetrator's *mens rea*.[22] Punishment was, in part, collective: an entire family or lineage could suffer the negative consequences of a wrongdoer's actions through the payment of compensation or spiritual harm, and as a result, all persons had a role to play in law enforcement. By contrast, the colonial state separated police from society and created a disciplined, uniformed unit that exercised violence and social control on behalf of the state.[23]

British colonialism was characterized by an overwhelming flexibility, guided by the policy of "indirect rule" in which the colonial system incorporated existing power structures, theoretically saving resources and inviting at least marginal African involvement in governance.[24] The system of indirect rule required chiefly hierarchies to provide local administration, confirming their existing authority or creating it in chiefless societies, and depended on separate court systems to administer African customary law among colonial subjects.[25] Customary law was uncodified law, based on the habits and social practices of the community through oral tradition, and courts established to apply such law in the colonial era typically operated with simplified rules of procedure and in local languages but

---

20 CHENWI, *supra* note 9 at 18–19 (noting that in some societies, sorcery or witchcraft, culpable homicide, treason, and some political offenses were seen as threatening the security of the community and beyond redress through compensation). Chenwi identifies, for instance, the Baganda (Uganda), Yoruba (Nigeria), and Luo (Kenya) as practicing the death penalty, and the Igbo (Nigeria) and Ama-Xosa (South Africa) as not possessing the death penalty. *Id.* The Tswana of Botswana apparently practiced capital punishment, while the Shona of Zimbabwe did not. *Compare* Andrew Novak, *Guilty of Murder with Extenuating Circumstances: Transparency and the Mandatory Death Penalty in Botswana*, 27 B.U. INT'L L.J. 173, 200–203 (2009) (note), *with* Enoch Dumbutshena, *The Death Penalty in Zimbabwe*, 58 REVUE INTERNATIONALE DE DROIT PENAL 521, 521 (1987). The Kikuyu in Kenya reserved the death penalty for habitual murderers and major sexual offenses, with compensation paid in less serious cases. Neil McGlashan, *Indigenous Kikuyu Education*, 63 AFR. AFF. 47, 51 (1964).

21 *See, e.g.*, H.F. Morris, *The Award of Blood Money in East African Manslaughter Cases*, 18 J. AFR. L. 104, 104 (1974); EMMET V. MITTLEBEELER, AFRICAN CUSTOM AND WESTERN LAW: THE DEVELOPMENT OF THE RHODESIAN CRIMINAL LAW FOR AFRICANS 164 (1976).

22 Daniel Ntanda-Nsereko, *Compensating the Victims of Crime in Botswana*, 33 J. AFR. L. 157, 157 (1989).

23 Justice Tankebe, *Colonialism, Legitimation, and Policing in Ghana*, 36 INT'L J. L., CRIME & JUST. 67, 69–70 (2008).

24 JOHN GUNTHER, INSIDE AFRICA 337 (1955) (noting the "divide-and-conquer" strategy behind indirect rule while acknowledging the administrative training it provided to low-level African officials); *but see* JOHN D. HARGREAVES, WEST AFRICA: THE FORMER FRENCH STATES 139–41 (1967) (holding that the direct rule of French, Portuguese, and Belgian colonies did not differ that greatly from British indirect rule as both were products of resource constraints and paternalism).

25 A.L. Bostock, *Political Institutions: British Colonial Policy*, *in* AFRICA SOUTH OF THE SAHARA: AN ASSESSMENT OF HUMAN AND MATERIAL RESOURCES 76–7 (Anne Welsh ed., 1951).

yielded to the supremacy of European law in a conflict.[26] Reliance on precolonial systems of local authority and law enforcement allowed the British to bring large populations under its control without overt military force. British African colonies received nearly identical penal codes modified from the Indian Penal Code and its predecessors, making few concessions to their African contexts.[27] However, some precolonial conceptions of criminal justice, such as payment of compensation for both civil and criminal offenses, did survive British rule, and the division between civil and criminal cases was never as complete as it was in Britain.[28]

The penal code served as a tool of social control. The colonial criminal justice system was both gendered and racialized, reflecting the same prejudices inherent in the imperial project itself.[29] Stereotypes of traditional gender roles influenced the treatment of female offenders in male-dominated criminal justice systems, and "black peril" laws in white settler colonies such as Kenya and Rhodesia harshly punished sexual transgressions between a black male and a white female, often with death.[30] While death sentences were readily dispensed in British Africa, executions were relatively rare. It was not unusual for half of all death sentences handed down in a given year to be commuted, even sparking opposition from community elders and traditional leaders in their leniency.[31] When executions did take place, they were often for premeditated crime, brutal murders, or attacks on colonial officials or white settlers. With the exception of the Mau Mau Emergency in Kenya in the 1950s, the British only sparingly used the death penalty for political crimes, though capital punishment was robustly used to punish political dissent in apartheid South Africa and white minority-ruled Rhodesia.[32]

Although British African colonies had customary courts that could apply local law in family, probate, and land tenure cases, murder and other serious crimes fell squarely in the province of European-style courts. The death penalty in British colonial Africa was a "stark

---

26 A. Arthur Schiller, *Law*, in THE AFRICAN WORLD: A SURVEY OF SOCIAL SCIENCE RESEARCH 166, 167 (Robert A. Lystad ed., 1965); Abdulmumini Oba, *The Future of African Customary Law*, in THE FUTURE OF AFRICAN CUSTOMARY LAW 58 *et seq*. (Jean Marie Fenrich, Paolo Galizzi & Tracy E. Higgins eds., 2011).

27 James S. Read, *Crime and Punishment in East Africa: The Twilight of Customary Law*, 10 HOW. L.J. 164, 165 (1964). *See also*, Simon Coldham, *Criminal Justice Policies in Commonwealth Africa: Trends and Prospects*, 44 J. AFR. L. 218, 219 (2000) (noting the importance of the 1899 Queensland Penal Code and the 1877 Gold Coast Criminal Procedure Code on the development of African penal codes).

28 Douglas Brown, *The Award of Compensation in Criminal Cases in East Africa*, 10 J. AFR. L. 33, 34 (1966).

29 Stacey Hynd, *Deadlier Than the Male? Women and the Death Penalty in Colonial Kenya and Nyasaland, c. 1920–57*, 12 WIENER ZEITSCHRIFT FÜR KRITISCHE AFRIKASTUDIEN (VIENNA J. AFR. STUD.) 13, 15 (2007).

30 J. Pape, *Black and White: The "Perils of Sex" in Colonial Zimbabwe*, J. SOUTH. AFR. STUD. 699, 700 (1990); David M. Anderson, *Sexual Threat and Settler Society: "Black Perils" in Kenya, c. 1907–30*, 38 J. IMPERIAL & COMMONW. HIST. 47, 62–3 (2010).

31 Stacey Hynd, *Killing the Condemned: The Practice and Process of Capital Punishment in British Africa, 1900–1950s*, 49 J. AFR. HIST. 403, 405 (2008); Ralph Tanner, *Crime and Punishment in East Africa*, 21 TRANSITION 35, 36 (1965).

32 DAVID ANDERSON, HISTORIES OF THE HANGED: THE DIRTY WAR IN KENYA AND THE END OF EMPIRE 6 (2005); Andrew Novak, *Abuse of State Power: The Mandatory Death Penalty for Political Crimes in Southern Rhodesia, 1963–1970*, 19(1) FUNDAMINA: J. LEGAL HIST. 28, 45 (2013); George Devenish, *The Historical and Jurisprudential Evolution and Background to the Application of the Death Penalty in South Africa and Its Relationship with Constitutional and Political Reform*, 5 S. AFR. J. CRIM. JUST. 1, 12–14 (1992).

enactment of colonial power," a crucial element of the state's coercive capacity, but also illustrative of its resource constraints and inefficiency.[33] In early years, executions were often public, designed to have deterrent effects and to impress settlers and subjects alike. In addition to capital punishment, both imprisonment and corporal punishment reflected culturally British penal goals. The prison was unknown in most of precolonial Sub-Saharan Africa, but grew rapidly with the onset of colonial rule.[34] Kenya, for instance, imprisoned a larger proportion of its population than any other colony in the British Empire in unusually harsh conditions.[35] British colonies also inherited compulsory corporal punishment, with a prescribed number of cane strokes for a given crime.[36] Colonial justice revealed the contradictions of colonial rule, viewing African subjects as violent and dangerous, but also as defendants entitled to individual due process rights. Anderson described British justice as "a blunt, brutal and unsophisticated instrument of oppression," and yet obsessed with the most parsimonious courtroom procedures, highly detailed recordkeeping, and meticulous adherence to the formal letter of penal and procedure codes.[37]

After independence, Ghana, Kenya, Malawi, and Uganda each endured three decades of one-party dictatorship, gross human rights violations, and severe economic underdevelopment. The regime of President for Life Hastings Banda in Malawi oscillated between violent repression and paternalistic authoritarianism, demanding absolute, unquestioned loyalty to Banda himself even as living conditions deteriorated markedly under his rule.[38] Hundreds of people were executed under the thirty-year Banda regime, and following Banda's electoral loss to Baliki Muluzi in 1994, the new president commuted all death sentences to life imprisonment.[39] Most notoriously, Malawian security officials abducted prominent politician Orton Chirwa from his refuge in Zambia in 1981 and sentenced him to death for treason to international outrage.[40] The erosion of democratic rule in Kenya likewise threatened due process rights even in capital cases. Under Kenyan strongman Daniel arap Moi, constitutional protections for prisoners and criminal defendants eroded and judges were removed from office for expressing a desire for greater independence. Lawyers were arrested for representing detainees and filing habeas petitions.[41] The Moi regime was particularly fond of abusing the prosecution of the crime of robbery with violence, which carried a mandatory death sentence but did not entitle an indigent defendant to free legal aid. Such charges were brought against opposition politician and human right attorney Koigi wa Wamwere in November 1993, which sharply inflamed ethnic

---

33 Hynd, *Killing the Condemned*, supra note 31 at 403.

34 Daniel Branch, *Imprisonment and Colonialism in Kenya, c. 1930–1952: Escaping the Carceral Archipelago*, 38 INT'L J. AFR. HIST. STUD. 239, 244 (2005).

35 ANDERSON, supra note 32 at 313.

36 Tanner, supra note 31 at 37.

37 ANDERSON, supra note 32 at 7.

38 Kings Phiri & Kenneth Ross, *Introduction: From Totalitarianism to Democracy in Malawi*, in DEMOCRATIZATION IN MALAWI: A STOCKTAKING 10–11 (Phiri & Ross eds., 1998).

39 *Malawi Retains Death Penalty*, MAIL & GUARDIAN (S. Afr.), May 24–30, 1996.

40 Chirwa was denied legal representation, held in solitary confinement, and denied adequate food and medical care. He died in prison while appealing his case to the African Commission on Human and Peoples' Rights. Chirwa v. Malawi, Comm. 64/92, 68/92, and 72/92, AHG/Res.240 (November 3, 1994) (A.C.H.P.R.).

41 Stanley D. Ross, *The Rule of Law and Lawyers in Kenya*, 30 J. MOD. AFR. STUD. 421, 424 (1992); Makau Mutua, *Justice Under Siege: The Rule of Law and Judicial Subservience in Kenya*, 23 HUM. RTS. Q. 96, 97 (2001).

tensions throughout the country.⁴² Amnesty International condemned "widespread report of torture and ill-treatment of prisoners," and prisoners experienced overcrowding, inadequate food rations, rampant disease, and physical mistreatment.⁴³ Similarly, under President Milton Obote, Uganda suffered economic ruin as one of the most corrupt administrations in postcolonial Africa. His regime was surpassed in its devastation by Idi Amin, after a coup in 1971; Amin militarized politics, imprisoned and executed political opponents, and seized property from elites for redistribution.⁴⁴ Uganda had a notoriously prolific history of extrajudicial executions, torture, killings in detention, and abductions.⁴⁵ Ghana as well had a legacy of human rights violations during the administrations of President Kwame Nkrumah and the military rulers who succeeded him.⁴⁶ During the military rule of Jerry Rawlings from 1981 until 1993 when he was democratically elected to the first of his two civilian terms, the death penalty by firing squad in Ghana was most often used to punish political dissidents, sometimes sentenced to death in abstentia.⁴⁷ Since 1993, Ghana has been de facto abolitionist, though more than 400 prisoners remained on death row as of 2009.⁴⁸ The death penalty's legacy of abuse undoubtedly contributed to abolitionist sentiment on the continent.

The Constitutional Framework of the Death Penalty in Common Law Africa

The independence constitutions of Commonwealth Africa were negotiated by departing British colonial officials and incoming nationalist representatives with little public input, often replicating British parliamentary democracy and containing extensive provisions relating to fundamental rights and freedoms.⁴⁹ Beginning with the Nigerian independence constitution in 1959, colonial officials required constitutional protections of fundamental rights and freedoms as a precondition to independence, coinciding with British interests in

---

42   David Bryan Sullivan, *Kenya: The Trial of Koigi wa Wamwere et al.*, 22 REV. AFR. POL. ECON. 262, 265–6 (1995).

43   Yash Vyas, *Alternatives to Imprisonment in Kenya*, 6 CRIM. L.F. 73, 76, 80 (1995); *Amnesty International Report 1995: Kenya*, AMNESTY INT'L, available at http://www.unhcr.org/refworld/docid/3ae6a9fb4c.html.

44   George Kanyeihamba, *Power that Rode Naked Through Uganda Under the Muzzle of a Gun*, in UGANDA NOW: BETWEEN DECAY & DEVELOPMENT 70, 72, 74, 77 (Holger Bernt Hansen & Michael Twaddle eds., 1988).

45   *See, e.g.*, Mamadou Tall, *Notes on the Civil and Political Strife in Uganda*, 12 ISSUE: J. OF OPINION 41, 41 (1982).

46   A. Kodzo Paaku Kludze, *Constitutional Rights and Their Relation with International Human Rights in Ghana*, 41 ISR. L. REV. 677, 683 (2008).

47   Joseph Appiahene-Gyamfi, *Violent Crime in Ghana: The Case of Robbery*, 26 J. CRIM. JUST. 409, 412 (1998). The second largest category of executions occurred for those convicted of robbery or theft, particularly white collar and other economic crimes, as these could be tried in political tribunals without judicial review. *Id.* at 415.

48   Joseph Appiahene-Gyamfi, *Crime and Punishment in the Republic of Ghana: A Country Profile*, 33 INT'L J. COMP. & APPLIED CRIM. JUST. 309, 320 (2009). *See also* Oswald K. Seneadza, *The Death Penalty in Ghanaian Law and Practice: Can Its Retention in Contemporary Time Be Justified?*, 37 COMMONW. L. BULL. 115, 130 (2011).

49   *See* William Dale, *The Making and Remaking of Commonwealth Constitutions*, 42 INT'L & COMP. L.Q. 67, 67-8 (1993).

protecting the land rights of white settlers and other business interests from expropriation.[50] These fundamental rights provisions, based on the European Convention of Human Rights, were hardly absolute, subject to detailed limitations and derogations clauses.[51] Within a decade, however, few of these constitutions survived unaltered: they were suspended, abrogated, or amended beyond recognition. Perhaps because of the strong role played by British colonial officials in drafting the original documents, these early constitutions failed to strike a durable political balance and were ill-suited to the political realities of the postcolonial world in which ambitious new governments sought to expand their power.[52] Not until the late 1980s and early 1990s did changing international pressures allow for the rewriting of African constitutions, as former one-party states enshrined multiparty politics, former socialist regimes enacted capitalist systems, and former military regimes transitioned to civilian rule.[53]

Except for those of South Africa and Namibia, which possess absolute right to life clauses, every constitution in former British West, East, and Southern Africa has a limitation on the right to life provision that explicitly or implicitly saves the death penalty from constitutional challenge.[54] Most of these clauses mirror the counterpart in the European Convention on Human Rights: "No one shall be deprived of his life save in the execution of a sentence of a court following his conviction of a crime for which

---

50 Anthony Wambugu Munene, *The Bill of Rights and Constitutional Order: A Kenyan Perspective*, 2 AFR. HUM. RTS. L.J. 135, 154 (2002). Ghana and Tanzania are exceptions. While Ghana's independence in 1957 preceded the impetus to enshrine fundamental rights in the constitution, Tanzania explicitly rejected the need for codifying fundamental rights. However, in 1984 a bill of rights was added to the constitution by amendment. JENNIFER A. WIDNER, BUILDING THE RULE OF LAW: FRANCIS NYALALI AND THE ROAD TO JUDICIAL INDEPENDENCE IN AFRICA 154, 161–3, 170 (2001). Ghana has also since added a bill of rights. Kludze, *supra* note 46 at 683–4.

51 Muna Ndulo & Robert Kent, *Constitutionalism in Zambia: Past, Present, and Future*, 40 J. AFR. L. 256, 263 (1996).

52 Stephen B. Pfeiffer, *Notes on the Role of the Judiciary in the Constitutional Systems of East Africa Since Independence*, 10 CASE W. RES. J. INT'L L. 11, 30 (1978) (noting that the fundamental rights portions of the constitutions often remained intact).

53 The literature on this "third wave" of constitution-making is voluminous. *See, e.g.*, James Thuo Gathii, *Popular Authorship and Constitution Making: Comparing and Contrasting the DRC and Kenya*, 49 WM. & MARY L. REV. 1109, 1109 n. 1 (2008) (noting that as many as twenty-five new constitutions entered into force in Africa after 1989); Bereket Habte Selassie, *Creating a Constitution for Eritrea*, 9 J. DEMOCRACY 164, 173–4 (1998); Muna Ndulo & Robert Kent, *Constitutionalism in Zambia: Past, Present, and Future*, 40 J. AFR. L. 256 (1996); Margaret Hall & Tom Young, *Recent Constitutional Developments in Mozambique*, 35 J. AFR. L. 102, 114 (1991) (describing the new Mozambican constitution, which installed a capitalist economy and a multiparty democracy).

54 *See* BOTSWANA CONST. art. 4(1); GAMBIA CONST. art. 18(1); GHANA CONST. art. 13(1); LESOTHO CONST. art. 5(2); MALAWI CONST. art. 16; MAURITIUS CONST. art. 4(a); NIGERIA CONST. art. 33(1); SIERRA LEONE CONST. art. 16(1); SUDAN CONST. art. 33(1); SWAZILAND CONST. art. 15(1); UGANDA CONST. art. 22(1); ZAMBIA CONST. art. 12(1); ZIMBABWE CONST. art. 12(1) (1980), art. 48(2) (2013). *Compare* KENYA CONST. art. 26 (2010). Again Tanzania is the exception; it does not possess a true death penalty savings clause, but Tanzanian courts have interpreted a general savings clause protecting existing laws and permitting limitations on fundamental rights if they are in the public interest as protecting the death penalty from constitutional challenge. *See* TANZ. CONST. art. 30(2); Mbushuu v. Republic, [1995] T.L.R. 97 (Tanz. C.A.), *reversing* Republic v. Mbushuu, [1994] 2 L.R.C. 335 (Tanz. H.C.). The death penalty is abolished in South Africa and Namibia. *See* NAMIBIA CONST. art. 6; S. AFR. CONST. art. 11. South Sudan's transitional constitution, effective at independence on July 9, 2011 until a permanent constitution enters into force, explicitly saves the death penalty for "extremely serious offences," though it does not define these. S. SUDAN CONST. art. 21.

this penalty is provided by law."⁵⁵ Recently, several constitutions have departed from this generic wording. Swaziland's constitution specifically prohibits the mandatory death penalty.⁵⁶ The Gambian constitution appears to prohibit the death penalty for crime other than aggravated or premeditated murder, although the Supreme Court construed the clause as permitting the death penalty for treason in October 2012.⁵⁷ Several constitutions narrow the classes of persons who could be subjected to the death penalty. Sudan's constitution prohibits the death penalty for persons below age 18 or on pregnant or lactating women, or those above the age of 70 except for certain offenses under Islamic law.⁵⁸ Similarly, the new constitution of Zimbabwe, overwhelmingly passed in a March 2013 referendum, prohibits the death penalty for women and persons under age 21 or over age 70. The new constitution also restricts the death penalty to "murder committed in aggravating circumstances" and requires that courts have "discretion whether or not to impose the penalty."⁵⁹

Also relevant for constitutional challenges to the mandatory death penalty are the prohibitions on cruel, inhuman, or degrading punishment, a provision that exists in every constitution in common law Africa.⁶⁰ While courts in Africa have resisted finding the death penalty itself or individual methods of execution to be cruel and degrading form of punishment, they have been more receptive to incremental or collateral challenges. One starting place has typically been challenges to adult and juvenile corporal punishment, which have succeeded in a number of common law African countries.⁶¹ Kenya, Malawi, and Uganda each abolished corporal punishment before considering mandatory death challenges.⁶² Finally, more modern African constitutions largely avoid the minefield posed by broad Caribbean-style savings clauses. Only four African constitutions contain a partial savings clause on the Caribbean model, prohibiting constitutional challenges to forms of punishment based on the cruel and inhuman punishment clauses: Botswana, Lesotho,

---

55   European Convention for the Protection of Human Rights and Fundamental Freedoms, 213 U.N.T.S. 222, *entered into force* Sept. 3, 1953, art. 2.
56   SWAZILAND CONST. art. 15(2).
57   GAMBIA CONST. art. 18(2) ("...[N]o court in The Gambia shall be competent to impose a sentence of death for any offence unless the sentence is prescribed by law and the offence involves violence, or the administration of any toxic substance, resulting in the death of another person"); Badjie v. State, S.C. Crim. App. 1–7/2011 (October 19, 2012) (Gambia S.C.). This case was an appeal of the death sentences for treason for coup plotter Lt. Gen. Lang Tombong Tamba and six associates.
58   SUDAN CONST. arts. 33(1)–(2).
59   ZIMBABWE CONST. art. 48(2) (2013).
60   BOTSWANA CONST. art. 7(1); GAMBIA CONST. art. 21; GHANA CONST. art. 15(2); KENYA CONST. art. 29(f); LESOTHO CONST. art. 8(1); MALAWI CONST. art. 19(3); MAURITIUS CONST. art. 7(1); NIGERIA CONST. art. 34(1) (a); S. SUDAN TRANSITIONAL CONST. art. 18; TANZ. CONST. art. 13(6) (3); UGANDA CONST. art. 24; ZAMBIA CONST. art. 15; ZIMBABWE CONST. art. 53. Sudan's constitutional provision follows a slightly different format, but nonetheless prohibits torture. SUDAN CONST. art. 20.
61   *See, e.g.*, Petrus v. State, 1984 Bots.L.R. 14 (C.A.) (abolishing repeated or delayed corporal punishment for adults); State v. Ncube, 1987 2 Zim.L.R. 246 (S.C.) (abolishing adult corporal punishment); Ex Parte: Attorney-General, In Re: Corporal Punishment by Organs of State, [1991] NASC 2 (Namib. S.C.) (abolishing adult and juvenile corporal punishment); State v. Williams, 1995 (3) S.A. 632 (C.C.) (abolishing adult and juvenile corporal punishment); Banda v. People, (2002) A.H.R.L.R. 260, (Zam. H.C. 1999) (abolishing adult corporal punishment).
62   KENYA CONST. art. 29(e) (prohibiting infliction of corporal punishment for both adults and juveniles); MALAWI CONST. art. 19(4) (same); Kyamanywa v. Uganda, Crim. App. 16 (1999) (unreported) (Uganda C.C.), *confirmed in* Oryem Richard & Another v. Uganda, [2003] UGSC 30 (invalidating corporal punishment in Uganda).

Mauritius, and Sierra Leone.[63] No constitution contains a general savings clause similar to those in Barbados and Trinidad and Tobago that save all existing laws from constitutional challenge based on fundamental rights provisions, and indeed the more recent constitutions in Sub-Saharan Africa contain clauses that expressly *fail* to save unconstitutional pre-existing laws.[64] More troubling from a human rights perspective are constitutional provisions that authorize broad derogations or suspensions of human rights during states of emergency. While the right to life and the prohibition on cruel and degrading punishment are never subject to suspension or derogation, many procedural and due process rights are subject to limitation, including the ban on detention without trial.[65]

Several African countries have had mass commutations or are under unofficial moratoria.[66] As in the Caribbean, the anti-death penalty movement has achieved a measure of success in the courtroom, pursuing an incremental strategy. Zimbabwean advocates pioneered challenges based on the death row phenomenon due to undue delay or conditions on death row.[67] The Zimbabwean Supreme Court built on other death row syndrome decisions arising out of the European Court of Human Rights, the Supreme Courts of Canada and India, and the Privy Council.[68] During this "golden era of human rights litigation" in the country, challenges in Zimbabwean courts resulted in successful challenge to solitary confinement, reduced diet, adult and juvenile whipping, retroactive punishments, and punishments premised on "mute confessions."[69] Some of these victories were later reversed by constitutional amendments and a pending challenge to hanging as a method of execution was pre-empted by the legislature, but the decisions are still persuasive in

---

63 BOTSWANA CONST. art. 7(2); LESOTHO CONST. art. 8(2); MAURITIUS CONST. art. 7(2); SIERRA LEONE CONST. art. 20(2). While the constitutions of Botswana (1967) and Mauritius (1964) are independence constitutions, the clauses in Lesotho's (1993) and Sierra Leone's (1991) constitutions are more troubling because they were drafted in the "third wave" of constitutionalism in Africa. As discussed below, Kenya's former constitution contained such a clause, but the 2010 replacement does not. KENYA CONST. art. 74(2) (1963).

64 Generally, these laws require interpreting existing laws in conformity with the new constitution to the extent possible. They vary in wording and some are contained in transitional schedules to the constitution, but they reference the judicial prerogative to strike down pre-existing unconstitutional laws. *See, e.g.*, GHANA CONST. art. 5–6; KENYA CONST. sched. 6, art. 7(1); MALAWI CONST. art. 200; NIGERIA CONST. art. 315(1); UGANDA CONST. art. 214(1). Tanzania's constitution allows the High Court to certify unconstitutional laws to the legislature for revision within a certain time period. TANZ. CONST. art. 30(5).

65 JOHN HATCHARD, MUNA NDULO, & PETER SLINN, COMPARATIVE CONSTITUTIONALISM AND GOOD GOVERNANCE IN THE COMMONWEALTH: AN EASTERN AND SOUTHERN AFRICAN PERSPECTIVE 276 et seq. (2004). For a table comparing Southern African constitutions and the rights that are permissibly limited during states of emergency, see *id.* at 286.

66 *Death Row Prisoners Freed in Nigeria*, AMNESTY INT'L NEWS, August 26, 2009, http://www.amnesty.org/en/news-and-updates/good-news/death-row-prisoners-freed-nigeria-20090826; Report, *Death Sentences and Executions 2011*, AMNESTY INT'L, ACT 50/001/2012 (March 2012) (noting commutations in Sierra Leone, Swaziland, and Zambia and indicating that a number of other countries, such as Malawi and Zimbabwe, have no intention of carrying out executions).

67 Catholic Commission for Justice and Peace in Zimbabwe v. A.G., (1993) L.R.C. 277 (Zimbabwe S.C.).

68 Soering v. U.K., 11 E.H.R.R. 439 (1989) (Eur. Ct. H.R.); Pratt & Morgan v. A.G. Jamaica, 43 W.I.R. 340 (P.C.); Triveniben v. State of Gujarat, (1989) 1 S.C.R. 509 (India); U.S. v. Burns, [2001] S.C.R. 283 (Can.).

69 Adrian de Bourbon, *Human Rights Litigation in Zimbabwe: Past Present and Future*, 3 AFR. HUM. RTS. L.J. 195, 209–10 (2003).

other jurisdictions.[70] While the incremental strategy bore fruit, direct challenges to the constitutionality of the death penalty uniformly failed. In 1998, the Supreme Court of Nigeria upheld the constitutionality of the death penalty in *Kalu v. State* after widely citing other Commonwealth authority, indicating that the Nigerian constitution clearly permitted the sentence even if it was otherwise cruel and degrading.[71]

The most significant constitutional challenge to the death penalty in the African context is *State v. Makwanyane*, in which the Constitutional Court of South Africa unanimously struck down the death sentence for murder as contrary to the right to life and human dignity and the right to be free from cruel, inhuman, or degrading punishment.[72] While the decision provided a gold standard for abolitionists elsewhere on the continent, the persuasive value of the Constitutional Court's decision is limited by the unique wording of the South African constitution.[73] Perhaps the Constitutional Court's greatest bequest to the rest of common law Africa is not the direct holding in *Makwanyane*, but the Court's liberal interpretation of the constitution's fundamental rights provisions, reading them in a manner that promotes the values of a democratic society and that favors the rights of the individual over the powers of the state.[74] Future incremental challenges to the death penalty on the African continent will require at least that much.

The African Mandatory Death Penalty Challenges

Death penalty abolition in Sub-Saharan Africa is an incremental process, nurtured by small steps such as stays of execution, grants of clemency, and appellate clarification. Because former British African colonies inherited similar fundamental rights protections in their postcolonial constitutional orders, including fair trial rights and prohibitions on cruel or degrading punishments, these countries possess a common constitutional vulnerability as the mandatory nature of the death penalty is not specifically required by any modern African constitution.[75] Constitutional challenges to the mandatory death penalty in Kenya, Malawi, and Uganda relied heavily on the Privy Council's Caribbean jurisprudence and the earlier case law from India and the United States. At the same time, these challenges made their own contribution to the corpus of global death penalty jurisprudence, which will be cited in the future as the mandatory death penalty yields not only in Africa but elsewhere in the common law world.

---

70 Anthony Gubbay, *Human Rights in Criminal Justice Proceedings: The Zimbabwean Experience*, *in* THE PROTECTION OF HUMAN RIGHTS IN AFRICAN CRIMINAL PROCEEDINGS 312 (M. Cherif Bassiouni & Ziyad Motala eds., 1995). *Catholic Commission* may well be the most cited decision ever written by an African court of final appeal. *See, e.g.*, Kobedi v. State, [2003] BWCA 22 (Botswana C.A.); Attorney General v. Kigula, [2009] 2 E.A.L.R. 1; *see also* Knight v. Florida, 528 U.S. 990 (1999) (Breyer, J., dissenting to denial of cert.).

71 Kalu v. State, [1997–1998] All N.L.R. 407, 443 (Nigeria S.C. 1998).

72 State v. Makwanyane, 1995 (3) S.A. 391.

73 *But see*, SANGMIN BAE, WHEN THE STATE NO LONGER KILLS: INTERNATIONAL HUMAN RIGHTS NORMS AND ABOLITION OF CAPITAL PUNISHMENT 61 (2007).

74 HATCHARD, NDULO, & SLINN, *supra* note 65 at 181.

75 The one exception, analyzed below, appears to be Ghana's constitutionally authorized mandatory death penalty for treason. GHANA CONST. art. 3(3).

The Constitutional Court of Malawi: Kafantayeni

According to Malawi's Penal Code, dating from 1930, five crimes carried the death penalty: treason, rape, murder, armed robbery, and burglary. Only for murder was it mandatory.[76] In 2007, the Constitutional Court of Malawi found the mandatory death penalty violated the right to be free from cruel, inhuman punishment; the right to a fair trial; and the right of access to the court system.[77] The decision cited other Caribbean jurisprudence extensively, finding *Reyes v. Queen* to be particularly persuasive, as well as the South African Constitutional Court's decision in *Makwanyane*. Ultimately, the Court determined that the lack of individualized sentencing discretion could result in the infliction of capital punishment on a defendant whose crime did not warrant the penalty, and therefore constituted cruel and degrading punishment.[78]

The Constitutional Court also found that the penalty violated the right to a fair trial because it denied an accused person an individualized sentencing determination.[79] The International Covenant on Civil and Political Rights required that every person convicted of a crime must be permitted effective appellate review, the Court reasoned, and the mandatory nature of a death sentence precluded a higher court from reviewing a sentence on its own merits.[80] For a similar reason, the Court also found that a mandatory death penalty violated the right of access to justice as enshrined in Malawi's constitution, a ground raised *sua sponte* by the Court.[81] Because the mandatory death penalty did not permit a sentencing hearing and precluded appellate review of a sentence, it effectively denied an accused person's right to access the judicial system for resolving legal disputes.

Although the state did not appeal in *Kafantayeni*, the Supreme Court of Appeal, Malawi's highest court, confirmed the judgment in *Jacob v. Republic*.[82] The Court affirmed *Kafantayeni* in its entirety and indicated that it was "largely persuaded" by the jurisprudence of the Privy Council.[83] Using a more textual approach than the Constitutional Court, the Supreme Court interpreted Article 42 of the constitution, the "right to adduce and challenge evidence," as a basis for finding that the mandatory death penalty violated an accused's right to a fair trial by not permitting consideration of mitigating factors.[84]

Although the Constitutional Court avoided reliance on the right to life provision of the Malawi Constitution in *Kafantayeni*, lower courts have cited the decision for the proposition that the right to life is inviolable except in the application of a discretionary death penalty.[85] In *Republic v. Cheuka*, the Malawi High Court convicted a police officer of manslaughter due to police brutality, holding that extrajudicial police killing was a violation

---

76 Malawi Law Commission, Discussion Paper No. 1, Human Rights Under the Constitution of the Republic of Malawi 2 (2006), *available at www.lawcom.mw/docs/discussion_paper1_human_rights.pdf;* Mwiza Jo Nkhata, *Bidding Farewell to Mandatory Capital Punishment: Francis Kafantayeni and Others v Attorney General*, 2007 Malawi L.J. 103, 110.
77 Kafantayeni v. Attorney-General, [2007] MWHC 1.
78 *Id.* at 9.
79 *Id.* at 12.
80 *Id.* at 12–13.
81 *Id.* at 14, *citing* Malawi Const. art.41(2).
82 Jacob v. Republic, MSCA Crim. App. No. 16/2006 (July 19, 2007) (Malawi S.C.A.) (unrep.). The plaintiff in *Jacob* claimed that he had been acting in a state of temporary insanity induced by a narcotic, which could have qualified as a mitigating circumstance.
83 *Id.* at 3–5.
84 *Id.* at 6.
85 *See* Malawi Const. art. 16.

of the right to life.[86] In *Cheuka*, the judge wrote that "the right to life ranks supreme to all other rights guaranteed by [the] Constitution," the "most fundamental of all rights in that it is a prerequisite for the enjoyment or exercise of all other rights."[87] After analyzing the jurisprudence of the European Court of Human Rights and the United Nations Code of Conduct for Law Enforcement, the judge concluded that an extrajudicial killing at the hands of a police officer fell below international law enforcement standards. This case suggests that lower courts in Malawi will apply the *Kafantayeni* rationale in other contexts.

Progress in resentencing death row prisoners after *Kafantayeni* has been slow. As of 2010, only a handful of the nearly 200 persons on death row had even consulted a lawyer and not a single resentencing hearing had taken place.[88] Despite a theoretical constitutional right of legal aid at state expense, the shortage of legal representation in Malawi is particularly acute as only a handful of legal aid lawyers serve the entire country.[89] Following the trend elsewhere in Sub-Saharan Africa, Malawi is experimenting with allowing non-lawyers such as paralegals and law students in university legal clinics to shoulder some of the burden in representing indigent criminal defendants.[90] In addition, Malawi's prison system is vastly overcrowded, with shortages of food, clothing, and medical supplies common. In 2009, the Constitutional Court found that prevailing prison conditions, which resulted in more than 200 deaths due to lack of ventilation over two years, were unconstitutionally cruel, inhuman, and degrading.[91] The Court gave Parliament eighteen months to allocate sufficient resources to ensure that Malawi's prisons met minimal international standards.[92] As in *Kafantayeni*, the Court looked to international and foreign sources in analyzing Malawi's cruel and degrading treatment clause.

The Supreme Court of Uganda: Kigula

The decision of the Ugandan Constitutional Court in *Kigula v. Attorney General* determined that the mandatory death penalty and inordinate delay in carrying out executions violated the constitution, while upholding a discretionary death penalty and hanging as a method of execution in an omnibus challenge.[93] The Court closely interpreted domestic precedent and engaged in a textual constitutional analysis. The concurring opinions used a range of constitutional interpretive methods, including cultural arguments, framers' intent, and popular opinion.[94] The dissents argued that the criminal justice system provided sufficient

---

86   Republic v. Cheuka et al., Crim. Case No. 73/2008 (Apr. 2, 2009) (Malawi H.C.).
87   *Id.*
88   Chesa Boudin, *Making an Impact in Malawi*, CHICAGO LAWYER MAGAZINE, May 27, 2010, *available at* http://www.chicagolawyermagazine.com/Archives/2010/06/01/7530.aspx.
89   Hillery Andersen, *Justice Delayed in Malawi's Criminal Justice System: Paralegals v. Lawyers*, 1 INT'L J. CRIM. JUST. 2 (2006); *see also* MALAWI CONST. art. 42(1) (c).
90   Boudin, *supra* note 88.
91   Masangano v. Attorney General, (2009) A.H.R.L.R. 353 (Malawi H.C. 2009).
92   *See also*, Michael Wines, *The Forgotten of Africa, Wasting Away in Jails Without Trial*, N.Y. TIMES, November 6, 2005, http://www.nytimes.com/2005/11/06/international/africa/06prisons.html.
93   Kigula et al. v. Attorney General, Constitutional Petition No. 6/2003 at 61–3 (2005) (Uganda C.C.).
94   *Id.* at 68–9, 116. *See also*, *id.* at 117–18 (Twinomujuni, J., concurring); 17–23 (Byamugisha, J., concurring).

safeguards against arbitrariness, including legal aid for indigent defendants, the right of automatic appeal, and the right to petition for clemency.[95]

Both parties cross-appealed the Constitutional Court decision to the Supreme Court of Uganda. The Supreme Court voted unanimously to uphold the death penalty per se, but to strike down the mandatory death sentence for murder and unconstitutional delay and conditions on death row.[96] The Court also voted 6 to 1 to turn away the challenge to hanging as a method of execution, emphasizing the conclusions of the Constitutional Review Commission ten years earlier as evidence of drafters' intent, finding that the "inclusion of the death penalty in the Constitution was therefore not accidental or a mere afterthought. It was carefully deliberated upon."[97] In addition to a savings clause, the Constitution contemplated existence of the death penalty through a right to legal representation for capital defendants at state expense and the right to seek clemency.[98]

The Supreme Court agreed with the lower court's finding that a fair trial included both conviction and sentencing stages and that a defendant was entitled to present mitigating evidence subject to appellate review.[99] The Court also addressed a novel separation of powers argument, finding that a mandatory death penalty tied the hands of judges in their inherent constitutional power to determine both conviction and sentence. Both the Constitutional Court and the Supreme Court interpreted domestic precedent on cruel and inhuman punishment closely, relying on *Kyamanywa v. Uganda*, which invalidated adult corporal punishment, and *Abuki v. Attorney General*, which invalidated banishment as a penalty for witchcraft.[100]

In accepting the argument concerning the death row syndrome, the Supreme Court looked in detail at "demeaning" prison conditions.[101] The Court found that the mandatory death penalty was a sentence in itself and consequently fell within the scope of *Abuki*, which laid out guidelines for determining whether a sentence constituted cruel and inhuman punishment. However, hanging was only a method of execution; consequently, *Abuki* did not apply. This distinction is in tension with the Privy Council's jurisprudence holding that the mandatory death penalty is not a judicial punishment per se (and therefore subject to Caribbean-style partial savings clauses), but rather simply a method of sentencing. The dissent by Justice Egonda-Ntende laid out in detail the harsh effects of hanging and argued that, like the mandatory nature of the death penalty, hanging was not specifically saved under the constitution and could be found unconstitutional.[102]

Kigula has led to a revolution in criminal sentencing. In April 2010, the Ugandan Court of Appeal upheld two death sentences after considering mitigating factors such as a three-year delay in prison before trial, remorse for the murder of a relative, and dependents of

---

95 *Id.* at 159–64, 169–73 (Mapagi-Bahigeine J, dissenting); 179 (Kavuma, J, dissenting).
96 Attorney General v. Kigula, [2009] 2 E.A.L.R. 1, 30 (Uganda S.C.).
97 *Id.* at 12.
98 UGANDA CONST. arts. 22(1), 28(3) (e), 121(5).
99 *Kigula*, [2009] 2 E.A.L.R. at 20, 22.
100 Abuki v. Attorney General, [1999] UGCC 5, *aff'd by* Attorney General v. Abuki, [2001] 1 L.R.C. 63 (Uganda S.C.); Kyamanywa v. Uganda, Const. Ref. No. 10 of 2000 (Dec. 14, 2001) (Uganda C.C.) (referred from Uganda Supreme Court in Crim. App. No. 16 of 1999, dated July 4, 2000). *Kyamanywa* was confirmed by the Supreme Court in Richard Oryem & Another v. Uganda, [2003] UGSC 30 (September 16, 2003).
101 *Kigula*, [2009] 2 E.A.L.R. at 24.
102 *Id.* at 43–6 (Egonda-Ntende, J., dissenting).

the defendants.[103] In a similar case, the Court ruled that aggravating factors outweighed mitigating factors where the defendant violently murdered an elderly woman.[104] In mitigation, the defendant-appellant argued that he was a first-time offender, that he was on remand for four years before conviction, and that he had a wife and five children. He also raised defenses of intoxication and provocation, which were legal defenses raised at trial.

The Ugandan Court of Appeal reversed a death sentence in June 2010 where mitigating factors outweighed aggravating factors in the case of *Jino v. Uganda*.[105] In that case, the defendant-appellant was convicted of armed robbery. He pleaded in his defense that he was a first-time offender, that he had been in prison for over three years before conviction, and that he had a wife and four children.[106] The Court found that the trial judge had properly convicted the defendant of armed robbery, but determined that a death sentence was inappropriate because even though three gunshots were fired, no life was lost.[107] In October 2011, the Ugandan newspaper *The Monitor* reported that the Ugandan High Court reduced three death sentences for convicts in aggravated robbery trials to imprisonment of fifteen and twenty years, respectively, evidencing the Court's continued skepticism of death sentences for non-murder crimes.[108]

By ruling that all prisoners on death row for longer than three years should have their sentences commuted to life imprisonment "without remission," the Supreme Court's decision in *Kigula* created an interpretive problem since the Prisons Act defined "imprisonment for life" as twenty years' imprisonment rather than "whole life" imprisonment.[109] In addition to the twenty-year rule under the Prisons Act, prison officials retained some discretion to shorten the sentence for good behavior.[110] The Supreme Court squarely confronted the issue of the meaning of life imprisonment under Section 47(6) of the Prisons Act. In *Tigo v. Uganda*, the Supreme Court clarified *Kigula* by indicating that whole life or natural life imprisonment was warranted for those prisoners who were spared the death penalty, rather than imprisonment for twenty years, because *Kigula* intended to impose the next most severe sentence, and term sentences longer than twenty years existed.[111] As Mujuzi writes, however, the decision conflicts with a growing international trend to limit life imprisonment terms to a period of years rather than whole or natural life.[112]

The legal systems of both Uganda and Malawi have recently come under intense international scrutiny because of the criminalization of homosexuality. In Malawi, a same-sex couple was sentenced to fourteen years' imprisonment with hard labor following a

---

103 Calvin Omasige and James Okia v. Uganda, Crim. App. No. 179 of 2003 (April 6, 2010) (Uganda C.A.).
104 Yasin Feni v. Uganda, Crim. App. No. 51 of 2006 (June 28, 2010) (Uganda C.A.).
105 Adama Jino v. Uganda, Crim. App. No. 50 of 2006 (June 23, 2010) (Uganda C.A.).
106 *Id.* at 3.
107 *Id.* at 8.
108 Anthony Wesaka, *Three Convicts on Death Row Survive Hangman*, THE MONITOR, Oct. 20, 2011. On the other hand, the Ugandan High Court has handed out discretionary death sentences after consideration of mitigating circumstances in an armed robbery case. *See, e.g.*, Uganda v. Aurien, Crim. Case No. 12/2010, [2010] UGHC 102.
109 JAMIL DDAMULIRA MUJUZI, LIFE IMPRISONMENT IN INTERNATIONAL CRIMINAL TRIBUNALS AND SELECTED AFRICAN JURISDICTIONS—MAURITIUS, SOUTH AFRICA AND UGANDA 272–5 (May 13, 2009) (LL.D. Thesis, University of the Western Cape).
110 Prisons Act, 2006, No. 17, §§ 84–6 (Uganda).
111 Tigo v. Uganda, Crim. App. No. 170 of 2003 (Mar. 23, 2009) (Uganda S.C.).
112 MUJUZI, *supra* note 109 at 283–90.

sodomy conviction.[113] After the sentence was upheld on appeal, international pressure forced President Bingu wa Mutharika to pardon the couple.[114] After Mutharika died in office in 2012, his successor President Joyce Banda committed to repeal of Malawi's anti-sodomy law, a priority of HIV/AIDS activists and donors.[115] In Uganda, the Anti-Homosexuality Bill of 2009 authorized a mandatory death sentence for persons convicted of "aggravated" sodomy or HIV transmission, eliciting worldwide condemnation despite facial unconstitutionality of the death penalty provision after *Kigula*.[116] While neither country is likely to increase criminal penalties of this nature given the demands of international HIV-related donor assistance, both cases underscore the extent to which harsh criminal punishments for homosexuality retain popular support. Like Malawi, Uganda has also faced legal aid shortages in post-*Kigula* challenges. A new initiative, developed in October 2011 and funded by the Uganda-based Foundation for Human Rights Initiatives and the British government, will provide free legal assistance to fifteen inmates on death row who are challenging their sentences.[117]

In June 2013, Uganda issued sentencing guidelines to promote uniformity in criminal sentencing. The guidelines were the product of a twenty-five member committee appointed by the Chief Justice. According to the guidelines, a judge has the discretion to sentence an offender to between thirty years and life imprisonment, as well as a possible death sentence, for offenses in which death is the maximum sentence. The guidelines explicitly discourage judges from sentencing prisoners to death, emphasizing that the penalty is only for the "rarest of the rare" cases. The guidelines provide the factors that a judge should consider in determining a sentence, including the offender's state of mind, the impact of the crime on the community, and the circumstances of the offense itself, deducting any time served prior to conviction.[118]

The Court of Appeal of Kenya: Mutiso

In July 2010, the Kenyan Court of Appeal invalidated the mandatory death sentence for murder in *Mutiso v. Republic*.[119] The defendant was convicted of a premeditated murder and sentenced to death, although his sentence was reduced to life imprisonment in the August 2009 mass commutation of all death row prisoners by President Mwai Kibaki.[120] The Court accepted jurisdiction notwithstanding the commutation or the attorney general's concession that the mandatory death penalty was unconstitutional. Ultimately, the Court

---

113 Jamil Ddamulira Mujuzi, *Discrimination Against Homosexuals in Malawi: Lessons from the Recent Developments*, 11 INT'L J. DISCRIMINATION & L. 150, 156 (2011).

114 *Malawi Gay Couple Released After Presidential Pardon*, BBC NEWS, May 30, 2011 available at http://www.bbc.co.uk/news/10194057.

115 Godfrey Mapondera & David Smith, *Malawi Suspends Anti-Gay Laws as MPs Debate Repeal*, GUARDIAN (U.K.), Nov. 5, 2012, www.guardian.co.uk/world/2012/nov/05/malawi-gay-laws-debate-repeal.

116 Anti-Homosexuality Bill, No. 18 of 2009, Uganda Gazette No. 47, Sept. 25, 2009. *See also*, Cecilia Strand, *Kill Bill! Ugandan Human Rights Organizations' Attempts to Influence the Media's Coverage of the Anti-Homosexuality Bill*, 13 CULTURE, HEALTH & SEXUALITY 917, 917–19 (2011).

117 Ephraim Kasozi and Betty Ndagire, *Death Sentence Inmates to Get Free Legal Services*, THE MONITOR, Oct. 15, 2011.

118 Edward Ssekika & Sulaiman Kakaire, *Order, Certainty in New Sentencing Guide*, THE OBSERVER (Kampala), June 19, 2013 (retrieved from AllAfrica.com).

119 Mutiso v. Republic, [2011] 1 E.A.L.R. 342 (Kenya C.A.).

120 Republic v. Mutiso, Crim. Case No 55/2004 (Feb. 29, 2008) (Kenya H.C.).

invalidated the mandatory death penalty for murder on the grounds that the sentence violated the right to life, that it constituted cruel, inhuman, and degrading punishment, and that it violated the right to a fair trial.[121] A week after the decision in *Mutiso*, Kenyan voters went to the polls and overwhelmingly ratified a new constitution.[122] The new constitution contains a death penalty savings clause, although it is deliberately vaguer than the former constitution.[123]

In *Mutiso*, the Court of Appeal's framing of the right to life violation was unique. The Malawian court did not reach the issue, and the Ugandan court avoided it by finding that the death penalty was saved and thus could not violate the right to life.[124] According to the Kenyan court, where the mandatory death penalty fell on defendants who did not necessarily merit the special penalty of death, a right to life violation occurred.[125] Constitutional litigation over the right to life is particularly prolific in Kenya, and legal debates implicating the right to life clause have arisen out of the Court of Appeal and the constitutional reform process concerning abortion access, domestic violence, and environmental rights.[126]

The decision had other similarities to *Kigula* and *Kafantayeni*. Although the Court did not explicitly find that the mandatory death penalty violated the separation of powers because of legislative constraints on judicial sentencing discretion, it quoted this holding from *Kigula*.[127] The Court's caution was warranted because the separation of powers was drastically altered under Kenya's new constitution. In line with Privy Council jurisprudence, the Court dismissed the argument that sentencing discretion was unnecessary because of the executive pardon and clemency power.[128] The Kenyan Court of Appeal noted it was "satisfied" that foreign case law was "persuasive in our jurisdiction and we make no apology for applying" it.[129] Like the Ugandan court, the Kenyan court issued strong dicta indicating that the mandatory death penalty for crimes other than murder was also unconstitutional, including treason, robbery with violence, and attempted robbery with violence.[130] The Court also provided strong dicta receptive to a death row syndrome challenge in the future.[131]

Finally, the Court successfully bridged the gap between Kenya's independence constitution and the 2010 constitution. Unlike Malawi and Uganda, which have more modern constitutions, Kenya's original constitution possessed a Caribbean-style partial savings clause.[132] The Court interpreted the clause in accordance with the Caribbean cases *Reyes*, *Fox*, and *Hughes*, holding that the mandatory death penalty was a manner of sentencing, not a judicial punishment, and thus was not saved.[133] Like the Ugandan Supreme

---

121 *Mutiso*, [2011] 1 E.A.L.R. at 354–5 (Kenya C.A.).
122 *See* Jeffrey Gettleman, *Kenyan Constitution Opens New Front in Culture Wars*, N.Y. TIMES, May 14, 2010), at A6.
123 *Compare* KENYA CONST. art. 71(1) (1969), *and* art. 29(f) (2010).
124 *C.f.* Kafantayeni v. A.G., [2007] MWHC 1 at 6–7; Kigula v. A.G., [2009] 2 E.A.L.R. 1, 17 (Uganda S.C.).
125 *Mutiso*, [2011] 1 E.A.L.R. at 353.
126 *See, e.g.*, Waweru v. Republic, (2006) 1 K.L.R. 677, 677, 681, 684 (Kenya H.C.); Eunice Brookman Amissah & Josephine Banda Moyo, *Abortion Law Reform in Sub-Saharan Africa: No Turning Back*, 12 REPRODUCTIVE HEALTH MATTERS 227, 231 (2004).
127 *Mutiso*, [2011] 1 E.A.L.R. at 356–7.
128 *Id.* at 350.
129 *Id.* at 355.
130 *Id.* at 357–8.
131 *Id.* at 350.
132 KENYA CONST. art. 74(2) (1969) (there is no equivalent in the 2010 constitution).
133 *Mutiso*, [2011] 1 E.A.L.R. at 353.

Court, the Kenyan court looked to drafters' intent, noting that the new constitution "was arrived at through a consultative and public process," and consequently one could assume "that the people of Kenya, owing to their own philosophy and circumstances, have resolved to qualify the right to life and retain the death penalty in the statute books."[134] The Court appeared to close the door on a direct challenge to the constitutionality of the death penalty.[135]

Though the Court of Appeal claimed to close the door on a direct challenge to the constitutionality of the death penalty under the new constitution, it did not engage a searching comparison between the old constitution and the new one. The death penalty under the old constitution was clearly saved at Article 71(1), modeled on that of the European Convention on Human Rights: "No person shall be deprived of his life intentionally save in execution of the sentence of a court in respect of a criminal offence under the law of Kenya of which he has been convicted."[136] In comparison, however, the new constitution is more ambiguous:

26(1) Every person has the right to life.

26(2) The life of a person begins at conception.

26(3) A person shall not be deprived of life intentionally, except to the extent authorized by this constitution or other written law.

26(4) Abortion is not permitted [with exceptions omitted].[137]

The new right to life provision at Article 26 contains two ambiguities. First, the clause that could be construed as "saving" the death penalty is a separate clause from, and not a modifying subclause of, the grammatically absolute right to life. Second, 26(3) appears to be circular, because it states that a person shall not be deprived of life except where constitutionally authorized, and provides no constitutional authorization except for abortion exceptions. According to one of the experts on the Constitutional Review Commission, this ambiguity was intentional, to reconcile Kenyan popular opinion with global trends toward the death penalty.[138]

On June 10, 2011, High Court Judge John Matthew Anyara Emukule found the death penalty per se unconstitutional under the new constitution, highlighting both of the ambiguities in Article 26 of the new constitution.[139] In accepting the mitigating factors of the case, including the defendant's young age and the ethnic and political dimension of the murder, Judge Emukule held "that Article 26(2) (on deprivation of life) is inconsistent with the right to life preserved under Article 26(1) of the Constitution."[140]

---

134 *Id.* at 352.
135 However, the High Court has extended *Mutiso*'s mandatory death penalty holding to the crime of robbery with violence. Evanson Muiruri Gichane v. Republic, Crim. App. No. 277 of 2007 (Dec. 10, 2010) (Kenya H.C.).
136 KENYA CONST. art. 71(1) (1969).
137 KENYA CONST. art. 26 (2010).
138 Email from member of Committee of Experts, to author (June 21, 2011) (on file with author).
139 Republic v. John Kimita Mwaniki, Crim. Case No. 116 of 2007 (June 10, 2011) (Kenya H.C.).
140 *Mwaniki*, Crim. Case No. 116 of 2007 at 26. Judge Emukule again reiterated his opposition to the death penalty under the new constitution in dicta in Republic v. Milton Kabulit, Crim. Case No. 115/2008 (Jan. 26, 2012) (Kenya H.C.).

In December 2011, High Court Judge M. Warsame came to the opposite conclusion, not only upholding the constitutionality of the death penalty, but also rejecting *Mutiso* and finding that the new constitution authorized a mandatory death penalty.[141] Judge Warsame compared the wording of the old constitution to the new constitution and found that the new constitution actually expanded the application of the death penalty because the phrase "the extent authorized by this constitution or other written law" in Article 26(3) of the new constitution was broader than "save in execution of the sentence of a court" in Article 71(1) of the former constitution. He rejected the belief that the death penalty was cruel and inhuman punishment. He made his disagreement with Judge Emukule explicit, believing that murder itself was a form of inhuman treatment and that a perpetrator "must pay for it in equal measure." The decision of Judge Warsame is an outlier. In nearly all other capital sentencing cases at the High Court, including both murder cases in which the High Court sits as a trial court and in robbery with violence cases in which the High Court sits as an appellate court, the accused was permitted to offer mitigating evidence in accordance with *Mutiso*.[142]

The split among High Court judges is creating pressure on the Court of Appeal to clarify its earlier ruling in *Mutiso*. In March 2012, the Kenya Court of Appeal upheld two discretionary death sentences that were imposed on defendants after they had the opportunity to present mitigating evidence.[143] This is in keeping with the spirit of *Mutiso* that the death penalty was lawful so long as it was not mandatory. However, in October 2013, a five-judge panel of the Court of Appeals, including former High Court Judge Warsame, issued a decision that appeared to reject the rationale of *Mutiso*. In this decision, *Mwaura v. Republic*, the Court of Appeal addressed for the first time the constitutionality of capital punishment under the new constitution, upholding it despite the circular nature of the right to life clause and the prohibition on cruel and degrading punishment.[144] The Court also rejected the argument that the death penalty was too harsh for the crime of robbery with violence, writing that severity of sentence was a question of fact and outside the appellate court's jurisdiction, a surprising holding as the challenge was to the disproportionality of the sentence *as a matter of law*. The Court concluded that the authorization of the death penalty in the penal code constituted "other written law" as required by Article 26 of the new constitution. The Court noted that it had "the power to depart from [prior] decisions where we consider that in the circumstances, it is correct to do so."[145] In the end, the Court sharply curtailed *Mutiso*'s reach: "We hold that the decision in [*Mutiso*] to be per incuriam in so far as it purports to grant discretion in

---

141 Republic v. Dickson Mwangi Munene, Crim. Case No. 11 of 2009 (Dec. 10, 2011) (Kenya H.C.).

142 *See, e.g.*, Vincent Jared Ogutu v. Republic, Crim. App. No. 89/2010 (Nov. 1, 2011) (Kenya H.C.); Boaz Onyango v. Republic, Crim. App. 53 & 55/2010 (Sept. 23, 2011) (Kenya H.C.). For homicide, see Republic v. Jacob Juma Msituni, Crim. Case No. 10/2008 (March 12, 2012) (Kenya H.C.) and Republic v. Mbaruk Mwangeti, Crim. Case No. 15/2008 (March 16, 2012) (Kenya H.C.). In both cases, the High Court judges weighed the evidence in the first instance and then proceeded to a sentencing phase where the defendant was permitted to offer mitigating evidence.

143 Benard Mutua Matheka v. Republic, Crim. App. No. 155/2009 (March 15, 2012) (Kenya C.A.); James Maina Magare et al. v. Republic, Crim. App. No. 224/2009 (March 16, 2012) (Kenya C.A.). Interestingly, the Court of Appeal noted at the end of the *Magare* judgment that one of the judges on the three judge panel refused to sign the decision. The Court of Appeal also expressed some skepticism of the death penalty for armed robbery in David Njoroge Macharia v. Republic, Crim. App. 497/2007 (March 18, 2011) (Kenya C.A.).

144 Mwaura v. Republic, Crim. App. 5/2008 (Oct. 18, 2013) (Kenya C.A.)

145 *Id*. at 23.

sentencing with regard to capital offences."¹⁴⁶ The decision in *Mwaura* does not square with the intent of the constitution's drafters and fails to interpret an ambiguous constitutional provision in a manner consistent with Kenya's international human rights obligations and its internal political culture.

In the end, the Supreme Court of Kenya will need to resolve the split among the High Court panels, and such an appeal has been filed.[147] There are some indicators for optimism: a number of pending judicial candidates have told the Judicial Services Commission during the vetting process that they believe the death penalty is unconstitutional under Article 26, hints of jurisprudence yet to be written.[148] In the interim, however, the Court of Appeal's vindicating decision in *Mutiso* remains in constitutional limbo.

The Supreme Court of Ghana: Johnson

In March 2011, the Supreme Court of Ghana defied the trend in common law Africa toward abolition of the mandatory death penalty, upholding it in a 4 to 1 decision that carefully considered and rejected the emerging Commonwealth consensus that a discretionary death penalty regime more closely aligned with existing human rights norms.[149] The lengthy opinions by Justices Rose Constance Owusu and Jones Dotse held that the mandatory death penalty was consistent with the Constitution of Ghana, and the establishment of a discretionary death penalty regime was a policy decision that must be made by the legislature rather than the Court, a holding with which the other two members of the majority concurred. By contrast, a strong dissenting opinion by Justice Samuel Date-Bah intensively analyzed the jurisprudence of other Commonwealth jurisdictions, especially Kenya and Uganda, which are based on constitutional frameworks similar to Ghana's. The decision in *Dexter Johnson v. Republic* was a missed opportunity, but it failed to provide a comprehensive philosophical alternative to the emerging consensus in the common law world that the mandatory nature of the death penalty is not constitutionally required and violates fundamental rights.

The opinions by Justices Owusu and Dotse engaged in a purely textual analysis of the disputed provisions of the constitution and the penal code and used the cloak of judicial restraint to avoid reconciling this analysis with contrary persuasive authority from other common law jurisdictions. Justice Owusu, known to be a proponent of capital punishment, noted the similarities between the constitutions of Ghana and Kenya, but determined that the Ghanaian provisions were clear and unambiguous and therefore did not require reference to authority from other jurisdictions.[150] She also found that the mandatory death sentence was not overly rigid, as juveniles, pregnant women, and persons found to be insane are exempted, though these cases do not greatly narrow the full range of moral culpability attached to the crime of homicide. Finally, Justice Owusu raised an argument rejected by the Privy Council, that the ability of the defendant to seek clemency following his conviction

---

146   *Id.* at 25.
147   Sam Kiplagat, *Death Row Convict Goes to Supreme Court to Overturn Sentence*, THE STAR, Nov. 5, 2013 (retrieved from AllAfrica.com).
148   *Death Penalty Cruel, JSC Told*, DAILY NATION, July 6, 2011; *Magistrates Push for Repeal of Death Penalty*, DAILY NATION, Aug. 4, 2011.
149   Dexter Johnson v. Republic, [2011] 2 S.C.G.L.R. 601.
150   *See* Sylvanus Nana Kumi, *Do We Reform or Abolish This Law?*, BUSINESS GUIDE (Ghana), August 30, 2010, http://www.businessguideghana.com/?p=3066. *See also*, Seneadza, *supra* note 48 at 126.

satisfies his or her right to a fair trial because it allows a defendant an opportunity to present mitigating evidence.[151] The shadowy and quasi-political proceedings of a clemency committee, however, are very different from courtroom criminal procedure and remove from the decision-making process the single person most familiar with the case, the trial judge.[152] In refusing to follow *Mutiso* in confirming the death sentence as discretionary even where the statute read "is liable to suffer death," instead of "shall suffer death," Justice Owusu explained that "nothing short of death shall be the appropriate sentence" in light of the appellant's gruesome murder.[153] This is a judicially activist holding disguised as judicial restraint; it does not comport with the legislative intent to restrict application of the death penalty in Ghana.

In his opinion upholding the mandatory death penalty, Justice Jones Dotse likewise acknowledged the comparative precedent from other jurisdictions but ultimately determined that the Constitution of Ghana was clear and unambiguous. His opinion, however, misconstrued the nature of a discretionary death penalty regime and conflated the division of murder into degrees with judicial sentencing guidelines. If the mandatory death penalty were found unconstitutional, Justice Dotse wrote, Ghana would have to divide murder into degrees and develop sentencing guidelines for each degree; he distinguished the United States in this regard, where murder was already divided into degrees before the development of sentencing guidelines.[154] This is an illogical argument because it merges the guilt inquiry and the sentencing one; dividing murder into degrees is a separate policy determination from the development of capital sentencing guidelines that require aggravating factors to trigger a death sentence. Justice Dotse's opinion was heavily concerned with the principle of certainty, and he argued that leaving criminal sentencing to the determination of the trial judge would lead to arbitrary results.[155] As a consequence, his argument created a straw man, predicting the chaos that would result if judges had to determine both guilt and degree of murder, weighing the gruesomeness of the crime, the number of victims, the premeditation of a crime, and other factors in the absence of sentencing guidelines. His decision is unpersuasive because he mischaracterizes the nature of a discretionary death penalty regime; his analysis simply does not comport with the real experiences of Kenya, Malawi, Uganda, and other developing countries.

His opinion is also notable for two additional arguments. The first relates to Article 3(3) of the Constitution of Ghana, which mandates the death penalty for any person convicted of high treason.[156] According to Justice Dotse, the existence of Article 3(3) indicates that the 1992 constitution "does not directly or indirectly abhor or frown upon the imposition of the death sentence on the class of cases where the law provides for it."[157] The essence

---

151 *Johnson*, [2011] 2 S.C.G.L.R. at 655, 658 (Owusu, J.S.C., concurring).

152 As Chenwi writes, "in practice, there is very little information as to the extent to which the prerogative [of mercy] is exercised, since the process is shrouded in secrecy." The mercy reports prepared by the trial judge are confidential in some countries. Lilian Chenwi, *Fair Trial Rights and Their Relation to the Death Penalty in Africa*, 55 INT'L & COMP. L.Q. 609, 632 (2006).

153 *Johnson*, [2011] 2 S.C.G.L.R. at 658.

154 *Id.* at 699 (Dotse, J.S.C., concurring).

155 *Id.* at 692–3.

156 GHANA CONST. art. 3(3), which states: "Any person who (a) by himself or in concert with others by any violent or other unlawful means, suspends or overthrows or abrogates this Constitution or any part of it, or attempts to do any such act; or (b) aids and abets in any manner any person referred to in paragraph (a) of this clause; commits the offence of high treason and shall, upon conviction, be sentenced to suffer death."

157 *Johnson*, [2011] 2 S.C.G.L.R. at 688 (Dotse, J.S.C., concurring).

of this argument is that the drafters of the constitution contemplated the existence of the mandatory death penalty and intended to create a constitutional order that included it. Justice Dotse's holding may also be criticized for its failure adequately to appreciate the difference in text between the constitutional treason provision and the penal code's murder provision, as Article 3(3) stated that a defendant "shall, upon conviction, be sentenced to suffer death" while Section 46 of the Penal Code stated that a person who "commits murder is *liable to suffer* death."[158] The second interesting point made by Justice Dotse is his wholesale rejection of the separation of powers argument. "The principle of the separation of powers has been carried too far" by the Ugandan Supreme Court in *Kigula*, Justice Dotse wrote. "[T]he concept as interpreted in the *Kigula* case meant that the Judiciary was interfering with the work of the Legislature."[159] He reasoned that mandatory sentences did not unconstitutionally constrain judicial power.

Unlike the majority opinions, the dissent in *Johnson* closely followed the reasoning of the Kenyan, Malawian, and Ugandan decisions, and extensively cited the Privy Council's Caribbean jurisprudence. The dissenter, Justice Samuel Date-Bah, found the persuasive authority from other common law jurisdictions "irrefutable" and "irresistible," extensively quoting the Kenyan *Mutiso* decision over five pages.[160] *Mutiso* is particularly relevant because the former Kenyan constitution under which the case was decided contained a partial savings clause similar to Ghana's that immunized pre-existing punishments from challenge.[161] On matters of human rights, Justice Date-Bah wrote in dissent, "when interpreting Ghanaian constitutional provisions *in pari materia* with other Commonwealth jurisdictions and international human rights instruments," the Court should depart from their holdings "only for tangible policy reasons." And here there were none: "The countervailing argument that all murders are murders and should be treated equally is an unreasonably inflexible ideological position, belied by actual human experience."[162] Because of the universal nature of human rights, interpretations of constitutional provisions nearly identical to Ghana's and drawn from jurisdictions with similar postcolonial histories were particularly weighty.

In addition to finding that the mandatory nature of the death sentence was cruel, inhuman, and degrading and therefore a violation of Article 15(2) of Ghana's constitution, the justice also found that "[a] punishment that does not distinguish between the gravity of the particular cases that trigger the punishment is inherently arbitrary," and a violation of Article 13(1) of the constitution prohibiting arbitrary deprivation of life.[163] This was a holding of the Kenyan Court of Appeal in *Mutiso*. Reframing the issue, Justice Date-Bah also found a violation of the right to a fair trial, contained at Article 19(1) of the Constitution of Ghana: "The inability of trial judges to exercise...discretion to make the

---

158 HENRIETTA J.A.N. MENSA-BONSU, THE ANNOTATED CRIMINAL OFFENCES ACT OF GHANA 70, 175 (5th ed. 2008). The difference between "shall suffer" and "shall be liable to suffer" is extremely important, and several courts have found death sentences to be discretionary where the "liable" language is used. Some examples elsewhere in this book include decisions from Sri Lanka and Papua New Guinea. *See* Van Der Jhultes v. Attorney General, (1989) 1 Sri L.R. 204 (June 28, 1988); Ume v. State, [2006] PGSC 9, S.C. 836 (May 19, 2006). In both cases, the courts read the "shall be liable to suffer" language as discretionary.
159 *Johnson*, [2011] 2 S.C.G.L.R. at 695.
160 *Id.* at 622 (Date-Bah, J., dissenting).
161 *Id.* at 633.
162 *Id.*
163 *Id.* at 634.

punishment fit the crime in cases of murder infringes the right of the accused to a fair trial."[164] Finally, the dissent addressed the separation of powers argument developed by the Ugandan Supreme Court in *Kigula*: "It is judges who must exercise final judicial power and this power includes the power to determine what sentence is appropriate on the facts of individual cases."[165] Indeed, the most striking quality of the dissent is how sweepingly it vindicated prior persuasive authority.

The dissent also addressed an argument unique to Ghana's 1992 constitution: the provision at Article 3(3) providing for the mandatory death sentence for high treason. Justice Date-Bah distinguished the mandatory death penalty for murder, "a criminal offence with a very wide range of moral culpability scenarios," from high treason, which had a range of moral culpability "of a more limited nature," as it was, for instance, premeditated.[166] This was a novel argument based on the Ghanaian context, but it may have relevance for jurisdictions that still possess the mandatory death penalty for specific-intent crimes such as drug trafficking, a crime that also typically requires premeditation and does not encompass heat of passion conduct.

The decision of the Supreme Court of Ghana in *Dexter Johnson* complicates the continent-wide trend toward abolition of the mandatory death penalty. However, unlike the case law from Malaysia and Singapore, the Ghanaian decision falls short of a comprehensive and philosophical defense of the mandatory nature of the death penalty; the Court failed to consider the very different constitutional contexts of Malaysia and Singapore, and perhaps missed an opportunity to distinguish Ghana's constitution from those. Despite the decision of the Supreme Court in *Dexter Johnson*, the death penalty may well be abolished in the near future. The sensational case of Benard Tagoe, who was acquitted after twenty-four years on death row in Ghana by the Court of Appeal, was a cold reminder that wrongful convictions do occur.[167] The fact that the mandatory death penalty overpunishes for homicides that do not necessarily deserve death is undoubtedly one factor that has contributed to capital punishment's eroding legitimacy.[168] After the decision in *Dexter Johnson*, the London-based Death Penalty Project and the Human Rights Advocacy Center in Accra filed a communication with the United Nations Human Rights Committee on Johnson's behalf.[169] As the Committee has already favorably ruled on similar mandatory death petitions arising from the Caribbean, Johnson's petition may help further clarify the obligations of state parties in death penalty cases under international law.

---

164   *Id*. at 638.
165   *Id*.
166   *Id*. at 633.
167   Editorial, *Abolish Death Penalty*, PUBLIC AGENDA (Accra), July 30, 2010 (retrieved from AllAfrica.com).
168   Interestingly, one consequence of the mandatory nature of the death penalty in Ghana is that it increases suicides by perpetrators, as evidenced by the relatively high rate of suicide among husbands who have murdered their wives, a category of homicide that possesses unique characteristics of motive and criminal prosecution. Mensah Adinkrah, *Husbands Who Kill Their Wives: An Analysis of Uxoricides in Contemporary Ghana*, 52 INT'L J. OFFENDER THERAPY & COMP. CRIMINOLOGY 296, 305 (2008).
169   Death Penalty Project UK, *UN Human Rights Committee*, http://www.deathpenaltyproject.org/where-we-operate/international/un-human-rights-committee/ (last accessed May 13, 2013).

Conclusion

Commonwealth Africa is following the emerging global consensus that not all murders are equally heinous and deserving of death, that the right to a fair trial includes a right to a sentencing hearing, and that a disproportionately harsh sentence is cruel and degrading punishment. The courts of Malawi, Uganda, and Kenya followed the lead of the Privy Council's Caribbean jurisprudence because African constitutions are *in pari materia* with their Caribbean counterparts. But these courts are not simply the passive recipients of comparative jurisprudence on the death penalty: they have made their own contributions to this persuasive authority. Just as *Edwards v. Bahamas* is cited for the proposition that the mandatory death penalty violates the right to a fair trial and *Reyes v. Queen* is cited for the finding that the penalty is cruel and inhuman punishment, so too will *Kafantayeni, Kigula,* and *Mutiso* be cited for their novel holdings that the mandatory death penalty violates the right of access to courts, the separation of powers, and the right to life.

The mandatory death penalty decisions from Ghana and Kenya broadly considered jurisdictional objections and found that each defendant could raise constitutional claims on appeal without lower courts having considered them.[170] The Kenyan Court of Appeal did so in a case in which the defendant was no longer under sentence of death, believing the constitutional issue at stake to warrant consideration nonetheless. This is a holding that extends beyond the substance of the mandatory death challenges; a more restrictive holding by either court (including dismissal on mootness grounds in *Mutiso*) would have pre-empted many other death penalty challenges completely and limited the role that international human rights attorneys could play in finding test cases for bringing fundamental rights cases and further developing local constitutional jurisprudence. The appellate courts in both jurisdictions reached the constitutional issues presented, and that was a victory in itself.

Constitutional challenges to the mandatory death penalty are planned or pending in a number of other jurisdictions in common law Africa, including Nigeria, Sierra Leone, Tanzania, and Zambia.[171] These challenges present an opportunity further to strengthen the constitutional sharing of death penalty jurisprudence across borders. The strong trend in common law Africa is toward abolition of the mandatory death penalty, a trend engineered by a small network of anti-death penalty advocates based in London and their partners on the ground. Even the decision of the Supreme Court of Ghana upholding the mandatory death penalty is part of this trend: the justices widely cited jurisprudence from other common law jurisdictions. Through this constitutional sharing process, African courts are instilling international human rights norms in domestic law.

---

170 *Johnson*, [2011] 2 S.C.G.L.R. at 649–50, 678–9; Mutiso v. Republic, [2011] 1 E.A.L.R. 342, 348, 351.

171 *See* Death Penalty Project UK, *Where We Operate: Africa*, http://www.deathpenaltyproject.org/where-we-operate/africa/ (last accessed May 13, 2013).

Chapter 7
The Doctrine of Extenuating Circumstances: The Rise of Judicial Sentencing Discretion in Southern Africa

The mandatory death penalty is on the rapid retreat in common law East Africa after prominent court decisions in Kenya, Malawi, and Uganda. In Southern Africa, however, where Roman-Dutch law served as a counterweight to English common law, a different set of principles applied. In the countries that border South Africa, the death penalty may be substituted for a lesser penalty if the judge finds that extenuating circumstances existed at the time of the offense warranting such a reduction; if not, the death penalty was mandatory. The rise of the doctrine of extenuating circumstances in apartheid South Africa was an attempt to mitigate the harshness of the common law mandatory death penalty by constructing a hybrid of mandatory and discretionary sentencing regimes. In this respect, the rise and fall of the doctrine of extenuating circumstances in Southern Africa fits within a continent-wide trend toward judicial sentencing discretion in capital cases.

Under the traditional application of the doctrine, upon a conviction for murder the burden shifted to the accused to show, beyond a fair preponderance of the evidence, that circumstances existed at the time of the crime that "reduce[d] the moral blameworthiness of the accused, as distinct from his legal culpability."[1] The definition had two limitations. First, only those circumstances existing at the time of the crime fell within the scope of the doctrine, although courts have been inconsistent about applying this limitation in practice: previous convictions if any; remorse or good behavior; or medical or familial exigencies could not, at least in theory, be included. Second, the circumstances must bear on the accused's moral blameworthiness, and not his legal culpability, so failed defenses at trial such as provocation, heat of passion, or intoxication, which would otherwise reduce a murder conviction to manslaughter were relevant at sentencing. Common extenuating circumstances typically included witchcraft, youth, lack of intent to kill, provocation, and lack of premeditation, though variations exist in different jurisdictions.

While the doctrine of extenuating circumstances introduced a measure of sentencing discretion to mandatory capital punishment regimes, in practice it lacked the analytical clarity and rationality of a discretionary regime. First, it allowed a judge full discretion to consider mitigating factors, but, if no factors were found, permitted a judge to hide behind the law to impose a death sentence. The result was that judges did not have to take responsibility for the death sentences they handed down, and could shift responsibility to other actors in the system.[2] Second, in the absence of sentencing guidelines and robust

---

1 State v. Letsolo, 1970 (3) S.A. 476, 476 (A.D.).
2 University of Houston Law Professor David Dow's memoir very memorably illustrates this point in the American death penalty system. "It's easier to kill somebody if it's someone else's decision, and if somebody else does the killing. Our death-penalty regime depends for its functionality on moral cowardice." DAVID DOW, THE AUTOBIOGRAPHY OF AN EXECUTION 218–19 (2010).

appellate review, wide sentencing disparities existed among judges and across jurisdictions.[3] In general though, as former Chief Justice of Zimbabwe Enoch Dumbutshena wrote, it was "common practice among judges to lean towards a finding of manslaughter or finding extenuating circumstances. Judges are reluctant to sentence people to death."[4] Third, by shifting the burden to the defendant to show extenuating circumstances, the doctrine acted as a rebuttable presumption in favor of death. This placed the greatest burden on the weakest link in the criminal justice system—that is, defense counsel—in a region that had only skeletal legal aid schemes for indigent defendants. Finally, the doctrine did not provide a coherent method of weighing *aggravating* factors, and different courts in Southern Africa came to differing conclusions about whether and when aggravating factors were relevant.

The doctrine arose as a political compromise in South Africa in 1935 as a result of a historically high rate of commutation and pardon by the governor-general. The Rhodesian legislature followed suit in 1949, and when the penal codes of Botswana, Lesotho, and Swaziland were revised before independence, each included the doctrine. In 1965, the provision entered into the law of Papua New Guinea, an Australian colony in the South Pacific, likely as a result of the recommendations of the United Kingdom's Royal Commission on Capital Punishment in 1949 that favored the doctrine of extenuating circumstances as an alternative to the mandatory death penalty. In a later reform of its own death penalty laws, Zambia adopted the doctrine in 1990, just as South Africa was abolishing it in favor of a discretionary system. Swaziland's courts eventually overturned the burden-shifting nature of the doctrine and finally abolished the mandatory death penalty in the 2005 constitution. Papua New Guinea established a discretionary death penalty in a constitutional challenge in 2006, although the country had long rejected the onus placed on the defendant and the limited definition of extenuating circumstances. Zimbabwe's new constitution, adopted in March 2013, prohibits the mandatory death penalty even in the absence of extenuating circumstances. The doctrine survives in modified form in Botswana, Lesotho, and Zambia. As the doctrine of extenuating circumstances is extinguished, Southern Africa is following the international trend of abolishing the common law mandatory death sentence in favor of pure discretionary sentencing regimes.

The Origins of Judicial Sentencing Discretion in South Africa

The legal system of twentieth-century South Africa reflected the country's complicated political and social history, as a hybrid of English common law, Roman-Dutch civil law, and African customary law. The criminal code, however, was almost entirely British in origin, and South Africa "inherited the wide definition of murder, the mandatory death sentence, and the secret process of mercy in death-penalty cases from the English after they colonized the Cape in 1806."[5] Precolonial law often did not distinguish between premeditated and impulse killings, and sharp variations existed as to the existence and extent of capital punishment. The element of executive mercy, which introduced some

---

3 *See* John Hatchard and Simon Coldham, *Commonwealth Africa*, *in* CAPITAL PUNISHMENT: GLOBAL ISSUES AND PROSPECTS 167 (Peter Hodgkinson & Andrew Rutherford eds., 1996) (noting wide disparities in sentencing).

4 E. Dumbutshena, *The Death Penalty in Zimbabwe*, 58 REVUE INTERNATIONALE DE DROIT PENAL 521, 524, 530 (1987).

5 ROBERT TURRELL, WHITE MERCY: A STUDY OF THE DEATH PENALTY IN SOUTH AFRICA 4 (2004).

discretion into the capital sentencing process, helped close the "chasm between customary and colonial homicide law."[6]

South Africa established a statutory mandatory death penalty in 1917, codifying common law practice, though some judges did not previously consider the death penalty to be mandatory.[7] The crimes of infanticide by new mothers and murders committed by those under age 16 were exempted, and treason and rape merited a discretionary death sentence.[8] Upon conviction, the judge wrote a confidential report as to whether he believed the sentence should be carried out, and the governor-general reviewed the report in his clemency deliberations. The system was opaque and unaccountable, and "only contribute[d] very marginally to exclude all risk of judicial error."[9] Criticism arose over the governor-general's frequent use of the commutation and pardon power.[10] In the decade before 1935, only 24% of capital sentences were actually carried out, with the remainder receiving clemency or reprieve: "only in theory did the mandatory death sentence for murder apply."[11] Following adoption of the doctrine, the number of murder convictions doubled over the next decade as juries were less hesitant to convict as the death penalty was no longer the only possible punishment.[12]

The high rate of commutation by the governor-general generated calls for reform of capital sentencing. In early 1935, the South African House of Assembly considered as alternatives a discretionary death penalty regime similar to the punishments for rape, treason, and infanticide by a new mother; the division of common law murder into capital and non-capital murder, the former of which would still carry a mandatory death sentence; and the doctrine of extenuating circumstances.[13] Judges sought the broadest discretion possible, but then-Prime Minister Jan Smuts only sought a proposal that reduced the number of death sentences and the high proportion of reprieves. "[T]o Smuts it was a practical matter, not a moral one—he was not an abolitionist."[14] Initially, there was general acceptance of the new law. Judges generally did not complain of the burden imposed on them in having to exercise final discretion, even as the jury system faded in favor of assessors.[15]

Over time, however, the application of the death penalty reflected the social realities of the South African population: it was biased against the ethnic minorities and in favor of women. The poor attracted less concern as individuals and were often unable to afford a competent defense. Beginning in the 1930s, with the political consolidation of the white state, the death penalty was "transformed from a form of class self-defense into a form of

---

6   *Id.* at 6, 20–21.

7   Laurel Angus & Evadné Grant, *Sentencing in Capital Cases in the Transvaal Provincial Division and Witwatersrand Local Division: 1987–1989*, 7 S. AFR. J. ON HUM. RTS. 50, 51 (1991).

8   Criminal Procedure and Evidence Act 33 of 1917 § 338.

9   B. v. D. van Niekerk, *...Hanged by the Neck Until You Are Dead: Some Thoughts on the Application of the Death Penalty in South Africa*, 86 S. AFR. L.J. 457, 461 (1969), *continued in* 87 S. AFR. L.J. 60 (1970).

10   Criminal Procedure and Evidence (Amendment) Act 46 of 1935 § 61.

11   George Devenish, *The Historical and Jurisprudential Evolution and Background to the Application of the Death Penalty in South Africa and Its Relationship with Constitutional and Political Reform*, 5 S. AFR. J. CRIM. JUST. 1, 8 (1992).

12   TURRELL, *supra* note 5 at 233, 236.

13   Ellison Kahn, *How Did We Get Our Lopsided Law on the Imposition of the Death Penalty for Common-Law Crimes? And What Should We Do About It?*, 2 S. AFR. J. CRIM. JUST. 137, 146–50 (1989) (hereinafter, "Kahn, *Lopsided Law*").

14   *Id.* at 150.

15   *Id.* at 155–6.

racial self-defense."[16] Before adoption of the doctrine of extenuating circumstances, the heaviest burden of capital punishment fell on poor white South Africans or those of Indian or mixed-race descent; prevailing attitudes held that black Africans had innate "violent tendencies."[17] During the 1940s, however, the death penalty became overtly racist, inflicted on the black majority by the white state. South Africa was the only country in the world with a rising murder rate between 1900 and 1950; the high violence rate among black South Africans reinforced paternalistic, even racist, white views of the violence that pervaded black society. In this era, evident trends about executions and reprieves are discernible: cases of infanticide, offenses by juveniles or women, or political crimes were usually reprieved; similarly, crimes involving witchcraft, provocation, or intoxication, or where the offender had a mental disorder also had a high reprieve rate. Death sentences of black men for the rape of white women served the purposes of racial self-defense and purity and were almost never reprieved.[18]

From the creation of the Union of South Africa in 1910 until the moratorium on executions in 1990, about 4,200 people were hanged in South Africa. While the death penalty originally applied only for murder, rape, and treason, since 1958 the South African parliament expanded the list to include kidnapping, child-stealing, robbery or attempted robbery, and aggravated housebreaking or attempted housebreaking, as well as terrorism.[19] These sentences were rarely imposed; some 90% of executions were for murder. In 1959, the age limit for the discretionary death sentence for juveniles was raised from 16 to 18.[20] The doctrine of extenuating circumstances was recommended by the Royal Commission on Capital Punishment for possible use in the United Kingdom.[21]

While the doctrine fulfilled its primary aim of reducing the number of prisoners on death row, it failed properly to guide judicial discretion. Under South Africa's criminal procedure code, where a judge was of the opinion that a death sentence might be imposed, he sat with assessors. In such cases, the majority decided on the guilt of the accused and, in the case of murder, on the existence of extenuating circumstances. Upon conviction, judges often consulted with their assessors on appropriate sentences; although the existence of extenuating circumstances was a majority vote, the imposition of the death sentence was not.[22] In at least one case, a judge who apparently found extenuating circumstances was outvoted by his assessors, although this was said to happen very rarely.[23] The accused had no automatic right of appeal; he or she had to apply to the trial court for leave to appeal, which the court was to grant if there was a reasonable possibility that another

---

16 TURRELL, *supra* note 5 at 21.

17 *Id.* at 236–7.

18 *Id.* at 21–2, 234–5.

19 Symposium, *The Relaunch of the Society for the Abolition of the Death Penalty in South Africa*, 106 S. AFR. L.J. 39, 40 (1989) (Ellison Kahn). The expansion of capital punishment for these crimes (housebreaking and robbery had not been capital crimes in South Africa since at least 1840) was justified in deterrence grounds. The first executions took place in February 1959. Ellison Kahn, *Crime and Punishment 1910–1960: Reflections on Changes since Union in the Law of Criminal Punishment and its Application*, 1960 ACTA JURIDICA 191, 202–3 (1960) (hereinafter, "Kahn, *Crime and Punishment*").

20 Criminal Law Amendment Act 16 of 1959 § 25.

21 Kahn, *Crime and Punishment, supra* note 19 at 202–3.

22 Janos Mihalik, *The Death Penalty in Bophuthatswana: A New Deal for Condemned Prisoners?*, 107 S. AFR. L.J. 465, 484 (1990).

23 T.P. McNally, *Capital Punishment: An Orange Free State Perspective*, 2 S. AFR. J. CRIM. JUST. 239, 249 (1989).

court could have come to a different conclusion. If the trial court denied such leave, the accused had to petition the Chief Justice, adding an additional layer of human judgment that risked arbitrariness.[24]

The first case to define the limits of the doctrine of extenuating circumstances was *R. v. Mfoni* in 1935, in which the court stated that "only such circumstances as are connected with or have a relation to the conduct of the accused in the commission of the crime should have any weight at all," and sentimental factors or factors too remotely connected should be disregarded.[25] This was to be an enduring feature of the doctrine. A trial judge was to consider both the physical aspects of the crime and the mental strain and stress of the perpetrator.[26] Three years later, in *R. v. Biyana*, the court defined extenuating circumstances any fact "associated with a crime which serves in the minds of reasonable men to diminish, morally albeit not legally, the degree of the prisoner's guilt."[27] In 1947, the Appellate Division determined that onus of showing extenuating circumstances on the balance of probabilities rested with the accused.[28] In *R. v. Fundakubi*, the Appellate Division provided further guidance to trial judges: "no factor not too remote or too faintly or indirectly related to the commission of the crime, which bears on the accused's moral blameworthiness in committing it, can be ruled out from consideration."[29] The procedure grew ever more complex over time, and large tracts of case law parsing the doctrine's essential features developed in South African courts.

The most authoritative expression for the theory of extenuating circumstances was the judgment in *State v. Letsolo* in 1970, still widely cited in Southern African jurisprudence:

> [T]he trial judge has a discretion, to be exercised judicially on a consideration of all relevant facts including the criminal record of the accused, to decide whether it would be appropriate to take the drastically extreme step of ordering him to forfeit his life; or whether some alternative, short of this incomparably utter extreme, would sufficiently satisfy the deterrent, punitive and reformative aspects of sentence. The possibility of such an alternative should be considered by the trial Judge…[a]nd it should be weighed with the most anxious deliberation, for it is, literally, a matter of life and death.[30]

In 1971, the Appellate Division upheld a death sentence where the judge found a limited degree of extenuation but nonetheless determined that the death penalty was appropriate.[31] This was permissible under the statute, which held that the court *may* (but was not required to) impose a lesser sentence upon a finding of extenuating circumstances, but the "seeming incongruity" of sentencing a person to death upon a finding of extenuating circumstances attracted scholarly criticism.[32]

---

24 Christina Murray, Julia Sloth-Nielsen & Colin Tredoux, *The Death Penalty in the Cape Provincial Division: 1986–1988*, 5 S. AFR. J. ON HUM. RTS. 154, 159 (1989).
25 R. v. Mfoni, 1935 O.P.D. 191.
26 Stanley Evans, *Extenuating Circumstances*, 72 S. AFR. L.J. 385, 389 (1955).
27 R. v. Biyana, 1938 E.D.L. 310, 311.
28 R. v. Lembete, 1947 (2) S.A. 603, 609 (A.D.).
29 R. v. Fundakubi, 1948 (3) S.A. 810, 818 (A.D.).
30 State v. Letsolo, 1970 (3) S.A. 476, 476–7 (A.D.).
31 State v. Matthee, 1971 (3) S.A. 769, 770 (A.D.) (see headnote; decision is reported in Afrikaans).
32 D. Zeffertt, *Recent Cases: Extenuating Circumstances*, 88 S. AFR. L.J. 416, 417 (1971). *See also* James Lund, *The Decision to Kill: Discretionary Death Sentences Purposes, Principles and*

The doctrine had an additional fundamental weakness that highlighted its internal inconsistency, even its absurdity: by bifurcating a murder trial into two, a convicted defendant who pled innocent had to change his or her story to admit guilt and claim extenuating circumstances in order to save his or her life.[33] Invariably, the prosecution claimed that the defendant lied at trial and therefore his testimony on extenuating circumstances could not be trusted. On the other hand, a defendant who continued to maintain innocence at the sentencing phase of the trial failed to carry his or her burden of showing that extenuating circumstances existed. Although the accused was typically called on to testify at the extenuating circumstances phase of the trial, "as his testimony has in most instances already been rejected by the court he starts with a lack of credibility."[34] His version of events, which could possibly be true, might not be accepted on the balance of probabilities. "In these circumstances" Koyana writes, "the surprising aspect is not the fact that the doctrine of extenuating circumstances fell when it did in 1989/90, but that it lasted as long as it did over so many years."[35]

The doctrine of extenuating circumstances, what Davis calls a "halfway house" between a mandatory and a discretionary sentencing regime, required judges to perform a discretionary act in finding extenuating circumstances before they could even consider whether imprisonment was an acceptable alternative in the present case, whether the accused person had some potential for reform, or whether the death sentence was the only appropriate punishment.[36] In other words, a judge had to perform two separate and unrelated discretionary acts instead of one—finding extenuating circumstances in the first place, and then crafting an individualized sentence.

A final criticism of the doctrine of extenuating circumstances was the weakness and inexperience of *pro deo* counsel, practicing lawyers who were paid a nominal sum by the state to represent an indigent accused person.[37] The South African constitution did not include a substantive right to counsel during the apartheid era, and the Appellate Division rejected attempts to interpret the right to a fair trial to encompass the right to be provided with legal representation at state expense.[38] If an accused could not afford the representation of counsel, he or she could apply to the Legal Aid Board. A financial means test was used to determine whether the defendant qualified. For the crime of murder, the Legal Aid Board paid for an attorney to defend an accused before trial courts, but not before appellate courts, which used a *pro deo* system in which the bar appointed counsel for an accused.[39]

---

the Courts, 2 S. Afr. J. Crim. Just. 189, 198–202 (1989) (noting different judicial philosophies on sentencing, which produced different results).

33 D.S. Koyana, *The Demise of the Doctrine of Extenuating Circumstances in the Republics of South Africa and Transkei*, 4(2) Consultus 115, 118 (Oct. 1991).

34 Dirk van Zyl Smit, *Judicial Discretion and the Sentence of Death for Murder*, 99 S. Afr. L.J. 82, 86 (1982).

35 Koyana, *supra* note 33 at 118.

36 D.M. Davis, *Extenuation: An Unnecessary Halfway House on the Road to a Rational Sentencing Policy*, 2 S. Afr. J. Crim. Just. 205, 211–12 (1989).

37 Van Zyl Smit, *supra* note 34 at 93.

38 *See* State v. Khanyile, 1988 (3) S.A. 795 (Natal Prov. Div.), *State v. Rudman*, 1992 (1) S.A. 343 (A.D.). *Rudman* essentially reversed the progress made in *Khanyile* and other cases toward establishing such a right. D.M. Davis, *An Impoverished Jurisprudence: When is a Right Not a Right?*, 8 S. Afr. J. on Hum. Rts. 90, 91, 96 (1992).

39 Wilfried Scharf & Rona Cochrane, *World Factbook of Criminal Justice Systems: South Africa*, U.S. Bureau of Justice Statistics (1994), http://www.ojp.usdoj.gov/bjs/pub/ascii/wfbcjsaf.txt.

A shortage of funds made it impossible for the Board to represent every indigent defendant facing imprisonment, and as many as 85% of criminal defendants were unrepresented.[40]

By the 1980s, the system of capital punishment in South Africa became unsustainable. An analysis of death sentences in the Orange Free State between 1984 and 1987 revealed the rareness of executive clemency, occurring in one out of thirty cases, while a reduction or acquittal on appeal was more likely.[41] Throughout the 1980s, as the number of death row prisoners increased, the length of time that each prisoner was on death row also increased, as apparently did execution volunteerism and prisoner suicides to escape the torments of delay and prison conditions.[42] In addition, decisions of the Appellate Division vastly expanded the common purpose doctrine in political cases, and large numbers of defendants were sentenced to death even though they had played only a trivial role in a crime, which sparked international condemnation after the convictions of several violent protest groups.[43]

By the 1980s, statistics on death sentences imposed in South Africa showed wildly sharp disparities among judges. In the scholarly literature and in the popular press, the most prolific judges were known as "hanging judges." Such disparities included not only how frequently each judge imposed the punishment, but also whether they granted leave to appeal and how often they imposed discretionary death sentences. As Angus and Grant noted, "one of the vital factors contributing to these disparities is the personal disposition towards capital punishment of the individual judges," leading them to conclude that "judicial attitudes towards the death penalty play a material role" in sentencing inconsistencies.[44] The disparities in discretionary capital sentences were especially obvious, because sentencing discretion was not concealed by the formality of whether extenuating circumstances were found. Judges "apply widely differing approaches to the consideration of youth as a factor in extenuation," while at the sentencing phase of the trial, judicial personality appeared to determine the weight given to evidence such as social worker reports, testimony of psychologists, and expert criminological studies.[45]

Only once in South African legal history did the government open an inquiry into the application of the death penalty: the Lansdown Commission of 1947, which confirmed public support of the death penalty, though it was inconclusive as to whether capital punishment provided the deterrent effects claimed by supporters.[46] Influenced by a similar movement among civil rights leaders in the United States, legal scholar Barend van Niekerk conducted an exhaustive study of the racial application of the death penalty in South Africa and Rhodesia, publishing his conclusions in the *South African Law Journal* in 1969 and 1970.[47] His views were unpopular as they were subversive of the racial order. Though acquitted of a contempt charge, his harassment by state officials dampened independent academic inquiry into the death penalty until the late 1980s, when its overuse during late apartheid uprisings sparked a campaign of abolition that finally won effective abolition by 1990.[48]

---

40 *Id.*
41 McNally, *supra* note 23 at 247.
42 Janos Mihalik, *The Death Penalty in Bophuthatswana: A New Deal for Condemned Prisoners?*, 107 S. AFR. L.J. 465, 473–5 (1990).
43 Kahn, *Lopsided Law*, *supra* note 13 at 162 n. 99.
44 Angus & Grant, *supra* note 7 at 69 (including a detailed statistical analysis of the capital sentences of about fifty judges).
45 Murray, Sloth-Nielson & Tredoux, *supra* note 24 at 168–9.
46 Devenish, *supra* note 11 at 9.
47 Van Niekerk, *supra* note 9, *passim*.
48 TURRELL, *supra* note 5 at 10.

Two brief historical moments—van Niekerk's founding of the Society for the Abolition of the Death Penalty in 1971, and the relaunch of the Society in 1989—both resulted in reduced short-term numbers of executions from 81 (1970) to 43 (1973), and from 164 (1987) to 53 (1989).[49] Even slight public pressure could have outsized consequences.

In early 1990, the African National Congress set a moratorium as a precondition for negotiations with the South African government. President F.W. de Klerk announced a moratorium on February 2, 1990. The resulting implementing legislation abolishing the doctrine of extenuating circumstances, the Criminal Law Amendment Act of 1990, was greatly welcomed by lawyers and human rights organizations. However, the death penalty was still in crisis: "Hanging black persons to maintain an oppressive government by a racially elite minority is indubitably a gross abuse of criminal law and procedure that is incompatible with the political and constitutional reform that is so earnestly desired by the people of South Africa," a penalty "perceived by blacks as a logical consequence of inherent unfairness in the administration of justice."[50] Some commentators made comparisons to the United States, where sentencing guidelines directed judicial discretion and due process protections, but where this guided discretion had not solved the underlying problems of racial and economic disparities on death row.[51] But the time for abolition had not yet come.

The Criminal Law Amendment Act went into effect on July 27, 1990, abolishing the mandatory death sentence for murder and substituting a discretionary death sentence in all cases.[52] The legislation required that the death penalty be imposed only after full consideration of both mitigating and aggravating factors and that the court be satisfied that death was the only proper sentence. Under the new rules, the state carried the onus to prove that mitigating circumstances did not exist or were outweighed by aggravating ones. Finally, the Act created an automatic right of appeal and review so that the Appellate Division was required to scrutinize death sentences even where the defendant did not appeal. The Appellate Division had enhanced power to substitute a more appropriate sentence on appeal.[53] The legislation included a procedure for reconsidering the sentences of all death row prisoners whose appeals were final. A committee composed of former judges and other appointees was empowered to hear petitions, recommend lesser sentences, or refer cases for a new trial. The Act's discretionary provisions were applicable to all pending cases, effectively ordering the resentencing of prisoners whose cases were still on appeal.[54]

---

49 Devenish, *supra* note 11 at 11–12.
50 *Id.* at 28.
51 Ursula Bentele, *The False Promise of Discretionary Imposition of the Death Penalty in South Africa*, 9 S. Afr. J. on Hum. Rts. 255, 256 (1993).
52 Criminal Law Amendment Act 107 of 1990. In addition to the features listed in the paragraph above, the legislation also removed the definition of "aggravating circumstances" in the Act (so that courts would consider a broader range of aggravating circumstances), removed aggravated housebreaking and attempted housebreaking from the list of capital crimes, and allowed the Minister of Justice to submit statements to the Appellate Division on behalf of the death row prisoner where he has doubt as to the correctness of the sentence. The Amendment also abolished the discretionary death sentence for persons under age 18. *Id.*
53 Evadné Grant & Laurel Angus, *Capital Punishment*, 2 S. Afr. Hum. Rts. Y.B. 1, 2–8 (1991). This change may have been related to the case S. v. S., 1988 (1) S.A. 120 (A.D.), in which the appeals court upheld a death sentence for rape as reasonable even though a long prison sentence would also have been reasonable. *See* Janos Mihalik, *Mr Justice Braam Lategan, the Appellate Division and the Abolitionists*, 4 S. Afr. J. Crim. Just. 187, 191 (1991).
54 Criminal Law Amendment Act 107 of 1990 §§ 19–20.

Following the change of law, the Appellate Division gave guidance to lower courts on how to weigh aggravating and mitigating factors in lieu of an extenuating circumstance analysis.[55] In *State v. Senonohi*, the Court took the view that the death penalty could only be imposed when no other sentence was appropriate.[56] In *State v. Nkwanyana*, the Court ruled that the new provision required judges to weigh aggravating and mitigating factors in order to determine whether the death sentence was the only appropriate sentence under the circumstances.[57] The statute did not define aggravating or mitigating factors, but the Court found that "mitigating factors" was intended to be broader than "extenuating circumstances," and judges were to look to "the degree of planning, the manner of the commission of the murder, its motive, the circumstances of the victim and an accused's previous convictions...in deciding whether there are aggravating factors."[58] According to one analysis, these early decisions provided guidance as to how aggravating and mitigating factors should be *weighed*, but not *weighted* (i.e., according each factor relative weight) so that some decisions only recited a laundry list of factors.[59]

The Penal Code amendment failed to include a reference to which party bore the burden of proof. Unlike the prior extenuating circumstances regime, the new statute required a judge specifically to articulate the presence or absence of aggravating or mitigating factors, and consequently, the burden of showing these factors had to be assigned. According to the Court, proof of aggravating factors rested on "the State to establish their presence. And in order to discharge such onus, proof beyond reasonable doubt will be required."[60] The Court applied a similar rule to mitigating factors, placing the onus "on the State to negative, beyond reasonable doubt, the existence of such mitigating factors as are relied on by an accused. It follows that if there remains a reasonable possibility that mitigating factors exist, the onus is not discharged."[61] The Court believed that the burden on the issue of proving a negative may seem unfair, but "the problem will often be more apparent than real," as a mitigating factor had to have a factual basis. If both aggravating and mitigating circumstances existed, the Court wrote, "their respective force or significance will have to be weighed in order to determine whether the death sentence is the proper one."[62]

---

55 The first reported case, *State v. Masina*, reversed a death sentence under the new law but did not articulate the process of balancing mitigating and aggravating factors. State v. Masina, 1990 (4) S.A. 709 (A.D.).

56 This is because the amendment required that a court find the death penalty to be "*the* appropriate sentence" rather than "an appropriate sentence." State v. Senonohi, 1990 (4) S.A. 727, 728 (A.D.) (see headnote; decision reported in Afrikaans).

57 State v. Nkwanyana, 1990 (4) S.A. 735 (A.D.).

58 *Id.* at 743.

59 Jan H. Van Rooyen, *South Africa's New Death Sentence: Is the Bell Tolling for the Hangman?*, 7 S. AFR. J. CRIM. JUST. 79, 80 (1991).

60 *Nkwanyana*, 1990 (4) S.A. at 743–4.

61 *Id.* at 744.

62 *Id.* at 745. The Court cited an earlier case in which a judge reviewed precedent from other jurisdictions and concluded that a discretionary death penalty was more rational than the doctrine of extenuating circumstances: "What is attractive about the approach is this: To an accused person the sentence is at least as important as the conviction, and it might seem, in a sense, anomalous to give him the benefit of all reasonable doubts before finding him guilty, and then, when dealing with a question which may make a vast difference to his sentence, to place an onus on him so that the Court, if it finds the probabilities equally balanced in relation to some mitigating fact, will punish him as if that fact did not exist." State v. Shepard, 1967(4) S.A. 170 (Wits. Local Div.), *quoted in Nkwanyana*, 1990 (4) S.A. at 744. For a later confirmation of the difference this onus made, see State v. Matshili, 1991 (3) S.A. 264, 273 (A.D.) ("We have to approach the matter on the basis that it was

Once the new Constitutional Court of South Africa came into existence in February 1995 under the Interim Constitution, the Court's first case was *Makwanyane v. State*, a constitutional challenge to the death penalty, heard the day after the eleven justices were sworn in.[63] The appellants challenged the death penalty as being incompatible with the rights to life, human dignity, and the prohibition on cruel, inhuman, and degrading punishment.[64] The Court unanimously found the death penalty was incompatible with the interim constitution, although each justice wrote separately. The decision, probably the most vindicating abolitionist decision ever handed down by a court of final appeal, was notable for its searching analysis of comparative jurisprudence from Canada, the European Union, and the United States.

Chief Justice Arthur Chaskalson, writing for the Court, found that judicial discretion did not prevent arbitrariness:

> Mitigating and aggravating factors must be identified by the Court, bearing in mind that the onus is on the State to prove beyond reasonable doubt the existence of aggravating factors, and to negative beyond reasonable doubt the presence of any mitigating factors relied on by the accused. Due regard must be paid to the personal circumstances and subjective factors which might have influenced the accused person's conduct, and these factors must then be weighed up with the main objects of punishment, which have been held to be: deterrence, prevention, reformation, and retribution. In this process "[e]very relevant consideration should receive the most scrupulous care and reasoned attention," and the death sentence should only be imposed in the most exceptional cases, where there is no reasonable prospect of reformation and the objects of punishment would not be properly achieved by any other sentence. [...]
>
> The argument that the imposition of the death sentence under section 277 [of the Criminal Procedure Act] is arbitrary and capricious does not, however, end there. It also focuses on what is alleged to be the arbitrariness inherent in the application of section 277 in practice. Of the thousands of persons put on trial for murder, only a very small percentage are sentenced to death by a trial court, and of those, a large number escape the ultimate penalty on appeal. At every stage of the process there is an element of chance. The outcome may be dependent upon factors such as the way the case is investigated by the police, the way the case is presented by the prosecutor, how effectively the accused is defended, the personality and particular attitude to capital punishment of the trial judge and, if the matter goes on appeal, the particular judges who are selected to hear the case. Race and poverty are also alleged to be factors.
>
> Most accused facing a possible death sentence are unable to afford legal assistance, and are defended under the *pro deo* system. The defending counsel is more often than not young and inexperienced, frequently of a different race to his or her client, and if this is the case, usually has to consult through an interpreter. *Pro deo* counsel are paid only a nominal fee

---

for the State to disprove the mitigating factors under consideration. In my view, it has not discharged this onus. Though appellants' credibility is suspect, their evidence stands uncontradicted. So does that of the experts.").

63 William Schabas, *African Perspectives on Abolition of the Death Penalty*, in THE INTERNATIONAL SOURCEBOOK ON CAPITAL PUNISHMENT: 1997 EDITION 30, 39 (Schabas ed., 1997).

64 S. AFR. INTERIM CONST. arts. 9, 10 & 11(2).

for the defence, and generally lack the financial resources and the infrastructural support to undertake the necessary investigations and research, to employ expert witnesses to give advice, including advice on matters relevant to sentence, to assemble witnesses, to bargain with the prosecution, and generally to conduct an effective defence. [...][65]

The Court concluded that the death penalty constituted an arbitrary deprivation of life.

The *Makwanyane* decision exemplified both the globalization of death penalty jurisprudence, and its reverse trend, the localization and indigenization of global human rights norms. Several of the justices cited the concept of *ubuntu*, a concept akin to human dignity in the Zulu and isiXhosa family of languages, and *botho* in the Tswana and Sotho languages, to emphasize the need for reconciliation and restoration in criminal justice.[66] The death penalty, according to this reasoning, was a form of institutionalized vengeance.[67] Because other African countries continued to possess death penalty savings clauses, the decision in *Makwanyane* was not specifically followed by death penalty abolition in the region. However, the decision was cited and distinguished in regional jurisprudence for the principle that human dignity plays a role in criminal sentencing, helping to mitigate the harshness of the death penalty.[68]

In 1998, South Africa passed mandatory minimum sentences, with premeditated and felony murder and aggravated rape warranting mandatory life imprisonment.[69] The poorly drafted legislation was originally intended to be temporary, but became permanent after the repeal of the provision requiring renewal of the legislation each year.[70] In 2001, the Supreme Court of Appeal indicated that mandatory sentences should ordinarily be imposed, but if a case calls for a departure from the prescribed sentence, a court should not hesitate to do so.[71] In *State v. Dodo*, the Constitutional Court upheld the constitutionality of mandatory sentences, as the legislation allowed a judge to depart from the scheme if necessary.[72]

The Rise and Fall of the Mandatory Death Penalty in Zimbabwe

In precolonial Zimbabwe, the Shona people did not practice the death penalty for murder, believing that taking another person's life would cause his spirit to return to torment the living, though the more centralized Ndebele did practice capital punishment.[73] The Ndebele

---

65 State v. Makwanyane, 1995 (3) S.A. 391, 418–19 (C.C.).

66 *Id.* at 481, 501.

67 Drucilla Cornell & Karin van Marle, *Exploring* ubuntu: *Tentative Reflections*, 5 AFR. HUM. RTS. L.J. 195, 207 (2005).

68 *See, for instance, Uganda v. Sekamatte*, [2012] UGHC 96 (September 20, 2012); *Rex v. Ntobo*, [2001] LSHC 133 (December 13, 2001) (citing *Makwanyane* for the proposition that death is reserved to only the narrowest and most heinous crimes).

69 Criminal Law Amendment Act 105 of 1997.

70 Stephen Terblanche & Geraldine Mackenzie, *Mandatory Sentences in South Africa: Lessons for Australia?*, 41 AUST. & N.Z. J. CRIMINOLOGY. 402, 410 (2008).

71 State v. Malgas, [2001] 3 All S.A. 220 (S.C.A.).

72 State v. Dodo, 2001 (3) S.A. 382, 408 (C.C.). The Constitutional Court has been strict as to the constitutionality of reverse onuses, such as that in the doctrine of extenuating circumstances, as these may infringe the presumption of innocence. State v. Manamela, 2000 (3) S.A. 1.

73 Dumbutshena, *supra* note 4 at 521.

had developed a system of fines, but incarceration was unknown.[74] As in other British African colonies, a dual legal system was established that codified and applied customary law in certain family, probate, and land disputes, while recognizing the supremacy of European-derived law.[75] The court system that developed in colonial Southern Rhodesia was more complex, with different forums and avenues of appeal based on a litigant's race and residence and the amount of money involved in the dispute.[76]

As elsewhere in Southern Africa, the criminal law of the territory operated as a means of social control. Criminal sentencing was "profoundly paternalistic" toward women.[77] It also reflected racial biases as well, as evidenced in "black peril" laws, which became at times "a fully hysterical obsession within colonial Zimbabwe's white settler community."[78] At least formally, a single criminal and penal code applied to both black and white Rhodesians, but prosecutorial discretion in bringing charges, and prison regulations authorizing the amount and quality of food, clothing, and other essentials an inmate might receive produced overt patterns of racial discrimination.[79]

The death penalty is authorized by Chapter 59, Section 314 of Zimbabwe's penal code. Zimbabwe inherited a wide array of capital crimes from the colonial period, including attempted murder, conspiracy, treason, rape and attempted rape, aggravated robbery and attempt, certain political offenses under Rhodesian security legislation, and felony murder.[80] While Zimbabwe retained an array of capital offenses after independence, the death sentence was restricted to cases of murder and treason in 1992.[81] The doctrine of extenuating circumstances was passed in the Southern Rhodesian Legislative Assembly in 1949, introducing some judicial discretion to capital sentencing.[82] Then-Minister of Justice Thomas Beadle told the all-white legislature that "only half the death sentences which are passed in this Colony are ever carried out in fact."[83] One member noted that the doctrine provided clarity to the law since the current mandatory death penalty regime created "a tendency to strain the law against the finding of murder," and instead convict of

---

74 A. MITTLEBEELER, AFRICAN CUSTOM AND WESTERN LAW: THE DEVELOPMENT OF THE RHODESIAN CRIMINAL LAW FOR AFRICANS 163–4 (1976).

75 T.W. Bennett, *Conflict of Laws: The Application of Customary Law and the Common Law in Zimbabwe*, 30 INT'L & COMP. L.Q. 59, 68 (1981).

76 Western-style courts included magistrate's courts, the High Court, and the Appellate Division in Salisbury, from which appeals could be taken to the Appellate Division in South Africa (to 1955), the Federal Court of Rhodesia and Nyasaland (1955–63), or the Rhodesian Supreme Court (after 1963). Rhodesia permitted appeals to the Privy Council for a time. In African customary disputes, in urban areas disputes arose in a district commissioner's court, with appeals to the Native Appeal Court (later the Court of Appeal for African Civil Cases). In rural areas, chiefs' courts and headmen's courts appealed to the Tribal Appeals Court. These court systems were merged at Zimbabwe's independence. Tapiwa Zimudzi, *African Women, Violent Crime and the Criminal Law in Zimbabwe*, 30 J. SOUTH. AFR. STUD. 499, 502 (2004); A. Ladley, *Changing the Courts in Zimbabwe: The Customary Law and Primary Courts Act*, 26 J. AFR. L. 95, 96 (1982).

77 Zimudzi, *supra* note 76 at 505–7.

78 J. Pape, *Black and White: The 'Perils of Sex' in Colonial Zimbabwe*, 16 J. SOUTH. AFR. STUD. 699, 700 (1990).

79 C. Zimmerli, *Human Rights and the Rule of Law in Southern Rhodesia*, 20 INT'L & COMP. L.Q. 239, 286 (1971).

80 G. FELTOE, A GUIDE TO SENTENCING IN ZIMBABWE 26–7 (1990).

81 Criminal Laws Amendment Act 2 of 1992. *See* Criminal Procedure and Evidence Act, 1 STATUTE LAW OF ZIMBABWE, Cap. 9:07, § 337 (1996 ed.).

82 Criminal Procedure and Evidence Amendment Act 52 of 1949.

83 Debates of the Legislative Assembly of Southern Rhodesia, October 18, 1949, at 2643.

manslaughter. Allowing a judge a measure of sentencing discretion would "enable the law to be administered more logically."[84]

Like South Africa, colonial Rhodesia relied on the death penalty to punish political crimes and deter political dissent. Increasing African nationalist political activity during the early years of the Rhodesian War revived the mandatory death penalty for the political crimes of throwing a "petrol bomb" (Molotov cocktail) and for possession of arms of war. Neither crime permitted consideration of extenuating circumstances.[85] Both pieces of legislation were doggedly opposed in Parliament by white liberal MPs and by the black African and South Asian MPs first elected in 1962.[86] Introduced in February 1963, the mandatory death penalty for petrol bombing generated intense media coverage as the "Hanging Bill," which the opposition opposed on grounds that the death penalty was mandatory and did not include a provision for extenuating circumstances.[87] However, the conservative Rhodesian Front played on white settler fears that a victorious African nationalist administration would free political prisoners, undermining the deterrent effects of imprisonment.[88] With the increasing dominance of the Rhodesian Front over settler politics after 1965, opponents were powerless to prevent passage of the mandatory death penalty for possession of arms of war.[89] Less than a year later, however, the Rhodesian legislature abolished the mandatory death penalty for both crimes, finding them to be unenforceable in practice.[90] In 1974, the Rhodesian legislature passed the death penalty for terrorist recruitment and training, but the bill allowed a judge to substitute life imprisonment based on consideration of several statutorily defined "special circumstances."[91]

The mandatory death penalty for petrol bombing inevitably faced constitutional challenge under the prohibition on cruel, inhuman, or degrading punishment under the 1961 and 1965 Rhodesian constitutions. In a series of challenges before Rhodesian courts and the Privy Council, defendants argued that the mandatory death penalty was overly harsh because it did not consider mitigating circumstances.[92] The challenges were brought by sympathetic defendants, guilty only as accomplices, in cases where the petrol bombs did not ignite or caused only minor property damage. All three challenges ended with the

---

84   *Id*. at 2651.

85   *See generally*, Andrew Novak, *Abuse of State Power: The Mandatory Death Penalty for Political Crimes in Southern Rhodesia, 1963–1970*, 19 FUNDAMINA: J. LEGAL HIST. 28, 35 *et seq*. (2013).

86   Anthony Lemon, *Electoral Machinery and Voting Patterns in Rhodesia, 1962–1977*, 77 AFR. AFF. 511, 511 (1978) (on Rhodesia's electoral system). IAN HANCOCK, WHITE LIBERALS, MODERATES, AND RADICALS IN RHODESIA 98 (1984).

87   *"Hanging Bill" is Read*, BULAWAYO CHRONICLE, February 15, 1963; *"Hanging Bill" Under Fire*, BULAWAYO CHRONICLE, February 19, 1963. *See also*, Law and Order (Maintenance) Amendment Act 12 of 1963.

88   Debates of the Legislative Assembly of Southern Rhodesia, Feb. 26, 1963, at 603, 630.

89   The legislation on possession of arms of war contained an insidious clause that reversed the burden of proof, requiring the defendant to show absence of intent. Rhodesian Constitutional Council determined that the provision violated the presumption of innocence under the Rhodesian Declaration of Rights contained in the new 1965 Constitution, but the Council was overruled by a two-thirds vote of the legislature. Richard Hodder-Williams, *Rhodesia's Search for a Constitution: Or, Whatever Happened to Whaley?*, 69 AFR. AFF. 217, 220 (1970).

90   Law and Order (Maintenance) Amendment Act 41 of 1968; Debates of the Legislative Assembly of Rhodesia, Sept. 25, 1968, at 1573.

91   Debates of the Legislative Assembly of Rhodesia, Nov. 14, 1974, at 914–15, 935, 941, 951-2.

92   Regina v. Runyowa, 1966 R.L.R. 42 (P.C.) (appeal taken from Rhodesia & Nyasaland); Gundu v. Sheriff of Southern Rhodesia, 1965 R.L.R. 301 (Rhodesia A.D.); Regina v. Mapolisa, 1964 R.L.R. 591 (P.C.) (appeal taken from Rhodesia & Nyasaland).

rulings that the prohibition of cruel, inhuman, and degrading punishment related only to kind, type, or method of punishment and not to severity, quantum, or appropriateness of punishment. The 1961 Rhodesian constitution possessed a partial savings clause, excluding from constitutional challenge any form of punishment that was lawful in Southern Rhodesia at the time the constitution entered into force.[93] Because there had been a mandatory death penalty in 1961, even if it had not existed for petrol bombing, the penalty was immune from challenge. In addition, the Appellate Division extended these holdings in 1968, when it ruled that it had no jurisdiction to assess whether delay on death row, including delay in considering a petition for clemency or pardon, was cruel and degrading, an early death row syndrome challenge.[94] The window for bringing these constitutional claims closed: the 1969 Rhodesian constitution rendered the bill of rights non-justiciable, and courts could no longer "inquire into or pronounce upon the validity of any new law on the ground that it is inconsistent with the Declaration of Rights."[95] The Rhodesian challenges to the mandatory death penalty at the Privy Council, however, had a destructive reach far beyond Zimbabwe. The holding that the cruel and degrading punishment clause did not apply to severity, amount, or appropriateness of punishment (only to the type, nature, or manner of punishment) remained good law, confirmed by the Privy Council in *Ong Ah Chuan*, the Singapore drug trafficking case, in 1981.

In 1987, the seven-year sunset provision of Zimbabwe's independence Constitution constraining fundamental rights challenges finally expired (similar to the sunset savings clause in Belize's 1981 constitution).[96] Litigation on the basis of cruel, inhuman, and degrading punishment came almost immediately. In 1987, the full bench of the Supreme Court of Zimbabwe unanimously held that the sentence of whipping for adults constituted cruel, inhuman, and degrading punishment contrary to Section 15(1) of the Zimbabwean Constitution, looking both to international trends against judicial caning and whipping and to the decline in the penalty's use domestically.[97] Two years later, the Court found in a 3 to 2 vote that corporal punishment of juveniles also violated Section 15(1), although this decision was later reversed by constitutional amendment.[98] One by one, challenges succeeded: against solitary confinement, reduced diet, retroactive punishments, and punishments based on mute confessions.[99]

The pinnacle of this era was the Supreme Court's famous decision in *Catholic Commission for Justice and Peace v. Attorney General*, in which the Court found that the dehumanizing factor of prolonged delay on death row, viewed in conjunction with the harsh and degrading conditions in the holding prison, meant that the executions of appellants would have constituted inhuman and degrading treatment contrary to Section 15(1).[100]

---

93 SOUTHERN RHODESIAN CONST. art. 60(3) (1961).
94 Dhlamini v. Carter, 1968 R.L.R. 136 (Rhodesia A.D.).
95 RHODESIAN CONST. art. 84 (1969).
96 *See* ZIMBABWE CONST. art. 26 (1980).
97 State v. Ncube, 1988 (2) S.A. 702, 721 (Zim. S.C.).
98 Juvenile v. State, [1989] L.R.C. 1774 (Zim. S.C.), *reversed by* Constitution of Zimbabwe Amendment Act, No. 11 of 1990. However, nearly a year after the amendment, Parliament had not drafted implementing legislation. For more about corporal punishment in Zimbabwe see John Hatchard, *The Fall and Rise of the Cane in Zimbabwe*, 35 J. AFR. L. 198, 198–200, 202 (1991).
99 Adrian de Bourbon, *Human Rights Litigation in Zimbabwe: Past Present and Future*, 3 AFR. HUM. RTS. L.J. 195, 209–10 (2003).
100 Catholic Commission for Justice and Peace in Zimbabwe v. A.G., (1993) L.R.C. 277 (Zim. S.C.).

Several aspects of the Court's decision were notable: a holding that a defendant was not penalized for seeking to exercise his or her constitutional right to appeal; a broad standing ruling allowing a human rights organization to bring a suit on behalf of a group of prisoners; and a broad range of international authorities cited, including decisions of the United States, India, Canada, the Privy Council, and the United Nations Human Rights Committee.[101]

The doctrine of extenuating circumstances survived unreformed in Zimbabwean homicide law. Zimbabwean courts clearly adhered to the traditional rule placing the burden of proof on the accused.[102] Courts were permitted to adopt either of two approaches to weighing extenuating circumstances. The first required a judge to weigh all mitigating factors against all aggravating factors to determine whether extenuating circumstances existed in order to justify the non-imposition of the death penalty. The second required a court to *first* find that extenuating circumstances existed, no matter how weak they were, and *then* balance mitigating and aggravating factors. As Feltoe notes, the second approach was truer to the wording of the penal code because it allows a court to impose a death sentence even if extenuating circumstances were found.[103] The lack of clarity as to how aggravating factors were to be weighed against extenuating circumstances was an enduring legacy of the doctrine.

One unique aspect of Zimbabwe's doctrine of extenuating circumstances was the degree of deference given to a trial court's decision, and the Supreme Court was powerless to change a sentence in the absence of misdirection or irregularity, even if it would have imposed a lesser sentence.[104] Feltoe referred to judicial discretion in capital cases as "wide and vague."[105] If the Supreme Court upheld a death sentence, the evidence and rulings were transmitted to the President, who had to confirm the death sentence before it was carried out.[106]

Recent case law confirms the Supreme Court's overwhelming deference to trial court decisions. In one recent case, the Court upheld a trial court's finding that no extenuating circumstances existed in a felony murder case, indicating that the law was "clear" that a "murder committed in the course of a robbery attracts the death penalty unless there are weighty extenuating circumstances."[107] In making a determination on extenuating circumstances, "the trial court exercises what is essentially a moral judgment" and the

---

101 John Hatchard, *Delay and the Death Sentence: The Zimbabwean Approach*, 37 J. AFR. L. 185, 192 (1993).

102 *See, e.g.*, Jongwe v. State, [2002] ZWSC 62 (Aug. 8, 2002). The Court stated in that case that "[t]he onus to establish the defense of provocation and extenuating circumstances is on the appellant. Should the trial court reject his version of events the appellant will have problems establishing extenuating circumstances." *Id*. For an even more recent case, see State v. Wairosi, [2011] ZWHHC 53 (Feb. 15, 2011) ("The convicted person in this case did not advance any statutory reason why the death sentence should not be imposed on him. He did not advance anything warranting the recalling of the court's findings on extenuating circumstances or the conviction. He merely repeated what he had said in his defence which was not believed by the court. There is therefore no basis on which this court can pass a sentence other than the death sentence"). In other words, the defendant carries the burden; if the defendant says nothing, the death sentence is mandatory.

103 G. Feltoe, *Extenuating Circumstances: A Life and Death Issue*, 4 ZIM. L.REV. 60, 63 (1986).

104 John Hatchard, *Capital Punishment in Southern Africa: Some Recent Developments*, 43 INT'L & COMP. L.Q. 923, 925 (1994).

105 Feltoe, *supra* note 103 at 82–3.

106 Dumbutshena, *supra* note 4 at 531.

107 Morgan Matondo Matongo v. State, Crim. App. No. 108/04, Judgment No. SC 61/05 (Nov. 14, 2005).

Supreme Court on appeal "cannot substitute its own view." The Court could only "interfere if persuaded that the conclusion of the trial court could not reasonably have been reached; or where the court had regard to the wrong factors; or had mistakenly excluded factors proper to be taken into account, or had, in some other way, erred in principle."[108] This was a high threshold. In another case, the Supreme Court found that a trial court had erred in finding a murder premeditated, but nonetheless upheld a death sentence without extenuating circumstances as the murder was still intentional.[109] This level of deference contrasts markedly with the efforts of other appellate courts in Southern Africa to seek uniformity in sentencing. In refusing to reduce a sentence for murder with extenuating circumstances from twenty-five years to twenty years, the justices wrote that it was "not for this Court to interfere with a sentence passed by a court of first instance merely because it might have imposed a different sentence."[110] This level of deference suggests a lack of robust appellate review in capital cases.

Courts in Zimbabwe never developed a clear method of weighing aggravating and mitigating circumstances. Even in the presence of possible extenuating circumstances, the Supreme Court of Zimbabwe upheld death sentences where aggravating factors outweighed mitigating ones.[111] The Court showed willingness to dispense death sentences for felony murder and accomplice liability in which the defendant had only constructive intent to kill.[112] Intent to commit a serious felony such as armed robbery if death was foreseeable was not an extenuating circumstance. The Court has ruled, however, that lack of actual intent to kill is an extenuating circumstance where the "foreseeability of the possibility of death...was rather remote."[113] In a later case, the Court clarified its holdings on constructive intent: "The finding of a constructive intent to kill in a murder case will not necessarily lead to an overall finding...that there are extenuating circumstances justifying a sentence other than death, but it is a factor which must be put [o]n the credit side in the accused's favour in that weighing-up process."[114] The court ruled that constructive intent, on its own or with other factors, can constitute an extenuating circumstance, and a trial court must "balance carefully the mitigating features and aggravating features" before making a final determination.

In May 2013, President Robert Mugabe signed into law a new constitution, one that was overwhelming ratified by voters. The constitution went through several drafting phases before the detailed death penalty provisions were finalized. The 2001 National Constitutional Assembly draft permitted the death penalty for "the most heinous murders," but only after public debate about which types of murder should attract the death penalty, and only where aggravating circumstances are precisely defined in law. The 2007 Kariba Draft exempted pregnant women and persons under 18 years of age; it also required courts to have discretion in imposing death, and granted all defendants the right to seek pardon or

---

108   State v. Woods, 1993 (2) Zim.L.R. 258, 284 (S.C.).
109   Mbembe Porusingazi v. State, Crim. App. No. 119/06, Judgment No. S.C. 63/07 (June 9, 2008).
110   Pfungwa Mamvura v. State, Crim. App. No. 127/2003, Judgment no. S.C. 22/05 (June 20, 2005).
111   Irvine Kanhumwa & Others v. State, Crim. App. No. 189/2002, Judgment No. SC 71/07 (November 29, 2004) (finding that the defendant's youth and status as a first time offender were "totally eclipsed by the aggravating circumstances").
112   Piniel Murijo v. State, Crim. App. No. 124/04, Judgment No. SC 150/04, [2005] ZWSC 139 (September 22, 2005).
113   Robert Mugwanda v. State, Crim. App. No. 215/2001, Judgment No. SC 19/02 (June 6, 2002).
114   Siluli v. State, 2005 (2) Zim.L.R. 141, 146.

commutation of sentence. The 2010 proposed Law Society of Zimbabwe draft abolished the death penalty and forbade executions from taking place in the country. The version that was ultimately ratified abolishes the death penalty for treason and sharply curtails the death penalty for murder, requiring it to be committed in "aggravating circumstances." With ratification, the death penalty became a prohibited sentence for women and persons under the age of 21 at the time of the offense or over the age of 70. The provision states that "the law must permit the court a discretion whether or not to impose the penalty," which provides a judge discretion to impose a lesser sentence even in the absence of extenuating circumstances.[115] The effective abolition of the doctrine of extenuating circumstances in Zimbabwe fits with a continent-wide trend toward abolition of the mandatory death penalty.

Transparency and the Doctrine of Extenuating Circumstances in Botswana

In Botswana, the death penalty existed in precolonial Tswana law for crimes such as murder, sorcery, incest, and conspiracy against a chief, with executions often occurring swiftly and secretly.[116] Section 26 of the penal code authorizes that any person sentenced to death be "hanged by the neck until dead" for the crimes of murder, treason, and piracy with intent to murder.[117] According to Section 203(2) of the penal code, "[w]here a Court in convicting a person of murder is of the opinion that there are extenuating circumstances, the Court may impose any sentence other than death." Despite the phrasing of this provision, the sentencing court *must* impose a sentence other than death if it finds extenuating circumstances.[118]

As in Zimbabwe, South African jurisprudence is an important source of law in capital sentencing. Decisions of South African courts are of "strong persuasive force," but "on the question of extenuating circumstances, the decisions of the courts of South Africa have a perhaps even stronger persuasive force because the concept of 'extenuating circumstances' in sentences for murder as introduced into the Penal Code was plainly derived...from and based on legislation in South Africa."[119] While this process is no longer "living," as South African jurisprudence after abolition of the death penalty in 1995 has been found to be inapplicable to Botswana, death penalty cases from the pre-abolition period are still widely cited.

In Botswana, a court must inquire as to whether any factors might have influenced an accused's state of mind at the time he committed the offense; whether those factors did in fact influence the accused; and whether the influence on the accused's mind was such that the act could be considered less morally reprehensible.[120] A court must consider the defendant's social background, considering the standards of behavior of an ordinary person in the defendant's community, and judging the accused's behavior according to his own peculiar circumstances—his weaknesses, foibles, defects, and beliefs. The Court of Appeal has clearly thwarted attempts to use an objective "reasonable man" standard.[121] In weighing

---

115   ZIMBABWE CONST. art. 48(2) (2013).
116   IAN SCHAPERA, A HANDBOOK OF TSWANA LAW AND CUSTOM 260–61 (1970).
117   Daniel D. Ntanada Nsereko, *Extenuating Circumstances in Capital Offenses in Botswana*, 2 CRIM. L.F. 235, 267 (1991). No convictions have occurred under the latter two crimes.
118   *Id.* at 246.
119   Clement Kobedi Gofhamodino v. State, Crim. App. No. 4/1984 (June 1984) (Bots. C.A.).
120   Nsereko, *supra* note 117 at 261.
121   *Id.* at 262–3.

whether extenuating circumstances exist, Botswana courts must consider the totality of all factors, both mitigating and aggravating.[122]

The Botswana Court of Appeal has generously interpreted extenuating circumstances to include a wide range of factors. Absence of premeditation alone may be an extenuating circumstance in Botswana, unlike in Zimbabwe, which is a strong indicator that judges attempt to restrict the death penalty only to the narrowest class of cases.[123] Botswana clearly permits provocation as an extenuating circumstance, having found that the proper inquiry is whether the totality of the circumstances that existed at the time the crime was committed had a bearing on the accused's state of mind.[124] In Zimbabwe, by contrast, if a defense of provocation fails at trial, it is likely to fail as an extenuating circumstance because the accused's version of events was rejected.[125]

The Constitution of Botswana grants the president the power to substitute, reduce, or lift a criminal sentence.[126] Like many other common law constitutions, Botswana's constitution also provides for an advisory committee on the prerogative of mercy, consisting of the attorney-general and a cabinet minister and medical practitioner designated by the president.[127] The committee regulates its own procedure, which must, as a constitutional minimum, require a judge to write a report of the capital case to be considered by the advisory committee in secret proceedings.[128] The president invokes the pardon power extremely rarely.[129] "The president is not...obliged to follow the Committee's advice," but should he not, he must personally sign the death warrant. "The exercise of the prerogative of mercy constitutes a serious interference with the judicial process, and is exercised only for good cause," and as a consequence, the president will likely intervene "only in the most exceptional and unusual situation" to reverse a judicially imposed sentence.[130]

Persons sentenced to death in Botswana need not apply for pardon or commutation, as the constitution obligates the president to consider exercising the mercy power to all capital convicts.[131] The committee's lack of transparency has come in for particularly brutal criticism from human rights NGOs, as its proceedings are not available to the defendant, the defense counsel, or the public.[132] Because the state does not notify family members,

---

122 Generally, aggravating factors include premeditation, use of a weapon, excessive cruelty, murder during a rape or robbery, or peculiar vulnerability of the victim. Extenuating circumstances include belief in witchcraft, provocation, absence of actual intention to kill, intoxication, youth, and factors peculiar to the individual defendant. A court may not consider prior convictions unless it has found extenuating circumstances to exist. *Id.* at 246, 267.

123 Masono v. State, [2000] 1 Bots.L.R. 46 (C.A.).

124 Ndlovu v. State, [1995] Bots.L.R. 432, 438 (C.A.).

125 Jongwe v. State, Crim. App. No. 251/2002, Judgment No. S.C. 62/02, [2002] ZWSC 62 (Aug. 8, 2002).

126 BOTSWANA CONST. art. 53.

127 *Id.*, art. 54.

128 *Id.*, art. 55.

129 ELIZABETH MAXWELL & ALICE MOGWE, IN THE SHADOW OF THE NOOSE 105 (2006); Nsereko, *supra* note 117 at 266.

130 Charles Manga Fombad, *The Separation of Powers and Constitutionalism in Africa: The Case of Botswana*, 25 B.C. THIRD WORLD L.J. 301, 331 (2005).

131 Nsereko, *supra* note 117 at 266.

132 FEDERATION INTERNATIONALE DES LINGUES DES DROITS DE L'HOMME (FIDH) & DITSHWANELO BOTSWANA CENTRE FOR HUMAN RIGHTS, THE DEATH PENALTY IN BOTSWANA: HASTY AND SECRETIVE HANGINGS 26 (2007).

lawyers, or human rights monitoring organizations of pending executions, the secrecy makes appeal to regional and international tribunals more difficult.[133]

The Botswana Court of Appeal made an important modification to the traditional doctrine, at least formally removing the evidentiary burden on the accused to show extenuating circumstances. In a case under the traditional rule, the Court of Appeal noted that "the appellant's mental state during the attack on the deceased was left very much in the dark" and the judges knew "virtually nothing about [his] personality, his motive, his mentality, his past history, experiences, and upbringing," because the defendant's attorney failed to make a showing of extenuating circumstances.[134] The fault, however, was on the defendant: "The onus was on the Defence to provide the trial court with evidence from which extenuating circumstances might be inferred.... Appellant did not do so and his motivation remains unexplained."[135] Over time, however, the Court has softened the rule, holding that if the defendant does not show extenuating circumstances, the judge may find them on his own, *sua sponte*: "the law has not put any onus on an accused to prove even on balance of probabilities that extenuating circumstances exist in his case."[136] Instead, the trial judge has the responsibility to examine the evidence after conviction, regardless of any showing by the defendant.

This innovation in the doctrine of extenuating circumstances derived from a series of decisions in January 1995. The first was *Kelaletswe v. State*, in which the Court determined that the burden of showing extenuating circumstances no longer rested on the accused.[137] The prosecutor often had more resources at its disposal than the defendant to show the severity of a crime and surrounding circumstances, but the accused was often the only person present when the crime was committed, so he or she was better-placed to testify to personal factors. For these reasons, the Court determined that the judge and counsel themselves had the responsibility to inquire as to the existence or not of extenuating circumstances. The benefit of the doubt belonged to the accused.[138]

In the second case, *Ntesang v. State*, the Court upheld the constitutionality of the death penalty and hanging as a method of execution based on Botswana's partial savings clause, as death by hanging was legal at the time the constitution entered into force.[139] Additionally, in determining the issue of extenuating circumstances, the Court confirmed that the law does not "cast any onus on...a person to show that such extenuating circumstances exist," and the determination "may be arrived at independently of whether or not the accused gives any evidence in that regard," so long as the trial judge provides an opportunity for the accused to present such evidence.[140] The Botswana Court of Appeal confirmed that the trial judge is to engage in only a single step, weighing aggravating and extenuating factors together to determine whether extenuating circumstances exist. In *Tshabang v. State*, the third of the trio, the Court found that even though the defendant was only 21 at the time of his crime and acted without premeditation, the manner in which he carried out the crime in the course

---

133 *See* Interights (on Behalf of Bosch) v. Botswana, Comm. No. 240/2001, 2003 A.H.R.L.R. 55 (A.C.H.P.R. 2003) In that case, the defendant was executed while her case was still on appeal to the African Commission. MAXWELL & MOGWE, *supra* note 129 at 106–7 (on the secrecy of executions).
134   Sibanda v. State, [1984] BWCA 13 at 6 (Bots. C.A.).
135   *Id.* at 7.
136   Molale v. State, [1995] Bots.L.R. 146, 149 (C.A.).
137   Kelaletswe v. State, [1995] Bots.L.R. 100 (C.A.).
138   *Id.* at 124.
139   Ntesang v. State, [1995] Bots.L.R. 151 (C.A.).
140   *Id.* at 155–6.

of an armed robbery "indicate[d] a cold calculation on his part," which "negative[d] the characteristics of immaturity and impetuosity attached to youth."[141] Although the Court held that there were no extenuating circumstances, the Court's *reasoning* implied that such factors did exist, but that they were outweighed by aggravating factors. This lack of analytical clarity persists in Botswana's case law.

In recent years, the reputation of the death penalty in Botswana has suffered, both domestically and internationally. In 2001, Botswana executed Mariette Sonjaleen Bosch, a white South African woman, for murdering the wife of a man she later married. The case had several irregularities that attracted widespread criticism, including a misstatement of law by the trial judge that was found to be harmless on appeal.[142] The Court upheld the conviction of murder without extenuating circumstances, finding that her emotional jealousy could not be an extenuating circumstance when the murder was so carefully planned. The trial had a circus-like quality to it due to the sordid facts, and the speed with which Bosch was executed after confirmation of her appeal raised objections from human rights organizations. The Government also failed to respond to the request by the African Commission on Human and Peoples' Rights not to carry out the execution until her application could be considered.[143] Although the Commission upheld use of the death penalty under international law in a posthumous decision and determined that the lack of transparency and speed of execution did not create an arbitrary deprivation of life, it cautioned that the criminal justice system "must have a human face in matters of execution," including time to organize one's affairs, visit with family members, receive spiritual advice, and have a proper burial.[144]

An even more consequential case arose two years later when the Court revisited the constitutionality of the death penalty in *Kobedi v. State* and considered a death row "syndrome" challenge.[145] In *Kobedi*, the Court distinguished the Privy Council's recent invalidation of the mandatory death penalty in Belize in *Reyes v. Queen*, noting that the death penalty in Botswana was not strictly mandatory. *Kobedi* also provided an occasion to challenge another aspect of the doctrine of extenuating circumstances, one that never fully developed in South African jurisprudence. This was a fair trial challenge against Botswana's *pro deo* system of legal representation in which criminal defendants could be assigned inadequate or inexperienced defense counsel. The Court was not persuaded: "It is not for this Court to criticise the Botswana *pro deo* system," as the "country has a large number of competent and skilled legal practitioners" who adequately represent most indigent capital defendants.[146] Kobedi had adequate counsel, the Court found, finding his attorney's cross-examination of witnesses to be "searching and vigorous" and his submissions to the court "full and detailed." But this decision masks the shortcomings of such a system. The Constitution of Botswana guarantees the right of a defendant "to defend himself before the court in person or, at his own expense, by a legal representative of his own choice."[147] Standard practice for murder trials has been for the state to assign counsel at nominal cost to an indigent accused person, but "the quality of such representation mostly leaves a lot

---

141 Tshabang v. State, [1995] Bots.L.R. 132, 142 (C.A.).
142 Bosch v. State, [2001] 1 Bots.L.R. 71 (C.A.).
143 Tim Curry, *Cutting the Hangman's Noose: African Initiatives to Abolish the Death Penalty*, 13 HUM. RTS. BRIEF 40, 43 (2006).
144 Interights (on Behalf of Bosch) v. Botswana, Comm. No. 240/2001, 2003 A.H.R.L.R. 55 (ACHPR 2003).
145 Kobedi v. State, [2003] BWCA 22 (Bots. C.A.) (March 19, 2003).
146 *Id.* at 42.
147 BOTSWANA CONST., ch. II, art. 10(d).

to be desired" and the average amount received for a *pro deo* case is one-tenth that made by an attorney in private practice for a single court appearance.[148] State-appointed lawyers often received briefs only shortly before the trial date. "The result is that most *pro deo* cases are handled by inexperienced lawyers who lack the skills, resources, and commitment to handle such serious matters [affecting] the rights of the accused."[149]

Kobedi also raised a vagueness challenge on the basis that the definition of "extenuating circumstances" was unconstitutionally narrow. The defendant argued that the Court's inability to consider mitigating factors as opposed to extenuating ones violated his right to a fair trial as mitigating factors were broader in scope and could include factors such as a lack of previous convictions, good behavior, religious conversion, medical needs, familial obligations, remorse after the fact, or others that do not bear on an accused's moral guilt at the time of the offense. In Kobedi's case, those factors included his good academic record and close family life. The Court dodged the argument, writing that nothing stopped the defendant from raising such arguments.

Finally, Kobedi also raised a death row syndrome challenge as five years had passed from his initial conviction to the final disposition of his appeal. Distinguishing the Zimbabwean case *Catholic Commission*, the Court ruled that delay in Kobedi's case was caused by his own actions in dismissing and hiring new counsel and seeking extensions for court submissions. The Court did not reject the theory of a death row syndrome challenge in the event of an inordinate delay after a defendant has exercised his rights of appeal, noting that such a circumstance could be unconstitutional, but "it is inherent in the [death] penalty that any person upon whom it is imposed is likely to experience mental strain and suffering. He is confined in prison and usually in segregated conditions. His life in prison is a lonely one. He has to cope with the uncertainty as to when his execution will occur, although he is aware that execution is a certainty."[150] The Court issued a stay of Kobedi's death sentence pending his mercy application, a meaningless gesture given that the constitution obliges the president to consider exercising his prerogative of mercy over all capital convicts.[151] The Court did nothing more than shift its responsibility for Kobedi's death sentence to the President.

Judicial Innovation and Constitutional Reform in Swaziland

Swaziland's criminal law is generally based on English common law, though some South African legal concepts survive in Swazi law.[152] Swaziland possessed a Bill of Rights in

---

148 Duma Gideon Boko, *Fair Trial and the Customary Courts in Botswana: Questions on Legal Representation*, 11 CRIM. L.F. 445, 454 (2000). There is no constitutional right to a state-appointed attorney even in capital cases. *See also* FIDH & DITSHWANELO, *supra* note 132 at 21.
149 FIDH & DITSHWANELO, *supra* note 132 at 21.
150 *Kobedi*, [2003] BWCA 22 at 52 (Bots. C.A.).
151 As Bojosi writes, the Court of Appeal's reasoning understated the amount of time that the defendant spent on death row and unfairly excludes delay caused by the prosecutor. In addition, it also penalizes a defendant for exercising their constitutional rights of appeal, even though whether a sentence can become cruel and degrading after an undue amount of time and in certain conditions is irrelevant to the fault of the delay. Kealeboga N. Bojosi, *The Death Row Phenomenon Comes to Botswana: Lehlohonolo Bernard Kobedi v. The State*, 38 COMP. & INT'L L.J. SOUTH. AFR. 304, 310–12 (2005).
152 *See, e.g.*, Deogratias Mabirizi, *Reflections on the Defence of Provocation in Swaziland*, 9 JAHRBUCH FÜR AFRIKANISCHES RECHT (Y.B. AFR. L.) 61, 68–9 (1995).

the original 1963 Order in Council, which ushered in self-government, and in the 1967 and 1968 constitutions, the latter of which became effective at Swaziland's independence in September 1968. However, the monarch suspended the constitution in 1973 during a constitutional crisis, leaving the country without supreme fundamental rights protections.[153] The 2005 constitution provides an elaborate Bill of Rights, including the right to life and a prohibition on torture and other cruel, inhuman, and degrading treatment and punishment, a marked improvement over the prior constitutional regime.[154] However, the constitution failed to protect political freedoms or limit the power of the monarchy, and constrained important human rights provisions.[155]

The doctrine of extenuating circumstances passed into Swaziland's criminal law via the Criminal Law and Procedure (Amendment) Act of 1959, which allowed a judge to substitute a sentence other than death upon a finding of extenuating circumstances.[156] Swaziland has not carried out an execution since July 1983, when eight people were hanged for murder, including a woman convicted of the ritual killing of a child.[157] The country made news when it opened a job search for a hangman in 1998, though the attorney general conceded that the country could not afford to pay a full-time salary. News reports suggested the country would begin using lethal injection as a method of execution since these only required a qualified medical practitioner.[158]

Ratified in 2005, Section 15(2) of the Constitution of Swaziland prohibits the mandatory death penalty, the only constitution in Africa to do so until Zimbabwe's in 2013.[159] In practice, however, the doctrine of extenuating circumstances fell into disuse some years before this, after a series of decisions in which the Court of Appeal (renamed the Supreme Court in the new constitution) determined that the burden did not shift to a defendant to show extenuating circumstances; instead, the prosecutor maintained the burden of showing that there were none. This change made Swaziland's death penalty regime indistinguishable from a truly discretionary one. The most recent case law requires judges to weigh aggravating and mitigating factors even in cases where no extenuating circumstances are found. This revolutionary change toward a discretionary regime provides a path forward for other retentionist nations in Southern Africa.

Unlike Botswana and Zimbabwe, Swazi courts have clearly formulated a two-part extenuating circumstances analysis. The High Court used such a two-part sentencing analysis in *Rex v. Sean Blignaut*, determining in separate stages that extenuating circumstances existed, and then determining an appropriate sentence of imprisonment after weighing both mitigating and aggravating factors.[160] In the judgment on extenuating circumstances, the

---

153 B.P. Wanda, *The Shaping of the Modern Constitution of Swaziland: A Review of Some Social and Historical Factors*, 6 LESOTHO L.J. 137, 153–65.

154 S.M. Langwenya, *Recent Legal Developments: Swaziland*, 2 U. BOTS. L.J. 167, 169 (2005).

155 Sabelo Gumedze, *Human Rights and the Rule of Law in Swaziland*, 5 AFR. HUM. RTS. L.J. 266, 276 (2005); Chris Maroleng, *Swaziland: The King's Constitution*, 12(3) AFR. SECURITY REV. 45, 47 (2003).

156 Criminal Law and Procedure (Amendment) Act 47 of 1959.

157 *Swaziland Executes Eight*, N.Y. TIMES (July 3, 1983) (retrieved from LexisNexis).

158 *Swaziland Can't Afford a Full Time Hangman*, AFRICAN EYE NEWS SERVICE (Feb. 22, 2001) (retrieved from LexisNexis); *No Noose is Still Bad News*, THE EVENING STANDARD (London) (Jan. 17, 2002) (retrieved from LexisNexis).

159 *Compare* SWAZILAND CONST. art. 15(2) with ZIMBABWE CONST. art. 48(2).

160 Rex v. Sean Blignaut, Crim. Case No. 130/2002, [2002] SZHC 10 (Apr. 29, 2002). Mitigating factors included the defendant's status as a first-time offender, his youthfulness, and his lack of prior convictions, while aggravating factors included the fact that the killing was a brutal one,

Court cited *Daniel Dlamini v. Rex*, in which the Court had written, "[w]e find ourselves in respectful agreement with the conclusion of the Botswana Court of Appeal that no onus rests on the accused person" in the extenuating circumstances analysis, citing *Kelaletswe v. State*.[161]

In August 1998, a High Court judge sentenced a defendant to death with a finding that no extenuating circumstances existed in a case in which uncontradicted testimony from a doctor indicated that the defendant's "mental state is very close to that of an idiot." The judge was "unable to find that on a balance of probabilities the accused's mental capacity is that of a child of 15 years," believing the defendant's actions during the crime did not support the doctor's statements.[162] The Court of Appeal reversed; because the doctor's statement was not contradicted on the record, the prosecution had not shown the absence of the extenuating circumstances raised by the record.[163] In May 2001, the High Court found that extenuating circumstances existed in a murder case, as conceded by both prosecution and defense. "For a long time in the past, courts in Swaziland consistently [held] that extenuating circumstances were to be proved by an accused person on the balance of probability," the judge wrote. "However, the Court of Appeal has since authoritatively set the record straight by handing down judgment on sentence where it categorically stated that 'no such onus rests on the accused person.'"[164]

The High Court divided the sentencing stage of the trial between a judgment as to whether extenuating circumstances existed and a judgment weighing mitigating and aggravating factors to determine an appropriate sentence. In one case, a judge found the defendant's youthfulness and intoxication reduced his moral blameworthiness for the offense.[165] In the judgment on sentencing, the judge considered the nature and circumstances of the offense, the characteristics of the offender and his circumstances, and the impact of the crime on the community.[166] In considering the offender, a judge must consider age and background; level of education and position in society; family circumstances, including marriage and dependents; motive in committing the offence; whether the crime was committed for personal gain; prior convictions; the prospect of reformation; and a "perceptive understanding of the accused's human frailties."[167] In considering the crime, the court had to consider the moral and ethical nature of the offense. Finally, in considering the interests of the community, factors such as the protection of society and the maintenance of peace and tranquility were relevant.

With the new constitution, courts reconciled the new constitution's abolition of the mandatory death penalty with the existence of the doctrine of extenuating circumstances. In 2009, the High Court of Swaziland ruled that the constitutional prohibition on the

---

and from a position of trust as a family member. The defendant also lacked remorse. The final sentence was twenty years. *Id.*

161 Daniel Dlamini v. Rex, Crim. App. No. 11/1998 (Swaz. C.A.).

162 Rex v. Pikinini Simon Motsa & Anor., Crim. Case No. 72/1998, [1998] SZHC 31 (Oct. 8, 1998).

163 Pikinini Simon Motsa v. Rex, Crim. App. No. 36/2000, [2000] SZSC 27 (Dec. 1, 2000).

164 Rex v. Nhlanhla Charles Moratele & Anor., Crim. Case No. 93/1999, [2001] SZHC 16 (May 16, 2001). *See also*, Bongani Mkhwanazi v. Rex, Crim. App. No. 125/1998, [2001] SZCA 2 (Nov. 27, 2001) (witchcraft as extenuating factor).

165 Rex v. Majahonkhe Major Mazibuko, Crim. Case No. 3/2002, [2003] SZHC 32 (judgment May 22, 2003; sentence June 26, 2003).

166 *Id., citing* State v. Zinn, 1969 (2) S.A. 537 (A.D.) *and* State v. Scheepers, 1977 (2) S.A. 154 (A.D.).

167 *Id., citing* State v. Sigwahla, 1967 (4) S.A. 566 (A.D.).

mandatory death penalty rendered the extenuating circumstances analysis obsolete since a court *always* possessed the discretion to substitute a lesser sentence regardless of whether extenuating circumstances existed.[168] According to the judge, "the question of extenuating circumstances upon conviction of murder falls away and the court should look into mitigating and aggravating factors," and the extenuating circumstances provision at Section 291(1) of the Criminal Procedure and Evidence Act was unconstitutional to the extent that it was inconsistent with the prohibition on the mandatory death penalty.[169] In a separate case, the Supreme Court of Swaziland agreed that courts possessed discretion to substitute a lesser sentence regardless of whether extenuating circumstances existed.[170] The Supreme Court reasoned that the doctrine could still be *relevant* in determining a sentence as it could "fortify a decision to impose or not to impose the death penalty."[171] In determining sentences, the trial judges of the High Court were permitted to use either the old method of deciding whether extenuating circumstances existed and then weighing aggravating and mitigating factors, or the new method of weighing aggravating and mitigating factors in a single step.

Since the establishment of a purely discretionary death penalty in Swaziland, judges have been reluctant to dispense a death sentence even when they had discretion to do so. A judge of the High Court found that a defendant was guilty of murder with no extenuating circumstances *and* found that the aggravating factors "far outweigh[ed]" the mitigating factors, but nonetheless decided to "invoke section 15 (2) of the Constitution which provides that the death penalty shall not be mandatory in circumstances where no extenuating circumstances exist" as the defendant was a first offender.[172] He was sentenced to imprisonment. However, in the particularly sensationalized case of serial killer David Simelane, who was convicted of twenty-eight murders of women and girls over a two-year period, the court had no hesitation. In confirming the death sentence passed by the High Court, the presiding appeals judge wrote, "[t]his has been one of the most serious cases I have dealt with both in my career as a State Counsel or as a judge. The Appellant's conduct has sunk to the very depths of depraved and evil conduct...."[173] The case law suggests that death sentences in Swaziland are truly reserved for the rarest of the rare cases.

With the rise of a truly discretionary death penalty in Swaziland, the Supreme Court began strictly monitoring sentences of imprisonment from the High Court for consistency. A common law of sentencing is developing in Swaziland in lieu of legislative sentencing guidelines, and Swazi courts have even looked to courts elsewhere to determine the proper sentence length. In one case, the High Court cited a Botswana case to determine the appropriate sentence for a heat of passion murder.[174] In another, the Supreme Court cited to courts in Botswana and Lesotho in reducing a sentence from thirty years to twenty-five years, which Sec. 15(3) of the Constitution considered to be "the lowest end of a life sentence."[175]

---

168 Rex v. Musa Kotso Samuel Dlamini, Crim. Case No. 200/2007, [2009] SZHC 151 (May 29, 2009).
169 *Id.* at 15 (¶ 41).
170 Rex v. Ntokozo Adams, Crim. App. No. 16/2010, [2010] SZSC 10 (Nov. 30, 2010).
171 *Id.* at 15 (¶ 33).
172 Rex v. Nhlanhla Lucky Dludlu, Crim. Case No. 202/2010, [2012] SZHC 236 (Sept. 28, 2012).
173 David Thabo Simelane v. Rex, Crim. App. No. 13/2011, [2011] SZSC 54 (Nov. 30, 2012).
174 *See, e.g.*, Rex v. Sandile Mbongeni Mtsetfwa, Crim. Case 81/2010, [2010] SZHC 145 (Sept. 16, 2010).
175 Xolani Zinhle Nyandzeni v. Rex, Crim. App. No. 29/2010, [2012] SZSC 3 (May 31, 2012).

Besides looking to foreign law, the Supreme Court has also attempted to impose sentence uniformity by comparing recent domestic cases and discerning an acceptable range for an offense. In *Tsela v. Rex*, the Court listed the sentences of every murder case in the prior ten years, determining that all sentences fell between five and twenty five years, with fifteen years as the mean.[176] The Court held that judges should not deviate from this range without good reason. Interestingly, the Court noted "a controlled ratcheting upwards of sentences for the offence of murder" over the prior ten years, "evidently a reaction to the burgeoning prevalence of unlawful killings in this Kingdom coupled with a disturbing degree of brutality."[177] Multiple sentences should run concurrently if the charges arose out of the same sequence of events (*res gestae*). No other court in Southern Africa has so thoroughly enacted judicially created sentencing guidelines.

The final way in which the Supreme Court has monitored sentences for consistency is through reasoning by analogy to earlier cases. For instance, in *Tfwala v. Rex*, the Supreme Court upheld a sentence of fifteen years for murder, citing to several earlier cases in which the defendant acted without provocation but otherwise had no prior convictions and was young at the time of the offense. According to the Court, "[t]hese cases serve to show in rough and general terms, the judicial trend in sentencing for murder. In the light of the above range of sentences for murder, I am inclined to hold that the custodial sentence of 15 years for murder in this case is not too harsh or high in the peculiar circumstances of this case."[178] The Supreme Court has suggested that an overly long sentence may violate the constitutional ban on cruel, inhuman, and degrading punishment.[179]

A Doctrine Limited by Statute: Zambia

Under the Penal Code Amendment Act of 1990, the death penalty in Zambia was no longer mandatory upon a finding of extenuating circumstances, defined in the statutory amendment as any facts "associated with the offence which would diminish morally the degree of the convicted person's guilt."[180] The statute itself limited the definition to circumstances "associated with the offence," and thus youth, behavior after the crime, or lack of a prior criminal record are not formally relevant. The statutory definition also included a mixed subjective–objective test, in which the trial judge is obligated to "consider the standard of behaviour of an ordinary person of a class of the community to which the convicted person belongs." Overall, the new provision sharply narrowed the scope of the death penalty for murder, although it did not allow appellate courts to exercise independent discretion as to the existence of extenuating circumstances existed and it placed the burden on the accused.[181]

Courts have implemented the law narrowly. The Zambian Supreme Court determined that the doctrine of extenuating circumstances was not retroactive to crimes committed before the Penal Code amendment entered into force, upholding a death sentence for a murder committed in 1985 but still pending on appeal at the time of the amendment's

---

176   Samkeliso Madati Tsela v. Rex, Crim. App. No. 20/2010, [2011] SZSC 13 (May 31, 2012).
177   *Id.* at 30 (¶ 27).
178   Mandla Tfwala v. Rex, Crim. App. No. 36/2011, [2012] SZSC 15 (May 31, 2012).
179   Zwelithini Tsabedze v. Rex, Crim. App. No. 32/2012, [2012] SZSC 73 (Nov. 30, 2012).
180   Penal Code (Amendment) Act 3 of 1990, *codified at* Penal Code Act, Cap. 87, LAWS OF REP. OF ZAMBIA (1995), § 201.
181   John Hatchard, *Developing the Criminal Law in Zambia: The Penal Code (Amendment) Act, 1990*, 36 J. AFR. L. 103, 103–4 (1992) (statute note).

passage.[182] The Supreme Court has refused to extend the doctrine to armed robbery, a crime which triggers the mandatory death penalty.[183] According to the Court, "the law of extenuating circumstances was introduced in Zambia as a measure between the extremes of the offence of murder and manslaughter" and was not intended for any other criminal offense.[184] Section 201(1)(b) of the Penal Code, the extenuating circumstances provision, states that it "shall not apply to murder committed in the course of aggravated robbery with a firearm."[185]

The Supreme Court reversed a death sentence where the defendant believed that the victim had killed his children through witchcraft, noting that "a belief in witchcraft, though unreasonable, is prevalent in our community and…such a belief is an extenuating factor in cases of murder."[186] On the other hand, the Supreme Court has ruled in another case that neither the age of an accused nor the acquittal of an accomplice constituted extenuating circumstances.[187] The Court has found provocation to be an extenuating circumstance.[188] In one case, where the defendant and victim were in a fight before a fatal stabbing, the Court found the fight to be an extenuating circumstance even though the defendant never raised the defense of provocation.[189]

Zambian voters are expected to vote on a new constitution during 2014, which includes a right to life provision at Article 28. The provision lacks the analytical clarity of the right to life clause in Zimbabwe's new constitution, though it does create a constitutional right to seek commutation or pardon.[190] The death penalty may not be imposed on a pregnant woman or a child, or where "extenuating circumstances" exist relating to the commission of a crime.[191] The Zambian draft constitutionalizes the doctrine of extenuating circumstances in its current form, and therefore will continue to shift the burden to the defendant to rebut a presumption in favor of death. The death penalty in Zambia retains popular support in constitutional consultations, but Zambia is considered de facto abolitionist, with three presidents in succession who each personally opposed the death penalty and installed moratoria on executions.[192]

---

182   Mvula v. People, [1991] ZMSC 19 (August 1, 1991).
183   Zambia Penal Code Act, Cap. 87, § 294.
184   Chongo v. People, [1999] Zam.L.R. 58, 60.
185   Zambia Penal Code Act, Cap. 87, § 201(b)(2).
186   Moola v. People, [2000] Zam.L.R. 148, 153.
187   People v. Kashwenka, [2007] Zam.L.R. 37, 42.
188   Simusokwe v. People, [2002] Zam.L.R. 63, 65.
189   Phiri v. People, [2002] Zam.L.R. 107, 111.

190   For a comparison of the two drafts, see Andrew Novak, *The Death Penalty and the Right to Life in the Draft Constitutions of Zambia and Zimbabwe*, AFRICLAW (Apr. 18, 2013), http://africlaw.com/2013/04/18/the-death-penalty-and-the-right-to-life-in-the-draft-constitutions-of-zambia-and-zimbabwe.

191   For a copy of the pending draft constitution, see Technical Committee on Drafting the Zambian Constitution, *First Draft Constitution* (Apr. 30, 2012), http://zambianconstitution.org/downloads/First%20Draft%20Constitution.pdf.

192   Zambia abstained in the December 2012 resolution calling for a moratorium on the death penalty. Third Committee of the United Nations, Moratorium on the Use of the Death Penalty, A/C.3/67/L.44/Rev.1, Item No. 69, November 19, 2012, http://www.un.org/en/ga/third/67/docs/voting_sheets/l.44.Rev.1.pdf.

In the Process of Modernization: Lesotho

Lesotho still relies on the traditional conception of the doctrine of extenuating circumstances, but the country's jurisprudence has evolved in more progressive ways than in Zambia and Zimbabwe. The Constitution of Lesotho contains a death penalty savings clause, and the country retains the death penalty for murder, treason, and rape where a rapist knows or has reasonable suspicion to believe that he is infected with the Human Immunodeficiency Virus (HIV).[193] No person has been sentenced to death for treason or rape in Lesotho, and the country has never had a constitutional challenge to capital punishment.[194] In addition, the death penalty by law cannot be carried out on persons under the age of 18 or on pregnant women.[195]

In Lesotho, as elsewhere, a court must impose a death sentence in the absence of extenuating circumstances; if such circumstances are found, the court has discretion to impose a lesser sentence. The Court of Appeal has, in the past, upheld a trial judge's determination that no extenuating circumstances existed and that the accused should be sentenced to death.[196] However, at present, judges "show a distinct reluctance to impose the death penalty[;] therefore they often find extenuating circumstances where their existence is sometimes slender."[197] Owori puts the state of the doctrine in Lesotho in even more stark terms: "Of the 915 murder charges brought before the courts in the last five years, there is at the moment not a single convict on death row, partly due to the courts always looking for and *finding* extenuating circumstances."[198] In the few cases where the High Court has imposed the death penalty, the Court of Appeal reversed on appeal. Like Swaziland, Lesotho has robust appellate review. According to the Court of Appeal, upon a finding of extenuating circumstances, the imposition of a disproportionately harsh sentence of imprisonment is unconstitutional.[199] A judge can find extenuating circumstances and substitute a lesser punishment even where the assessors in the case do not agree.[200]

The seminal case in Lesotho on the doctrine of extenuating circumstances is *Letuka v. Rex*, in which the Court of Appeal developed a clear process for weighing extenuating circumstances, extensively citing case law from Botswana and South Africa in its decision.[201] In that case, the trial court imposed a death sentence over the dissent of an assessor, finding no extenuating circumstances.[202] According to the Court of Appeal, because many crimes include aggravating or mitigating factors, the accused has an opportunity to give evidence to rebut the prima facie view that the offense fell into the category of heinous crimes deserving of death, including matters personal to him or her. The extenuating circumstances

---

193   LESOTHO CONST. art. 5; Criminal Procedure & Evidence Act, Sec. 297; Sexual Offenses Act, No. 3 of 2003, Sec. 32(a)(vii).

194   Michael Mathealira Ramodibedi, *The Right to Life and the Death Penalty*, SUNDAY EXPRESS (Oct. 20, 2009), http://sundayexpress.co.ls/?p=1055.

195   Moses O.A. Owori, *The Death Penalty in Lesotho: The Law and Practice*, British Institute of International and Comparative Law (c. 2004), http://www.biicl.org/files/2298_country_report_lesotho_owori.pdf (last accessed June 5, 2013).

196   *See, e.g.*, Rex v. Mabaso, [1980–1984] L.A.C. 256, 259 (1984).

197   W.C.M. MAQUTU, CONTEMPORARY CONSTITUTIONAL HISTORY OF LESOTHO 55 (1990).

198   Emphasis original. Owori, *supra* note 195.

199   Lefu v. Rex, [2012] LSCA 19 (April 27, 2012), *citing* Gaborekwe v. State, [2009] BWCA 67 (29 July 2009) (Botswana CA).

200   Rex v. Moratha, [2004] LSHC 56 (April 2, 2004) at 53.

201   Letuka v. Rex, [1997–1998] L.L.R.-L.B. 346, 360 (February 4, 1998).

202   Rex v. Letuka, [1997] LSHC 66, CRI/T/45/92 (Lesotho HC) (August 20, 1997).

inquiry must be "conducted with diligence and with an anxiously enquiring mind" to determine whether extenuation is warranted.[203] After this evidence and any aggravating circumstances pointed out by the prosecution have been received by the judge, the Court must evaluate the evidence and testimony and weigh all features of the case.

In *Letuka*, the Court of Appeal determined that the trial judge could have found numerous extenuating circumstances, but failed to articulate her factual findings and placed too great of a burden on counsel to point out extenuating circumstances when the judge possessed the responsibility to analyze the evidence. The Court listed the extenuating circumstances recognized in Lesotho: youth, intoxication, emotional conflict, motive, provocation, sub-normal intelligence, general background, impulsiveness, minor role in crime, absence of *dolus directus*,[204] witchcraft, absence of premeditation, "heavy confrontation," and rage of an accused. As the Court explained, "the mere presence of one or more of these features do not automatically mean that they are extenuating in relation to the crime at issue," but rather each "must be weighed and assessed in light of the evidence as a whole."[205]

While the Court of Appeal did not specifically follow the Botswana case *Kelaletswe* and the derivative Swazi case law in holding that the burden of showing extenuating circumstances was not on the accused, the Court "caution[ed] against the use of the *onus* as the determining cause for holding that no extenuating circumstances exist," as this "bears the hallmark of ready recourse to a legal make-weight and can be employed to justify an overly retributive response to serious crime."[206] The Court extensively cited the holding in *Kelaletswe*, but noted, unlike Botswana, this situation was "not currently the law of the Kingdom of Lesotho," where the onus existed on the accused to prove the existence of extenuating circumstances "on a balance of probability." However, the Court warned that the ready invocation of the onus as a determining factor was "a course to be avoided by judicial officers" because it tended to "inhibit the employment of an enquiring mind directed at investigating the presence or absence of extenuating circumstances." Even though the accused did not testify in *Letuka*, the facts were such that the judge should have been able to discern extenuating circumstances.

The burden of showing extenuating circumstances still technically rests on the accused. However, in *Maliehe v. Rex*, the Court of Appeal reversed a death sentence where a judge found the accused had not discharged the onus of proving the existence of extenuating circumstances. According to the Court, "I doubt whether the learned Judge was right in finding that there was an onus on the accused but it is not necessary to decide that" because the prosecution conceded on appeal that extenuating circumstances existed.[207] In *Maliehe*, the Court found extenuating circumstances even where a person was hired to kill, a form of premeditation. This continued hedging as to whether the accused had the onus still occurs in the Court's jurisprudence. In reversing a death sentence in 2011, the Court noted that "[e]ven if there was an onus on the appellant, what he said about the bad relationship between him and the deceased was not challenged."[208]

High Court decisions from the 1980s explicitly pondered the question of extenuating circumstances but often provided little reasoning as to why a specific sentence of

---

203   *Letuka*, [1997–1998] L.L.R.-L.B. at 360.
204   In South African law, dolus directus is direct intent to commit the harm caused (as opposed to dolus eventualis, in which the accused intended to do the action but did not intend the harm).
205   *Letuka*, [1997–1998] L.L.R.-L.B. at 363.
206   *Id.*, p. 364.
207   Maliehe v. Rex, [1997–1998] L.L.R.-L.B. 168, 181 (February 5, 1997).
208   Kopano v. Rex, [2011] LSCA 19 (April 20, 2011).

imprisonment was imposed. The Court of Appeal now requires this, and the High Court performs it as a matter of course. In Lesotho, courts consider a broader range of factors in determining the sentence than they do in determining the existence or not of extenuating circumstances. In one case, these included cooperation with investigators, about which the judge wrote, "an accused person, who freely admits his guilt and helps all these concerned with the investigations of his crime, to such an accused, this Court will extend a hand of mercy."[209] In another case, the Court considered (but ultimately rejected) the defendant's significant health problems and his offer to pay compensation to the victim's family as mitigating factors.[210] Prior convictions also frequently appear at the sentencing stage and not in the extenuating circumstances analysis.

Finding that sentences over twenty-five years are only appropriate in the most exceptional circumstances, the Court found in *Monaleli v. Rex* that a sentence of forty years' imprisonment was "clearly excessive."[211] The Court has continued to cite *Monaleli* in cases where trial judges impose "excessively severe" sentences longer than twenty-five years except in "very exceptional circumstances," which has created some uniformity in sentencing.[212] At the sentencing phase of the trial, courts in Lesotho have found that spending an excessive amount of time in prison prior to trial warrants a sentencing reduction.[213] In one case where the lower court found extenuating circumstances, the Court halved a sentence of imprisonment where seventeen years elapsed in bringing the accused to trial.[214]

Lesotho courts now treat youth as an extenuating factor even in the absence of other extenuating factors, which is likewise a broader application of the doctrine than that used in Zambia or Zimbabwe.[215] Where a trial judge found that youth could only be an extenuating circumstance in the presence of other factors, the Court of Appeal reversed, finding that the trial judge "failed to appreciate sufficiently that this was prima facie evidence of immaturity and that the evidence did not support the conclusion that the offence of the appellant was committed purely from 'inherent wickedness.'"[216] Other extenuating circumstances are similar to those in neighboring jurisdictions. Where a provocation defense failed at trial, a judge of the High Court found that it succeeded in establishing an extenuating circumstance.[217] An accused's recklessness as to the life of the victim (in South African law, a mental state of *dolus eventualis*) is also an extenuating circumstance on the basis that the accused lacked actual intent to kill.[218]

The Court of Appeal is entitled to pass a different sentence where it believes the alternative sentence is warranted in law. Unlike in Swaziland, the Lesotho Court of Appeal has intervened with some frequency to *increase* a sentence imposed at the trial level. In 1981, the Court raised a ten year sentence to fifteen years because it was "manifestly inadequate

---

209 Rex v. Maphobole, [1981] LSHC 2 (January 29, 1981).
210 Rex v. Mbobo, [2012] LSHC 78 (May 8, 2012).
211 Monaleli v. Rex, [2005–2006] L.A.C. 24, 28 (2005).
212 *See* Lentso v. Rex, Crim. App. No. 3 of 2005 (Lesotho C.A.) (Oct. 7, 2005).
213 Rex v. Mothobi, [1999] LSHC 101 (Sept. 21, 1999) (defendant spent more than six years in custody).
214 Mokone v. Rex, [2012] LSCA 35 (Sept. 3, 2012).
215 Rex v. Raseotsana, [1995] LSHC 122 (Oct. 30, 1995). *See also*, Rex v. Mokalanyane, [2001] LSHC 44 (May 15, 2001).
216 Thebe v. Rex, [1985–1989] L.A.C. 33, 51 (1985), *reversing* Rex v. Thebe, [1984] LSHC 59 (June 4, 1984).
217 Rex v. Tsibela, [1986] LSHC 128 (November 3, 1986).
218 Rex v. Raleshoai, [1993] LSHC 48 (August 16, 1993).

and disproportionate to the gravity of the appellant's conduct," and the trial judge failed to "give sufficient weight to the aggravating features in the case."[219] In 2008, the Court used a more modern version of the test, determining whether there was "a striking disparity between the sentence that this Court would have imposed and that actually imposed by the Court a quo. If the answer is in the affirmative this Court is entitled to interfere with the sentence."[220]

Where a trial judge neglects to consider specific extenuating circumstances at the trial level, the Court of Appeal will alter the sentence. In one case, the Court found that the trial judge failed to adequately consider the accused's behavior after the offense (traditionally beyond the scope of the doctrine of extenuating circumstances), which included ensuring the deceased victim received medical care, inquiring about his health, and seeking to visit him in the hospital. The accused turned himself in once the victim died.[221] In those circumstances, the Court reduced a nine year sentence to three years. After reviewing the evidentiary record in an earlier case, the Court of Appeal reduced a death sentence to five years' imprisonment because the trial judge did not believe the accused's story and made adverse inferences against her. On appeal, the Court, in reinterpreting the evidence, drew a very different picture of the series of events.[222] The Court did not defer to the trial judge's original findings.

Once the Court found extenuating circumstances for a hired killer in *Maliehe*, lower courts became more liberal in their sentencing analyses. According to one trial judge, "If the Court of Appeal had not found a hit-man who was employed for gain to go and kill a person...[had] exterminating circumstances in that case, I would have found it impossible to have found extenuating circumstances in this case. But since this issue of extenuating circumstances has been made elastic...I find extenuating circumstances exist."[223] The judge continued, "I must add that, if we had chosen not to find extenuating circumstances we would be morally justified. Therefore, the accused is lucky."

In *Rex v. Mosili*, the High Court noted that in the particular case of ritual murder and murder in the course of a robbery, traditionally extenuating circumstances would not have been found. However, the trial judge acknowledged that the "finding of extenuating circumstances in the *Maliehe* case has in fact moved the goal posts a little," and "extenuating circumstances are now found in cases where in the past they" would not have been.[224] The Court of Appeal affirmed *Mosili*, but found non-prejudicial error in the trial judge's failure to specify the extenuating circumstances that he relied on in his decision. The appeals judge writing for the Court wrote, "I myself would have been inclined to impose a lesser sentence notwithstanding the seriousness of the appellants' conduct and the heinousness of the offences," because sentences that are too high "leave little or no hope for the offender's rehabilitation and reintegration into society. However, there is not a striking disparity between the sentence I would have imposed and that in fact imposed."[225] The Court's rulings that a judge should clearly articulate the extenuating circumstances he found in the case is a positive one for the interests of transparency.

---

219 Phaloane v. Rex, [1980–1984] L.A.C. 72, 88 (1981).
220 Director of Public Prosecutions v. Khama, [2008] LSCA 19 (October 17, 2008).
221 George v. Rex, [2000–2004] L.A.C. 379, 384 (2001).
222 Rex v. Metsing, [1980–1984] L.A.C. 170, 174–5 (1982).
223 Rex v. Ramaema, [2003] LSHC 83 (August 6, 2003).
224 Rex v. Mosili, [2001] LSHC 87 (August 23, 2001).
225 Mosili v. Rex, [2000–2004] L.A.C. 934, 942 (2004).

The Doctrine and Death Penalty Abolition in Namibia

Prior to independence, courts in Namibia (then South-West Africa) appealed to the Appellate Division of South Africa, with the High Court of South-West Africa construed as one of the country's provincial divisions and staffed by South African judges.[226] As a consequence, the Namibian variant of the doctrine of extenuating circumstances operated indistinguishably from South Africa. At independence, the death penalty was abolished in Namibia. According to the Namibian constitution, "the right to life shall be respected and protected. No law may prescribe death as a competent sentence. No Court or Tribunal shall have the power to impose a sentence of death upon any person. No executions shall take place in Namibia."[227]

The prohibition on cruel, inhuman, and degrading punishment in the Constitution of Namibia has also generated human rights litigation. In 1991, in a celebrated opinion, the Supreme Court of Namibia found that judicial corporal punishment was unconstitutional.[228] As the first abolitionist country in common law Southern Africa, Namibia was the first to face challenges to the most serious mode of punishment next to death: life imprisonment. In *State v. Tcoeib*, the Supreme Court of Namibia upheld the constitutionality of natural-term life imprisonment, so long as statutory mechanisms existed to consider the prisoner's rehabilitation in a parole proceeding.[229] Without such a procedure, natural-term life imprisonment would be, in effect, a death sentence. In *Tcoeib*, the Supreme Court reversed a lower court decision that had found life imprisonment to be unconstitutional as a violation of the rights to life and human dignity.[230]

In Namibia, courts have found the doctrine of extenuating circumstances and related case law as no longer relevant to criminal sentencing. In 2003, the Supreme Court of Namibia finally put the doctrine to rest in *State v. Alexander*, an appeal of a sentence of life imprisonment for murder and aggravated robbery.[231] In that case, the Supreme Court noted the grisly and random circumstances of the crime, committed in broad daylight, the defendant's prior convictions and persistent dishonesty at trial, his absence of genuine remorse, and the resulting public outcry. "These are all aggravating circumstances which are compelling and must be accorded due weight in the determination of an appropriate sentence," the Court ruled. "Precisely what the comparative weight thereof should be when measured against factors advanced in mitigation" and the emphasis given to each "in designing a fitting sentence to meet the objectives of punishment, falls pre-eminently within the sentencing discretion of the trial [c]ourt." The Court provided an elegant defense of sentencing discretion:

---

226 DAVID DYZENHAUS, HARD CASES IN WICKED LEGAL SYSTEMS: PATHOLOGIES OF LEGALITY xxii (2010); Sam K. Amoo, *The Structure of the Namibian Judicial System and Its Relevance for an Independent Judiciary*, in THE INDEPENDENCE OF THE JUDICIARY IN NAMIBIA 69, 69 (Nico Horn and Anton Bosl eds., 2008).
227 NAMIBIA CONST. art. 6.
228 Ex parte: Attorney General, In Re: Corporal Punishment by Organs of State, 1991 (3) S.A. 76 (Nam.S.C.) (Apr. 5, 1991).
229 State v Tcoeib, 1996 (1) S.A.C.R. 390 (Nam.S.C.).
230 State v. Nehemia Tjijo, September 4, 1991 (unreported), *quoted in Tcoeib*, 1996(1) S.A.C.R. at 390.
231 State v. Alexander, [2003] NASC 5 (February 13, 2003).

> Steeped in the atmosphere of the case, exposed to the emotions and demeanor of victims and perpetrators alike, alert to local circumstances such as prevalence and the community's legitimate interests in a fair and just judicial response to the crimes in question, the trial Judge is normally better positioned to tailor a fitting sentence than a Court of appeal which has but a transcript of the record to judge the matter. For these reasons a Court sitting on appeal against sentence will accord the trial Court a significant degree of appreciation in the exercise of its sentencing discretion.[232]

The Court engaged in robust appellate review, noting that it had the power to change a criminal sentence where a trial court committed an error of law or fact; where an irregularity occurred in the proceedings; where a sentence was manifestly inappropriate given the gravity of the offense; or if there had been an overemphasis of one of the sentencing interests at the expense of another. On appeal, the full bench of the High Court ruled that the trial judge, in dispensing a life sentence for murder, overemphasized the seriousness of the crime because the judge concluded that the imposition of the death penalty would have been mandatory had it not been abolished by the constitution because there were no extenuating circumstances.

The Supreme Court of Namibia agreed with the full bench of the High Court in reducing the sentence from life imprisonment: "It is fundamentally wrong to import and apply pre-independence norms for the imposition of the death penalty to the current sentencing criteria for the imposition of life imprisonment in appropriate instances." With constitutional abolition of the death penalty, a judge's sentencing discretion was "no longer tied up in the procedural straightjacket" of determining whether circumstances existed at the time of the offense that reduced the accused's moral blameworthiness before crafting a sentence other than death. "'Mitigating factors' not only encompasses, but also extends wider than 'extenuating circumstances,'" the Court ruled. In the present case, the Supreme Court found that the lack of premeditation would have been an extenuating circumstance, and, as a result, upheld the finding that the sentence of life imprisonment was "startlingly inappropriate."

The Globalization of the Doctrine of Extenuating Circumstances: Papua New Guinea

South Africa's robust reliance on the death penalty during the apartheid era ensured that the country's sizable jurisprudence influenced capital punishment law in other retentionist regimes, especially neighboring countries within the South African orbit. The adoption of the doctrine of extenuating circumstances in Papua New Guinea in 1965 illustrated the truly global reach of South African law. Papua New Guinea had several similarities with South Africa that likely made adoption of the doctrine attractive, including the relatively late imposition of a British-style penal code over a large indigenous population with very different customary notions of criminal punishment. By 1965, however, the defects in the doctrine of extenuating circumstances had become clear, and Papua New Guinea succeeded in removing its two most objectionable features by refusing to place the onus of showing extenuating circumstances on the accused and by not adopting the restrictive definition of "extenuating circumstances" as factors that existed at the time of the offense. Papua New Guinea's inconsistent adherence to and eventual abolition of the doctrine in 2006 accords

---

232 *Id.*

with the same trend in Southern Africa toward permitting judicial discretion in capital cases and narrowing the scope of the death penalty to only the most serious crimes.

Precolonial societies in New Guinea were relatively small, with a social order divided by extended family and clan. As in stateless societies in Sub-Saharan Africa, crimes such as homicide or robbery were addressed through a system of compensation, which accompanied an elaborate ceremony and served the triple purposes of deterrence, retribution, and restorative justice.[233] Papua New Guinea adopted a version of the Queensland Penal Code, which included the common law distinction between murder and manslaughter as well as the common law defenses and mental states.[234] British and Australian colonial administrations in both Papua and New Guinea territories used the death penalty, often with public executions, for homicide. Capital sentences were reviewed by the Executive Council and the lieutenant-governor. Murders of white settlers and the rape of white women were treated particularly harshly, but at least earlier in the colonial period capital punishment fell more heavily on settlers and "civilized" colonial subjects than on the majority indigenous population, again like South Africa. Not until the 1930s were Papuans regularly executed for the murder of other Papuans. The death penalty was used much more frequently under Australian military rule in the New Guinea League of Nations mandate than in Australian colonial Papua.[235]

Unified Papua New Guinea received its independence in 1975 from thirty years of Australian rule, with an independence constitution that stated, "No person shall be deprived of his life intentionally except in the execution of a sentence of a court following his conviction of an offence for which the penalty of death is prescribed by law."[236] The constitution also contains a prohibition on "punishment that is cruel or otherwise inhuman, or is inconsistent with respect for the inherent dignity of the human person."[237] Although the prohibition on cruel or otherwise inhuman punishments specifically exempts the death penalty, the constitution notes that "the manner or the circumstances" of the death penalty may violate the provision.[238]

In most criminal legislation, the maximum penalty is prescribed in the law, and a court has discretion as to the form and severity of the penalty, allowing judges to articulate the broader social policy behind a particular sentence.[239] Colonial officials were torn between the competing impulses of strictly applying the provisions of the penal code so as to require Papua New Guineans to conform their behavior to Australian notions of justice, and recognizing the essential injustice of imposing harsh sentences for failure to adhere to a penal code that they did not understand.[240] By the late 1960s, courts had resolved the tension by strictly applying the law while lessening the injustice inherent in its harsh application

---

233 Bruce L. Ottley & Jean G. Zorn, *Criminal Law in Papua New Guinea: Code, Customs and the Courts in Conflict*, 31 AM. J. COMP. L. 251, 257 (1983).

234 The Code was adopted in Papua (British New Guinea) in 1902 and in Australian-ruled New Guinea in 1921. *See generally*, R.S. O'Regan, *Provocation and Homicide in Papua and New Guinea*, 10 U.W. AUST. L. REV. 1 (1971–2).

235 *See generally* Hank Nelson, *The Swinging Index: Capital Punishment and British and Australian Administrations in Papua and New Guinea*, 13 J. PACIFIC HIST. 130, *et seq.* (1978).

236 PAPUA NEW GUINEA CONST. art. 35(1) (subsection markers omitted).

237 *Id.* at art. 36(1).

238 *Id.* at art. 36(2).

239 Sinclair Dinnen, *Sentencing, Custom and the Rule of Law in Papua New Guinea*, 27 J. LEGAL PLURALISM & UNOFFICIAL L. 19, 21 (1988).

240 Ottley & Zorn, *supra* note 233 at 264.

through permitting customary defenses or reducing sentences based on the customary law of the accused. The prevailing theory was that "reduced sentences were necessary due to the primitive culture and environment of the accused."[241]

As in South Africa, judges frequently took customary perceptions and practices as extenuating factors in homicide cases, where those practices were not "repugnant" to general principles of humanity.[242] Among the customary practices encountered in homicide cases were "payback" or retaliatory killings and homicide committed for spiritual reasons. The killing of a sorcerer occasioned a relatively light punishment, and judges would consider the sophistication of a defendant in determining an appropriate sentence.[243] In one "payback" homicide case, the trial judge explained his finding of extenuating circumstances based on the "ignorance" and "tribal traditions" of the accused, determining that the court's function was to "encourage acceptance of the general law as a step towards a more orderly, humane, and unified society."[244] Courts were more likely to accept defenses or mitigation if they could fit in the mold of a common law defense—e.g., a retaliatory sorcery murder would be more likely to succeed if framed as a defense of provocation than as a customary defense.[245]

The territories of Papua and New Guinea adopted the mandatory death sentence for willful murder under the Queensland Criminal Code, but in 1907 an amendment permitted judges to make mercy recommendations. In 1965, the united territory adopted the doctrine of extenuating circumstances, modeled on South African law, which allowed a court to impose a sentence of imprisonment for life or for a lesser prison term as the circumstances warranted; persons convicted of death could appeal against the severity of sentence. The new amendment stated that if a Court convicted a defendant of willful murder, "it shall thereupon consider whether there existed extenuating circumstances such that it would not be just to inflict the punishment of death, and if it finds that those circumstances existed the Court may impose a sentence of imprisonment for life or for such lesser term as the Court thinks just."[246] The provision likely entered Papuan law as a result of the British Royal Commission into Capital Punishment in 1949, which recommended South Africa's doctrine of extenuating circumstances in place of the mandatory death penalty as an alternative for Great Britain itself.[247]

The 1965 ordinance did not define "extenuating circumstances." In 1971, in *Ivoro v. Regina*, the Supreme Court cited South African case law as to the definition of extenuating circumstances, but did not adopt the South African definition.[248] The Court adopted a broader definition: "relevant circumstances which operate so as to diminish the culpability of the prisoner, not in the strict legal sense but broadly, regard being had not only to moral considerations but to all the considerations which might reasonably be taken into account"

---

241   *Id.* at 265.
242   Dinnen, *supra* note 239 at 25–7.
243   *Id.* at 33–5, *citing* Regina v. Asis and Bitimui, [1970] S.C. No. 5599 (unrep.) (three years' imprisonment with hard labor for a sorcery killing), Regina v. Lakalyo Neak and Others, [1971] S.C. No. 632 (Papua N.G. S.C.) (unrep.) (life imprisonment with hard labor for "payback" killing). In each case, judges found extenuating circumstances to exist, allowing them to impose a punishment other than death.
244   Regina v. Iu Ketapi, [1971–72] P.N.G.L.R. 44, 47.
245   Ottley & Zorn, *supra* note 233 at 266.
246   Criminal Code Amendment (Papua) Ordinance of 1965, *cited in* Regina v. Peter Ivoro, [1971–72] P.N.G.L.R. 374, 377 (Papua N.G. S.C. 1971).
247   *Ivoro*, [1971–72] P.N.G.L.R. at 387.
248   *Id.* at 381.

to determine whether it was unjust to inflict a death sentence. In *Ivoro*, the Court found that extenuating circumstances existed after analyzing psychiatric opinions, determining that the appellant's history of aggressiveness and violence indicated that he had difficulty controlling his actions. One judge in the case determined that the South African definition limiting extenuating circumstances only to issues affecting moral culpability "might be inapt and too restrictive for purposes of Papua New Guinea's legislation and social circumstances," and "any attempt to define or restrict what has been granted as unlimited judicial discretion to the judges should be resisted."[249]

Although the 1965 ordinance did not amend the underlying Criminal Code provision creating a mandatory death sentence, the Supreme Court ruled in 1973 that the doctrine of extenuating circumstances effectively made the death sentence discretionary. In *Regina v. Melin*, the Court found that no onus rested on the accused to prove extenuating circumstances; instead, the duty was on the trial judge to determine whether such circumstances existed, reminiscent of the Botswana Court of Appeal decision in *Kelaletswe* twenty years later.[250] In partially rejecting the South African variant of the doctrine, the Court wrote that the prosecution should present all considerations affecting the public good, and the defense counsel should present all mitigating evidence, but "the responsibility is the court's to decide whether extenuating circumstances exist and if they do what is the proper sentence to impose." *Melin* involved the state's appeal of a nominal sentence for a customary "payback" killing; the Supreme Court increased the sentences on appeal after finding them "inadequate" even though defendants were "primitive and simple tribesmen."[251]

In 1975, the Supreme Court distinguished sorcery murder from *Melin*'s holding as to payback murder in *Secretary for Law v. Amantasi*, reasoning that the accused were of the "most primitive type" and lived in the remotest jungle regions, "an extremely hard environment, with only the barest contact with other races, and minimal knowledge of the Government and the world that is advancing from outside to engulf them," unlike the more sophisticated Highlanders in *Melin*.[252] The murder at issue had been of a reputed sorcerer who had boasted of killing others with his sorcery, and the tribesmen acted in a desperate attempt to save the clan. The nominal sentences were not increased on appeal. A dissent argued that *Melin* stood for the proposition that robust sentences should be imposed despite the "primitiveness" of the accused, as victims, even suspected sorcerers, were entitled to the little protection the law could afford.[253]

In 1974, immediately prior to Papua New Guinea's independence, the death penalty was abolished and the Criminal Code was amended to prescribe life imprisonment for willful murder, and amended again to include "imprisonment with hard labour for life." Following abolition, judicial attitudes toward customary forms of homicide hardened; payback killings no longer warranted reduction of sentence while sorcery killings only received a reduced sentence between ten years and life imprisonment.[254] Although calls to reform Papua New Guinea's post-independence legal system to include customary law concepts and dispute resolution mechanisms came from the prime minister and from the Law Reform Commission, the country retained its English common law penal and procedure codes.[255]

---

249   *Id.* at 388 (Prentice, J., dissenting).
250   Regina v. Melin, [1973] P.N.G.L.R. 278, 280.
251   *Id.* at 280–81.
252   Secretary for Law v. Amantasi, [1975] P.N.G.L.R. 134, 137.
253   *Id.* at 141 (Saldanha, J., dissenting).
254   Dinnen, *supra* note 239 at 45–9.
255   Ottley & Zorn, *supra* note 233 at 252-3.

In 1975, the Law Reform Commission expressed disapproval of the mandatory life sentence for murder, noting that "there will be many instances where the sentence will be considered inappropriate and unacceptable in the eyes of the people and the reputation of the courts and of the government will suffer because of this."[256] The Commission recommended an extenuating circumstances provision for mandatory life imprisonment that closely mirrored the 1965 death penalty ordinance, though this was never adopted. In 1991, Papua New Guinea passed the Criminal Law (Compensation) Act, which created a legal basis for consideration of customary compensation in sentencing. A compensation order was to consider the nature if non-monetary, the amount, and the method of payment; the appropriate person to receive payment; and any custom which related to the amount of compensation based on the recipient's age.[257]

The death penalty was reinstated in 1991.[258] In 1992, the National Court of Justice (the country's trial-level court), determined that the reinstated death penalty was not mandatory and ruled that "the maximum penalty should be reserved for the worst kind of wilful murder."[259] However, an inkling of the doctrine of extenuating circumstances continued to survive. Two years later, the Court found that it had only "limited discretion" to substitute a lesser sentence as murder always involved the same culpable conduct in the intentional taking of human life.[260] According to the Court, the legislature specifically intended to restrict the circumstances that would merit a lesser punishment to factors such as a plea of guilty, youthfulness, remorse, or attempts at paying compensation. This constraint on judicial sentencing discretion was a holdover from Papua New Guinea's pre-abolition death penalty jurisprudence.

In a 2006 constitutional challenge, the Supreme Court established a discretionary death penalty that reserved murder for the rarest of the rare cases, drastically narrowing the scope of the punishment and removing all limitations on judicial discretion.[261] The Court in *Ume v. State* determined that the right to life provision and the prohibition on cruel and inhuman punishment contemplated the existence of capital punishment so long as it was carried out in a manner consistent with human dignity. Due to faulty drafting, the Court was able to read Papua New Guinea's death penalty statute as discretionary without invalidating the Criminal Code provision. The Criminal Code stated that "a person who commits willful murder shall be liable to be sentenced to death."[262] However, when the mandatory death penalty was reinstated in 1991, the legislature did not amend the Criminal Code's interpretive provision, which stated that, unless expressly provided otherwise, a "person liable to death may be sentenced to imprisonment for life or for any shorter term."[263] According to the Court, when the two sections were read together, the death penalty was discretionary.

The Court held that a trial judge must consider all relevant aggravating factors, extenuating circumstances, and mitigating factors and determine a punishment that fits

---

256 Law Reform Commission of Papua New Guinea, *Report on Punishment for Wilful Murder*, Report No. 3 (October 1975).
257 Criminal Law (Compensation) Act 25 of 1991, § 2 (Papua N.G.). *See generally*, Cyndi Banks, *Custom in the Courts: Criminal Law (Compensation) Act of Papua New Guinea*, 38 BRIT. J. CRIMINOLOGY 299 (1998).
258 Criminal Code (Amendment) Act of 1991, *supra* note 257.
259 State v. Komane, [1992] P.N.G.L.R. 524, 547.
260 State v. Paege, [1994] P.N.G.L.R. 65, 67.
261 Ume v. State, [2006] PGSC 9, S.C. 836 (May 19, 2006).
262 Criminal Code Act of 1994, Cap. 262, § 299(2), LAWS OF PAPUA N.G.
263 *Id.* at § 19(1)(aa).

the particular crime. The Court defined extenuating circumstances as those that related to the circumstances of the offense itself, while mitigating factors included all other factors, including a defendant's background and behavior after the crime was committed.[264] "The death penalty being the maximum punishment for wilful murder is reserved for the worst case of its kind," and each case required careful consideration. Because death was the ultimate penalty under the penal code, a judge must also consider community concerns, the need for deterrent or punitive sentences, customary beliefs, and the views of the victim's relatives.

Finally, the Court defined the types of murders that warranted the death penalty. Citing case law from across the Commonwealth, the Court determined that in countries where the death penalty was discretionary it was restricted to "the very worst case of its kind" or the "rarest of the rare," looking particularly to Indian and American cases. "Because human life is sacred, the emphasis is on ensuring that a man condemned to die should not be put to death unless all avenues for reviewing and correcting mistakes made in the sentencing process by the courts and executive bodies which decide on pardon are exhausted." The Court looked to Privy Council jurisprudence for a right to petition the executive for clemency. In the absence of legislative guidance, the Court generated a list of aggravating factors that placed certain murders among the "rarest of the rare" and deserving of death, such as murder of a vulnerable person or a law enforcement official, political or felony murder, murder for hire, and multiple murder. Through this decision, Papua New Guinea created a truly discretionary death penalty regime in which a judge is permitted to weigh aggravating and mitigating factors according to the circumstances of the offense, and consequently provides a model for the countries in Southern Africa that retain the doctrine of extenuating circumstances.

Conclusion

The doctrine of extenuating circumstances existed in Southern African criminal law as a means to reduce the harshness of the mandatory death sentence by essentially turning the sentence into a rebuttable presumption of death, requiring a judge to articulate a mitigating factor that allowed substitution of a lesser sentence. The strength of the doctrine was that it placed overwhelming emphasis on the most important of mitigating factors, namely, those that existed at the time the crime was committed that reduced the defendant's moral blameworthiness for the offense.[265] But the doctrine was not the only method of doing this, and certainly not the most transparent. As a hybrid between a mandatory death penalty and a discretionary one, the rise and fall of the doctrine of extenuating circumstances fits within the global-historical trend of reducing death sentences for all but the most serious crimes and allowing a trial judge, with his or her special expertise of the case at hand, the discretion to weigh aggravating and mitigating factors in a sentencing hearing. While the erosion of the doctrine in Southern Africa resulted more from the product of dozens, even hundreds, of individual appeals and not a single constitutional challenge, the replacement of the doctrine with discretionary death penalty regimes nonetheless fits the larger continent-wide trend

---

264 The Court specified as mitigating factors youth, family and personal background, good character, education, employment status, first-time offender, guilty plea, early confession to police, remorse, poor health, and compensation to victim.

265 Koyana, *supra* note 33 at 118.

toward individualized sentencing discretion in capital cases. As a result, Southern Africa's capital punishment regimes now operate closer to conformity with international human rights norms.

While the doctrine of extenuating circumstances originated in South Africa, where a large body of case law developed during the apartheid era, it has evolved with striking variation in the smaller legal systems of Botswana, Lesotho, Swaziland, Zambia, and Zimbabwe, especially after abolition of the death penalty in South Africa. The doctrine was also adopted in Papua New Guinea, where it adapted to local realities and permitted a level of judicial sentencing discretion broader than the Southern African jurisdictions. While the traditional form of the doctrine survives in Zambia (currently) and Zimbabwe (until 2013), the overly technical aspects of it—in particular, the shifting of the burden to the defendant and the constraining definition of extenuating circumstances—were softened in Botswana, Lesotho, Papua New Guinea, and Swaziland. The smaller legal systems of Southern Africa were not passive recipients of South African legal and constitutional doctrine, but, like Bangladesh vis-à-vis India, active contributors to a transnational body of death penalty jurisprudence that courts in the region and beyond have looked to for guidance.

Chapter 8
Conclusion: After the Mandatory Death Penalty

The penalty of death differs from all other forms of criminal punishment, not in degree, but in kind. It is unique in its total irrevocability. It is unique in its rejection of rehabilitation of the convict as a basic purpose of criminal justice. And it is unique, finally, in its absolute renunciation of all that is embodied in our concept of humanity.

Justice Potter Stewart, *Furman v. Georgia* (1972)[1]

Such a sentence [of life imprisonment], mandatorily imposed, was subject to almost all the vices held to be inherent in the mandatory death sentence itself. It permitted no distinction to be drawn between one offence of murder and another, despite the great and well-known disparity between the culpability of different murderers, even where an intention to kill is a necessary ingredient of the offence. It allowed no account to be taken of the youth, age, vulnerability or circumstances of the individual offender. It gave the defendant no opportunity to plead for a lesser penalty before being deprived of everything worth living for, save life itself.

Lord Bingham of Cornhill, *Boucherville v. Mauritius* (2008)[2]

Toward a Global Consensus on Mandatory Capital Punishment

In Chapter 1, this book explored the origins of the common law mandatory death penalty and its diffusion to the English-speaking world. In 1976, the U.S. Supreme Court became the first to invalidate the mandatory death penalty for murder in *Woodson v. North Carolina*, the subject of Chapter 2. The decision might have passed into history books as an outlier, distinguished by the unique phrasing of the Eighth Amendment, after its reasoning was rejected the following year by the Supreme Court of Canada. But the decision was transformational for another common law death penalty regime: India, the subject of Chapter 3. Like the United States, India would come to develop a death penalty regime that relied on guided judicial discretion in considering individualized circumstances of an offense.

Because of the efforts of a small group of anti-death penalty advocates, the decisions from the United States and India played a pivotal role in bringing human rights litigation before British colonies in the Caribbean, Africa, and South and Southeast Asia. The countries of the Commonwealth Caribbean, the subjects of Chapter 4, were peculiarly susceptible to European values concerning capital punishment because many of them maintained a line of appeal to the Judicial Committee of the Privy Council in London, before which practicing British lawyers could provide direct representation to Caribbean death row prisoners. As a result of persistent litigation, the mandatory death penalty has been extinguished throughout the Caribbean basin since 1999. By contrast, pending challenges failed in Malaysia and Singapore, the subjects of Chapter 5, as a result of their dissimilar constitutional structure

---

1 409 U.S. 15 (1972) (Potter, J., concurring).
2 [2008] UKPC 37 (9 July 2008), summarizing appellant's case.

and the strongly communitarian norms underlying their criminal justice policy. The truth is, however, that even Malaysia and Singapore are not immune to global trends on capital punishment as evidenced by the sweeping reform of Singapore's death penalty law in November 2012.

In common law Africa, the subject of Chapter 6, litigation against the mandatory death penalty has succeeded in establishing discretionary regimes in Kenya, Malawi, and Uganda. Each of these three decisions made their own unique contributions to the global body of shared death penalty jurisprudence. While such a challenge failed before the Supreme Court of Ghana, the overwhelming continent-wide trend favors abolition of the mandatory death penalty and its replacement with a discretionary one. Traveling south, perhaps no country in the world has endured such a profound and vindicating reversal on capital punishment in so short a time as South Africa, explored in Chapter 7. South Africa led the Western world in executions for much of the twentieth century and even exported to its neighbors its unique death penalty law creating a presumption in favor of death, known as the doctrine of extenuating circumstances. Today, by contrast, South Africa exports its abolition, and its seminal decision striking down capital punishment as unconstitutional in *Makwanyane* is one of the most internationally cited decisions ever handed down by an African court.

Challenges to Mandatory Life Imprisonment and Other Mandatory Sentences

The successful challenges to the mandatory death penalty in Africa, South and Southeast Asia, and the Caribbean were based on the principle that death is an extraordinary punishment and should only be reserved for the worst offenders after consideration of individualized circumstances. However, "lesser" punishments—up to and including life imprisonment without possibility of parole—are dispensed mandatorily upon conviction in some common law countries to prevent disparities and satisfy the public desire for certainty in criminal sentencing. The number of prisoners serving life sentences is growing, with increases of 75% reported in England and Wales between 1994 and 2004; 83% in the United States between 1992 and 2003; and more than 1,000% in South Africa between 1995 and 2005.[3] The rise of life imprisonment has the advantage of satisfying a retributivist impulse, as it, like the death penalty, is a total rejection of the rehabilitative purposes of punishment, but without the death penalty's irreversibility and risk of error. But it comes with its own disadvantages, perhaps most profoundly the extreme costs involved, including the attendant problems of overcrowding and poor prison conditions.

Nonetheless, a mandatory sentence of life imprisonment raises at least some of the theoretical problems of a mandatory death sentence.[4] A global consensus may be emerging that a mandatory sentence of life imprisonment must accompany a provision for amelioration through parole or reduction of sentence, or else it may be disproportionately excessive for a crime. Indeed, in systems where a mandatory life sentence is not accompanied by periodic review by a parole board, executive clemency plays the role of pressure valve in the most

---

3 Rachael Stokes, *A Fate Worse Than Death? The Problems with Life Imprisonment as an Alternative to the Death Penalty*, in AGAINST THE DEATH PENALTY: INTERNATIONAL INITIATIVES AND IMPLICATIONS 281, 285 (Jon Yorke ed., 2008).

4 DIRK VAN ZYL SMIT, TAKING LIFE IMPRISONMENT SERIOUSLY IN NATIONAL AND INTERNATIONAL LAW 198 (2002).

egregious cases. In Britain, the mandatory sentence of life imprisonment replaced the death penalty with the passage of the Murder (Abolition of the Death Penalty) Act of 1965, a successor piece of legislation to the Homicide Act of 1957, which divided the offense of murder into capital and non-capital offenses.[5] In the United States, the sentence of life imprisonment without parole came into prominence after *Furman v. Georgia* appeared to abolish the death penalty in 1972; in an indirect challenge in *Schick v. Read* in 1974, the Supreme Court appeared to uphold such a sentence.[6] Life without parole laws were introduced widely even after death penalty reinstatement in 1976, and it continues to be a mandatory sentence in several states and for certain federal crimes.

Despite the apparent popularity of life imprisonment, the abolition of the mandatory death penalty may render *mandatory* life imprisonment constitutionally vulnerable where no provision is made for parole. In 2008, the Privy Council found a mandatory sentence of life imprisonment unconstitutional in *Boucherville v. Mauritius* as it did not clearly permit a process for seeking parole, despite the existence of an executive clemency mechanism.[7] The Council distinguished the decision of the European Court of Human Rights in *Kafkaris v. Cyprus* upholding a life sentence *with* parole, as the existence of such a procedure did not render the applicant hopeless or without any prospect of intermediate release.[8] The U.S. Supreme Court has even extended the invalidation of juvenile capital punishment in *Roper v. Simmons* to juvenile life imprisonment without parole, an unusual development for a court that has strongly distinguished capital and non-capital cases under the Eighth Amendment.[9] These trends suggest that the global mandatory death jurisprudence may render other mandatory criminal sanctions such as life imprisonment without parole constitutionally vulnerable in the coming years.

Maintaining Sentencing Uniformity in Discretionary Regimes

A discretionary death penalty places the principles of proportionality and fairness above certainty and predictability. Countries that have abolished the mandatory death penalty and other mandatory sentences have responded differently to the challenge of sentencing disparities in which different judges or sentencing authorities treat like cases differently. A legal regime that fails to provide adequate guidance to judges in the sentencing process may result in erratic and arbitrary sentences. Worse, such variation provides an opportunity for discriminatory patterns of treatment as plagued South African courts in the 1970s and 1980s, threatening the legitimacy of the entire criminal justice system.

In practice, the countries explored in this book that have established discretionary death penalty regimes have responded to the challenge of sentencing uniformity in three primary ways. First, legislatures have enacted sentencing guidelines that provide judges with a baseline sentence, typically a term of imprisonment, and permit variations of that sentence

---

5 BARRY MITCHELL & JULIAN V. ROBERTS, EXPLORING THE MANDATORY LIFE SENTENCE FOR MURDER 33–4 (2012).
6 VAN ZYL SMIT, *supra* note 4 at 54, *citing* Schick v. Read, 419 U.S. 254.
7 Boucherville v. Mauritius, [2008] UKPC 37 (9 July 2008).
8 Kafkaris v. Cyprus, (2009) 49 E.H.R.R. 35.
9 Roper v. Simmons, 543 U.S. 551 (2005); Miller v. Alabama, 132 S.Ct. 2455 (2012).

based on enumerated aggravating or mitigating circumstances.[10] In April 2013, the Chief Justice of Uganda enacted sentencing guidelines for his country.[11]

Second, some appellate courts have strictly monitored lower court decisions for consistency, ensuring that judges do not depart from the usual parameters for the length of a sentence of imprisonment in the absence of weighty aggravating or mitigating circumstances. This is the case in Swaziland, where the Supreme Court routinely reduces overly harsh sentences passed by lower courts after comparing them to the typical range for such sentences and through reasoning by analogy to prior cases.[12]

Finally, mandatory minimum sentences, if used judiciously, may succeed in preventing wide sentencing disparities without overly constraining a judge's discretion. Though widely unpopular in Australia, the use of mandatory minimums in South Africa beginning in the late 1990s helped limit excessive variation in criminal sentencing.[13] Mandatory minimums shift sentencing discretion from a judge to a prosecutor who must determine the level at which to charge a defendant at the outset; guidance for prosecutors and judicial review of prosecutorial discretion may prevent misconduct and ensure that prosecutors do not overcharge for a crime.

The Future of Executive Clemency

The decline of the mandatory death penalty typically reduces the role of executive clemency or pardon by shifting sentencing discretion from an executive body to a trial judge in the sentencing phase of a trial. Executive clemency was always, and remains, an imperfect solution. The capital trial procedure at common law lost much of its deterrent value because pardon consideration came so late in the process, long after the public spectacle of a trial and a death sentence. Instead pardon was a random lottery, a secretive process that took place outside of public view, and the fact that most condemned prisoners would never be executed was widely known.[14] The increasing openness of the criminal sentencing process has created pressure to make the mechanics of clemency more transparent and accountable by, for instance, requiring executives to consult with other appointed officials, or even to give final clemency discretion to an independent body. India's executive clemency procedure contributed to the decline of the death penalty as it became more open and regulated; clemency decisions must be made on the aid and advice of cabinet ministers, not just executives alone, and may be subject to judicial review. Executions cannot take place while a clemency request is pending, and there is no limit to the number of petitions that may be filed, allowing a prisoner to indefinitely postpone execution.[15] Once again, Singapore has resisted this opening, and its Court of Appeal has refused to recognize executive clemency

---

10 *See* S.S. Terblanche, *Sentencing Guidelines for South Africa: Lessons from Elsewhere*, 120 S. Afr. L.J. 858 (2003).

11 Edward Ssekina & Sulaiman Kakaire, *Order, Certainty in New Sentencing Guide*, The Observer (Kampala), June 19, 2013 (retrieved from AllAfrica.com).

12 Tsela v. Rex, [2011] SZSC 13 (May 13, 2012).

13 *See* Stephen Terblanche & Geraldine Mackenzie, *Mandatory Sentences in South Africa: Lessons for Australia?*, 41 Aust. & N.Z. J. of Criminology 402 (2008).

14 Peter King, Crime, Justice, and Discretion in England, 1740–1820 at 338–9 (2000).

15 David T. Johnson, *The Death Penalty in India*, *in* Crime and Justice in India 365, 379 (2013).

as reviewable in court.[16] The South African Constitutional Court has upheld a presidential reprieve for incarcerated mothers of young children and not fathers, without finding the reprieve to be gender discriminatory.[17] Whether executive clemency will open itself to judicial review across the Commonwealth in coming years remains to be seen.

Concluding Remarks

The abolition of the mandatory death penalty in the common law world is a case study on the mutually reinforcing relationship between international human rights law and domestic constitutional law. The prohibition on cruel and degrading punishment in international law was a product of prevailing norms in domestic constitutional systems, most of which contain such a ban, but litigation before international tribunals produced a body of persuasive precedent that domestic courts used to help shape their own constitutional orders. In turn, the emerging consensus of domestic courts away from automatic capital sentencing is creating a new transnational norm that punishment disproportionate to a crime is cruel, inhuman, and degrading. The results are broader still, showing how a relatively small group of lawyers can take advantage of the increasing interdependence among legal systems to help professionalize the legal community, share legal resources and knowledge across borders, and ultimately help ground emerging notions of constitutionalism and judicial independence.

---

16   *See* Shubhankar Dan, *Presidential Pardon in Singapore: A Comment on* Yong Vui Kong v. Attorney General, 42 COMM. L. WORLD REV. 48 (2013).

17   President of the Republic of South Africa v. Hugo, 1997 (4) S.A. 1 (C.C.).

Index

accomplice liability, death penalty and *see* death penalty, accomplice liability and
advisory committee on the prerogative of mercy *see* clemency
African Charter on Human and Peoples' Rights 102
African Commission on Human and Peoples' Rights 102, 144
    Working Group on the Death Penalty, 102
African National Congress 132
Alabama 23, 24
    Supreme Court of 24
Ali, Sukur 45
American Convention on Human Rights 58, 60, 61, 62, 63
American Declaration on the Rights and Duties of Man 60, 61
Amin, Idi 106
Amnesty International 106
Anguilla 50
Antigua and Barbuda 47
    Constitution of 52
    executions in 49
    High Court of Justice of 66
apartheid 104, 127, 131, 132
arms offenses, death penalty and 39, 40, 76, 83, 85, 96
Australia 126, 157, 166

Bahamas 48, 56, 69
    Constitution of 52, 53, 57, 69
    executions in 49
Banda, Hastings 105
Banda, Joyce 115
Bangladesh 2, 31, 41, 44, 46
    Appellate Division of 42
    Constitution of 41, 42
    criminal procedure code of 42
    penal code of 41

banishment, *see* punishment, banishment as form of
Bar Council of Malaysia 80
Barbados 48, 56, 63, 71
    Constitution of 53, 63, 64, 66, 70
    Court of Appeal of 70
    executions in 49
Beadle, Thomas 136
Beale, Robert 15
Beccaria, Cesare 14
Belize 48
    Constitution of 52, 54, 65
    Court of Appeal of 65
    drug trafficking in 49
    Supreme Court of 66
Bermuda 50
    abolition of the death penalty in 50
Bingham, Lord 163
"black peril" laws 104, 128, 136
Blackmun, Harry 19, 22, 25
Bloody Assizes 14
Bloody Code 5, 32
Boko Haram 101
Bosch, Mariette Sonjaleen 144
Botswana 103, 108, 126, 146, 148, 162
    Constitution of 142, 143
    Court of Appeal of 141, 142, 143, 144
    penal code of 141
Brennan, William 19
Breyer, Stephen 29
Brightman, Lord 55
British colonialism, *see* colonialism
British Columbia 28
British Dependent Territories, *see* Anguilla, Bermuda, British Virgin Islands, Cayman Islands, Hong Kong Special Administrative Region, Montserrat, and Turks and Caicos Islands
    abolition of the death penalty in 50, 92

British Virgin Islands 50
Brown Commission, *see* National Commission on the Reform of Federal Criminal Laws
Brunei Darussalam 96, 97
    Constitution of 96
    penal code of 96
Burger, Warren 19

California 24, 25
    Supreme Court 16, 18
Canada 9, 28–9, 109
    Bill of Rights 28
    Charter on Rights and Freedoms 28
    Supreme Court of 9, 28, 163
Cape Colony 126
Caribbean, Commonwealth 47, 50, 163
    constitutions of 48, 56
    crime rates of 49, 51
    political conditions in 48
    proliferation of small arms in 49
    savings clauses in, *see* constitutions, comparative
Caribbean Court of Justice 70–71, 72
Cayman Islands 50
Chaskalson, Arthur 134
Chatterjee, Dhanajoy 33
China, People's Republic of 32, 73, 92, 93, 94
Chirwa, Orton 105
civil society, death penalty and *see* death penalty, civil society and
clemency 4, 13, 47, 67, 93, 95, 115, 126–7, 145, 158, 163
    judicial review of 35, 57, 89, 166, 167
    mercy committees 57
    process for seeking 89, 100, 127, 142
    rates of 127, 131
    right to seek 35, 61–2, 65, 70, 113, 119, 142, 150
    transparency 142, 166
Coard, Bernard 66
colonialism 104, 105, 157
Commonwealth Caribbean, *see* Caribbean, Commonwealth
communitarian values, death penalty and 77
compensation, homicide and 103, 160
constitutions, comparative 52
    death penalty savings clauses 107, 116, 155, 157

due process clauses 57 *or see* fair trial, due process rights
emergency provisions 109
general savings clauses 53, 66, 67, 68, 69, 109
interpretation of 88, 112, 117, 155, 160
partial savings clauses 52, 64, 65, 108, 116, 121, 143
prohibition on cruel, inhuman, or degrading punishment 73, 108, 157
right of access to justice 111
right to life clauses 107, 109, 110, 111, 116, 117, 121, 155
corporal punishment 4, 47, 53, 69, 81, 90, 108, 109, 138, 155
    juveniles and 138
    mandatory 73, 105
cruel and unusual punishment, *see* punishment, cruel and unusual
customary international law 88
customary (indigenous) law 103, 104, 136

Dahomey 100
Date-Bah, Samuel 119
de Klerk, F.W. 132
death penalty
    abolition of 92
    accomplice liability and 20, 43, 64, 89, 131, 137
    aggravating factors and 22, 36, 43, 71, 114, 115, 132, 133, 154, 155
    arms offenses and, *see* arms offenses, death penalty and
    civil society and 79, 90
    delay and, *see* death row phenomenon
    discretionary 20, 21, 37, 78, 108, 121, 125, 126, 130, 132, 140, 141, 146, 148, 155, 156, 159
    drug trafficking and 40, 45, 75, 80–81, 85, 86, 87, 89, 90, 91
    elderly and 61, 102, 108, 141
    foreigners and 80
    gender and 11, 42, 43, 104, 108, 127, 136, 141
    juveniles and 17, 61, 102, 108, 128, 141
    mandatory, *see* mandatory death penalty
    mental illness and 12, 17–18, 29, 64, 71–2
    military offenses 33

mitigating factors and 37, 113, 125, 128, 141, 145, 147, 156, 161
non-homicide offenses and 17, 114, 116
offenses 32, 75, 91, 128, 151
political crimes and 61, 104, 131, 136, 137
proportionality and, *see* punishment, proportionality of
prosecutorial discretion and 11, 21, 89
public opinion and 33–4, 80, 92, 102
race and 10, 29, 104, 127, 128, 132, 136
sentencing guidelines and, *see* sentencing guidelines
slavery and 47
terrorism and, *see* terrorism, death penalty and
witchcraft and 128, 150, 158, 159
Death Penalty Project (United Kingdom) 6, 51, 80, 99, 122
death row phenomenon 29, 35, 43, 55–6, 57, 109, 113, 116, 138, 139, 145
    delay and 54
    pre-trial delay and 57
    prison conditions and 52
death row syndrome, *see* death row phenomenon
Diplock, Lord 86
discretionary death penalty, *see* death penalty, discretionary
disparities in sentencing, *see* sentencing disparities
DNA evidence 12
doctrine of extenuating circumstances, *see* extenuating circumstances, doctrine of
Dominica 48
    Constitution of 65
    executions in 49
Dotse, Jones 119, 120, 121
Douglas, William 19
drug trafficking
    death penalty and *see* death penalty, drug trafficking *or* mandatory death penalty, drug trafficking
    presumption of trafficking 81, 82, 83, 84
due process, *see* constitutions, comparative and due process, *or* fair trial, due process and
Dumbutshena, Enoch 126

Eastern Caribbean Court of Appeal 64, 65

Economic Community of West African States (ECOWAS) 102
ECOWAS Community Court of Justice 102
Eighth Amendment, *see* United States Constitution, Eighth Amendment
Emukule, Matthew Anyara 117
encounter killings, *see* executions, extrajudicial
English Bill of Rights 13, 14, 15, 55
European Convention on Human Rights 6, 50, 52, 86, 87, 90, 107–8, 117
European Court of Human Rights 6, 50, 109
executions
    comparative rates 32
    delay and, *see* death row phenomenon
    extrajudicial 33, 106, 112
    method of 13, 35
        firing squad 106
        hanging 5, 34, 113, 143
        lethal injection 10, 29
        premodern methods 13, 14
    notification of 142, 144
    public 4–5, 35, 105
executive clemency, *see* clemency
extenuating circumstances, doctrine of 2, 125, 126, 127, 130, 136, 140, 142, 146, 147, 150, 158, 160, 161
    abolition of 132, 141, 156, 161
    appellate review of 154
    burden on defendant 133, 141, 143, 147, 152, 156, 159
    constitutionality of 145, 148
    definition of 128, 129, 149, 153, 154
    method of determining 139, 151
    origins of 128
    youth and 153
extradition 94

fair trial
    due process and 61, 90, 100, 105, 109
    right to 7, 44, 73, 110, 111, 121, 144
    right to appellate review and 128–9, 132, 139
    right to a sentencing hearing and 66, 111
felony-murder, mandatory death penalty and, *see* mandatory death penalty, felony-murder and
Foundation for Human Rights Initiatives (Uganda) 115

Gambia, The 101, 102, 108
Ghana 99, 101, 105, 106, 107, 163
   Constitution of 119, 120, 121, 122
   penal code of 121
   Supreme Court of 99, 100, 122
Gifford, Lord 71
Grassian, Stuart 54
Grazette, Clyde Anderson 71
Grenada 48
   executions in 49
Griffiths, Lord 55
Guatemala 62
Guyana 48, 60
   Constitution of 53
   executions in 49

hanging, *see* executions, method
Harlan, John Marshall (1899–1971) 18
Henry, Patrick 13
HIV/AIDS 115
   criminalization of transmission of 151
homosexuality, criminalization of 114–15
Hong Kong Special Administrative Region 92, 94, 97
   Basic Law of 93
   Bill of Rights of 92
   Court of Final Appeal of 93, 94, 95
   death penalty abolition in 73, 92–3, 95
   demographics of 92
   homicide rates 93
Human Rights Advocacy Center (Ghana) 122
human rights litigation 109, 123, 138–9

imprisonment 105
   see also life imprisonment
   conditions of 112
India 2, 5, 31–2, 38, 46, 109
   clemency process 166
   Constitution of 36, 38, 39, 79
   court system 33
   criminal procedure code 34
   establishment of discretionary death penalty in 163
   penal code of 32, 34, 38
   Supreme Court of 36, 37
ineffective assistance of counsel 12, 100, 144
infanticide 127
Inter-American Human Rights System 48, 67, 72

Inter-American Commission on Human Rights 6, 57, 60, 61, 62
Inter-American Court of Human Rights 6, 60, 63
International Covenant on Civil and Political Rights 3, 58, 77, 96
   First Optional Protocol to 59, 77
   "most serious crimes" doctrine 59, 63, 87
   Second Optional Protocol to 77
international tribunals, right to appeal to 56, 57
Islam
   death penalty and 73, 74, 100
   hudud offenses 74

Jamaica 47, 48, 56, 67, 70
   Constitution of 53
   executions in 49
   homicide rates in 49
   prison conditions in 51–2
   violent crime rates in 50
Japan 32
Judicial Committee of the Privy Council 9, 50, 53, 54, 55, 56, 57, 58, 67, 68, 70, 72, 78, 83, 84, 85, 87, 109, 110, 119, 137, 138, 163
Judicial Services Commission (Kenya) 119
jury nullification 21
jury trial 127
juveniles, *see* death penalty, juveniles *or* life imprisonment, juveniles

Kennedy, Anthony 23
Kenya 2, 99, 103, 104, 105, 163
   Constitution of 116, 117, 118
   Court of Appeal of 100, 115, 116, 123
   High Court of 118
   Supreme Court of 100, 119
Kibaki, Mwai 99, 115

Lansdown Commission 131
law enforcement 103
Law Reform Commission (Papua New Guinea) 160
Law Society of Singapore 79
Law Society of Zimbabwe 141
Lee, Martin 94
legal aid 12, 43, 70, 112, 113, 115, 130
Legal Aid Board (South Africa) 130

lethal injection, *see* executions, method
Lesotho 108, 126, 152–3, 154, 162
   Constitution of 151
   Court of Appeal of 151, 152, 153
life, right to *see* constitutions, comparative, right to life clauses
life imprisonment 114, 156, 163
   constitutionality of 114, 163
   discretionary 43
   juveniles and 17, 165
   mandatory 23, 94–5, 135, 163
   natural life term 114
   without possibility of parole 23, 163
Long Term Prison Sentences Review Board (Hong Kong) 93
Louisiana 20

Malawi 2, 99, 100, 105, 114–15, 123, 163
   Constitution of 111
   Constitutional Court of 111, 112
   penal code of 111
   Supreme Court of Appeal of 111
Malaysia 7, 81, 82, 84, 90, 91, 96, 97, 163
   Constitution of 73, 75
   Court of Appeal of 85
   court system of
   demographics of 74
   execution rates 77, 81
   Federal Court of 78, 84, 85
   penal code of 75
   political history 75
mandatory death penalty 2–3, 20–21, 38
   abolition of 116
   capital perjury and 41
   constitutionality of 83, 86, 87, 88
   drug trafficking and 40, 45, 75, 76, 78, 80, 81, 82, 83, 84, 85, 86, 87, 89, 91
   felony-murder and 59, 68, 78
   homicide of law enforcement and 60
   life term prisoners and 23, 24–5, 38–9, 44
   public opinion and 80
   right to life and 63
   treason and 120, 122
mandatory life imprisonment, *see* life imprisonment, mandatory
mandatory minimum sentences 16, 90, 135, 166
Marshall, Thurgood 18, 19
Mason, George 13, 14

Massachusetts
   Body of Liberties 15
   Mau Mau Emergency 104
Mauritius 109, 165
mental illness and the death penalty, *see* death penalty, mental illness
mercy, *see* pardons or clemency
Michigan
   Supreme Court of 16
Mills, John Atta 101
Model Penal Code 19, 25
Moi, Daniel arap 105
Montserrat 50
"most serious crimes" doctrine, *see* International Covenant on Civil and Political Rights
Mugabe, Robert 140
Mughal Dynasty (India) 31
murder, definition of 68, 79, 94, 161
Muluzi, Bakili 105
Murugesu, Shanmugam 80
Mutharika, Bingu wa 115

Namibia 107
   Constitution of 155
   Supreme Court of 156
National Association for the Advancement of Colored People Legal Defense Fund 18
National Commission on the Reform of Federal Criminal Laws (United States) 26
Ndebele people 135–6
Nevada 23, 25–6
New York 25
   Court of Appeals of 25
Niekerk, Barend van 131–2
Nigeria 101, 103, 106, 123
   Supreme Court of 110
Nkrumah, Kwame 106
North Carolina 20

Oates, Titus 14
Obote, Milton 106
Ohio 22
   Supreme Court of 22
Oklahoma 10, 22
Owusu, Rose Constance 119, 120

Papua New Guinea 3, 126, 156, 157, 158, 160, 161, 162

Constitution of 157, 160
history of retaliatory killing in, *see*
"payback" killing
legal reform in 159
penal code of 159
political history of 157
pardon, *see* clemency
parole 27, 95
"payback" killing 158, 159
penal transportation 3, 5
Philippines 15, 59
police, *see* law enforcement
political crimes, death penalty and, *see* death
penalty, political crimes and
Powell, Lewis 19
Privy Council, *see* Judicial Committee of the
Privy Council
pro deo legal representation 130, 134, 144
prosecutorial discretion, death penalty and *see*
death penalty, prosecutorial discretion
prosecutorial misconduct 12
provocation, as mitigating factor 142, 150, 153
psychiatric evaluations of prisoners, *see* death
penalty, mental illness
public executions, *see* executions, public
public opinion and the death penalty, *see* death
penalty, public opinion and
punishment 103, 158
    banishment as form of 113
    cruel and unusual 14, 15, 55, 57, 88, 108, 138
    cruel, inhuman, and degrading, *see*
        punishment, cruel and unusual
    hard labor as form of 158
    proportionality of 7, 13–14, 15, 16, 19, 23, 28, 29, 118, 137–8

race and the death penalty, *see* death penalty, race
"rarest of the rare" doctrine 161
    Bangladesh 43
    India 31, 36, 37, 40
Rawlings, Jerry 106
reprieve, *see* pardons or clemency
Rehnquist, William 19
rendition, *see* extradition
Rhode Island
    Supreme Court of 24

Rhodesia 9, 104, 136
    Appellate Division of 138
    Constitution of 136, 137, 138
Rhodesian Front 137
Roman-Dutch law 125
Royal Commission on Capital Punishment
    (United Kingdom) 2, 5, 126, 128, 158

Saint Kitts and Nevis 48
    executions in 49
    political conditions of 49
Saint Lucia 48
    Constitution of 64, 65
    Court of Appeal of 66
    executions in 49
Saint Vincent and the Grenadines 48
    Constitution of 64
    executions in 49
savings clauses, *see* constitutions, comparative
Scalia, Antonin 18, 23
Scarman, Lord 55
sentencing disparities 27, 131, 149, 153
sentencing guidelines 27, 115, 120, 165
separation of powers 42, 44, 86, 113, 116, 121, 146
Shadrake, Alan 79–80
Shah, Azlan 84
Shona people 135
Sierra Leone 109, 123
Simelane, David 148
Singapore 1, 2, 7, 32, 84, 96, 97, 163, 166
    comparison with Hong Kong 93
    Constitution of 73, 76, 78, 83, 88, 89, 90
    Court of Appeal of 78, 82, 86, 87, 88, 91, 166
    court system of 77
    demographics of 74
    developmental philosophy of 74
    execution rates 77, 80, 81, 93
    High Court of 91
    penal code of 76, 79, 88
    political history 75
Singh, Dara 33
Sixth Amendment, *see* United States
    Constitution, Sixth Amendment
slavery, death penalty and 47
small arms, proliferation of 49, 50
Smuts, Jan 127

Society for the Abolition of the Death Penalty (South Africa) 132
South Africa 2–3, 103, 107, 125, 127, 141, 156, 158, 162, 163, 165, 166
   Appellate Division of 129, 131, 132, 133
   Constitution of 130
   Constitutional Court of 110, 134, 135, 167
   execution rates in 128, 131
   Interim Constitution of 134
   legal system of 126
   penal code of 126
   Supreme Court of Appeal of 135
South Sudan 102, 107
South West Africa see Namibia
Southern Rhodesia see Rhodesia
Sri Lanka 31, 45, 46
   Constitution of 45
   Court of Appeal of 45
Stevens, John Paul 29
Stewart, Potter 19, 55, 163
Sudan 108
Swaziland 108, 126, 147, 162
   Constitution of 145–6, 147, 148
   establishment of discretionary death penalty in 166
   political history of 146

Tanzania 101, 107, 109, 123
terrorism, death penalty and 32, 33, 38, 40, 41, 42, 76, 96, 137
Texas 1, 10
torture 13, 106
transportation to penal colony, see penal transportation
treason, mandatory death penalty and, see mandatory death penalty, treason and
Trinidad and Tobago 48, 54, 56, 59, 63, 66
   Constitution of 53
   Court of Appeal of 72
   executions in 49
   homicide rates in 49, 51
   public opinion and the death penalty in 51
Tswana people 141
Turks and Caicos Islands 50
Tyburn 4

ubuntu 135

Uganda 2, 99, 100, 103, 105, 106, 163, 114, 116, 119, 123
   Constitution of 113
   Constitutional Court of 112, 113
   establishment of sentencing guidelines in 166
   Supreme Court of 113
United Kingdom 3–5, 165
United Nations 150
United Nations Human Rights Committee 6, 58, 59, 67, 72, 77, 102, 122, 139
United States 9–10, 26–7, 120, 165
   Parole Commission 26–7
   Sentencing Commission 27
   size of death row 99
   Supreme Court 15, 16–17, 18, 20–21, 23, 25, 29, 163
United States Constitution
   Eighth Amendment 9, 13, 14, 15–16, 17, 18, 20, 21, 22, 23, 25, 163, 165
   Fourteenth Amendment 16
   Sixth Amendment 12

Virginia 10
   Declaration of Rights 13

Wamwere, Koigi wa 105
Ward, Nathaniel 15
Warsame, M. 118
whipping, judicial see corporal punishment
White, Byron 19, 28
witchcraft, death penalty and see death penalty, witchcraft and
Woodson, James Tyrone 20
women and the death penalty see death penalty, gender
wrongful convictions 11, 100, 122

youth, as extenuating factor see extenuating circumstances, doctrine of, youth and

Zambia 101, 102, 104, 123, 162
   Constitution of 150
   penal code of 149, 150
   Supreme Court of 149, 150
Zimbabwe 101, 103, 108, 126, 135, 146, 150, 162
   Constitution of 138, 140
   penal code of 136
   Supreme Court of 139, 140

Table of Authorities

African Commission on Human and Peoples' Rights
    Amnesty International (on behalf of Orton and Vera Chirwa) v. Malawi 102, 105
    Constitutional Rights Project (in respect of Akamu and others) v. Nigeria 102
    Forum of Conscience v. Sierra Leone 102
    Interights et al. (on behalf of Bosch) v. Botswana 102, 143, 144

Antigua and Barbuda
    Queen v. Monelle 66

Bangladesh
    Abdul Awal v. State 43
    Anwar Hossain Chowdhury v. Bangladesh 42
    Arms Act of 1878 42
    Bangladesh Italian Marble Works Ltd. v. Bangladesh 42
    Bangladesh Legal Aid and Services Trust (BLAST) v. Bangladesh 44–5
    Biswas v. State 43
    Code of Criminal Procedure Act of 1898 42
    Criminal Law (Amendment) Act of 1958 41
    Explosive Substances Act of 1908 42
    Explosives Act of 1884 42
    Oppression of Women and Children (Special Enactment) Act of 1995 43, 45
    Sajenda Parvin v. Bangladesh 42
    Sarder v. State 43
    Special Powers (Amendment) Act of 1974 41, 42
    State v. Akkel Ali 43
    State v. Mohammed Monir Ahmed 43
    State v. Pinto 43
    State v. Sukur Ali 2, 43, 44, 45
    Women and Children Repression Prevention Act of 2000 43

Belize
    Lauriano v. Attorney General of Belize 65
    Queen v. Reyes 66

Botswana
    Bosch v. State 144
    Gofhamodino v. State 141
    Kelaletswe v. State 143, 152
    Kobedi v. State 110, 144–5
    Masono v. State 142
    Molale v. State 143
    Ndlovu v. State 142
    Ntesang v. State 143
    Petrus v. State 108
    Sibanda v. State 143
    Tshabang v. State 143–4

Brunei Darussalam
    Mohd Noh Bin Ramli v. Public Prosecutor 96
    Public Prosecutor v. Abdul Bin Turkey 96
    Public Prosecutor v. Samer Klom Klom 96

Canada
    Criminal Law Amendment Act (No. 2) 28
    Queen v. Latimer 9, 95
    Queen v. Luxton 95
    Queen v. Miller (British Columbia) 28
    Queen v. Oakes 90
    Queen v. Shand (Ontario) 28
    Queen v. Smith 29
    Miller v. Queen 9, 25
    United States v. Burns 6, 54, 109

Caribbean Court of Justice
    Attorney General v. Joseph 70–71
    Grazette v. Queen 71

Eastern Caribbean Court of Appeal
    Spence and Hughes v. Queen 64, 66, 72

Economic Community of West African States (ECOWAS) Community Court of Justice
S.E.R.A.P. v. The Gambia 102

European Court of Human Rights
Kafkaris v. Cyprus 165
Soering v. United Kingdom 6, 54, 109

The Gambia
Badjie v. State 108

Ghana
Dexter Johnson v. Republic 100, 119, 120, 121, 122, 123

Guyana
Criminal Law Offences (Amendment) Act of 2010 60

Hong Kong Special Administrative Region
Cheung Wai Bun v. Queen 93
Lau Cheong v. Hong Kong S.A.R. 94, 95
Tong Yu Lam v. Long Term Prison Sentences Review Board 95

India
Anamma v. State of Andhra Pradesh 36
Arms Act of 1959 39, 40, 41
Arms (Amendment) Act of 1988 40
Attorney General v. Devi 35
Bachan Singh v. State of Punjab 31, 36, 46
Bhagwan Bax Singh v. State of Uttar Pradesh 39
Code of Criminal Procedure Act of 1898 34
Deena v. Union of India 34–5
Dilip Kumar Sharma v. State of Madhya Pradesh 38
Gyasuddin Khan v. State of Bihar 40
Indian Harm Reduction Network (on behalf of Gulam Mohammed Malik) v. Union of India 40
Indian Penal Code Act of 1860 34, 38
Jagmohan Singh v. State of Uttar Pradesh 36
Kehar Singh v. Union of India 35
Kesavananda Bharati v. State of Kerala 42
Macchi Singh v. State of Punjab 37
Mahabir Gope v. State of Bihar 38
Maneka Gandhi v. Union of India 34, 36, 38
Maru Ram v. Union of India 35
Mithu v. State of Punjab 2, 30, 38
Narcotic and Psychotropic Drugs Act 39, 40, 41
Oyami Ayatu v. State of Madhya Pradesh 38
Pratap v. State of Uttar Pradesh 38
Rajendra Prasad v. State of Uttar Pradesh 36
Santosh Bariyar v. State of Maharashtra 37–8, 46
Scheduled Castes and Scheduled Tribes (Prevention of Atrocities) Act of 1989 41
Swaran Singh v. State of Uttar Pradesh 35
State of Punjab v. Dalbir Singh 40
State through CBI, Delhi v. Gian Singh 39
Subhash Chander v. Krishan Lal 34
Subhash Ramkumar Bind v. State of Maharashtra 39
Sunil Batra v. Delhi Administration 34, 38
Terrorism and Detention Act of 1985 39
Terrorist and Disruptive Activities (Prevention) Act of 1985 41
Triveniben v. State of Gujurat 6, 35, 54, 109
Vatheeswaran v. State of Tamil Nadu 35

Inter-American Commission on Human Rights
Aitkin v. Jamaica 62
Baptiste v. Grenada 61
Edwards v. Bahamas 61, 123
Jacob v. Grenada 61
Knights Grenada 61
Lallion v. Grenada 61
Lamey v. Jamaica 62
McKenzie v. Jamaica 62
Raxcocó-Reyes v. Guatemala 62
Sewell v. Jamaica 62
Thomas v. Jamaica 62

Inter-American Court of Human Rights
Boyce v. Barbados 63–4
Cadogan v. Barbados 64
Hilaire, Constantine and Benjamin v. Trinidad and Tobago 63

Judicial Committee of the Privy Council (United Kingdom)
Abbott v. Attorney General of Trinidad and Tobago 55

Balson v. State 65
Benjamin v. State 72
Boucherville v. Mauritius 165
Bowe v. Bahamas 69
Bowe v. Queen 9
Boyce and Joseph v. Queen 67–8
Bradshaw v. Attorney General of Barbados 56
Coard v. Attorney General of Grenada 65–6
De Freitas v. Benny 54
Fox v. Queen 2, 65
Griffith v. Queen 68
Guerra V. Baptiste 56
Henfield v. Attorney General of the Bahamas 56
Khan v. State 68
Lockhart v. Queen 72
Mathew v. State 67–8
Miguel v. State 68
Moses v. State 68
Ong Ah Chuan v. Public Prosecutor 78, 79, 83, 85, 87
Pratt and Morgan v. Attorney General of Jamaica 6, 55, 56, 58, 70, 109
Queen v. Hughes 2, 65
Queen v. Runyowa 9, 137
Regina v. Mapolisa 137
Reyes v. Queen 1, 2, 65, 72, 123
Riley v. Attorney General of Jamaica 55
Roodal v. State 66
Taitt v. State 72
Tido v. Queen 71
Trimmingham v. Queen 71
Watson v. Queen 67–8
White v. Queen 71

Kenya
    Gichane v. Republic 117
    Macharia v. Republic 118
    Magare v. Republic 118
    Matheka v. Republic 118
    Mutiso v. Republic 2, 99, 115, 116, 118, 119, 120, 121, 123
    Mwaura v. Republic 100, 118–19
    Ogutu v. Republic 118
    Onyango v. Republic 118
    Republic v. Kabulit 117
    Republic v. Msituni 118

Republic v. Munene 118
Republic v. Mutiso 115
Republic v. Mwangeti 118
Republic v. Mwaniki 117
Waweru v. Republic 116

Lesotho
    Director of Public Prosecutions v. Khama 154
    George v. Rex 154
    Kopano v. Rex 152
    Lefu v. Rex 151
    Lentso v. Rex 153
    Letuka v. Rex 151, 152
    Maliehe v. Rex 152
    Mokone v. Rex 153
    Monaleli v. Rex 153
    Mosili v. Rex
    Phaloane v. Rex 154
    Rex v. Letuka 151
    Rex v. Mabaso 151
    Rex v. Maphobole 153
    Rex v. Mbobo 153
    Rex v. Metsing 154
    Rex v. Mokalanyane 153
    Rex v. Moratha 151
    Rex v. Mosili 154
    Rex v. Mothobi 153
    Rex v. Raleoshoai 153
    Rex v. Ramaema 154
    Rex v. Raseotsana 153
    Rex v. Thebe 153
    Rex v. Tsibela 153
    Thebe v. Rex 153

Malawi
    Jacob v. Republic 111
    Kafantayeni v. Attorney General 2, 99, 111, 112, 116
    Masangano v. Attorney General 112
    Republic v. Cheuka 111–12

Malaysia
    Chiang Liang Sang v. Public Prosecutor 84
    Dangerous Drugs Act of 1952 76, 81
    Firearm (Increased Penalties) Act of 1971 78
    Ibrahim Mohamad v. Pendakwa Raya 82
    Internal Security Act of 1960 76, 85

Lee Kwan Who v. Public Prosecutor 78
Loh Hock Seng v. Public Prosecutor 84
Low Soo Song v. Public Prosecutor 78
Mohammed bin Hassan v. Public Prosecutor
Mohd. Amin bin Mohd. Razali v. Pendakwa
  Raya 78
Pathip Selvan s/o Sugumaran v. Public
  Prosecutor 78
Public Prosecutor v. Gunus Sagena 78
Public Prosecutor v. Lau Kee Hoo 83, 85
Public Prosecutor v. Mohamed Ismail 84
Public Prosecutor v. Neoh Wan Kee 84
Public Prosecutor v. Oon Lai Hin 84
Public Prosecutor v. Saubin Beatrice 85
Public Prosecutor v. Tan Gong Wai 84
Public Prosecutor v. Tan Hock Hai 84, 85
Security Offences (Special Measures) Act
  of 2012 76
Shamim Reza Bin Abdul Samad v. Public
  Prosecutor 78
Tan Ewe Huat v. Pendakwa Raya 78
Tan Tatt Eek v. Public Prosecutor 82
Yusri Bin Pialmi v. Pendakwa Raya 82

Namibia
  Ex Parte: Attorney-General, In Re: Corporal
    Punishment by Organs of State 108, 155
  State v. Alexander 155
  State v. Nehemia Tjijo 155
  State v. Tcoeib 155

Nigeria
  Kalu v. State 110

Papua New Guinea
  Criminal Law (Compensation) Act of 1991
  Regina v. Asis and Bitimui 158
  Regina v. Iu Ketapi 158
  Regina v. Lakalyo Neak 158
  Regina v. Melin 159
  Regina v. Peter Ivoro 158–9
  Secretary for Law v. Amantasi 159
  State v. Komane 160
  State v. Paege 160
  Ume v. State 121, 160

Rhodesia
  see also, Zimbabwe

Gundu v. Sheriff of Southern Rhodesia 137
Dhlamini v. Carter 138

Saint Lucia
  Moise v. Queen 66
  Phillip v. Queen 65

Singapore
  Criminal Procedure (Amendment) Act of
    2012 75, 90
  Daniel Vijay v. Public Prosecutor 91
  Jabar v. Public Prosecutor 79, 87
  Lee Chez Kee v. Public Prosecutor 78, 79
  Mimi Wong v. Public Prosecutor 79
  Mohd Halmi bin Hamid v. Public
    Prosecutor 82
  Misuse of Drugs Act of 1973 76, 81, 83,
    85, 86
  Misuse of Drugs (Amendment) Act of 2012
    75, 90
  Muhammed bin Kadar v. Public Prosecutor
    79
  Ng Yang Sek v. Public Prosecutor 82
  Nguyen Tuong Van v. Public Prosecutor
    83, 85–6
  Penal Code (Amendment) Act of 2012 75,
    90
  Public Prosecutor v. Mazan 90
  Rajeevan Edakalavan v. Public Prosecutor
    90
  Ramalingam Ravinthran v. Attorney-
    General 89
  Tan Kiam Peng v. Public Prosecutor 82
  Tang Hai Liang v. Public Prosecutor 82
  Yong Vui Kong v. Public Prosecutor 83, 86,
    87, 88, 89, 90, 91

South Africa
  Criminal Law (Amendment) Act 107 of
    1990 132
  Criminal Law (Amendment) Act 105 of
    1997 135
  Criminal Procedure and Evidence
    (Amendment) Act 46 of 1935, 2–3
  President of the Republic of South Africa v.
    Hugo 167
  R. v. Biyana 129
  R. v. Fundakubi 129

R. v. Lembete 129
R. v. Mfoni 129
State v. Dodo 135
State v. Letsolo 125, 129
State v. Makwanyane 110, 134–5, 163
State v. Malgas 135
State v. Manamela 135
State v. Masina 133
State v. Matshili
State v. Matthee 129
State v. Nkwanyana 133
State v. Scheepers 147
State v. Senonohi 133
State v. Shepard 133
State v. Sigwahla 147
State v. Williams 108
State v. Zinn 147

Sri Lanka
Van Der Jhultes v. Attorney General 45, 121
Weerawardane v. State 45

Swaziland
Bongani Mkhwanazi v. Rex 147
Criminal Law and Procedure (Amendment) Act 146, 148
Daniel Dlamini v. Rex 147
David Thabo Simelane v. Rex 148
Mandla Tfwala v. Rex 149
Pikinini Simon Motsa v. Rex 147
Rex v. Majahonkhe Major Mazibuko 147
Rex v. Musa Kotso Samuel Dlamini 148
Rex v. Nhlanhla Charles Moratele 147
Rex v. Nhlanhla Lucky Dludlu 148
Rex v. Ntokozo Adams 148
Rex v. Pikinini Simon Motsa 147
Rex v. Sandile Mbongeni Mtsetfwa 148
Rex v. Sean Blignaut 146
Tsela v. Rex 149, 166
Xolani Zinhle Nyandzeni v. Rex 148
Zwelithini Tsabedze v. Rex 149

Tanzania
Mbushuu v. Republic 107
Republic v. Mbushuu 107

Uganda
Abuki v. Attorney General 113
Adama Jimo v. Uganda 114
Attorney General v. Kigula 2, 99, 110, 113, 121
Calvin Omasige and James Okia v. Uganda 114
Kigula v. Attorney General 112, 113, 116, 122
Kyamanywa v. Uganda 108, 113
Oryem Richard v. Uganda 108, 113
Prisons Act of 2006 114
Tigo v. Uganda 114
Uganda v. Aurien 114
Yasin Feni v. Uganda 114

United Kingdom
see also, Judicial Committee of the Privy Council
Homicide Act of 1957 2
Murder (Abolition of the Death Penalty) Act of 1965
Queen v. Lambert 90

United Nations Human Rights Committee
Carpo v. Philippines 59–60
Chan v. Guyana 60
Kennedy v. Trinidad and Tobago 59
Lubuto v. Zambia 59, 102
Thompson v. St Vincent and the Grenadines 59

United States
Atkins v. Virginia 12, 18, 29
Baze v. Rees 29
Branch v. Texas
Cabana v. Bullock 17
Coker v. Georgia 17
Eberhart v. Georgia 17
Eddings v. Oklahoma 22
Ellridge v. Florida 29
Enmund v. Florida 17
Ewing v. California 16
Ford v. Wainright 12, 29
Foster v. Florida 29
Furman v. Georgia 18–19, 20, 165
Graham v. Florida 17
Gregg v. Georgia 20
Harmelin v. Michigan 23
Harris v. State (Alabama) 24

Hart v. Coiner 16
Hitchcock v. Dugger 23
Jackson v. Georgia 18
Jurek v. Texas 20
In re: Kemmler 15
Kennedy v. Louisiana 17
Knight v. Florida 29, 110
Lackey v. Texas 29
Lockett v. Ohio 22
In re: Lynch 16
McClesky v. Kemp 29
McGautha v. California 18
Miller v. Alabama 17, 165
The Paquete Habana 16
Penry v. Lynaugh 18
People v. Anderson (California) 18
People v. Lorentzen (Michigan) 16
People v. Smith (New York) 25
Pervear v. Massachusetts 15
Proffitt v. Florida
O'Neil v. Vermont 15
Roberts, Harry v. Louisiana 21, 22
Roberts, Stanislaus v. Louisiana 20, 21
Robinson v. California 16
Roper v. Simmons 17, 18, 165
Rudolph v. Alabama 18
Rummel v. Estelle 16
Schick v. Read 165
Sentencing Reform Act of 1984 27
Shuman v. State (Nevada) 25
Shuman v. Wolff 25
Solem v. Helm 16
Stanford v. Kentucky
State v. Cline (Rhode Island) 24
State v. Davis (New York) 22
Sumner v. Shuman 23, 25
Thigpen v. State (Alabama) 24

Thompson v. Oklahoma 17
Tison v. Arizona 17
Trop v. Dulles 15–16
Weems v. United States 15–16, 19
Wilkerson v. Utah 15
Witherspoon v. Illinois 16
Woodson v. North Carolina 1, 9, 20, 21, 23, 28, 30, 163

Zambia
  Banda v. People 108
  Chongo v. People 150
  Moola v. People 150
  Mvula v. People 150
  Penal Code (Amendment) Act 3 of 1990 149
  People v. Kashwenka 150
  Phiri v. People 150
  Simusokwe v. People 150

Zimbabwe
  see also, Rhodesia
  Catholic Commission for Justice and Peace v. Attorney General 6, 54, 109, 110, 138, 145
  Jongwe v. State 139, 142
  Juvenile v. State 138
  Kanhumwa v. State 140
  Mamvura v. State 140
  Matongo v. State 139
  Mugwanda v. State 140
  Murijo v. State 140
  Porusingazi v. State 140
  Siluli v. State 140
  State v. Ncube 108, 138
  State v. Wairosi 139
  State v. Woods 140